Controversies in American Federalism and Public Policy

This interdisciplinary collection presents a scholarly treatment of how the constitutional politics of federalism affect governments and citizens, offering an accessible yet comprehensive analysis of the U.S. Supreme Court's federalism jurisprudence and its effect on the development of national and state policies in key areas of constitutional jurisprudence. The contributors address the impact that Supreme Court federalism precedents have in setting the parameters of national law and policies that the states are often bound to respect under constitutional law, including those that relate to the scope and application of gun rights, LGBT freedoms, health care administration, anti-terrorism initiatives, capital punishment, immigration and environmental regulation, the legalization of marijuana and voting rights.

Uniting scholarship in law, political science, criminology, and public administration, the chapters study the themes, principles, and politics that traditionally have been at the center of federalism research across different academic disciplines. They look at the origins, nature and effect of dual and cooperative federalism, presidential powers and administrative regulation, state sovereignty and states' rights, judicial federalism and the advocacy of organized interests.

Christopher P. Banks, Kent State University, USA, combines his research and teaching interests by studying the political behavior of the judiciary, constitutional law, the judicial process and civil rights and liberties. He has published books and articles relating to judicial policy-making, federalism, the legal profession, the judicial process, human rights, American politics, terrorism, *Bush v. Gore* (2000), the politics of court reform and the judicial politics of the DC circuit.

Controversies in American Constitutional Law

Series Editors: Jon Yorke and Anne Richardson Oakes
Centre for American Legal Studies, School of Law, Birmingham City University, UK

Controversies in American Constitutional Law presents and engages with the contemporary developments and policies which mould and challenge US constitutional law and practice. It deals with the full spectrum of constitutional issues, publishing work by scholars from a range of disciplines who tackle current legal issues by reference to their underlying legal and political histories and the philosophical perspectives that they represent. Its cross-disciplinary approach encourages analysis of past, present and future challenges to the idea of US constitutionalism and the power structures upon which it rests. The series provides a forum for scholars to challenge the boundaries of US constitutional law and engages with the continual process of constitutional refinement for the protection of individual rights and liberties, within an evolving framework of legitimate government.

CALS promotes research, scholarship, and educative programs in all areas of US law and is the home of the *British Journal of American Legal Studies*. Faculty members have extensive experience in submitting *amicus curiae* briefs to the United States Supreme Court and lower federal courts and advising on criminal justice issues in many states. CALS coordinates the largest British law undergraduate internship program to the United States. Through this program, and members' research, CALS has created relationships with over 100 partners in over 25 states. CALS faculty advise public bodies, provide professional training, and speak at conferences across the USA.

Recent title in this series

https://www.routledge.com/Controversies-in-American-Constitutional-Law/book-series/CONTROVERSIES

Controversies in American Federalism and Public Policy

Edited by Christopher P. Banks

Routledge
Taylor & Francis Group

LONDON AND NEW YORK

First published 2018
by Routledge
2 Park Square, Milton Park, Abingdon, Oxon OX14 4RN

and by Routledge
711 Third Avenue, New York, NY 10017

Routledge is an imprint of the Taylor & Francis Group, an informa business

British Library Cataloguing-in-Publication Data
A catalogue record for this book is available from the British Library

Library of Congress Cataloging-in-Publication Data
Names: Banks, Christopher P., editor.
Title: Controversies in American federalism and public policy / edited by Christopher P. Banks.
Description: New York, NY : Routledge, 2018. |
Series: Controversies in american constitutional law | Includes bibliographical references and index.
Identifiers: LCCN 2017048639| ISBN 9781138036659 (hardback) | ISBN 9781138036642 (pbk.)
Subjects: LCSH: Federal-state controversies—United States. | Federal government—United States. | Political planning—United States. | State governments—United States. | United States. Supreme Court.
Classification: LCC KF4612 .C66 2018 | DDC 342.73/042—dc23
LC record available at https://lccn.loc.gov/2017048639

ISBN: 978-1-138-03665-9 (hbk)
ISBN: 978-1-138-03664-2 (pbk)
ISBN: 978-1-315-17844-8 (ebk)

Typeset in Galliard
by Keystroke, Neville Lodge, Tettenhall, Wolverhampton

Contents

Contributors

Christopher P. Banks is a Professor of Political Science at Kent State University. He has a law degree and earned his PhD at the University of Virginia. Before receiving his doctorate in American politics from the University of Virginia in 1995, he practiced law in civil and criminal litigation in Connecticut and was active in local and state politics. He is the author of *The American Legal Profession: Myths and Realities* (Sage/CQ Press, 2017) and *Judicial Politics in the D.C. Circuit Court* (John Hopkins University Press, 1999); the co-author of *The Judicial Process: Law, Courts, and Judicial Politics* (Sage/CQ Press 2015), *The U.S. Supreme Court and New Federalism: From the Rehnquist to the Roberts Court* (Rowman & Littlefield, 2012) and *Courts and Judicial Policymaking* (Prentice Hall, 2008); editor and chapter contributor of *The State and Federal Courts: A Complete Guide to History, Powers, and Controversy* (ABC-CLIO, 2017); and co-editor and chapter contributor of *The Final Arbiter: The Consequences of* Bush v. Gore *for Law and Politics* (State University of New York Press, 2005) and *Superintending Democracy: The Courts and the Political Process* (University of Akron Press, 2001). He has published numerous book chapters, book reviews, and journal articles on U.S. Supreme Court politics, judicial behavior, law and politics, federalism, terrorism, and human rights.

John C. Blakeman is the Eugene Katz Distinguished Faculty, professor, and chair of the political science department at the University of Wisconsin–Stevens Point. He is the author *The Bible in the Park: Federal District Courts, Religious Speech, and the Public Forum*, and co-author of *The U.S. Supreme Court and New Federalism*, and *The American Constitutional Experience*. He is the author of several journal articles and book chapters on religious liberty, religion ad politics, federalism, and terrorism. He regularly teaches courses on American constitutional law, the First Amendment, American political thought, and religion and politics.

Nelson Lund is University Professor at George Mason University's Antonin Scalia Law School. A graduate of St. John's College in Annapolis, Maryland, he holds advanced degrees in philosophy from the Catholic University of America (M.A. 1978), and in political science from Harvard University (A.M. 1979; Ph.D. 1981). He received his law degree in 1985 from the University of Chicago, where he was executive editor of the *University of Chicago Law Review* and chapter president of the Federalist Society for Law and Public Policy.

Professor Lund served as a law clerk for the Honorable Patrick E. Higginbotham of the United States Court of Appeals for the Fifth Circuit (1985–1986) and for the Honorable Sandra Day O'Connor of the United States Supreme Court (O.T. 1987). In addition to experience in the United States Department of Justice at the Office of the

Solicitor General and at the Office of Legal Counsel, Professor Lund served in the White House as Associate Counsel to the President from 1989 to 1992.

In addition to dozens of articles on the Second Amendment, Professor Lund has written on a variety of other subjects: constitutional interpretation, federalism; separation of powers, jurisprudence, federal election law, the Commerce Clause, the Speech or Debate Clause, the Uniformity Clause, employment discrimination and civil rights, the legal regulation of medical ethics, the application of economic analysis to legal institutions and to legal ethics, and political philosophy.

Mary Welek Atwell recently retired from Radford University where she was a Professor of Criminal Justice. She has published four books dealing with legal subjects: *Equal Protection of the Law? Gender and Justice in the United States* (Peter Lang, 2002); *Evolving Standards of Decency: Popular Culture and Capital Punishment* (Peter Lang, 2004); *Wretched Sisters: Examining Gender and Capital Punishment* (Peter Lang, 2007; 2nd ed., 2014); and *An American Dilemma: International Law, Capital Punishment, and Federalism* (Palgrave Macmillan, 2015), as well as numerous articles and reviews. She holds a PhD from Saint Louis University.

John Dinan is Professor of Politics and International Affairs at Wake Forest University. He received his PhD from the University of Virginia. He is the author of several books and various articles focusing on federalism, state constitutions, and American political development, including *The American State Constitutional Tradition* and *Keeping the People's Liberties: Legislators, Citizens, and Judges as Guardians of Rights*. He writes an annual entry on state constitutional developments for *The Book of the States*. He is the editor of *Publius: The Journal of Federalism* and is a past chair of the Federalism and Intergovernmental Relations Section of the American Political Science Association.

Nancy J. Knauer is a Professor of Law and the Director of Law & Public Policy Program in the Beasley School of Law at Temple University. She is an internationally recognized scholar writing in the areas of identity, sexuality, and gender, and she was selected as one of 26 law professors from across the nation to be featured in the book *What the Best Law Teachers Do*, published by Harvard University Press (2013).

Sam Kamin has emerged as an expert voice on marijuana law reform in Colorado and throughout the country. He sat on Colorado Governor John Hickenlooper's Amendment 64 Implementation Task Force and worked with the ACLU and California Lt. Governor Gavin Newsom to formulate a set of best practices for marijuana regulation in that state. In addition, he has written more than a dozen scholarly articles about marijuana law reform and co-authors the series "Altered State: Inside Colorado's Marijuana Economy" for *Slate Magazine*, chronicling the impact of Colorado's marijuana regulations on lawmakers, businesses and consumers. In the spring of 2015 he taught the nation's first law school course on representing marijuana clients and was named the Vicente Sederberg Professor of Marijuana Law and Policy, the first professorship of its kind in the country.

Robert L. Glicksman is the J. B. and Maurice C. Shapiro Professor of Environmental Law at the George Washington University Law School. He is a nationally and internationally recognized expert on environmental, natural resources, and administrative law issues. A graduate of the Cornell Law School, his areas of expertise include environmental, natural resources, administrative, and property law.

Pratheepan Gulasekaram is a Professor of Law at Santa Clara University School of Law, where he teaches constitutional law and immigration law. His research, which includes his co-authored book *The New Immigration Federalism*, currently focuses on the political and legal dynamics of state and local immigration regulations, and their effect on federal policies. Prior to academia, he was a litigation associate with O'Melveny & Meyers LLP and Susman Godfrey LLP, both in Los Angeles, and he clerked for the Honorable Jacques L. Wiener Jr. on the US Circuit Court of Appeals for the Fifth Circuit in New Orleans. In addition, he is the co-founder of the World Children's Initiative, Inc., a non-profit organization dedicated to improving health and educational infrastructure for children in developing areas around the world.

Franita Tolson is a Professor of Law at the University of Southern California Gould School of Law. She graduated from the University of Chicago Law School, where she was a member of the University of Chicago Law review and was a recipient of the Thomas Mulroy Prize for Oral Advocacy in the Hinton Moot Court Competition. Her scholarship and teaching focuses on areas of election law, constitutional law, legal history and employment discrimination, and she has publications on partisan gerrymandering, campaign finance reform, the Elections Clause, the Voting Rights Act of 1965, and the Fourteenth and Fifteenth Amendments. Her forthcoming book, *A Promise Unfulfilled: Section 2 of the Fourteenth Amendment and the Future of the Right to Vote*, will be published in 2018 by Cambridge University Press. Before entering academia, she clerked for the Honorable Ann Claire Williams of the United States Court of Appeals for the Seventh Circuit and the Honorable Ruben Castillo of the Northern District of Illinois.

Acknowledgments

This book would not have been possible if my colleague John Dinan, of the Department of Politics and International University at Wake Forest University, did not refer me to the series editors in charge of the robust and expanding *Routledge Series on American Constitutional Law*, Anne Richardson Oakes and Jon Yorke, both from the Centre for American Legal Studies at Birmingham City University Law School in the United Kingdom. The support each gave for this interdisciplinary research project was unwavering and very helpful in giving me the editorial discretion to develop the project from its inception to its final execution. John Dinan was also kind enough to agree to contribute to the book even though he is very busy as the editor of one of the leading federalism journals in the field, *Publius: The Journal of Federalism*. The quality of insight that John gave me was not surprising. I learned long ago, from our days at UVA, that John was a very special scholar, and I am very grateful for all of his help. John Blakeman, also from UVA and a fine scholar in his own right, also contributed to the project and his consistent support and assistance in collaborating with me in this book and also other research projects throughout the years is always much appreciated. Moreover, all of the contributors to this book, some of which I did not know that well before it started, did an excellent job in writing the book chapters. All of them were very easy to work with as well, and that made completing this admittedly ambitious project much easier. Many thanks to all. During the editorial and production process, the expertise and assistance from Alison Kirk and Alexandra Buckley, among others, were essential to getting the textbook published and marketed successfully. I would also like to thank the anonymous reviewers for their valuable insight and suggestions.

As in any research project that I have undertaken both in graduate school and in my academic professional life, my family—Diane, Zachary, and Samantha—remain the foundation for anything I do, and I am very lucky to be a part of their lives. Thank you, and I love you all.

Last, but certainly not least, I am pleased to acknowledge and dedicate this book to my father and lifelong mentor and role model, Richard V. Banks, who I lost this year, at the age of 94. Among many other things, he was my athletic coach, law partner, and inspiration for everything I could ever hope to accomplish as a professional. I was very fortunate to learn from all of the considerable business and legal experience he accumulated over the multiple careers he had, dating from the New Deal to the present, in banking, law, marketing, and real estate. I will miss you, Dad, but you will never be forgotten.

1 The U.S. Supreme Court, new federalism, and public policy

John C. Blakeman and Christopher P. Banks

In 2017, the federal system of government in the United States turned 230 years old. For over two centuries federalism has served to balance power between the national government and the states. Federalism is an embedded part of the United States Constitution, and it has proven to be an enduring structure. As with most aspects of the Constitution, though, the interpretation and application of federalism has often been in dispute. Federalism theory and practice in the American constitutional tradition is historically contentious and infused with considerable political and philosophical debate over its meaning. Included in that debate are ongoing arguments over the appropriate and constitutional relationship between states and the national government, and those arguments have ranged widely across several historical eras. For example, federalism prior to the Civil War focused on protecting state autonomy from an encroaching national government. By the New Deal Era in the 1930s, a progressive interpretation of federalism had developed that allocated significant power to the national government to address economic and social ills, even if national power contravened state power in some policy areas.

New federalism is a recent variant of American federalism. Typically, it views the Constitution's relationship between the states and federal government as structural and procedural. In this understanding, the federal system of government preserves and protects state sovereignty from national power through a series of procedural mechanisms and constitutional provisions that, in total, create structural barriers that impede federal oversight of state policymaking. The structural approach to federalism is accomplished through the U.S. Supreme Court's interpretations of a wide range of constitutional provisions, including the national government's power to regulate interstate commerce in Article I, Section 8, of the Constitution, its implied powers in the Necessary and Proper Clause (also in Article I, Section 8), and the roles and powers of the states protected by the Tenth and Eleventh Amendments.

The intellectual foundations of new federalism started with President Richard M. Nixon's administration in 1968 and were further developed and given constitutional prominence by the U.S. Supreme Court under the leadership of Chief Justice William H. Rehnquist in the 1980s to 2005. With the support of the conservative administration of President Ronald Reagan, new federalism thinking was used by the Court to reinvigorate states' rights in several key cases. In this time period, the Court interpreted the Constitution to protect state sovereignty and thus establish limits on the federal government's power in several important policy areas. Indeed, the term "new federalism" is associated with the revival or reassertion of federalism principles that pre-date the Civil War and placed "aggressive and affirmative constitutional limits on the central government while protecting the sovereignty, autonomy, or rights of state governments."[1]

To be sure, the Rehnquist Court was not fully consistent in its interpretation of federalism. While many federalism cases were closely decided, a majority of justices in the Rehnquist era nonetheless supported federal power over states in certain policy areas. Ironically, the Chief Justice himself may have been less consistent on state sovereignty than his jurisprudential leadership might indicate. However, a "federalism five" group of justices—albeit with a changing membership—emerged to sustain new federalism doctrine.[2]

New federalism's focus on state sovereignty did not reside solely with constitutional disputes in the federal judicial system. Although the Supreme Court is the primary institution that articulated more robust protections for states' rights, a wide range of institutions and actors now actively use new federalism principles to contest federal policymaking affecting the states and to protect state policymaking from federal interference. An increasing activism geared towards state sovereignty is embedded among state government institutions, such as governors, legislatures, and attorneys general. Interest groups too have become much more active in using federalism to limit federal power. Many policy disputes between states and the federal government are seemingly couched in terms of federalism and states' rights, so much so that substantive disagreements over policy outcomes are overshadowed by constitutional arguments over federalism.[3] An emerging state activism against federal policy has become part of a larger debate about the normative underpinnings and meaning of American federalism.

State activism against the federal government has taken on a partisan tint as well. States' rights arguments are often made by conservative states to halt the implementation of federal laws and regulations within their jurisdictions, whereas more liberal states likewise invoke states' rights to protect their socially progressive laws that might be in conflict with national law and policy. Several examples are readily apparent. State policymakers in conservative states opposed to the Patient Protection and Affordable Care Act (ACA) passed by Congress in 2010 enacted legislation and used litigation to halt the implementation of the ACA within their jurisdictions. Similarly, conservative states that were opposed to the Environmental Protection Agency's (EPA) expansive regulations during President Barack Obama's administration also adopted litigation and legislative strategies to block the impact of the EPA's regulations locally. Conversely, more liberal policymakers in progressive states—who viewed the federal government as too slow and unable to address certain social issues such as same-sex marriage or the legalization of marijuana—passed laws that advanced more progressive policies in their states. Policymakers relied on states' rights arguments as well to sustain their own state-level policies that seemed to defy or run counter to national policy. These developments suggest that federalism is malleable or opportunistic; accordingly, "invocations of federalism tend to be spurred by specific substantive concerns" about public policy and are less about theoretical or normative debates about the structure of federalism.[4] Thus, conservative red and liberal blue state views on federalism have emerged and are

---

1 CHRISTOPHER P. BANKS & JOHN C. BLAKEMAN, THE U.S. SUPREME COURT AND NEW FEDERALISM: FROM THE REHNQUIST COURT TO THE ROBERTS COURT 6, 68–69 (2012).

2 *Id.,* 78–100.

3 JOHN KINCAID, *State–Federal Relations: Obstructive or Constructive Federalism?* in THE BOOK OF THE STATES 25–35 (Audrey Wall ed., 2015).

4 Austin L. Raynor, *The New State Sovereignty Movement,* 90 IND. L.J. 614, 618 (2015).

conditioned more by specific policy issues and less by historical and normative views on states' rights versus national power.[5]

The evolution of the Supreme Court's new federalism jurisprudence is significant because its present-day application is much different than its political origin. As discussed next, new federalism was not necessarily destined to become a province of the judiciary. But, when it did take hold in the Rehnquist Court era, its ideological and conservative purpose was to reinvigorate state sovereignty. While individual justices may have had their own ideological motivations for coalescing around new federalism principles, the legacy of their doctrinal shift is now less of an enduring judicial approach to federalism (although new federalism precedents are still very much a part of American constitutional law). Instead, the legacy of new federalism is now, in large part, a statement about how far state sovereignty arguments can be inserted into contentious public policy debates that span a wide range of issues, a phenomenon that has in turn resulted in increasing activism by states and interest groups to advocate for states' rights and their own political interests in the judicial policymaking process.

The intellectual development of new federalism

New federalism's intellectual heritage originated in the Nixon administration as part of a larger strategy for bringing about political change in the late 1960s and early 1970s. One of its main purposes, for conservatives, is to scale back the federal government's role in administering economic and social policies vis-à-vis the states.[6] In its original formulation, President Richard Nixon's political advisors saw it as a tool for constructing a domestic policy agenda that reconciles "the contradictory demands of dual sovereigns trying to coexist in one polity."[7] Neither Nixon nor his principal advisors, though, considered that new federalism represented a strict separation of co-equal federal and state sovereign spheres, as some "dual federalism" advocates, and sometimes the Supreme Court, insist upon. Instead, it was more in line with the ideals of "cooperative federalism" because it sought to forge a partnership between federal, state, and local governments through block grants, revenue sharing, and improved intergovernmental information systems.[8] For William Safire (Nixon's special assistant and speech writer) and apparently for Nixon himself, new federalism replaced "true federalism" (decentralization) with a system of "administrative decentralization in which all significant policies will be made in Washington with their administration left in state and local hands."[9] For many conservatives in the Nixon administration new federalism was more about administering national policy by the most local level of government possible, and not so much an ideological, revolutionary change in constitutional doctrine.

---

5 Robert Shapiro, *Not Old or Borrowed: The Truly New Blue Federalism*, 3 HARV. L & POL'Y REV. 33 (2009). See also Kathleen M. Sullivan, *From States' Rights Blues to Blue States' Rights: Federalism After the Rehnquist Court* 75 FORDHAM L. REV. 799 (2006).

6 Beverly Takahaski, *A New Paradigm for the Labor Movement: New Federalism's Unintended Consequences* 17 INT'L J. POL., CUL. & SOC. 261 (2003).

7 BANKS & BLAKEMAN, *supra* note 1, at 51.

8 DAVID B. WALKER, THE REBIRTH OF FEDERALISM: SLOUCHING TOWARDS WASHINGTON 24 (2nd ed.1995).

9 Editor's Introduction, 2 PUBLIUS: J. OF FEDERALISM 95–97 (1972).

Safire's reform ideas were debated internally in the Nixon administration a series of internal unpublished "new federalist" papers.[10] Critics included "Cato," a pseudonym adopted by Tom Huston (a lawyer and special assistant) and "Publius" (Wendell Hulcher, Assistant Director of the Office of Intergovernmental Relations). Neither found administrative decentralization attractive, favoring instead classical notions of federalism, and both, tellingly, opted to leave the Nixon administration after the debate was settled.[11] While their voices were heard, the debate was ultimately resolved by the White House when it embraced the viewpoints of Safire and "Johannes Althusius" (or Richard P. Nathan, who wrote the essay under this pseudonym while in the Office of Management and Budget). Thus, the ideas of "Publius" and "Althusius" are a baseline for understanding new federalism's genesis because Safire ultimately became a principal voice in articulating Nixon's domestic agenda, while Nathan later served as Under Secretary for the Department of Health, Education and Welfare (the agency in charge of effectuating welfare reform), a defining administrative component of Nixon new federalism policy practice.[12]

In Publius' view, federalism cannot be characterized as a simple debate over centralized versus decentralized power. Instead, federalism was a more complex arrangement of public administration. In fact, new federalism was conceived as a type of "national localism," or a system of administrative decentralization that recognized the reality of centralization while returning power and governing decisions back to the states and its local citizens. Similarly, divisive claims of states' rights were dampened in order to highlight notions of state obligations that are fulfilled in a unified national interest; and, he hinted that the distribution of federal monies was an important element in preserving national unity and the diversity underlying state and local governance. As he explained, new federalism is:

> A sea-change in the approach to the limitation of centralized power- part of what is "new" in the new Federalism-is that "States' rights" have now become rights of first refusal. Local authority will now regain the right to meet local needs itself, *and gain an additional right to Federal financial help*; but it will not regain the right it once held to neglect the needs of its citizens. *States' rights are now more accurately described as States' duties*, this is a fundamental change in Federalism, removing its great fault without undermining its essential local-first character, and provides the New Federalists with two of their prime causes: the cause of regaining control, and the cause of fairness.[13]

As Nixon put it, "The essence of New Federalism is to gain control of our national destiny by returning control to the States and localities; [that is,] power, funds, and authority are channeled increasingly to those governments closest to the people."[14] Relatedly, under new federalism a national conscience, or "what most people" in the nation "believe is 'only fair'" emerges when administrative services are rendered in the states not only in accordance with local needs, but also national purposes and goals.[15]

10 *Id.*, 96.
11 *Id.*, 97. See also Cato, *Federalism: Old and New*, 2 PUBLIUS: J. OF FEDERALISM 116 (1972), and Publius, *In Support of Strengthening the American Federal System*, 2 PUBLIUS: J. OF FEDERALISM 138 (1972).
12 Editor's Introduction, *supra* note 9, at 96–97.
13 Publius, *New Federalist Paper No. 1*, 2 PUBLIUS: J. OF FEDERALISM 98, 99–100 (1972) (emphasis added).
14 *Id.*, 100.
15 *Id.*, 100–106.

With the conceptual framework set, Publius addressed specific policy areas where new federalism might be implemented. Welfare reform, and especially grants-in-aid and revenue sharing, were policy targets for New Federalist thinking, as was unemployment insurance and tax policy.[16] Following Publius, Althusius likewise defended new federalism principles and showed how it would work in practice. After first observing that President Nixon first used the term "new federalism" in the context of referencing the administration's revenue sharing plan in an August 1969 television address, Althusius wrote that the federal government is responsible for the type of welfare reform that allows for the transfer of income to those who need it in an equitable and need-based fashion, ostensibly through legislative proposals such as family assistance, food stamps, and a family health insurance plan. For its part, the federal government assumes a predominant role in regulating the post office, the draft, student aid, and environmental pollution control. In contrast, states manage areas of "responsible decentralization" that primarily fall into the realm of traditional state functions involving government services and policymaking. These include, among others, education, manpower, and public health. For example, under one Nixon initiative in 1969, the Comprehensive Manpower Act, federal authority is consolidated into the federal Department of Labor, but state governors and local mayors are given more control to plan for, coordinate, and administer manpower programs with "flexible [federal] funding, sensitive to State and local needs." Finally, new federalism embraces a robust revenue sharing component, a reform proposal that uses a refined federal income taxes and grants-in-aid program to give the states flexibility in determining it administrative policymaking priorities.[17] President Nixon echoed this sentiment when he said to the nation's governors that, "It's not only what we spend that matters, it is the way we spend it."[18]

Notably, Nixon's new federalism was designed to be pragmatic and not ideologically divisive. It was meant to encourage policymaking that met the needs of individuals— especially the poor and minorities—through national policies administered by state governments. New federalism was to merge national policy priorities with local concerns and, as such, opposed the "the artificial construction of regional, ideological, or ethnic blocs." Instead, it sought to "fuse two elements: a greater respect for conscience deeply examined, and a more compassionate understanding of the concerns of the individual in its local application."[19] Policies set by the national government can be applied by states and localities in ways that best fits their unique circumstances, thus facilitating the functions the federal government does well—like raising or borrowing money and managing foreign affairs—while persuading states to respond flexibly in deciding how to administers services— like implementing crime control and educational programs—that are attentive to national goals as well as local circumstances.[20] In an important sense, new federalism was set to be a relatively neutral mechanism for policy cooperation and implementation by national and state governments. Under a new federalism paradigm, the "old liberal-conservative and centralist-localist calibrations will lose meaning when applied to a fusion of certain elements of liberalism and conservatism, of central concern and local consent."[21]

---

16 *Id.*
17 Johannes Althusius, *New Federalist No. 3*, 2 PUBLIUS: J. OF FEDERALISM 133, 134–137 (1972).
18 Publius, *supra* note 13, 100.
19 Publius, *supra* note 13, 104–106.
20 *Id.*, 100.
21 *Id.*, 113.

The Nixon administration provided the intellectual heft and impetus for a rethinking of American federalism, and a more conservative Supreme Court provided the constitutional legitimacy. Several key appointments to the Court between 1969 and 1991 by Presidents Nixon, Reagan, and George H.W. Bush, including Justice William Rehnquist who was appointed by Nixon in 1972 and elevated to Chief Justice by President Reagan in 1986, created a critical bloc of justices who were inclined to interpret federalism in light of state sovereignty. Guided by Chief Justice Rehnquist, newly appointed Justices Sandra Day O'Connor, Antonin Scalia, Anthony Kennedy, and Clarence Thomas could often be relied upon to form a "federalism five" core of justices who were willing to protect state sovereignty. Other more liberal justices, such as John Paul Stevens and Stephen Breyer would occasionally provide votes in favor of new federalism outcomes too.

While changes to the Court's personnel were critical to establishing new federalism doctrine, its development was also bolstered in the 1980s by the Reagan and Bush administrations, which perceived it more as a political ideology and constitutional doctrine that protected states' rights. In contrast, Nixon thought federalism was a vehicle to achieve pragmatic, flexible governance.[22] Thus, as the Court was developing new federalism constitutional doctrine, the Reagan and Bush administrations provided support by heightening the ideological stakes through policy goals that sought to roll back federal power and that emphasized state autonomy and sovereignty.

The economic context of new federalism

Much of the Court's development of new federalism took place in the context of economic policymaking by Congress. Beginning with the New Deal, Congress has long sought to use its plenary powers over interstate commerce to regulate policy areas that traditionally fall under the states' police powers. The Court validated this approach in several New Deal era cases in which it upheld Congress' use of its commerce power to regulate labor relations, child labor, and agricultural production, among other things. For the Court, the power over interstate commerce was very broad when Congress used it to regulate activities within states that impeded national commerce. From the mid-1930s to the mid-1990s, the Court's expansive reading of commerce and federalism dominated constitutional doctrine until the Rehnquist Court began to place limits on the reach of federal interstate commerce power, especially if it affected the broad police powers of the states.

A few representative cases stand out. In several concurring and dissenting opinions as an associate justice, Rehnquist set the "long fuse" for new federalism in the 1970s, up to his appointment as Chief Justice of the United States Supreme Court in 1986.[23] In a series of contentious cases that addressed the constitutionality of extending the federal minimum wage to state and local government employees, Rehnquist orchestrated a more assertive role for the Court (and lower federal judges) that sought to protect state sovereignty. In *National League of Cities v. Usery* (1976)[24] the Court struck down Congress' attempt to force states to pay their workers the federal minimum wage. Then-Associate Justice Rehnquist, building

---

22 Banks & Blakeman, *supra* note 1, at 75.
23 Mark Tushnet, A Court Divided: The Rehnquist Court and the Future of Constitutional Law 277 (2005).
24 426 U.S. 833 (1976).

off of his lone dissent in *Fry v. United States* (1975)[25] (an earlier federal wage case), argued that federalism protects "traditional" state functions from federal control, and judges have the authority to delineate what those are in federalism litigation. Put differently, Congress overreached by passing a law that interfered with state functions and policy choices that were an inherent part of their sovereignty. The minimum wage issue arose again in 1985 when the *Usery* case was overturned by a very divided Court in *Garcia v. San Antonio Metropolitan Transit Authority* (1985).[26] This time, with Rehnquist in the minority, the Court ruled that since the "traditional state functions" approach to federalism was unworkable, states are best able to protect their interests through the national political process. *Garcia* emphasized what became known as the "political safeguards" approach to federalism, which was premised on the states' abilities to represent their own interests directly and indirectly in Congress and the executive branch.

Even though the Court's internal disagreements over federalism lingered throughout the 1980s and 1990s, shortly after *Garcia* was decided it became clear that enough justices were willing to return to Rehnquist's more robust protections for state sovereignty, *Garcia* notwithstanding. Thus, in a series of cases that concerned Congress' use of its plenary powers of federal spending or interstate commerce as means of regulating state policy, the Court gradually returned to a jurisprudence that more aggressively protected state sovereignty. One important case, *South Dakota v. Dole* (1987),[27] concerned Congress' use of its spending clause power to condition the receipt of federal highway monies by the states according to their adoption of a minimum drinking ages for alcoholic beverages to 21. Although seven justices approved of the constitutionality of the policy, several justices in the majority and dissent made clear that Congress could not use the receipt of federal money to coerce states into following federal policy. Thus, the Court concluded that Congress retained broad prerogatives over federal spending; yet those prerogatives were at some point limited by antifederalist notions of state sovereignty and state decision-making. *South Dakota* may not have been the clear-cut new federalism decision that conservative Court watchers hoped for, but subsequent cases certainly moved in that ideological direction.

Several cases after *South Dakota* the Court addressed other issues of state sovereignty and federalism. One, for example, concerned Congress' use of federal mandates to implement federal policy priorities through its interstate commerce power that regulated policy areas which historically fell under the realm of broad state police power. Thus, in *New York v. U.S.* (1992)[28] the Court struck down a provision of the Low-Level Radioactive Waste Policy Act of 1985 that forced states to take title to all low-level waste generated within the state, unless they entered a regional compact with other states to dispose of the waste collectively. For the Court, the Tenth Amendment prohibited Congress from using its interstate commerce powers to commandeer states to take ownership of nuclear waste. *New York's* anti-commandeering principle was extended in *Printz v. U.S.* (1997)[29] when the Court invalidated a provision in the Brady Handgun Violence and Prevention Act that forced states to administer temporarily background checks for firearm purchases pending the creation and implementation of federal process for conducting the checks. In other

25 421 U.S. 542 (1975).
26 469 U.S. 528 (1985).
27 483 U.S. 203 (1987).
28 505 U.S. 144 (1992).
29 521 U.S. 898 (1997).

words, Congress could not commandeer the states to administer a federal regulatory program.

In the analogous cases of *U.S. v. Lopez* (1995)[30] and *U.S. v. Morrison* (2000),[31] the Court nullified Congress' use of its interstate commerce powers to address criminal justice issues. In *Lopez* the Court ruled that Congress could not use its power over commerce to regulate the non-economic activity of possessing a firearm near a school, as per the Gun Free School Zones Act, passed by Congress in 1990. And in *Morrison*, the Court ruled that the exercise of Congress' commerce power to regulate gender-based violence in the Violence Against Women Act, passed in 1994, was improper as well. In both cases, the Court articulated limits on Congress' use of its commerce power to address policy issues that typically fall under state police power. Notably, the *Lopez* decision was the first time since the New Deal that the Court placed limits on the interstate commerce clause as it applied to the states.

In time, new federalism jurisprudence jelled around cases that put constraints on Congress' interstate commerce powers. But the Court supported its developing line of jurisprudence with decisions grounded in other areas constitutional doctrine too. For example, in *College Savings Bank v. Fla. Prepaid Postsecondary Expense Board* (1999),[32] *Alden v. Maine* (1999),[33] *Kimel v. Florida Board of Regents* (2000),[34] and *Federal Maritime Commission v. South Carolina State Ports Authority* (2002)[35] the Court invalidated several attempts by Congress to abrogate, or waive, state sovereign immunity protected by the Eleventh Amendment. By broadly interpreting the Eleventh Amendment to protect state sovereign immunity, the Court forbade Congress from nudging states to comply with federal policy by exposing them to liability against their will. However, the Court's sovereign immunity cases remain inconsistent, with several decisions from same era reaching opposite results. For instance, in *Nevada Department of Human Resources v. Hibbs* (2003)[36] the Court (including Chief Justice Rehnquist in the majority) ruled that Congress, acting under its enforcement powers of the Fourteenth Amendment, could waive state sovereign immunity and expose states to liability under the Family and Medical Leave Act.[37]

Throughout the 1980s and 1990s much of new federalism doctrine was created in the context of the national government's economic powers. Notably, by the early 2000s it was co-opted by several federalism stakeholders for litigation in non-economic policy areas. A major impetus for that transition can be attributable to Justice Clarence Thomas, one of the Court's most prolific supporters of new federalism. Indeed, Thomas is referred to as the "true revolutionary" on the Court in federalism issues since he has advocated for a return to a pre-New Deal federalism jurisprudence that sharply curtails federal power.[38] For Thomas, the starting point in limiting federal power lies with a reassessment of the federal government's power over interstate commerce, a line of thinking that is consistent with an originalist reading of that power which is premised on a narrow eighteenth-century

30 514 U.S. 549 (1995).
31 529 U.S. 598 (2000).
32 527 U.S. 666 (1999).
33 527 U.S. 706 (1999).
34 528 U.S. 62 (2000).
35 535 U.S. 743 (2002).
36 538 U.S. 721 (2003).
37 BANKS & BLAKEMAN, *supra* note 1, at 98–99.
38 TUSHNET, *supra* note 23, at 277–278.

understanding of commerce. Thomas' narrow reading of the clause limits federal power to the economic activities of buying, selling, and transportation, but it excludes traditional intrastate functions associated with manufacturing and production.[39] Although Justice Thomas has yet to garner support for his originalist reading of the interstate commerce power from other justices, he has remained a stalwart supporter of new federalism. As such, he remains a lone outlier.

Even so, Thomas is significant to new federalism because his suggestions about the direction of jurisprudential doctrine can, in theory, be extended to cover areas of constitutional law that typically do not fall under federalism. In a series of cases addressing the First Amendment's Establishment Clause, Thomas has argued that the prohibition on government establishment of religion can only be applied to the federal government and not the states. In *Zelman v. Simmons-Harris* (2002)[40] and *Elk Grove United School District v. Newdow* (2004),[41] for example, Thomas articulated his view that the Establishment Clause only limits the power of the federal government. Thus, it operates as a jurisdictional clause to prohibit the national government from interfering with state religious policymaking. As with his originalist reading of the commerce clause, Thomas' reading of the Establishment Clause has received no support from his colleagues on the bench. Even so, it has garnered support from several interest groups and conservative state governments that were involved in litigating religious liberty issues in the 1990s and early 2000s.

Interestingly, the federalism argument employed by interest groups and states seeking to insulate state religious policymaking from federal and constitutional oversight was also adopted by more progressive groups in litigation concerning the Second Amendment. Just as some conservatives contended that the Establishment Clause is a federalism provision that preserved state power over religious policies, progressives have maintained that the Second Amendment is also a federalism provision that safeguarded state firearm policies. Under this interpretation, the Second Amendment does not grant a specific constitutional right to possess firearms (just as the Establishment Clause is not a rights' granting provision either). Instead, it insulates state firearms policy, as arguments in two key gun rights cases demonstrate. In *District of Columbia v. Heller* (2008)[42] and *McDonald v. City of Chicago* (2010)[43], the Supreme Court ruled that the Second Amendment represents an individual right to possess firearms (*Heller*), and that right is incorporated against the states through the Fourteenth Amendment's Due Process Clause (*McDonald*). In *Heller*, a range of federalism stakeholders such as the U.S. Conference of Mayors and several states pressed the Court to uphold the District of Columbia's handgun ban by echoing the District's argument that the Second Amendment is not a rights-granting provision; rather, it is a federalism provision that helped define the federal-state relationship.[44] Further, the briefs used the key new federalism cases involving firearms, *Lopez* and *Printz*, to advocate for the right of states to experiment with gun regulations and thus serve as laboratories for public policy. A brief filed by the City of Chicago even cited Justice Thomas' concurring opinion in *Elk Grove* in which he articulated

---

39 BANKS & BLAKEMAN, *supra* note 1, at 134.
40 536 U.S. 639 (2000).
41 542 U.S. 1 (2004).
42 554 U.S. 570 (2008).
43 561 U.S. 742 (2010).
44 See Brief by Major American Cities, the United States Conference of Mayors, and Legal Community Against Violence, District of Columbia v. Heller, 2008 U.S. S.Ct. Briefs LEXIS 48.

a federalism reading of the Establishment Clause that supported his federalism reading of the Second Amendment.

The examples of how new federalism has infused religious liberty and gun rights litigation by a range of constitutional actors illustrates several important points. First, new federalism doctrine has continued to evolve. Although its intellectual and ideological heritage is grounded in the politics of Republican presidential administrations and conservative Supreme Court justices, new federalism has been set loose from its conservative ideology of state sovereignty moorings and is now being used to argue for both conservative and progressive policy outcomes at the state level. Next, American federalism is becoming increasingly partisan in its scope and application. Thus, the conservative doctrine of state sovereignty, which originally was articulated in the context of protecting states from an overreaching federal government bent on creating progressive social and economic policymaking, is being transformed into a device that protects state policy, regardless of whether the policy in question is conservative, progressive, or somewhere in between. In many different policy areas, from environmental regulation to health care, federalism arguments are being co-opted by a range of constitutional actors to contest federal policy or to protect state policy.

Finally, new federalism remains judge-centric in the sense that federal judges would be expected to play an active role in resolving federalism conflicts between states and the national government. While states could always use the national political process to protect their interests, as proponents of process federalism theory maintain, the reinvigoration of state sovereignty by the Supreme Court also meant that federal courts would serve as a backstop to state sovereignty. Arguably, where the political process failed to protect their rights, states could turn to federal courts and invoke new federalism doctrine. Still, the prominent role of judges in new federalism has become diminished by the expansive range of constitutional stakeholders that now use the doctrine in legal and policy disputes. Moreover, the increasing polarization of federalism disputes suggests that crucial place assigned to the federal judiciary in policing the boundary between the national government and states may now be exaggerated. As noted below, other political forces and constitutional stakeholders are now prominent in resolving federalism disputes.

American federalism and political polarization

The decades since the 1980s have seen a resurgence of state power. On the one hand, it seems likely that new federalism signaled the Court's interest in protecting state power, which emboldened states to seek ways to confront and oppose federal power. The shift in the Court's federalism jurisprudence sent clear cues to state policymakers that federal courts will be receptive to state challenges to federal policy. On the other hand, recent scholarship linking political polarization at the national and state levels to the changing structure of federalism implies that structural considerations play a prominent role in explaining state behavior. The polarization that now inheres in national and state institutions prompts the political group that is out of power at one level of government to seek alternative avenues at the other national or subfederal level to enact favorable policies. While changes in federalism jurisprudence might have encouraged more state activism to preserve a states' rights approach to national policymaking, the partisanship embedded in political institutions means that the structure of federalism itself encourages red and blue state policymakers to oppose federal policies in accordance their own political preferences. In effect, policymakers have become more utilitarian in their arguments and decision-making and use federalism as another outlet to establish policies to which they are ideologically committed. In this fashion, they are less concerned with asserting normative constitutional principles to safeguard states' rights or sovereignty interests. As one federalism scholar puts it, federalism has allowed policymakers to shift the political initiative away from "paralyzed national institutions" to states, cities, and localities; and instead of diffusing polarization, as theories of federalism stipulate, subfederal institutions have guided polarization and political division in new directions.[45]

Accordingly, partisan warfare on the national level increasingly has been a part of federalism theory and practice. The previously mentioned debates over the Affordable Care Act and immigration policy illustrate the trend. The passage of Obamacare prompted a polarized backlash from its opponents, with Republican policymakers in nearly thirty states immediately filing lawsuits challenging its constitutionality on state sovereignty grounds, even though the litigation ultimately proved futile.[46] The partisan use of federalism was adopted by Democrat policymakers in states opposed to the many of the nascent Trump administration's policies on border control, immigration, the environment, and sanctuary cities.[47] The common element in both the health care and border control policy disputes is the underlying rhetoric and application of new federalism politics, albeit with a slightly different twist. Whereas new federalism developed in the Nixon administration as a means to incorporate states into the administration of national policy, and became constitutional doctrine in the eyes of conservative Supreme Court justices devoted to states' rights, today's new federalism theory and practice has evolved to allow conservative and progressive states the means to either contest overreaching federal power, as in the Affordable Care Act example, or to protect progressive state policies from restrictive regulation, as in the ongoing dispute over border control and immigration. Indeed, as new federalism was articulated and developed often in the context of economic policy, its rhetoric and principles now appear in state policy responses that are increasingly conditioned on the most contentious social policy debates of our time in the nation's culture wars.[48]

The partisan use of federalism has led to "blue state" and "red state" federalism, in which progressive blue states use states' rights language to protect more liberal economic and social policies from federal interference, and conservative red states use similar rhetoric to protect more conservative policies from federal oversight.[49] There are a myriad of causes

45 James H. Read, *Constitutionalizing the Dispute: Federalism in Hyper-Partisan Times*, 46 PUBLIUS: J. OF FEDERALISM , 337, 338 (2016).

46 Jessica Bulman-Pozen, *Partisan Federalism*, 127 HARV. L. REV. 1078 (2014). See also Christopher P. Banks, *Of White Whales, Obamacare, and the Roberts Court: The Republican Efforts to Harpoon Obama's Presidential Legacy*, 50 PS: POL. SCI. & POL. 40 (2017).

47 Joel Rose and Parker Yesko, *After 2 Weeks in Office, Trump Faces More Than 50 Lawsuits*, NPR POLITICS, (February 2, 2017), www.npr.org/2017/02/02/513045408/after-2-weeks-in-office-trump-faces-more-than-50-lawsuits (last visited March 27, 2017). See also Glenn Thrush and Maggie Haberman, *Trump Becomes Ensnared in Fiery G.O.P. Civil War*, N.Y. TIMES, (March 25, 2017) www.nytimes. com/2017/03/25/us/politics/trump-health-care-defeat-gop-civil-war.html?_r=0 (last visited March 27, 2017). See also Ryan Levi and Alex Emslie, *S.F. and California Attorney-General Announce Lawsuit Challenging Latest Trump "Sanctuary City" Policies*, KQED, (August 14, 2017) ww2.kqed.org/news/2017/08/14/s-f-and-california-attorney-general-announce-lawsuit-challenging-latest-trump-sanctuary-city-policies/ (last visited August 17, 2017).

48 James H. Read, *supra* note 45, at 2016. See also Austin L. Raynor, *The New State Sovereignty Movement*, 90 IND. L. J. 614 (2015).

49 ELAINE B. SHAPIRO, CULTURE WARS AND LOCAL POLITICS (1999). See also Kathleen Sullivan, *From States Rights' Blues to Blue States' Rights: Federalism After the Rehnquist Court*, 75 FORDHAM L. REV. 799 (2006).

to the polarization of American federalism, with some scholars suggesting that it is conditioned by a long-standing debate in American federalism between nationalists, who favor greater centralization of policy at the national level, and states' rights supporters, who advocate for more decentralization of policy.[50] Others argue that the more recent political polarization of national political institutions, and a growing partisanship of state policymakers, has polarized the structure of federalism itself. In the past, federalism used to provide a means through which states reached agreement on the broad parameters of federal programs and then implemented them through bargaining over "modest differences in the pace and content of state implementation." Now, the structure of federalism is affected by "deep schisms between partisans who increasingly inhabit separate policy and media worlds."[51] Thus, the current political polarization and behavior of policymakers has made federalism simply another aspect of partisan warfare, regardless of longstanding theoretical debates about the appropriate limits on federal and state power.

To be sure, other federalism scholars see the relationship between the states and the national government as conditioned by the levels of partisanship within and between both levels of government. Instead of states acting against the federal government to assert and protect a decentralized federalism, states now act in their own interests based on their partisan makeup. Therefore, federal politicians who support state power are often in alignment with state politicians opposed to federal power because they both come from the same political party, and that party is either in the minority at the national level or otherwise shut out of the national policymaking process. Federalism as an idea and structure serves to advance the partisan goals of some state and federal policymakers.[52]

State policymakers pursue different approaches too.[53] Some policymakers will simply refuse to implement federal policy when given a choice. Thus, many conservative states refused to expand Medicare under the Affordable Care Act, even though they would receive compensation from the national government.[54] Some states refused federal stimulus money for "shovel ready" projects during the Great Recession in part due to partisan opposition to Obama administration policies. Other states have more aggressively passed "sovereignty laws" that reflect legislative and regional resistance to federal laws regulating firearms, drugs, immigration, and health care, to name a few.[55] Such laws assert that a state may protect its own citizens from an overreaching federal law or policy, and while not a nullification of federal policy *per se*, sovereignty laws seek to impede the implementation of national polices with which the state disagrees. Sovereignty laws are rare, and interestingly reflect both red and blue state policies too. For example, red states have passed expansive firearms ownership laws designed to circumvent federal policy, and blue states have passed laws asserting the rights of the citizens to use medicinal marijuana in contravention of federal policy.

50 Kincaid, *supra* note 3, at 25.
51 Timothy L. Conlan and Paul Posner, *American Federalism in an Era of Partisan Polarization: The Intergovernmental Paradox of Obama's "New Nationalism"*, 46 PUBLIUS: J. OF FEDERALISM 281, 301 (2016).
52 Bulman-Polzen, *supra* note 46, at 1092.
53 See Raynor, *supra* note 48.
54 Bulman-Polzen, *supra* note 46, at 1050.
55 Raynor, *supra* note 48. *See also* John Dinan, *Contemporary Assertions of State Sovereignty and the Safeguards of American Federalism*, 74 ALB. L. REV. 1635 (2011).

New Federalism, political actors and constitutional stakeholders

Given the polarization of national and state politics and its broad impact on the structure of federalism, and its encouragement of states to use federalism to oppose national policy, other scholars have focused attention on types of state policymakers. Studies show, for example, that a state's opposition to federal policy correlates with the professionalization of state legislators.[56] A state's political culture, constitution, and statues might also direct or prompt policymakers, like attorneys general, to protect actively the interests of citizens against the national government.[57] State supreme court justices and judicial federalism itself likewise create yet another avenue through which policymakers within a state can oppose (or support) national policy.[58] Not surprisingly, state attorneys general (AG) are prominent too. State AGs have historically been active litigants in the U.S. Supreme Court, both as direct participants in lawsuits or as *amicus* friends of the court.[59] Indeed, state AG litigation has become much more coordinated over the past thirty years, with AGs from several often joining in multistate lawsuits to both oppose and support federal policies. Attorneys general often respond to state business demands for economic policy litigation, or to interest group demands to address social issues through litigation, and AGs act upon their own ideological interests too. The federal government and Congress have also encouraged state AGs to take on more enforcement of federal policy, and some national policymakers have encouraged states to oppose and litigate against national policy.[60]

Actors who are engaged in federalism disputes and are stakeholders and participants, to varying degrees, in the structure of American federalism, account for some of the changes to new federalism.[61] Actors such as state attorneys general, interest groups, and others are situated at several different points in the structure of American federalism and capable of influencing disputes over that structure through litigation. As stakeholders, they are concerned with specific, substantive outcomes in certain policy areas, and they are also concerned with the definition and redefinition of the structure of federalism. In sum, federalism participants will use the structure of federalism to seek policy outcomes in certain areas to which they are ideologically committed, and will also in parallel seek to interpret federalism a certain way to achieve that outcome. For instance, state AGs can initiate litigation directly against the national government or can join with other AGs to oppose or sustain federal policy through litigation. AGs can also serve as *amicus*—friends of the court—in federalism lawsuits, through which they make their preferences known to judges even though they are not direct litigants. Interest groups and groups of legislators and governors can serve similar functions by either sponsoring federalism litigation directly,

56 Pamela J. Clouse McCann, Charles R. Shipan, and Craig Volden, *Top Down Federalism: State Policy Responses to National Government Discussions*, 45 PUBLIUS: J. OF FEDERALISM 495 (2015).

57 Saikrishna Prakash, *The Boundless Treaty Power Within a Bounded Constitution*, 90 NOTRE DAME L. REV. 1499 (2015).

58 Simon Zschirnt, *Gay Rights, the New Judicial Federalism, and State Supreme Courts: Disentangling the Effects of Ideology and Judicial Independence*, 37 JUST. SYS. J. 348 (2016).

59 PAUL NOLETTE, FEDERALISM ON TRIAL: STATE ATTORNEYS GENERAL AND NATIONAL POLICYMAKING IN CONTEMPORARY AMERICA (2015). See also Colin Provost, *When to Befriend the Court? Examining State Amici Curiae Participation Before the U.S. Supreme Court*, 11 STATE POL. & POL'Y QUARTERLY 4 (2011).

60 *Id.*, 198–219.

61 Read, *supra* note 45, at 340.

or more likely by serving as amicus in cases in which they have an interest. By considering actors within the structure of federalism, we are better able to see how new federalism doctrine resonates throughout the policy process.

New federalism and public policy

Given the growth of litigation that centers upon the strategic use of federalism arguments for partisan gain, the remaining chapters address their significance and impact in different areas of public policy—a topic that has been generally been minimized in the controlling literature and public law scholarship. The authors that contribute to the edited volume represent an interdisciplinary approach: while many are lawyers and law professors, others are within the political or social science disciplines. All are experts in their field and their perspectives provide invaluable insights about the importance of federalism and how it affects the scope and nature of American policymaking debates and legal disputes.

In Chapter 2, "The right to keep and bear arms in the Roberts Court," Nelson Lund, a university professor at George Mason University's Antonin Scalia Law School, traces the legal and historical origins of the Second Amendment and it federalism implications in U.S. Supreme Court gun regulation jurisprudence. After supplying a legal and historical picture of the Second Amendment, Lund examines two key decisions, *District of Columbia v. Heller*[62] and *McDonald v. City of Chicago*,[63] that nullified state gun regulations in the District of Columbia and Chicago and which had the effect of extending *Heller's* principle that the Amendment protects an individual right to self-defense in the home to all state governments through the Fourteenth Amendment's incorporation doctrine. In observing that both decisions unleashed a spate of litigation that tested the limits of the Second Amendment's constitutional boundaries in laws aiming to regulate the possession and use of firearms, he concludes that the courts will continue to read *Heller* principle narrowly which, in turn, constricts its practical impact in shaping gun laws. As a result, state legislatures will continue to have significant discretion to regulate firearms and related gun control issues, especially since the Supreme Court to date has shown it has little inclination to review federal circuit court decisions addressing *Heller* and its constitutional implications.

In Chapter 3, political scientist Christopher P. Banks, an American politics professor at Kent State University, examines the different way states, and state actors such as states' attorney generals, have challenged President Donald Trump's use of federal executive orders restricting entry of foreign nationals into the United States on the grounds of national security in "National security and anti-terrorism policies: The federalism implications of Trump's travel ban." After surveying the President's executive orders declaring the ban, Banks details the principal litigation challenging them in the Fourth and Ninth Circuits, as well as in the Supreme Court. He finds that state attorney generals have been at the forefront of shaping the contours of judicial precedents affecting anti-terrorism initiatives such as the Trump travel ban, a phenomenon that increasingly demonstrates the politicization of the nation's culture wars and of federalism itself. Not surprisingly, he also observes that state institutions and actors that are challenging the ban are still taking advantage of new federalism rhetoric in their legal arguments, a finding that is consistent with the growing perception

62 554 U.S. 570 (2008).
63 561 U.S. 742 (2010).

that they need to establish a global profile in safeguarding their interests against federal overreaching on immigration and foreign policy issues.

In Chapter 4, "Capital punishment and federalism: International obligations and domestic standards," Mary Welek Atwell, a professor of criminal justice from Radford University, explores the public and legal policy implications of capital punishment, an issue that she describes as "a paradigm of federalism in the United States, a contested site of debates over how to balance state versus national interests." Against the backdrop of the Rehnquist Court's new federalism decisions, such as *United States v. Morrison* (2000),[64] which mandated that there had to be a constitutional separation between national and state interests in controlling their criminal justice punishment regimes, Atwell concludes that making any meaningful distinctions about what is being separated is problematic for two reasons. First, the Supreme Court has had difficulty in articulating how international legal standards align with the constitutional requirements of state criminal procedure, in part because there is wide disagreement between the justices about whether foreign law should be a part of interpreting the U.S. Constitution. Second, equally problematic is the Court's uneven decision-making in using the "evolving standards of decency" principle, a cornerstone of Eighth Amendment jurisprudence, as a basis for determining what a national consensus might be in determining if capital punishment runs afoul of constitutional requirements. The inability of ascertaining national consensus, in turn, frustrates the efforts by state governments to enact capital punishment laws that are in line with the public policy choices States make as sovereign entities.

Chapter 5, "The Supreme Court and the Affordable Care Act: The consequences of the *NFIB v. Sebelius* decision for health care policy," is written by John Dinan, a professor of politics and international affairs at Wake Forest University. His analysis focuses on the Supreme Court's landmark *National Federation of Independent Business v. Sebelius*[65] (*NFIB*) decision which, among other things, established the constitutional validity of requiring individuals to buy health insurance as well as authorizing Medicaid expansion in the states, subject to constitutional limitations, through Obamacare, or the federal Affordable Care Act. After taking stock of the effects of *NFIB* over a five-year period, he concludes that it has enhanced the capacity of state officials to leverage their interests in bargaining with the federal government over how to implement Medicaid expansion which, in turn, has allowed several states to resist the pressure exerted by federal officials to expand. Dinan also finds that *NFIB* has also been used as leverage by state officials to exact concessions from the federal government about the design and structure of Medicaid expansion in states that were more favorably disposed to expansion. These effects are important for federalism theory, says Dinan, because the Court's new federalism decisions are not necessarily insurmountable constitutional barriers that limit federal powers; instead, they have become the basis to strengthen the capacity of state governments to resist federal overreaching through complex and nuanced negotiation and bargaining strategies or practices that serve state public policy interests.

Nancy J. Knauer, the director of the law and public policy program at Temple University Beasley School of Law and a professor of law, examines the interplay between federalism and LGBT rights in Chapter 6, "Federalism, marriage equality, and LGBT rights." While

---

64 U.S. v. Morrison, 529 U.S. 528 (2000).
65 National Federation of Independent Business v. Sebelius, 132 S.Ct. 2566 (2012).

surveying the legal strategy that led up to the landmark marriage equality *U.S. v. Windsor*[66] and *Obergefell v. Hodges*[67] rulings, Knauer observes that advocacy on both sides of the issue have used federalism opportunistically for political purposes in taking positions that advanced their interests in a fluid political environment. Although *Windsor* reaffirmed the state's prerogative to control the definition of marriage and *Obergefell* did the opposite, she reasons that both decisions are compatible with a federalism ideal that give state legislatures the authority to define and regulate marriage relationships so long as they enact laws that comport with the due process and equality safeguards of the Fourteenth Amendment. In this regard, she concludes, "federalism has proven to be a pragmatic, but also imperfect, institutional choice for LGBT rights advocates because state level civil rights protections are generally not portable, and they remain especially vulnerable to majoritarian measures such as citizens' initiatives."

The federalism implications of federal and state regulation of marijuana is the focus of Chapter 7, "The legalization of marijuana and the interplay of federal and state laws," written by Sam Kamin, the Vicente Sederberg Professor of Marijuana Law and Policy at the University of Denver Sturm College of Law. Kamin first observes that state governments have the unique responsibility to authorize, tax, and regulate marijuana even though federal law prohibits it. While the specter of federal prohibition cannot stop the states from enacting their own laws to legalize and regulate marijuana, the federal ban places the states in the uncomfortable position of not being able to protect their citizens from criminal and civil enforcement of federal laws, and it impedes state legislatures from enacting laws that either are directed at reform or helping marijuana businesses, patients, and users comply with activities that are in compliance with state law. Given the complex and uneven interplay of federal and state laws on the issue, Kamin asserts that a cooperative federalism approach, such as the one being implemented in Canada, is needed to reconcile the competing interests of the federal government and states in enacting, regulating, or enforcing marijuana laws.

Robert L. Glicksman, the J.B. and Maurice C. Shapiro Professor of Environmental Law at the George Washington University Law School, also acknowledges that environmental regulation is based upon a cooperative federalism framework. Yet, in Chapter 8, "The firm constitutional foundation and shaky political future of environmental cooperative federalism," Glicksman argues that the Supreme Court's new federalism approach, as manifested by the interpretation the Rehnquist and Robert Courts have given to the Commerce or Spending Clauses and the Tenth Amendment, has not been able to derail the federal government's capacity to pass laws that regulate the environment in the states. Instead, he concludes, the vital role that states play in the cooperative federalism model is threatened more by executive rather than judicial action in light of the Trump administration's commitment to devolution. A devolutionary approach, he concludes, will damage the states' ability to help the federal government to regulate the environment because federal funding will be slashed or the preemption doctrine may be invoked to hinder state efforts to impose environmental constraints.

Immigration law and its impact on the federal and state level is the center of the analysis in Chapter 9, "Immigration federalism," an essay authored by Pratheepan Gulasekaram, a professor of law at the Santa Clara University School of Law. Gulasekaram reminds us that

---

66 U.S. v. Windsor, 133 S.Ct. 2675 (2013).
67 Obergefell v. Hodges, 135 S.Ct. 2071 (2015).

immigration is hardly the exclusive province of federal congressional legislation. In fact, he argues, immigration federalism has been a growing but variable source of integrationist or restrictive regulation from states and localities that are on the front lines of managing the immigrant population in different areas of the country. For its part, the Supreme Court has given mixed signals through its precedents that either support, reject or fail to give guidance as to the permissible constitutional boundaries of state regulations, a problem that is exacerbated by the highly contentious nature of the political debate surrounding the issue. As a result, Gulasekaram finds that "the nation is now a landscape of variegated immigration policies" that is substantially defined by the significant role the states play in immigration regulation, a trend that is likely to continue into the future amidst ongoing political contestations that are fueled, in part, by Trump administration restrictionist initiatives.

Franita Tolson, a professor of law at the University of Southern California Gould School of Law, examines the linkages between voting rights and federalism in Chapter 10, "The equal sovereignty principle as federalism sub-doctrine: A reassessment of *Shelby County v. Holder.*" She describes the Supreme Court's ruling in *Shelby County v. Holder,*[68] which struck down the preclearance formula of the federal Voting Rights Act of 1965, as an "aggressive pro-federalism" decision that has had the effect of shifting the onus of regulating elections from the federal government back to the states. Even so, she suggests that the forceful use of the equal sovereignty principle that is at the base of *Shelby County's* rationale is inconsistent with the text, structure, and history of the Fourteenth and Fifteenth Amendments, a problem that is made worse by the Court's increasing insistence in its case law to view that the reauthorized Voting Rights Act is the product of special interest group advocacy that works to advantage minority groups at the expense of majority will.

In Chapter 11, the book's conclusion, Christopher P. Banks brings all of the perspectives offered in the book together by identifying the common themes of the essays and offering some new insights about their significance in light of evolving federalism doctrine in the Supreme Court and the impact that the Trump presidency may have in altering the balance of power between the federal government and the states with devolutionary policies and new appointments to the federal bench.

68 Shelby County v. Holder, 133 S.Ct. 2612 (2013).

2 The right to keep and bear arms in the Roberts Court

Nelson Lund

> *A well regulated Militia, being necessary to the security of a free State, the right of the people to keep and bear Arms, shall not be infringed.*

Like everything else in the Bill of Rights, the Second Amendment originally restrained only the new federal government. This left the states free to regulate weapons as they saw fit, just as they were free to regulate such matters as speech and religion. The Supreme Court did not invalidate a federal statute under the Second Amendment until 2008, and it was only in 2010 that a regulation adopted pursuant to state law was struck down. These two decisions—*District of Columbia v. Heller*[1] and *McDonald v. City of Chicago*[2]—prompted a stream of litigation that may eventually put significant constraints on legislative efforts to regulate the possession and use of weapons. As this is written in the summer of 2017, however, the Court's decisions have had very limited practical effects. It is worth recalling the Rehnquist Court's Commerce Clause decision in *United States v. Lopez*,[3] which set off celebrations and lamentations about a federalism revolution that has yet to come about. Similarly, the Roberts Court has so far shown only that the Second Amendment does not leave governments with absolutely limitless regulatory power.

This chapter begins with a brief sketch of the legal and historical background that set the stage for *Heller* and *McDonald*. After a description of those cases, the chapter surveys the application of the decisions by the lower courts. The chapter concludes with an analysis of the Supreme Court's response to the case law developed by the lower courts.

The long road to *Heller* and *McDonald*

The Second Amendment is a unique element of the Bill of Rights in at least two respects. First, it contains a prefatory phrase that refers to a reason for protecting the substantive right with which it deals. Second, that phrase addresses an issue that caused considerable vexation during the Constitutional Convention and the ensuing ratification debates.

The lineage of the Second Amendment can be traced back to the English Bill of Rights, which provided: "That the subjects which are Protestants may have arms for their defence

---

1 554 U.S. 570 (2008).
2 561 U.S. 742 (2010).
3 514 U.S. 549 (1995).

suitable to their Conditions and as allowed by Law."[4] This provision reflected the outcome of a struggle between Parliament and the Crown for authority over military power in an insular country that did not need to maintain standing armies. For many years, England's cash-strapped governments sought to keep up a militia consisting of most able-bodied men, who were required to supply their own arms and undergo part-time unpaid training. For foreign wars, the Crown had to ask Parliament for funds with which to pay and equip full-time soldiers.

This arrangement broke down during the reign of Charles I, when King and Parliament began to contend with each other for control of the militia. During the ensuing civil wars, the population experienced military rule as well as concerted efforts by various political coalitions to disarm their political opponents and impose unpopular laws. The right to arms provision adopted after the Glorious Revolution reflected a belief that an armed citizenry was an important safeguard against the imposition of tyranny.[5]

Before our revolution, Americans had managed their own colonial militias and experienced their own share of unpleasant relations with regular troops. This led to a strong public prejudice against standing armies and in favor of keeping up the militia as an alternative. The delegates at Philadelphia were acutely sensitive to popular opinion on this issue, but the Convention faced a conundrum. Although standing armies were considered a serious threat to liberty, experience during the Revolutionary War convinced many leading Americans that the militia could not provide a sufficiently reliable tool for defending the nation against sudden threats.

A strong militia system might at least deprive the federal government of an excuse for unnecessarily raising armies during peacetime. But that approach had problems of its own. If control over the militia were left with the state governments, the resulting lack of uniformity in training and equipment would prevent the creation of a really effective fighting force. On the other hand, if control of the militia were lodged in the federal government, a full-time "select militia" could become an instrument of federal policy, hardly less dangerous to liberty than a standing federal army. Or the militia could be allowed by the federal government to fall into desuetude, deprived of training and discipline, so that it would be unable to act effectively when it was most needed as a counterweight to federal power.

There was no way out of the conundrum. Requiring the federal government to rely exclusively on the traditional militia would have imperiled national security because such forces could not be expected to provide a match for regular troops. But giving the federal government discretion to maintain an effective military establishment for national defense entailed a risk that this force would be used to oppress the citizens. Faced with a difficult choice, the Convention chose to give the new federal government almost unlimited authority to maintain armies and to regulate the militia.[6]

This massive increase in federal military authority became one of the leading complaints by Anti-Federalists who were skeptical about the proposed replacement for the Articles of Confederation. When the First Congress took up the drafting of a bill of rights, there was

---

4 1 W. & M., ch. 2, sess. 2 (1688) (Eng.).
5 For more detailed discussions, see JOYCE LEE MALCOLM, TO KEEP AND BEAR ARMS: THE ORIGINS OF AN ANGLO-AMERICAN RIGHT (1994); Nelson Lund, *The Past and Future of the Individual's Right to Arms,* 31 GA. L. REV. 1, 6–14 (1996).
6 See Lund, *Past and Future, supra* note 5, at 30–31.

absolutely no willingness to satisfy Anti-Federalist sentiment on this issue by subtracting from the federal government's military power. But that did not mean that fears about possible abuse of the new federal authority should be treated disrespectfully. The words of praise for the militia in the Second Amendment are best understood as a bow to the widespread fear of standing armies, and as an acknowledgement of the value placed on the traditional militia system.[7]

The Second Amendment provoked no serious opposition when proposed. Nobody had ever advocated that the federal government be given any power to disarm American citizens, just as no one proposed that it be given power to abridge the freedom of speech or the free exercise of religion. For a long time after the Bill of Rights was adopted, moreover, there was little occasion for controversies about the meaning of the Second Amendment. The federal government made at least a show of keeping up the militia for a while, and it never did raise armies or create a select militia in order to oppress the people. Nor did Congress enact what we would think of today as gun control regulations.

After the Civil War, the nation adopted the Fourteenth Amendment. There is good, if not absolutely compelling, historical evidence that the Privileges or Immunities Clause[8] was meant to protect the individual rights listed in the first eight Amendments against state action. But shortly after it was adopted, the Supreme Court virtually repealed that clause by giving it an extremely narrow interpretation.[9]

The twentieth century brought two developments that were crucial steps on the road to *Heller* and *McDonald*. First, the Supreme Court began "incorporating" specific provisions of the Bill of Rights into the Fourteenth Amendment through its Due Process Clause.[10] This was done on a piecemeal basis, notwithstanding a serious effort by Justice Hugo Black to show that the Privileges or Immunities Clause made the whole Bill of Rights applicable to the states.[11] Second, the federal government began enacting restrictions on civilians' access to firearms, and some states began to regulate weapons more aggressively than they had done during the nineteenth century.

The first significant federal gun control statute in our history was enacted just as Prohibition ended. Congress imposed a registration requirement and an extremely high tax on certain "gangster weapons," including machineguns and short-barreled shotguns. When two men were indicted for possessing an unregistered short-barreled shotgun, the district court quashed the indictment on Second Amendment grounds. In *United States v. Miller*,[12] the Supreme Court reversed and remanded, leaving the court below to determine whether such a weapon "has some reasonable relationship to the preservation or efficiency of a well regulated militia."[13] For several decades thereafter, the lower federal courts interpreted *Miller* to mean that the Constitution does not protect an individual right to keep and bear

---

7 For more detail, see *id.* at 20–29, 32–39.

8 "No State shall make or enforce any law which shall abridge the privileges or immunities of citizens of the United States."

9 *See* Slaughter-House Cases, 83 U.S. 36 (1873); United States v. Cruikshank, 92 U.S. 542 (1875).

10 "No State shall . . . deprive any person of life, liberty, or property, without due process of law."

11 See Adamson v. California, 332 U.S. 46, 68–123 (1947) (Black, J., dissenting).

12 307 U.S. 174 (1939).

13 *Id.* at 178. The defendants, who had fled after the indictment was quashed, were not represented in the Supreme Court, and the trial court took no further action after the Court's remand.

arms, but rather a collective right connected with regulating the militia.[14] The Second Amendment appeared to be a dead letter.

Later in the twentieth century, legislatures became more aggressive in regulating firearms. In response to several political assassinations and a wave of urban riots, Congress enacted the Gun Control Act of 1968.[15] This law sought to channel gun sales through federally licensed dealers, who were forbidden to transfer firearms to felons, illegal drug users, or those with serious mental illnesses. In succeeding years, the statutory regime has been modified in various ways, usually in the direction of broader regulation.[16] In response to rising rates of violent crime in the 1970s and 1980s, some state and local governments adopted additional regulations.[17] Many others, however, did not. Generally speaking, jurisdictions with large urban populations regulated guns more aggressively, and rural jurisdictions less so or not at all.[18]

During this period, significant political pushback against gun control developed. One seminal event occurred at the annual meeting of the National Rifle Association in 1977. A grassroots effort of the membership succeeded in removing the group's leadership, which was seen as insufficiently committed to resisting legal restrictions on gun rights.[19] During the same period, a small group of practicing lawyers began producing scholarly analyses that challenged the militia-centered "collective right" interpretation of the Second Amendment that had become completely dominant in the federal courts.[20] According to this new body of scholarship, the Second Amendment had been put into the Constitution to protect the right of individuals to keep and bear arms for defense against criminals as well as against tyrannical governments. Except for one isolated case in 2001,[21] no federal courts accepted this interpretation. Nevertheless, two developments outside the courts

---

14 This was a very dubious interpretation of the cryptic opinion in *Miller*, but the Supreme Court declined to review any of the decisions that adopted it. For a brief review of the cases, see Nelson Lund, *The Ends of Second Amendment Jurisprudence: Firearms Disabilities and Domestic Violence Restraining Orders*, 4 TEX. REV. L. & POL. 157, 184–88 (1999).

15 Pub. L. No. 90-618, 82 Stat. 1213.

16 Amendments include the following: Pub.L. 93-639, § 102, Jan. 4, 1975, 88 Stat. 2217; Pub.L. 99-308, § 101, May 19, 1986, 100 Stat. 449; Pub.L. 99-360, § 1(b), July 8, 1986, 100 Stat. 766; Pub.L. 99-408, § 1, Aug. 28, 1986, 100 Stat. 920; Pub.L. 101-647, Title XVII, § 1702(b)(2), Title XXII, § 2204(a), Nov. 29, 1990, 104 Stat. 4845, 4857; Pub.L. 103-159, Title I, § 102(a)(2), Nov. 30, 1993, 107 Stat. 1539; Pub.L. 103-322, Title XI, §§ 110102(b), 110103(b), 110105(2), 110401(a), 110519, Title XXXIII, § 330021(1), Sept. 13, 1994, 108 Stat. 1997, 1999, 2000, 2014, 2020, 2150; Pub.L. 104-88, Title III, § 303(1), Dec. 29, 1995, 109 Stat. 943; Pub.L. 104-208, Div. A, Title I, § 101(f) [Title VI, § 658(a)], Sept. 30, 1996, 110 Stat. 3009-371; Pub.L. 105-277, Div. A, § 101(b) [Title I, § 119(a)], (h) [Title I, § 115], Oct. 21, 1998, 112 Stat. 2681-69, 2681-490; Pub.L. 107-273, Div. C, Title I, § 11009(e)(1), Nov. 2, 2002, 116 Stat. 1821; Pub.L. 107-296, Title XI, § 1112(f)(1) to (3), (6), Nov. 25, 2002, 116 Stat. 2276; Pub.L. 109-162, Title IX, § 908(a), Jan. 5, 2006, 119 Stat. 3083.

17 The handgun bans at issue in *Heller* and *McDonald*, for example, were enacted in 1976 and 1982, respectively. In 1989, California adopted the Roberti-Roos Assault Weapons Control Act, which became the model for the 1994 federal statute and other similar laws discussed below.

18 See, e.g., Joseph Blocher, *Firearms Localism*, 123 YALE L.J. 82 (2013).

19 See, e.g., Reva B. Siegel, *Dead or Alive: Originalism as Popular Constitutionalism in* Heller, 122 HARV. L. REV. 191, 210–11 (2008).

20 None of these lawyers was a credentialed academic, which tells us something about the orientation of the legal academy and about the lingering tradition of law as a scholarly profession. See Nelson Lund, *Outsider Voices on Guns and the Constitution*, 17 CONST. COMM. 701 (2000).

21 United States v. Emerson, 270 F.3d 203 (5th Cir. 2001).

helped prepare the ground for its acceptance by the Supreme Court seven years later in the *Heller* decision.

In 1987, Florida became the first state with large urban population centers to enact a statute requiring that a license to carry a concealed firearm in public be issued to almost all law-abiding adults who apply for one. Notwithstanding predictions of disaster by many putative experts, violent crime went down instead of up, and permit holders almost never misused their guns. Florida's successful experiment with a "shall issue" law has now been repeated in all but a handful of jurisdictions, and 14 states do not even require citizens to obtain a license. These liberalized laws have seemed to operate without adverse effects on public safety.[22]

The second important development occurred in 1994, when Congress enacted a statute that essentially froze the civilian supply of "assault weapons," as well as magazines holding more than ten rounds of ammunition. The disfavored weapons consisted mostly of rifles that bore a superficial resemblance to the fully automatic machineguns used by the military. Machineguns, however, had been tightly restricted since 1934,[23] and the small supply in the hands of civilians had been frozen in 1986.[24] The 1994 law applied only to *semi*-automatic rifles that operated no differently than many other firearms that were unaffected by the new statute.

A disinterested observer might have regarded this initiative as a clever piece of political grandstanding. By making the law sound like something aimed at high-firepower machineguns, its proponents may have hoped that voters who worried about violent crime would be pleased that something was being done. At the same time, the fact that the law focused primarily on cosmetic features might have been expected to dampen opposition from hunters and other gun enthusiasts, who would realize that their access to functionally identical rifles would be unimpaired.

If that was the thinking behind the new statute, it turned out to be a miscalculation. In the mid-term elections that year, opposition to the statute was a prominent issue and the Democratic Party lost control of both houses of Congress for the first time in four decades. In 2000, Al Gore nonetheless campaigned in favor of new gun regulations, which may well have caused him to lose the very close election that year. Since that time, no significant new federal regulations affecting the general population have been adopted, even when the Democrats enjoyed overwhelming congressional majorities after the 2008 elections. Consistent with earlier patterns, highly publicized crimes like the Sandy Hook massacre have prompted new restrictions in some heavily Democratic states, and either no action or further liberalization elsewhere.

Heller and *McDonald*

By the time the *Heller* case arose, the body of scholarship challenging the "collective right" interpretation of the Second Amendment had become very large and was increasingly accepted within the legal academy. Most of this work involved textual and historical analysis aimed at recovering the original meaning of the Amendment. For that reason, it had become

---

22 See, e.g., JOHN R. LOTT, JR., MORE GUNS, LESS CRIME (3d ed. 2010); Nat'l Research Council of the Nat'l Academies, *Firearms and Violence: A Critical Review* 2 (2004).

23 National Firearms Act, Pub. L. No. 73-474, 48 Stat. 1236.

24 See 18 U.S.C. § 922(o).

unthinkable that a leading proponent of originalism would casually endorse the collective-right interpretation, as Robert Bork had repeatedly done in the past.[25] Nor could one have imagined that the Chief Justice of the United States would say, as Warren Burger did in 1990, that the individual-right interpretation is "one of the greatest pieces of fraud, I repeat the word 'fraud,' on the American public by special interest groups that I've ever seen in my lifetime. The real purpose of the Second Amendment was to ensure that state armies—the militia—would be maintained for the defense of the state."[26] Notwithstanding what virtually all of the lower courts had said, moreover, the Supreme Court itself had never adopted the collective-right theory.

Sensing an opportunity, a group of libertarian lawyers arranged a test case challenging the District of Columbia's broad ban on the possession of handguns by civilians. The plaintiffs had respectable backgrounds and appealing reasons for seeking relief, thus avoiding the bad "litigation optics" that plague Second Amendment challenges brought by criminal defendants. Although the trial court upheld the statute, the D.C. Circuit reversed, becoming the first federal court of appeals in history to invalidate a gun control law under the Second Amendment.[27]

By a vote of 5–4, the Supreme Court affirmed, in a decision that turned out to be a test case for the interpretive theory of originalism.[28] With almost no precedent to constrain its analysis, the Court had an opportunity to look for the original meaning of a constitutional text that is manifestly puzzling. The chief justice seized the moment by assigning the opinion to Antonin Scalia, the Court's most prominent advocate of originalism.

Not surprisingly, Scalia drew heavily on the revisionist scholarship that had built up over the previous decades, and he emphasized the majority's commitment to the principles of originalist interpretation. The result was a strong opinion concluding that the Second Amendment protects an individual right whose core purpose is rooted in the inherent or natural right of self-defense.[29] Justice John Paul Stevens wrote an opinion, joined by all of the dissenters, that defended the collective-right interpretation as a correct reading of the Amendment's original meaning.[30] Whichever side had the best of the debate, which is too complex to summarize here, the issue has now been settled for all practical purposes as far as the courts are concerned.

The *scope* of the individual right to arms, however, is far from settled. *Heller* held that there is a constitutional right to keep a handgun in one's home for self-protection, but the Court's opinion can be read to imply little or nothing beyond that narrow holding. In this respect, it resembles *Lopez*, which held that a statute banning guns in local schools exceeded congressional authority under the Commerce Clause. With a slight adjustment to the statute's jurisdictional provision, the same law was reenacted and remains on the books today.[31] Except for one minor statutory provision that might have been reframed so as to

---

25 See, e.g., Andrew D. Herz, *Gun Crazy: Constitutional False Consciousness and Dereliction of Dialogic Responsibility*, 75 B.U. L. REV. 57, 106 n.218 (1995) (collecting quotations).

26 See Silveira v. Lockyer, 312 F.3d 1052, 1063 (9th Cir. 2002) (quoting Warren E. Burger, *The Right to Bear Arms*, PARADE MAGAZINE, Jan. 14, 1990, at 4).

27 Parker v. District of Columbia, 478 F.3d 370 (2007).

28 District of Columbia v. Heller, 554 U.S. 570 (2008).

29 For an analysis that emphasizes some of the opinion's weaknesses, see Nelson Lund, *The Second Amendment, Heller, and Originalist Jurisprudence*, 56 UCLA L. REV. 1343, 1349–68 (2009).

30 554 U.S. at 636–80.

31 See 18 U.S.C. § 922(q); United States v. Danks, 221 F.3d 1037 (8th Cir. 1999).

pass constitutional review,[32] only the extraordinary individual mandate in the Affordable Care Act has been found to exceed the bounds of the Commerce Clause.[33] And even that statute was saved by Chief Justice John Roberts' heroic re-characterization of the regulatory penalty as a tax.[34]

The *Heller* opinion does contain a lot of rhetoric pointing toward a broad and robust right to arms. In that respect, it resembles *Brown v. Board of Education*,[35] which could easily have been read to apply only to public schools. As everyone knows, that case was soon interpreted to mean that virtually all forms of racial segregation in public facilities are unconstitutional. We cannot know yet whether *Heller* will eventually turn out to bear a closer resemblance to *Lopez* or to *Brown*. The evidence currently available, however, suggests that *Heller* may be read quite narrowly.

In sharp contrast with the detailed textual and historical analysis that Scalia set forth in defense of the individual-right interpretation of the Second Amendment, his discussion of the specific question actually at issue in the case is supported by no such evidence:

> The handgun ban amounts to a prohibition of an entire class of "arms" that *is* overwhelmingly chosen by American society for that lawful purpose [*viz.* self defense]. The prohibition extends, moreover, to the home, where the need for defense of self, family, and property is most acute. . . . [T]he American people have considered the handgun to be the quintessential self-defense weapon. There are many reasons that a citizen may prefer a handgun for home defense: It is easier to store in a location that is readily accessible in an emergency; it cannot easily be redirected or wrestled away by an attacker; it is easier to use for those without the upper-body strength to lift and aim a long gun; it can be pointed at a burglar with one hand while the other hand dials the police. Whatever the reason, handguns *are* the most popular weapon chosen by Americans for self-defense in the home, and a complete prohibition of their use is invalid.[36]

Even more arresting is the opinion's endorsement of several types of modern gun controls, all without any effort to connect such regulations with the original meaning of the Second Amendment. *Heller* offers a non-exhaustive list of "longstanding" regulations that are "presumptively lawful."[37] These include firearms disabilities imposed on felons and the mentally ill, bans on taking firearms into "sensitive places such as schools and government buildings," and the imposition of conditions and qualifications on the commercial sale of arms. In addition to the vagueness and ambiguity in some of its formulations, the Court's

---

32 See United States v. Morrison, 529 U.S. 598 (2000). The case involved a statute that created a federal civil remedy for victims of "gender-motivated violence." Had Congress cared to insist on establishing such a remedy, which largely duplicated what was available under state laws, it might have added a jurisdictional provision similar to the one it used to revive the gun-free school zones law. Alternatively, it might have induced the states to fashion remedies that fit congressional specifications, using conditions on federal grants of money. See South Dakota v. Dole, 483 U.S. 203 (1987).

33 See Nat'l Federation of Indep. Business v. Sebelius, 132 S. Ct. 2566 (2012).

34 See *id.* at 2593–2600.

35 347 U.S. 483 (1954).

36 554 U.S. at 628–29 (emphasis added).

37 *Id.* at 626–27 & n.26.

opinion is equivocal about whether these comments were meant to be treated as binding rules by the lower courts.[38]

The opinion also refers with apparent approval to nineteenth-century state cases upholding prohibitions on bearing concealed weapons in public, although it does not expressly endorse them. In addition, *Heller* interprets the Court's one significant precedent to mean roughly the opposite of what it says. Whereas *Miller* indicated that particular types of weapons, such as short-barreled shotguns, would be protected by the Second Amendment only if they have military utility, *Heller* says that short-barreled shotguns are not protected by the Second Amendment because they are not typically possessed by *civilians*; handguns, moreover, are protected by the Second Amendment, without regard to their military utility, because they *are* popular with civilians.[39]

The absence of any effort to ground these various pronouncements in an originalist analysis is particularly noteworthy because the Court's comments are hard to distinguish on methodological grounds from Justice Stephen Breyer's approach. All of the *Heller* dissenters joined his opinion arguing that even if an individual right is assumed to exist, courts should defer to reasonable efforts by legislatures to reduce gun violence, which would include handgun bans in high-crime urban areas. Breyer provided a fairly detailed cost/benefit analysis that compared the government's interest in public safety with the interests of individuals who want to keep a gun for self-defense. Scalia implicitly conducted the same kind of analysis in rejecting the D.C. handgun ban and endorsing several other forms of gun control. Notwithstanding some sarcastic comments aimed at Breyer,[40] Scalia's approach to specific cases seems to differ from Breyer's primarily in his omission of reasoned explanations for the conclusions he reached.

Two years after *Heller*, *McDonald v. City of Chicago* held that the Second Amendment applies to state and local regulations in the same way that it applies to federal regulations. This was a perfectly straightforward application of well-settled substantive due process doctrine, under which almost all the other provisions of the Bill of Rights had been "incorporated" into the Fourteenth Amendment. Nevertheless, the four *Heller* dissenters dissented again. For his part, Justice Clarence Thomas wrote a concurrence rejecting the Court's due process precedents but coming to a similar result under the Privileges or Immunities Clause. Significantly, Justice Samuel Alito's plurality opinion expressly repeats *Heller*'s assurances about the validity of several longstanding regulatory measures.[41]

The aftermath of *Heller* and *McDonald*

In the years since *Heller* and *McDonald* were decided, most federal circuit court decisions have had more in common with Breyer's *Heller* dissent than with Scalia's majority opinion. The dominant framework dictates a two-step procedure. The court first asks whether the challenged regulation impinges on a right protected by the Second Amendment. If not,

---

38 *Heller* does not say how the presumptions might be rebutted. At the end of the opinion, moreover, Scalia seems to treat them as established "exceptions." See *id*. at 635.

39 See *Miller*, 307 U.S. at 178; *Heller*, 554 U.S. 624–25. For further detail, see Nelson Lund, Heller *and Second Amendment Precedent*, 13 LEWIS & CLARK L. REV. 335 (2009).

40 See, e.g., 554 U.S. at 634–35.

41 For a detailed discussion of the principal opinions, see Nelson Lund, *Two Faces of Judicial Restraint (Or Are There More?) in* McDonald v. City of Chicago, 63 FLA. L. REV. 487 (2011).

the regulation is sustained. Otherwise, the court applies what it regards as the appropriate level of constitutional scrutiny. *Heller* ruled out the lowest tier, rational basis review, under which challenges almost always fail.[42] Strict scrutiny, which is typically very difficult to satisfy, applies in theory to regulations that impose a severe burden on the constitutional right,[43] but this demanding standard of review has not yet been applied to any gun control law. Instead, courts usually invoke the notoriously manipulable standard of intermediate scrutiny,[44] which is the approach that Breyer considered appropriate.[45] Gun regulations are almost never struck down under that rubric.[46]

The pattern I have just described holds true as a general matter, but there are a few cases that do not quite fit. There have also been panel opinions that would have been exceptions had they not been vacated when the case was taken before the en banc court. In addition, there are a number of dissenting opinions that indicate resistance by a minority of judges to the consensus view. One can get a sense of the current legal landscape by considering a few decisions dealing with distinct types of regulations.

Regulations endorsed by the Heller Majority

Courts never strike down regulations that were specifically approved in *Heller*. Some courts have gone further, concluding that *all* "longstanding" regulations are at least presumptively valid.[47] On the other hand, one court refused to use *Heller*'s reference to gun bans involving "the mentally ill" to uphold a lifetime firearms disability imposed on a currently healthy individual who had been briefly committed for an episode of depression 30 years earlier.[48]

Other regulations upheld at step one

In addition to the laws specifically approved by *Heller*, regulations considered to have only slight effects on the right to arms may be upheld without applying heightened scrutiny.[49] More dramatically, the Fourth Circuit, sitting en banc, upheld Maryland's ban on "assault

---

42 This standard requires only that a court be able to imagine some rational connection between the statute and a legitimate government interest.

43 Under this standard, a court must find that a law is narrowly tailored to serve a compelling government interest.

44 A statute may be sustained under this standard if a court concludes that it substantially advances an important government interest.

45 See *Heller*, 554 U.S. at 704–05 (Breyer, J., dissenting).

46 For a rare exception, see Heller v. District of Columbia, 801 F.3d 264 (D.C. Cir. 2015) (*Heller III*). Several provisions of D.C.'s endlessly evolving gun laws failed intermediate scrutiny because they did nothing to promote the ostensible purpose of the regulations, namely to promote public safety.

47 See, e.g., Drake v. Filco, 724 F.3d 426, 434 (3d Cir. 2013); Nat'l Rifle Ass'n v. Bureau of Alcohol, Tobacco, Firearms & Explosives, 700 F.3d 185, 196–97 (5th Cir. 2012); Heller v. District of Columbia, 670 F.3d 1244, 1253 (D.C. Cir. 2011) (*Heller II*); United States v. White, 593 F.3d 1199, 1205–06 (11th Cir. 2010); United States v. Seay, 620 F.3d 919, 925 (8th Cir. 2010). In fact, the Supreme Court merely *characterized* a few regulations as longstanding, without necessarily implying anything at all about other longstanding regulations. See *Heller*, 554 U.S. at 626–27.

48 Tyler v. Hillsdale Cty., 837 F.3d 678 (2016) (en banc).

49 See, e.g., *Heller III*, 801 F.3d at 274; United States v. Decastro, 682 F.3d 160, 166–69 (2d Cir. 2012); United States v. Mazzarella, 614 F.3d 85, 94–95 (3d Cir. 2010).

weapons" and high-capacity magazines, arguing that such devices are not covered by the Second Amendment at all. This statute was modeled on the 1994 federal statute, which had expired and not been renewed in 2004. The court's 10–4 decision in *Kolbe v. Hogan*[50] was unusual. First, similar laws had previously been upheld under the rubric of intermediate scrutiny, and the Fourth Circuit itself offered an intermediate-scrutiny analysis as an alternative holding. The more aggressive holding therefore seems gratuitously provocative. The dissenting opinion is also provocative, for it contends that the statute should have been subjected to strict scrutiny. For our purposes here, the most interesting aspect of the case is that both the majority and the dissent claimed that their conclusions were compelled by *Heller*, and both of them were wrong. Although *Heller* does not clearly rule out either conclusion, neither does it come close to compelling one result or the other.[51]

Intermediate scrutiny and "feel good" regulations

Bans on so-called assault weapons and high-capacity magazines are examples of laws that seem to aim primarily at making a political statement. A typical example of the judicial treatment of such laws is the D.C. Circuit's decision in *Heller v. District of Columbia* (*Heller II*).[52] After the Supreme Court struck down its handgun ban, the District adopted an elaborate new gun control statute, several provisions of which were challenged in this case. Among the challenged provisions was a ban, similar to the 1994 federal law, on certain semi-automatic rifles and on magazines with a capacity of more than ten rounds of ammunition. The court analogized the semi-automatic rifles to fully automatic machineguns (which *Heller* seemed to assume are outside the protection of the Second Amendment), on the ground that they can fire almost as rapidly.[53] The analogy is dubious because the Supreme Court treated machineguns as an unexplained special case, without suggesting any underlying rationale based on rates of fire. And even if the analogy were valid, the regulation appears to be arbitrary because its cosmetic criteria have little relation to its supposed public safety-purpose.

The court's analysis of the magazine ban is similarly questionable. First, the court accepted testimony that high-capacity magazines give an advantage to "mass shooters."[54] Intermediate scrutiny, however, is supposed to require more than mere speculation that the challenged law might have some effect on some person in some circumstances. Accordingly, the court also credited testimony that high-capacity magazines can tempt legitimate self-defense shooters to fire more rounds than necessary. This may be true, and there might be some cases in which the magazine ban could prevent an unfortunate accident. But exactly the same thing could be said about the D.C. handgun ban that was declared unconstitutional by the Supreme Court in *Heller*. The D.C. Circuit cited no evidence that the magazine ban would actually save any lives, and it did not even consider the possibility that innocent citizens would lose their lives because they ran out of ammunition while trying to defend themselves against criminals. This looks a lot like rational basis review masquerading as intermediate

---

50 849 F.3d 114 (4th Cir. 2017).
51 For a detailed discussion of the case, see Nelson Lund, *Fourth Circuit Shootout: "Assault Weapons" and the Second Amendment*, GEO. MASON L. REV. (forthcoming).
52 670 F.3d 1244 (D.C. Cir. 2011).
53 *Id.* at 1263.
54 *Id.*

scrutiny, and the Supreme Court has emphasized that the level of scrutiny is determined by the analysis actually applied, not by the label placed on the analysis.[55]

Intermediate scrutiny and public carry laws

One prominent form of gun control that is actually meant to have a real effect on public safety also has serious effects on Second Amendment rights. Most states now permit law-abiding citizens to carry concealed weapons in public. Usually, the government issues a license to anyone who meets criteria that are fairly easy to satisfy, and a growing number of states do not require a license at all.[56] A few states, however, will issue licenses only to individuals who can persuade a government official that they have an extraordinary need to carry a gun.

In *Drake v. Filco*,[57] for example, the court considered a challenge to one of these "may issue" statutes. A New Jersey law forbade almost all adults to carry a handgun in public without a license. In order to obtain a license, applicants were required to demonstrate an "urgent necessity for self-protection, as evidenced by specific threats or previous attacks which demonstrate a special danger to the applicant's life that cannot be avoided by means other than by issuance of a permit to carry a handgun."[58] An estimated 0.02 percent of New Jersey citizens were able to obtain a permit.[59]

The court found that the New Jersey regulation survived intermediate scrutiny. The court's entire analysis was comprehended in this sentence: "The predictive judgment of New Jersey's legislators is that limiting the issuance of permits to carry a handgun in public to only those who can show a 'justifiable need' will further its substantial interest in public safety."[60] Obviously, this is not actually an analysis, and the court made no effort to show the legally required fit between the goal of public safety and the restriction imposed by the challenged regulation.[61] Instead, it offered a vague allusion to "history, consensus, and simple common sense."[62] Here again, what the court called intermediate scrutiny looks more like the rational basis review that *Heller* forbade the lower courts to use.

In jurisdictions that enforce "may issue" statutes like New Jersey's, openly carrying handguns is completely banned. Since a tiny number of concealed carry permits are issued, almost all law-abiding citizens are effectively disarmed when they leave their homes.

---

55 See Fisher v. University of Texas, 133 S. Ct. 2411, 2419–21 (2013).
56 See Crime Prevention Research Center, *Concealed Carry Permit Holders Across the United States: 2017* (July 20, 2017).
57 724 F.3d 426 (3d Cir. 2013).
58 *Id.* at 428.
59 Petition for Certiorari, Drake v. Jerejian, No. 13–827, at 6; see also Crime Prevention Research Center, *Concealed Carry Permit Holders Across the United States: 2017* (July 20, 2017), at 34 (providing an estimate of 0.017 percent).
60 724 F.3d at 437.
61 See, e.g., Ward v. Rock Against Racism, 491 U.S. 781, 800 (1989) (intermediate scrutiny requires that the means chosen must not be "substantially broader than necessary to achieve the government's interest"); Bd. of Trustees of State Univ. of N.Y. v. Fox, 492 U.S. 469, 480–81 (1989) ("[S]ince the State bears the burden of justifying its restrictions, it must affirmatively establish the reasonable fit we require." [citation omitted]).
62 724 F.3d at 438 (quoting IMS Health, Inc. v. Ayotte, 550 F.3d 42, 55 [1st Cir. 2008]).

Courts that have upheld such laws under intermediate scrutiny have applied that standard of review more in name than in fact.

A seventh circuit trilogy

Although most courts have adopted the two-step framework described above, and have generally used a lax version of intermediate scrutiny when they reached the second step, there have been exceptions. Three cases from the Seventh Circuit illustrate the wide range of possibilities left open by *Heller*.

Moore v. Madigan[63] struck down an Illinois statute that forbade virtually all civilians to carry a firearm in public, whether openly or concealed, and made no provision for licenses to be issued in any circumstances. The court did not employ the two-step framework that other circuit courts had adopted. Somewhat surprisingly, the majority opinion was written by Judge Richard Posner, who had used the *New Republic* as a platform for blasting *Heller* as "an exercise [in] freewheeling discretion strongly flavored with ideology."[64] Apart from its faux originalism, in Posner's view, *Heller* made the same mistake the Court had made in *Roe v. Wade*, namely imposing a uniform rule on a diverse nation.[65]

As the dissent in *Moore* by Judge Ann Claire Williams showed, it would have been possible for Posner to uphold the Illinois law by interpreting *Heller* narrowly. Nonetheless, he concluded that the statute must be invalidated under *Heller*. The Illinois statute was so sweeping on its face that it would have been hard to uphold it without reading the word "bear" out of the Second Amendment. Not quite impossible, as Williams showed by interpreting *Heller* to mean only that people have a right to "bear" a handgun within the home.[66] But hard to do with a straight face.

Posner apparently believed that the Supreme Court would reverse a decision upholding the Illinois statute, and he stayed the mandate for six months in order to give Illinois an opportunity to enact a new gun law.[67] This gave the state a chance to adopt a restrictive "may issue" regulation like New Jersey's, thus effectively replicating the effects of the law that had just been struck down. Apparently expecting this to happen, the attorney general refrained from seeking Supreme Court review. In an ironic twist, Illinois—the state that had adopted the most restrictive gun regulations in the nation—ended up adopting a new "shall issue" law that permits most law-abiding citizens to carry a concealed weapon in public. This outcome illustrates how much public opinion has changed in the wake of Florida's 1987 experiment with liberalization.

Like *Moore*, *Friedman v. City of Highland Park*[68] avoided using the standard two-step framework. This case involved another ban on so-called assault weapons and high-capacity magazines, like the laws upheld in *Heller II* and *Kolbe*. Writing for the majority, Judge Frank Easterbrook essentially concluded that the Supreme Court's *Heller* decision was relevant

---

63 702 F.3d 933 (7th Cir. 2012).
64 Richard A. Posner, *In Defense of Looseness*, NEW REPUBLIC, Aug. 27, 2008, https://newrepublic.com/article/62124/defense-looseness.
65 *Id.*
66 702 F.3d at 946 (Williams, J., dissenting).
67 *Id.* at 942 (majority opinion).
68 784 F.3d 406 (7th Cir. 2015).

only with respect to issues on which Scalia's opinion was crystal clear. And those issues were very few:

> *Heller* and *McDonald* set limits on the regulation of firearms; but within those limits, they leave matters open. The best way to evaluate the relation among assault weapons, crime, and self-defense is through the political process and scholarly debate, not by parsing ambiguous passages in the Supreme Court's opinions. The central role of representative democracy is no less part of the Constitution than is the Second Amendment: when there is no definitive constitutional rule, matters are left to the legislative process.[69]

To get a sense of just how open Easterbrook thinks the Supreme Court has left matters, consider the following statement: "If it has no other effect, Highland Park's ordinance may increase the public's sense of safety. Mass shootings are rare, but they are highly salient, and people tend to overestimate the likelihood of salient events. If a ban on semiautomatic guns and large-capacity magazines reduces the perceived risk from a mass shooting, and makes the public feel safer as a result, that's a substantial benefit."[70] The same benefit could be said, with even more plausibility, to result from the D.C. handgun ban, yet *Heller* never even mentioned its possible relevance.

Similarly, Easterbrook lays great stress on the fact that the Highland Park regulation leaves citizens with what he considers ample means of self-defense. *Heller* had seemed to reject such reasoning, but Easterbrook brushes that problem aside: "*Heller* held that the availability of long guns does not save a ban on handgun ownership. The justices took note of some of the reasons, including ease of accessibility and use, that citizens might prefer handguns to long guns for self-defense. But *Heller* did not foreclose the possibility that allowing the use of most long guns plus pistols and revolvers, as Highland Park's ordinance does, gives householders adequate means of defense."[71]

If Posner's opinion in *Moore* is an acknowledgment that the Supreme Court would probably not approve absolute bans that openly conflict with the text and purpose of the Second Amendment, Easterbrook's opinion in *Friedman* reads *Heller* to signal a tolerance for just about anything short of such absolute and sweeping bans. Those positions are not inconsistent, and both of them probably reflect impatience with what these two former law professors see as the silly formalism of the standard two-step analytical model adopted by other circuits.

A third case from the Seventh Circuit takes a very different approach. Like the District of Columbia, Chicago replaced its unconstitutional handgun ban with an elaborate new gun control law. In *Ezell v. City of Chicago*,[72] the Seventh Circuit reviewed one of the new regulations: a requirement that citizens undergo one hour of range training as a prerequisite to lawful gun ownership, while simultaneously banning from the city any range at which this training could take place. Judge Diane Sykes set out a framework that bears a superficial resemblance to the standard two-step analysis adopted by most other courts. In fact, however, her approach is quite different. Briefly stated, she interpreted the Supreme Court's opinions as follows.

---

69 *Id.* at 412 (citation to *McCulloch v. Maryland* omitted).
70 *Id.* (citations omitted).
71 *Id.* at 411.
72 651 F.3d 684 (7th Cir. 2011).

First, just as some categories of speech, like defamation and fraud, are unprotected by the First Amendment as a matter of history and tradition, some activities involving arms are categorically unprotected by the Second Amendment.[73] These are the activities properly identified at step one of the standard analysis. Unlike other courts, Sykes maintains that such activities should be identified by looking for actual evidence of the original meaning of the right to arms.[74] This is in some tension with the way that *Heller* identified certain presumptively lawful regulations. But it is consistent with *Heller*'s rhetorical emphasis on originalism and with Scalia's unsubstantiated claim that the exceptions to Second Amendment protection mentioned in his opinion have "historical justifications."[75]

Second, if an activity is within a protected category, courts should evaluate the regulatory means chosen by the government and the public benefits at which the regulation aims. "Borrowing from the Court's First Amendment doctrine, the rigor of this judicial review will depend on how close the law comes to the core of the Second Amendment right and the severity of the law's burden on the right."[76] Broadly prohibitory laws restricting the core Second Amendment right—like the handgun bans at issue in *Heller* and *McDonald*—are categorically unconstitutional.[77] All other laws must be judged by one of the standards of means-end scrutiny used in evaluating other enumerated constitutional rights, and the government always has the burden of justifying its regulations. This resembles the formulas used by other courts at step two of the analysis, but Sykes' application of the framework looks very different.

She concluded that firing ranges are not categorically excluded from Second Amendment protection. Historical evidence approvingly cited in *Heller* (albeit not on this issue) supported the conclusion,[78] and a variety of other evidence cited by Chicago fell "far short of establishing that target practice is wholly outside the Second Amendment as it was understood when incorporated [by the Fourteenth Amendment] as a limitation on the States."[79]

The more difficult question involved which standard of review to apply. *Heller* repeatedly invoked the First Amendment, and Sykes began by summarizing the rather intricate set of legal tests generated by the Supreme Court in that area. From those cases, she distilled an analogous approach that she thought applicable to the Second Amendment. Severe burdens on the core right to self-defense will require an extremely strong public-interest goal and a close means-ends fit. As a restriction gets farther away from this core, it may be more easily justified, depending on the relative severity of the burden and its proximity to the core of the right.

Applying this test to the gun-range ban, the court concluded that the right to maintain proficiency in the use of weapons is an important corollary to the meaningful exercise of the core right. This requires a rigorous review of the government's justifications, "if not quite 'strict scrutiny.'"[80] Chicago did not come close to satisfying this standard. It produced no evidence establishing that firing ranges necessarily pose any significant threat to public safety,

---

73 *Id.* at 702.
74 *Id.* at 702–03.
75 554 U.S. at 635.
76 *Ezell*, 651 F.3d at 703.
77 *Id.*
78 See *id.* at 704.
79 *Id.* at 706.
80 *Id.* at 708.

and at least one of its arguments was so transparently a makeweight that "[t]o raise it at all suggests pretext."[81]

Sykes' use of First Amendment analogies enabled her to treat *Heller* as a binding precedent at the same time that she sought to improve on Scalia's intellectually unsatisfying combination of originalist rhetoric and naked assertions about specific applications of the Second Amendment. The kinship that she sees between the First and Second Amendments is also what distinguishes her approach from that of other circuit courts. All federal courts treat the freedom of speech as an enormously valuable right that judges should carefully protect from dubious government infringements. Consistently with a pointed dictum in *McDonald*,[82] Sykes seems to think that the Constitution requires courts to treat the right to keep and bear arms with the same respect. This is what most clearly distinguishes *Ezell* from almost all other post-*Heller/McDonald* decisions.

The Supreme Court's response to the Lower Courts

Each of the circuit court cases discussed in the previous section has generated a dissent or an opinion concurring only in the judgment, which reflects the lack of clear guidance from the Supreme Court in an area where judges (like many citizens) tend to have strong policy views. At least for the moment, however, there is wide agreement that the Court's opinions should be read narrowly and that legislatures should be given a great deal of latitude in regulating firearms.

Many petitions for certiorari have been filed, but the Supreme Court has declined to review any of the decisions reached by the federal circuit courts. This acquiescence does not imply that the justices agree with the results, but it does at least suggest that they are reluctant to disturb the existing consensus. There is additional evidence that supports this conclusion.

First, the Court did grant one petition for certiorari, in a case from the Supreme Judicial Court of Massachusetts. *Caetano v. Massachusetts*[83] summarily vacated that court's decision to uphold a ban on stun guns, a type of non-lethal weapon. The state court had thumbed its nose at the Supreme Court by basing its decision on three rationales that *Heller* had very clearly rejected. Rather than review the ban on stun guns, however, the Court merely sent the case back to the state court to try again.

Justice Alito, joined by Justice Thomas, concurred in the judgment but issued a strongly worded opinion accusing the majority of an inappropriately mild response to the state court's contemptuous treatment of *Heller* and to its cavalier attitude toward the right of self-defense.[84]

There are also three cases in which Thomas has dissented from the Court's refusal to grant a petition for certiorari. Scalia joined Thomas in the first two and Justice Neil Gorsuch joined him in the most recent. The theme running through all three dissents is that the lower courts have been eviscerating *Heller* and therewith the Second Amendment. Attacking Easterbrook's

---

81 *Id.* at 710.
82 561 U.S. at 778–79 (Second Amendment should not be "singled out for special—and specially unfavorable—treatment").
83 136 S. Ct. 1027 (2016).
84 *Id.* at 1028–1023 (2016) (Alito, J., concurring in the judgment). The case was decided by an eight-member Court after the death of Scalia.

opinion in *Friedman*, for example, Thomas wrote that "[i]f a broad ban on firearms can be upheld based on conjecture that the public might *feel* safer (while being no safer at all), then the Second Amendment guarantees nothing."[85]

Similarly, in objecting to the Court's refusal to review a decision upholding a law requiring homeowners to lock up their guns, Thomas wrote that "nothing in our decision in *Heller* suggested that a law must rise to the level of the absolute prohibition at issue in that case to constitute a 'substantial burden' on the core of the Second Amendment right. And when a law burdens a constitutionally protected right [in other areas of the law], we have generally required a higher showing than the Court of Appeals demanded here."[86]

In the most recent case, Thomas and Gorsuch objected to the Ninth Circuit's en banc decision in *Peruta v. County of San Diego*,[87] which left intact a California "may issue" regime similar to the New Jersey statute upheld in *Drake v. Filco*.

> The Court's decision to deny certiorari in this case reflects a distressing trend: the treatment of the Second Amendment as a disfavored right. . . . For those of us who work in marbled halls, guarded constantly by a vigilant and dedicated police force, the guarantees of the Second Amendment might seem antiquated and superfluous. But the Framers made a clear choice: They reserved to all Americans the right to bear arms for self-defense. I do not think we should stand by idly while a State denies its citizens that right, particularly when their very lives may depend on it.[88]

When the Court denies a petition for certiorari, it is not signaling agreement with the decision of the court below. Similarly, the decision of a Justice not to join a dissent from such a denial does not necessarily imply anything about his views on the merits of the case. Alito, for example, indicated in *Caetano* that he does take the Second Amendment seriously, but he did not join any of Thomas' dissents from the denial of certiorari. Nevertheless, the vigor of the repeated protests in the Thomas dissents indicates that there is a significant split among the justices who formed a majority in *Heller* and *McDonald*.

This split may reflect substantive differences about the reach of the Second Amendment and thus about the proper interpretation of *Heller*. Indeed, such differences might account for the ambiguities and inconsistencies in *Heller* itself. Or the split might indicate that some fraction of the *Heller* majority hopes that future appointments to the Court will produce a more cohesive majority on this issue. Or there might be differences of opinion about the effect of controversial Second Amendment decisions on the Court's reputation.

Whatever the exact cause, it is striking that the Court has passively accepted the accumulation of a great deal of precedent that leaves legislatures with nearly unbounded discretion to regulate firearms. The legal analysis of the lower courts in many of these cases is pretty perfunctory at best and rather outlandish at worst. Some of the regulations they have upheld, moreover, have very serious effects on the right of self-defense, which *Heller* called the core of the Second Amendment.

The Supreme Court has not yet been presented with a petition for certiorari in a case where the lower court struck down a major gun control statute like those at issue in

---

85 Friedman v. City of Highland Park, Illinois, 136 S. Ct. 447, 449 (2015).
86 Jackson v. City and Cty. of San Francisco, 135 S. Ct. 2799, 2801 (2015).
87 824 F.3d 919 (2016).
88 Peruta v. California, 137 S. Ct. 1995, 1999–2000 (2017).

Drake v. Filco and *Peruta*. Just before the deadline for submitting this chapter to the publisher, a divided panel of the D.C. Circuit struck down a "may issue" statute similar to the ones upheld in those cases. In *Wrenn v. District of Columbia*,[89] Judge Thomas Griffith's opinion emphasized the similarity of this law to the handgun ban struck down in *Heller*:

> [A]t a minimum, the [Second] Amendment's core must protect carrying [a weapon] given the risks and needs typical of law-abiding citizens. *That* is a right that most D.C. residents can never exercise, by the law's very design. In this way, the District's regulation *completely* prohibits most residents from exercising the constitutional right to bear arms as viewed in the light cast by history and *Heller I*. . . . [U]nder *Heller I*, "complete prohibition[s]" of Second Amendment rights are always invalid. It's appropriate to strike down such "total ban[s]" without bothering to apply tiers of scrutiny because no such analysis could ever sanction obliterations of an enumerated constitutional right.[90]

In the panel opinion in *Peruta*, Judge Diarmuid O'Scannlain had conducted a detailed textual and historical inquiry that led him to the same conclusion:

> To reason by analogy, it is as though San Diego County banned all speech, but exempted from this restriction particular people (like current or former political figures), particular places (like private property), and particular situations (like the week before an election). Although these exceptions might preserve small pockets of freedom, they would do little to prevent destruction of the right to free speech as a whole. As the [Supreme] Court has said: 'The Second Amendment is no different.' It too is, in effect, destroyed when exercise of the right is limited to a few people, in a few places, at a few times.[91]

The legal arguments set forth by Judges O'Scannlain and Griffith are much stronger than the opposing arguments set out in such cases as *Drake v. Filco*.[92] The stakes involving the right to self-defense and the government's interest in public safety are also higher than in most other Second Amendment cases. A Supreme Court opinion resolving the new circuit split would tell us a lot about whether *Heller* will prove to be a truly seminal case or whether *Heller*'s rediscovery of the right to keep and bear arms will resemble the revival of the principle of limited and enumerated federal powers in *United States v. Lopez*. The District of Columbia, however, has decided not to ask for Supreme Court review in *Wrenn*, leaving the answer in the womb of time.

---

89 No. 16-7025 (D.C. Cir. July 25, 2017).

90 *Id.*, slip op. at 26 (citations to *Heller* omitted).

91 742 F.3d 1144, 1169–70 (2014) (citation to *Heller* omitted), *vacated by the en banc court*.

92 Notably, the Ninth Circuit's en banc opinion in *Peruta* strained to avoid the issue presented by the case, thereby escaping an obligation to respond to O'Scannlain's legal arguments.

3 National security and anti-terrorism policies

The federalism implications of Trump's travel ban

Christopher P. Banks

The United States government reacted to 9/11 by focusing its efforts on strengthening the criminal law but also adopting preventative anti-terrorism strategies with executive action, including enforcing rendition policies, using military commissions, and creating a new Department of Homeland Security agency. Congress also enacted legislation, such as the USA PATRIOT Act, and amending the Foreign Intelligence Surveillance Act of 1978.[1] The response was based on the need to prevent another catastrophic attack on the U.S. homeland, a concern that has not abated with time. In fact, the rise of the Islamic State of Iraq and the Levant (ISIL/ISIS) and the general destabilization of the Middle East following the U.S. invasion of Afghanistan and Iraq accentuate a growing concern that the most immediate terrorism threat to the homeland comes from unpredictable a diverse range of small transnational groups, including al-Qa'ida and its affiliates or allies, and a loose network of individual violent extremists (cells), and lone wolves. Airplane and suicide bombings, weaponized car attacks, mass shootings, and knife attacks by radicalized terrorist actors or lone wolves in London, Manchester, Paris, Nice, Berlin, Brussels, San Bernardino, Boston, and other cities have intensified the ongoing Western fear of impending foreign or domestic terrorism incidents, not only in Europe but increasingly on U.S. soil.[2]

As the violence accompanying the White Nationalist protest to remove Confederate symbols in Charlottesville, Virginia, reminds us, an evolving post-9/11 counter-terrorism landscape brings into sharp relief federalism issues that relate to national and state-led initiatives or responses that are directed at stopping not only international terrorist provocations, but also ones committed by domestic terrorists.[3] While U.S. law enforcement officials typically categorize domestic terrorists as those groups or individuals that are inspired to act due to extremist ideologies based in the United States,[4] the ISIL/ISIS-inspired radicalization of those who reside in the country present an analogous and equally potent threat to national security because their ability to wreak havoc does not

---

1 See Christopher P. Banks & Steven Tauber, *U.S. District Court Decision-Making in USA PATRIOT Act Cases after September 11*, 35 JUSTICE SYST. J. 139–161 (2014).

2 KRISTIN ARCHICK, PAUL BELKIN & DEREK E. MIX, CONG. RESEARCH SERV. CRS-2017-FDT-0397, EUROPEAN SECURITY AND ISLAMIST TERRORISM, CRS INSIGHT (2017).

3 JEROME P. BJELOPERA, CONG. RESEARCH SERV. R42536, THE DOMESTIC TERRORIST THREAT: BACKGROUND AND ISSUES FOR CONGRESS (2013). See also Charles Savage and Rebecca R. Ruiz, *Sessions Emerges as Forceful Figure in Condemning Charlottesville Violence*, N. Y. TIMES. August 14, www.nytimes.com/2017/08/14/us/politics/domestic-terrorism-sessions.html?_r=0.

4 *Id.*

necessarily depend upon their direct connection with a foreign terrorist group. With the rise of neo-jihadi communication transpiring through the Internet, homegrown terrorist incidents are of particular alarm because "the threat was already in the West, from self-radicalizing militants, and not from the outside through infiltration of foreign militants, resulting in an increase in homegrown attacks, disconnected from foreign terrorist organizations."[5] Not surprisingly, and in light of the terror that 9/11 inspired, the growing frequency of terrorist acts across Europe since then has increasingly prompted U.S. presidential administrations and congressional representatives to devise counter-terrorism policy strategies that will protect the nation from similar attacks on U.S. soil.[6]

Two days after Independence Day in the United States, and against a theme promoting his "America First" campaign, President Donald Trump delivered a symbolic address in Warsaw, Poland, that encapsulated the concern to safeguard America's borders from terrorist attacks.[7] While lambasted by progressives[8] and cheered by conservatives,[9] the President not only reminded NATO allies to pay their fair of expenses in keeping the world safe, but also asked whether the West could answer the "fundamental question of our time"; that is, "whether the West has the will to survive" and to "defend" Western values "at any cost?"[10] One key to answering that challenge, said the President, is to "protect our border," for it "will always be closed to terrorism and extremism of any kind."[11] Trump's Warsaw speech is consistent with his campaign promises to build a wall between the United States and Mexico and to secure the border by getting rid of the "bad hombres."[12] Moreover, after

5 MARC SAGEMAN, MISUNDERSTANDING TERRORISM (2017), at 11. Sageman's empirical analysis reports that 86 percent of global jihadi attacks since 9/11 are from "the bottom-up," coming from "a homegrown movement of people self-radicalized, with a few volunteering to go abroad for training with a foreign terrorist organization and returning home to carry out attacks." *Id.*, 52. See also MITCHELL D. SILBER, & ARVIN BHATT, RADICALIZATION IN THE WEST: THE HOMEGROWN THREAT (2007), www.jcrcny.org/wp- content/uploads/2016/01/NYPD_Report-Radicalization_in_the_West.pdf. The NYPD report illustrates that the Western perspective about terrorism threats began to change after 2004–05 because the London and Madrid bombings of mass transit systems revealed that "homegrown threats" increasingly originate from "unremarkable" citizens or residents that have become radicalized under jihadist-inspired movements. MARTHA CRENSHAW & GARY LAFREE, COUNTERING TERRORISM (2017) at 10.

6 See ARCHICK, BELKIN, & MIX, *supra* note 2, at 3.

7 Donald Trump, REMARKS BY PRESIDENT TRUMP TO THE PEOPLE OF POLAND | JULY 6, 2017 (2017), www.whitehouse.gov/the-press-office/2017/07/06/remarks-president-trump-people-poland-july-6-2017. See also Rosalind S. Helderman, *Stephen Miller: A Key Engineer for Trump's "America First" Agenda,* WASHINGTON POST, February 11, 2017, https://www.washingtonpost.com/politics/stephen-miller-a-key-engineer-for-trumps-america-first-agenda/2017/02/11/a70cb3f0-e809-11e6-bf6f-301b6b443624_story.html?utm_term=.4a8528c1d020.

8 Sarah Wildman, VOX, TRUMP'S SPEECH IN POLAND SOUNDED LIKE AN ALT-RIGHT MANIFESTO (2017), www.vox.com/world/2017/7/6/15927590/trump-alt-right-poland-defend-west-civilization-g20.

9 Marc A. Thiessen, AEIDEAS, TRUMP'S WARSAW SPEECH WASN'T AN OUTRAGE. IT WAS A CLEAR STATEMENT OF AMERICAN VALUES (2017), www.aei.org/publication/trumps-warsaw-speech-wasnt-an-outrage-it-was-a-clear-statement-of-american-values/.

10 Trump, *supra* note 7.

11 *Id.*

12 Janell Ross, *From Mexican rapists to bad hombres, the Trump campaign in two moments,* WASHINGTON POST, October 20, 2016, www.washingtonpost.com/news/the-fix/wp/2016/10/20/from-mexican-rapists-to-bad-hombres-the-trump-campaign-in-two-moments/?utm_term=.e088c5505aec; Parker, Ashley & Amy Chozick, *Donald Trump Pledges to "Heal Divisions" (and Sue His Accusers),* NEW YORK TIMES, October 22, 2016, www.nytimes.com/2016/10/23/us/politics/donald-trump-hillary-clinton.html?_r=0&auth=login-email.

winning the White House, Trump converted his campaign promises into action by issuing his controversial "travel bans," or executive orders designed to keep alien extremists from select Muslim countries from entering the United States to commit terrorist acts.[13]

This chapter explores the federalism implications of the Trump administration's decision to fight the terrorist threat by executive action that instituted border control through travel bans. In doing so, the relationship between national executive action (which aims to protect the homeland) and responses by U.S. state actors (that are obliged to follow it in a constitutional system informed by U.S. Supreme Court precedent) is investigated. The analysis focuses on the litigation surrounding the Trump administration's travel bans to determine how state attorney generals have challenged them. Of particular interest is to uncover whether the new federalism principles, namely those which maintain that state sovereignty interests are a bulwark against encroachments by the federal government, are part of the legal strategy and arguments of states that have resisted enforcement of the travel bans. An underlying theme is to assess if constitutional provisions and principles, such as the Supremacy Clause, the preemption doctrine, the anti-commandeering doctrine, the Tenth Amendment, and the various protections afforded through the Bill of Rights, among others, interfere or otherwise limit state governments from developing or implementing anti-terrorism policies in conjunction with the national interest. In this respect, the chapter sheds light on whether federalism and constitutional principles facilitate or impede the ability of the nation to speak with one voice on critical issues of national security and anti-terrorism policies.

National security and its (new) federalism implications

Western fears of terrorist attacks on the homeland intensified in the middle of the 2016 U.S. presidential campaign—a time when, in June, Omar Mateen, an American citizen, massacred 49 patrons dancing at PULSE, an Orlando LGBTQ-community bar. Occurring in the aftermath of the 2015 terrorist attacks on a Paris satirical newspaper, a U.S. San Bernardino County Department of Public Health training event and holiday party, and a Brussels airport and metro stop, the deadliest mass shooting in the U.S. exacerbated "an already rancorous political debate over the dangers of homegrown violent extremism and the links between terrorism and immigration as well as religion."[14] After the PULSE tragedy, then-presidential candidate Trump railed against a "dysfunctional immigration system" that let "[t]he killer [who] was born in Afghan, of Afghan parents, [and] who immigrated to the United States" to come to "America in the first place, [since we] allowed his family to come here."[15] Thus, he promised that if elected he would "suspend immigration

---

13 Michael D. Shear & Helene Cooper, *Trump Bars Refugees and Citizens of 7 Muslim Countries*, NEW YORK TIMES, January 27, 2017, https://www.nytimes.com/2017/01/27/us/politics/trump-syrian-refugees. html; Glenn Thrush, *Trump's New Travel Ban Blocks Migrants From Six Nations, Sparing Iraq*, NEW YORK TIMES, March 6, 2017, www.nytimes.com/2017/03/06/us/politics/travel-ban-muslim-trump.html. Notably, the Warsaw speech was allegedly written by Steve Miller, the main draftsman of the first executive order. Manchester, Julia, *Travel ban architect writing Trump Poland speech*. THE HILL, July 5, 2017, http://thehill.com/homenews/administration/340686-travel-ban-architect-writing-trump-poland-speech-report.
14 CRENSHAW & LAFREE, *supra* note 5, at 13–14.
15 Ryan Teague Beckwith, *Read Donald Trump's Speech on the Orlando Shooting*, TIME, June 13, 2016, http://time.com/4367120/orlando-shooting-donald-trump-transcript/.

from areas of the world where there's a proven history of terrorism against the United States, Europe or our allies until we fully understand how to end these threats."[16]

Shortly after his inauguration, on January 27, 2017, President Trump issued Executive Order 13769,[17] "Protecting the Nation from Foreign Terrorist Entry into the United States," an order designed to safeguard Americans from "terrorist attacks by foreign nationals admitted into the United States." The Order, which drew its authority from the president's constitutional powers and the Immigration and Nationality Act (INA),[18] banned for 90 days entry of foreign nationals from seven predominately Muslim countries (Iraq, Syria, Iran, Sudan, Libya, Somalia, and Yemen).[19] The Order explained that the ban was necessary to stop foreign-born individuals from exploiting immigration laws by doing terrorist harm to the United States after gaining entry into the country by visitor, student, or employment visas, or through the U.S. refugee settlement program. Among other things, the Order: a) directed the Secretary of State to bar Syrian refugees indefinitely; b) instructed Secretary of State, the Secretary of Homeland Security, the Director of National Intelligence, and the Director of the Federal Bureau of Investigation to implement a system of uniform screening procedures for those seeking entry into the United States; c) suspended for 120 days the U.S. Refugee Admissions Program (to afford time to review refugee application and adjudicative processes to ensure that admissions do not present a national security threat); d) prioritized the admission of refugees who were religious minorities in their country of nationality; and, e) capped the total amount of refugee admissions for 2017 at 50,000 (downsizing the 110,000 limit set by the Obama administration).[20] Whereas administration officials defended the ban as fulfilling Trump's longstanding promise to keep the nation safe from terrorist attacks on the homeland,[21] critics lambasted it as discriminatory "Muslim ban" that was an unconstitutional violation of the First and Fourteenth Amendments, all under the pretext of national security rationales.[22]

Within days of its issuance, EO 13769 caused nationwide protests and multiple court challenges that successfully blocked the travel ban's enforcement under injunctive relief principles and due process or equal protection rationales.[23] Instead of trying to vindicate

---

16 *Id.*

17 Exec. Order No. 13769, 82 Fed. Reg. 8977 (January 27, 2017).

18 Immigration and Nationality Act, 8 U.S.C. 1100, et. seq.

19 A main criterion for including countries on the list was whether Congress, in the Immigration and Nationality Act, restricted use of the Visa Waiver Program for nationals in countries designated by the Secretary of State as a state sponsor of terrorism, or whether the country was designated as a country of concern by the Secretary of Homeland Security, in consultation with the Secretary of State and the Director of National Intelligence. Exec. Order No. 13780 §1(b)(i), *infra* note 24.

20 See Bridget Stubblefield, *Executive Orders 13769 and 13780 "Protecting the Nation from Foreign Terrorist Entry into the United States,* 31 GEORGET. IMMIGR. LAW J. 177–187 (2017).

21 Barnini Chakraborty, *Trump signs executive order for "extreme vetting" of refugees,* FOX NEWS POLITICS, January 27, 2017, www.foxnews.com/politics/2017/01/27/trump-signs-executive-order-for-extreme-vetting-refugees.html.

22 Erwin Chemerinsky, *Trump's cruel, illegal refugee executive order,* LOS ANGELES TIMES, January 29, 2017, www.latimes.com/opinion/op-ed/la-oe-chemerinsky-trump-refugee-order-20170129-story.html. For the full scope of the litigation the travel ban order produced, see Litigation Documents & Resources Related to Trump Executive Order on Immigration, LAWFARE (2017), https://lawfareblog.com/litigation-documents-resources-related-trump-executive-order-immigration#Ninth%20Circuit.

23 Protests occurred in airports in New York, New Jersey, Massachusetts, California, Colorado, Texas and the District of Columbia; and federal judges in Massachusetts, New York, California, and Washington

the legality of the first order on appeal, on March 6, 2017, President Trump revoked and then replaced EO 13769 with Executive Order 13780,[24] also styled "Protecting the Nation from Foreign Terrorist Entry into the United States." Grounded in the same legal authority as the first order, but aspiring to fix the original edict's legal defects, the new directive dropped language that indefinitely banned Syrian refugees and had established a priority for refugees that were religious minorities in their home countries.[25] Because the administration took notice of Iraq's joint commitment with the United States to combat terrorism, and of its resolve to strengthen its immigration and vetting processes, the new command removed Iraq from the list of banned countries.[26] While the Order banned for 90 days entry from the remaining six predominately Muslim countries, it explicitly created a number of limitations, exceptions, and waiver possibilities to the travel ban, and it contained more detail about the national security justifications underlying the ban, including making references that hundreds of refugees now in the U.S. are the targets of counter-terrorism investigations, and to two Iraqi refugees and a naturalized U.S. citizen who came from Somalia that committed terrorist acts on the homeland.[27]

For example, under the new Order, suspension was inapplicable for green card (lawful permanent resident) holders; dual citizens with passports issue from a non-banned country; asylees; or refugees already admitted in the U.S.[28] Moreover, waivers could be granted, on a case-by-case basis, for entries if denials cause "undue hardship" where, for instance, a foreign national that had been previously admitted was seeking to return to resume a "continuous period" of "work, study, or other long-term activity," or a foreign national sought to visit or reside with a U.S. citizen that was a "close family member (e.g. a spouse, child, or parent)."[29] Furthermore, the new Order retained the 120-day suspension of the U.S. Refugee Admissions Program and the 50,000 total refugees' cap for 2017.[30]

President Trump is not the first leader to use executive orders in fighting terrorism soon after assuming office. In the first week of his presidency, Barack Obama issued three executive orders that reversed anti-terrorism policies that pertained to the military detention of suspected terrorists and the use of enhanced interrogation techniques that were established under George W. Bush's administration.[31] While crafting executive orders in times of war or emergency has notable historical and judicial support—the Supreme Court upheld President Franklin Delano Roosevelt's orders to try German saboteurs by military commissions[32]

---

refused to enforce all or part of the first travel ban. Notably, President Trump fired acting Attorney General Sally Yates for refusing to defend the travel ban. Steve Almasy & Darran Simon, *A Timeline of President Trump's Travel Bans*, CNN, March 30, 2017, www.cnn.com/2017/02/10/us/trump-travel-ban-timeline/index.html.

24 Exec. Order No. 13780, 82 Fed. Reg. 13209 (March 9, 2017).
25 Stubblefield, *supra* note 20, at 183-184.
26 Exec. Order No. 13780, *supra* note 24, at §1(g).
27 Id., at §§ 1(b), 1(d), 1(h). See also id. §§ 3, 12, respectively.
28 Id., at § 3(b). *See also* The White House, Office of the Press Secretary, Press Gaggle by Press Secretary Sean Spicer (2017), www.whitehouse.gov/the-press-office/2017/03/06/press-gaggle-press-secretary-sean-spicer.
29 Exec. Order No. 13780, *supra* note 24, at §§3(c)(i) and (c)(iv).
30 *Id.*, at §§ 6(a) and 6(b).
31 Daphne Barak-Erez, *Terrorism Law between the Executive and Legislative Models*, 82 Am. J. Comp. Law 877–896 (2009).
32 Ex parte Quirin, 317 U.S. 1 (1942).

and to segregate Japanese-Americans in military detention camps[33]—their use is controversial since sanctioning unilateral executive action in the post-9/11 context invariably runs the risk of compromising the rule of law and human rights' norms, a cornerstone of Western democratic values.[34]

Additionally, the invocation of presidential authority by executive order in foreign affairs or in the confines of national security has increasingly significant federalism implications.[35] As discussed in the next section, Trump's travel ban inspired an immediate litigation response by States that were negatively affected by it, claiming that their proprietary interests as sovereign entities were being compromised in different ways. Moreover, the Trump administration's approach to issues affecting border control and national security interests intuitively represent an expansion of national powers that have hurt at least some of the states that oppose it. As Goelzhauser and Rose observe,[36] the president's policy agenda in regard to related issues, such as immigration (and LGBTQ or health care), is not always neatly aligned with the traditional Republican GOP view that advocates stronger states' rights—a theme, as well, that is registered by new federalism decisions that sought to constrain federal powers that were decided in the conservative Rehnquist Court.[37]

The realignment of partisan positions on federalism questions is thus important because it raises the question of whether the Supreme Court, now under the leadership of Chief Justice John Roberts and composed of new justices that have replaced the core of the pro-states' rights "federalism five" coalition[38] (notably, William Rehnquist, Sandra Day O'Connor, Anthony Kennedy and Antonin Scalia), will use "new federalism" precedents, such those representing the anti-commandeering doctrine,[39] or Tenth Amendment-based rationales,[40] to counteract federal encroachment in the area of national security or immigration, even if they result in outcomes favoring progressive values. Where those precedents sit in conjunction with longstanding precedents favoring foreign affairs preemption,[41] or those giving the president almost plenary authority in the area of national security,[42] is also an open question in relation to the Trump travel ban. Furthermore, the fluidity of partisan federalism conflicts, as well as the constitutional dynamics underlying disputes over executive action and state policy prerogatives, may not only transcend conventional ideological positions. They also register the underlying reality that lawsuits, as commenced by state actors, have become one

33 Korematsu v. United States, 323 U.S. 214 (1944).
34 See Barak-Erez, *supra* note 31.
35 See, e.g., MICHAEL J. GLENNON & ROBERT D. SLOANE, FOREIGN AFFAIRS FEDERALISM: THE MYTH OF NATIONAL EXCLUSIVITY (2016); Matthew C. Waxman, NATIONAL SECURITY FEDERALISM IN THE AGE OF TERROR, 64 STAN. LAW REV. 289–350 (2012).
36 Greg Goelzhauser & Shanna Rose, *The State of American Federalism 2016–2017: Policy Reversals and Partisan Perspectives on Intergovernmental Relations*, 47 PUBLIUS J. FED. 285–313 (2017).
37 CHRISTOPHER P. BANKS & JOHN C. BLAKEMAN, THE U.S. SUPREME COURT AND NEW FEDERALISM: FROM THE REHNQUIST COURT TO THE ROBERTS COURT (2012). *See also* John Dinan, *The Rehnquist Court's Federalism Decisions in Perspective*, 15 J. L. & POL. 127 (1999);
38 John Q. Barrett, *The "Federalism Five" as Supreme Court Nominees, 1970–1991*, 21 ST JOHNS J. LEG. COMMENT. 485–496 (2007).
39 See, e.g., New York v. United States, 488 U.S. 1041 (1992); Printz v. United States, 521 U.S. 898 (1997).
40 See, e.g., Bond v. United States, 564 U.S. 211 (2011).
41 See, e.g., American Insurance Association v. Garamendi, 539 U.S. 396 (2003).
42 U.S. v. Curtiss-Wright Corp., 299 U.S. 304 (1936).

of the foremost vehicles to protect sovereignty interests against federal incursions.[43] These issues are considered next in the federalism context of how the states opposing the travel ban took their arguments to federal court.

The judicial response to the Trump travel bans

President Donald Trump's first Executive Order (January 27, 2017) produced several immediate challenges in court. A week after it was issued, in *Washington v. Trump*,[44] a Washington District Court granted a nationwide temporary restraining order. Six days later, the Ninth Circuit, in *Washington v. Trump*,[45] denied the federal government's emergency motion to stay that order, pending appeal. After Trump revoked the first order and replaced it with the second Executive Order (March 6, 2017), another round of litigation commenced in two separate cases in three different district courts in Maryland (*International Refugee Assistance Project v. Trump*[46]) and Hawaii (*Hawaii v. Trump*[47]; *Hawaii v. Trump*[48]).

In each case, the district courts granted injunctive relief that prevented nationwide enforcement of the 90-day travel ban and the 120-day suspension of refugee entry. The federal government appealed, which led to rulings against the federal government from a unanimous divided *en banc* court in the Fourth Circuit in *International Refugee Assistance Project v. Trump*[49] and a unanimous three-judge panel in the Ninth Circuit in *Hawaii v. Trump*.[50] Whereas both circuits (mostly) upheld the lower court injunction orders, the Fourth Circuit concluded that the government would likely lose its case on First Amendment (Establishment Clause) grounds; and the Ninth Circuit held that the President exceeded his authority to issue the second Executive Order under the Immigration and Nationality Act.

After granting the government's *certiorari* petition in *Trump v. International Refugee Assistance Project*[51] at the end of its 2016–2017 term, the Supreme Court allowed part of the travel ban to be enforced while keeping other injunctive relief in effect. Specifically, the Court removed the injunctions against the entry ban, refugee suspension, and the refugee cap. Those rulings had the effect of enforcing the travel ban against those lacking any United States connection. Yet it denied the government's request to implement the order against those who did if they had a credible or "bona fide" relationship with a United States person or entity. Moreover, in late September the Court agreed with Trump administration lawyers to block a Ninth Circuit court ruling that would have let up to 24,000 refugees that were

---

43 Goelzhauser & Rose, *supra* note 36, at 286 (observing that Democrats, instead of Republicans, are adopting states' rights positions that resist federal overreaching by the Trump administration in order to maintain or effectuate progressive policy change). Likewise, before Trump's election, Texas and other states sued to safeguard their interests to challenge President Obama's executive action that eased restrictions on undocumented aliens. at 2147.

44 Washington v. Trump, 2017 WL 462040 (WD Wash., February 3, 2017).

45 Washington v. Trump, 847 F.3d 1151 (9th Cir. 2017).

46 International Refugee Assistance Project v. Trump, 2017 WL 1018235 (D. Md., March 16, 2017).

47 Hawaii v. Trump, 2017 WL 1011673 (D. Hawaii Mar. 15, 2017).

48 Hawaii v. Trump, 2017 WL 1167383 (D. Hawaii Mar. 29, 2017).

49 International Refugee Project v. Trump, 857 F.3d 554 (4th Cir. 2017).

50 Hawaii v. Trump, 2017 WL 2529640 (9th Cir. June 12, 2017).

51 Trump v. International Refugee Assistance Project, 582 U.S. ___ (2017). The case is consolidated with Trump v. Hawaii.

already working with resettlement agencies enter the United States before October's end.[52] The Court's compromise initially positioned the justices to hear oral arguments and render a decision on the merits at the beginning of its 2017–2018 term but, notably, only if the non-justiciable claims of mootness and lack of standing that the federal government allege were dismissed.[53]

Additionally, as discussed shortly, whether the travel ban is dismissed as non-justiciable or resolved on its merits by the Supreme Court remains an open question in light of the Trump administration's decision to issue an executive proclamation that announced new travel restrictions in late September 2017. Still, the legal arguments raised by the parties in the underlying lower court rulings are highly germane because they illustrate the conflicting federalism interpretations of the federal government and the states regarding the travel ban's enforceability. Although the second Executive Order and the September 24, 2017, executive proclamation are the crux of the government's appeal in the Supreme Court, the underlying litigation leading up to those last two executive actions are considered next.

The first Executive Order (January 27, 2017)

Three days after the first Executive Order (EO-1) was issued, Washington Attorney General Bob Ferguson sued the President and other high-ranking administration officials in federal district court. He alleged that the travel ban must be enjoined because it "is separating Washington families, harming thousands of Washington residents, damaging Washington's economy, hurting Washington-based companies, and undermining Washington's sovereign interest in remaining a welcoming place for immigrants and refugees." An injunction is

---

52 Order in Pending Case (Trump v. Hawaii, 17A275, September 12 2017), www.supremecourt.gov/orders/courtorders/091217zr_h3ci.pdf; and, Associated Press, *Supreme court sides with Trump on refugee policy in travel ban case*, THE GUARDIAN, September 12, 2017, www.theguardian.com/us-news/2017/sep/12/trump-travel-ban-supreme-court-refugee-policy. Additionally, before the Court's September action, on July 19, 2017, in a separate order, the Court upheld Hawaii district court judge Derrick Watson's ruling as to what constitutes a "close" relative under the travel ban, but also did not weigh in on that judge's determination as to which refugees could enter the United States. Amy Howe, COURT RELEASES OCTOBER CALENDAR SCOTUSBLOG (2017), www.scotusblog.com/2017/07/court-releases-october-calendar/. Under Judge Watson's ruling, grandparents, grandchildren, brothers-in-law, sisters-in-law, aunts, uncles, nieces, nephews, and cousins are exempt from the ban, in addition to the Trump administration's list that includes a parent, spouse, fiancé, son, daughter, son-in-law, daughter-in-law, or sibling already in the U.S. Associated Press, *Grandparents are exempt from Trump's travel ban, refugees aren't—for now, Supreme Court says*, LOS ANGELES TIMES, July 19, 2017, www.latimes.com/politics/washington/la-na-essential-washington-updates-justices-allow-strict-enforcement-of-1500484504-htmlstory.html. See also ORDER GRANTING IN PART AND DENYING IN PART PLAINTIFFS' MOTION TO ENFORCE, OR, IN THE ALTERNATIVE, TO MODIFY PRELIMINARY INJUNCTION (in Hawaii v. Trump, CV. NO. 17-00050 DKW-KSC, July 13, 2017), https://assets.documentcloud.org/documents/3894554/Hawaii-Ruling.pdf.

53 Oral argument is scheduled for October 10, 2017. Howe, *supra* note 52. The effect of Supreme Court's June 26, 2017, ruling is explained in Leah Litman, *Symposium: The mootness games*, SCOTUSBLOG (2017), www.scotusblog.com/2017/07/symposium-mootness-games/. On the issue of whether what the Supreme Court will decide is moot is discussed *infra*, nn. 95–97 and accompanying text. See also *id*. In both cases, the federal government has questioned whether the states or group at issue have standing to challenge the executive order, so the Supreme Court is poised to answer that justiciability question as well.

necessary, too, because Washington has a "quasi-sovereign interest" in protecting its residents from economic and physical harm.[54]

Noting that thousands of non-citizen immigrants reside and work in Washington, the complaint, along with its supporting declarations that are compiled on the AG's "Executive Order Lawsuit" website,[55] outlined the negative impact EO-1 would have on the H-1B visa program, which allows high-tech foreign nationals to work in the state's technology industry at major businesses such as Expedia, Amazon, and Microsoft. For residents that were still in the state and for those who had left the country with an expectation of being able to return, the unforeseen travel restrictions interfered with their right to travel and caused chaos at Washington airports, state lines, and ports of entry. The resulting family turmoil, economic disruption, and loss of state revenues impaired businesses and interfered with the research missions (and enrollments, tuition revenues, and state expenditures) at public higher educational institutions, including the University of Washington, Washington State University, and community colleges. Citing Trump campaign promises suggesting that the ban was motivated by religious preference and an anti-Muslim animus, the AG argued that EO-1 violated several constitutional and statutory provisions, among them the Fifth Amendment's Equal Protection and procedural Due Process clauses, the First Amendment's Establishment Clause, the Immigration and Nationality Act, the Foreign Affairs Reform and Restructuring Act, the Religious Freedom Restoration Act, and the Administrative Procedure Act.

A couple of days later, Minnesota's attorney general, Lori Swanson, joined the Washington lawsuit. She asserted that the Order caused similar harm to Minnesota residents, businesses, and public universities. The amended complaint, as well, added a Tenth Amendment allegation, arguing that the reserved powers of the states prevent the federal government from "commandeering state legislative processes" that would force states "to enact and enforce federal law."[56] Moreover, a supplemental pleading and brief were filed to counter the federal government's claim that Washington lacked standing to pursue the challenge, arguing that travel ban adversely affected the state's proprietary interests; and that the state, in exercising its *paren patriae* role, had a quasi-sovereign right to protect its residents' well-being.[57] Shortly thereafter, federal district Judge James L. Robart, a President George W. Bush appointee, granted Washington and Minnesota's request for a temporary restraining order (TRO). He also denied the federal government's emergency stay motion, ruling that the plaintiffs met their burden in showing that EO-1 caused sufficient harm by imposing a 90-day travel ban, a 120-day refugee suspension, an indefinite Syrian refugee ban, and

54 COMPLAINT FOR DECLARATORY AND INJUNCTIVE RELIEF (in Washington v. Trump, U.S. District Court, Western District of Washington, January 30, 2017), http://agportal-s3bucket.s3.amazonaws.com/uploadedfiles/Another/News/Press_Releases/Complaint%20as%20Filed.pdf.

55 Executive Order Lawsuit, WASHINGTON STATE, OFFICE OF THE ATTORNEY GENERAL (www.atg.wa.gov/executive-order-lawsuit).

56 FIRST AMENDED COMPLAINT FOR DECLARATORY AND INJUNCTIVE RELIEF (in Washington and Minnesota v. Trump, U.S. District Court, Western District of Washington, Feburary 1, 2017), http://agportals3bucket.s3.amazonaws.com/uploadedfiles/Another/News/Press_Releases/Amended%20Complaint%20as%20Filed.pdf.

57 PLAINTIFF STATE OF WASHINGTON'S SUPPLEMENTAL BRIEF REGARDING STANDING (in Washington v. Trump, U.S. District Court, Western District of Washington at Seattle, February 1, 2017), http://agportal-s3bucket.s3.amazonaws.com/uploadedfiles/Another/News/Press_Releases/Supplemental%20Pleading%20Regarding%20Standing_0.pdf.

establishing an entry preference for refugees of a minority religion (namely, Syrian Christians and select non-Muslim refugees).[58]

Shortly before the TRO was granted, Hawaii's attorney general, Douglas Chin, filed a complaint for declaratory and injunctive relief in a Hawaii federal district court.[59] Thereafter, it moved to intervene in the federal government's appeal that sought to overturn Judge Robart's ruling in the U.S. Court of Appeals for the Ninth Circuit in *Washington v. Trump*.[60] In restating the legal grounds that supported Hawaii's declaratory and injunctive relief complaint, AG Chin's motion to intervene in the Ninth Circuit litigation averred that EO-1 not only violated constitutional provisions, but also that Trump impermissibly went beyond the grant of authority that Congress gave the President to regulate immigration under the Immigration and Nationality Act (INA). Hawaii's argument claimed that the law prevented the President from issuing a travel ban that violated the INA's prohibitions against using nationality and religion-based classifications; and, that Section 212(f) of the INA only gave the President limited discretion to suspend the entry of immigrants and non-immigrants through the travel ban. Moreover, the ban disrupted Hawaii's unique sovereign interests in facilitating tourism and compelled the State to participate in religious discrimination that contravenes not only Hawaii state constitutional law, but also imperils "Hawaii's hard-won reputation as a place of openness and inclusion" by "forc[ing] the State to abandon its commitment to pluralism and respect."[61]

Fifteen other states and the District of Columbia filed an *amicus curiae* ("friend of the court") brief[62] to support Washington, Minnesota, and Hawaii in opposing EO-1 and contesting the federal government's appeal in the Ninth Circuit. Citing similar harm to their business, medical, educational, and tourism institutions, the *amici* States argued that the travel ban adversely affects their proprietary, sovereign, and quasi-sovereign interests. Consistent with Hawaii's allegations, the brief observed that since "[r]esidents and businesses in many of the amici States . . . are *prohibited by state law* from taking national origin and religion into account in determining to whom to extend employment and other opportunities," States can curb federal overreaching whenever "the force of law impairs their legitimate, sovereign interest in the continued enforceability of their own statutes."[63]

58 Washington v. Trump, *supra* note 44.
59 See STATE OF HAWAII'S EMERGENCY MOTION TO INTERVENE UNDER FEDERAL RULE 24 AND CIRCUIT RULE 27–3 (in Trump v. Washington, U.S. Court of Appeals for the Ninth Circuit, February 5, 2017), http://agportal-s3bucket.s3.amazonaws.com/Mot.%20to%20Intervene%20-%20Hawai%27i.pdf.
60 Washington v. Trump, *supra* note 45. See also STATE OF HAWAII'S EMERGENCY MOTION TO INTERVENE UNDER FEDERAL RULE 24 AND CIRCUIT RULE 27–3 (in Trump v. Washington, U.S. Court of Appeals for the Ninth Circuit, February 5, 2017), *supra id.*
61 STATE OF HAWAII'S EMERGENCY MOTION TO INTERVENE UNDER FEDERAL RULE 24 AND CIRCUIT RULE 27–3 (in Trump v. Washington, U.S. Court of Appeals for the Ninth Circuit, February 5, 2017), *supra* note 59.
62 MEMORANDUM OF LAW OF THE STATES OF NEW YORK, CALIFORNIA, CONNECTICUT, DELAWARE, ILLINOIS, IOWA, MAINE, MARYLAND, MASSACHUSETTS, NEW MEXICO, OREGON, PENNSYLVANIA, RHODE ISLAND, VERMONT, AND VIRGINIA, AND THE DISTRICT OF COLUMBIA AS *AMICI CURIAE* STATES IN SUPPORT OF PLAINTIFFS-APPELLEES (in Trump v. Washington, U.S. Court of Appeals for the Ninth Circuit, February 6, 2017), http://agportal-s3bucket.s3.amazonaws.com/uploadedfiles/Another/News/Press_Releases/States%27%20Amicus%20Brief.pdf.
63 *Id.*, at 14.

Notably, the States' legal arguments that opposed the ban were all crafted by attorney generals affiliated with the Democratic party.[64]

Within the context of deciding if the lower court's ruling granting the TRO should be stayed, the Ninth Circuit considered four federal government arguments: 1) the States' lacked standing to bring an action that contested the President's authority to use the immigration laws to protect the nation's borders; 2) it was beyond the court's power to review the President's decision to promulgate EO-1; 3) a stay is warranted because there is strong proof that the EO-1 satisfied due process, anti-religious discrimination, and equal protection principles; and, 4) absent a stay, there will be irreparable harm to the public interest of safeguarding the nation against terrorist attacks. In *Washington v. Trump*,[65] none of these claims prevailed in a *per curiam* opinion written by Ninth Circuit Judges William Canby (a Carter appointee), Richard Clifton (a G.W. Bush appointee), and Michelle Friedland (an Obama appointee).

The three-judge panel first reasoned that the EO-1 injured the States' proprietary interests in advancing the academic missions of their public universities; hence they had "third party" standing to assert the rights of their students and faculty who could not come into or leave Washington or Minnesota to work, attend school, or do research because of the travel restrictions. Although the judges acknowledged the well-established principle that courts must afford the political branches substantial deference in deciding immigration, foreign affairs, or national security cases, the notion that the judiciary lacks any power to review them was also dismissed. The panel stressed that the government's bold assertion of unreviewability "runs contrary to the fundamental structure of our constitutional democracy," in part because courts must ensure that the government's 'authority and expertise in [such] matters do not automatically trump the Court's own obligation to secure the protection that the Constitution grants to individuals,' even in times of war."[66] After bypassing the First Amendment religion or equality issues, the panel held that there was ample evidence to show that EO-1 compromised the procedural due process rights of "persons" in the United States, whether they were in the country lawfully or not.[67] Lastly, the court refused to issue the stay since EO-1 created many hardships for the States, and those outweighed the purported harm to the government, especially since administration officials did not offer any convincing proof that any foreign nationals under the ban's restrictions were responsible for any homeland terrorist attacks.[68]

The second Executive Order (March 6, 2017)

Even though it tried to fix original edict's legal defects,[69] Executive Order 13780[70] (EO-2) was immediately challenged in a Maryland federal district court. In *International Refugee*

---

64 National Association of Attorneys General, WHO'S MY AG?, www.naag.org/naag/attorneys-general/ whos-my-ag.php.

65 Washington v. Trump, *supra* note 45.

66 *Id.*, at 1163 (citing Holder v. Humanitarian Law Project, 561 U.S. 1 (quoting *id.* at 61, Breyer, J., dissenting). See also *id.*, at 1161.

67 Washington v. Trump, *supra* note 45. See also Zadvydas v. Davis, 533 U.S. 678 (2001).

68 *Id.*, at 1168.

69 The second executive order removed the indefinite ban of Syrian refugees and eliminated the entry preferences for religious minority refugees. STUBBLEFIELD, *supra* note 20, at 183–184.

70 Exec. Order No. 13780, 82 Fed. Reg. 13209 (March 9, 2017), *supra* note 24.

Assistance Project v. Trump,[71] District Court Judge Theodore D. Chuang (an Obama appointee) delivered a nationwide injunction that stopped enforcement of the 90-day entry ban. After finding that the plaintiffs had standing to assert both statutory and constitutional claims, he reasoned that Trump, along with his official surrogates, made consistent comments during the presidential campaign that a Muslim ban was needed to stop the entry of nationals from select dangerous countries from committing terrorist acts in the United States. As a result, the evidence showed that national security concerns were a pretext for issuing the ban which, in turn, violated the First Amendment's Establishment Clause.

Close to fifty *amicus* briefs were filed in *International Refugee Project Assistance v. Trump*,[72] the federal government's appeal to the Fourth Circuit. Among them, two coalitions of States representing different ideological interests made opposing legal arguments about the travel ban's enforcement. A dozen states led by Republican attorney generals, including those of Texas, Arizona, Florida, South Dakota, and West Virginia, contended that states must defer to the federal government's policy decisions to establish the terms of alien entry into the United States for national security reasons. The brief added that non-resident aliens situated outside of and seeking entry into the United States do not have any constitutional rights; and, if they did, EO-2's nationality-based classifications are legitimately based in concerns for national security rather than being grounded in religious bias. As such, the lower court exceeded its authority because EO-2 was a lawful exercise of the foreign affairs and immigration powers that Congress delegated to the President through the Immigration and Nationality Act.[73]

In contrast, in a brief supported by Democratic attorney generals of 16 states (plus the District of Columbia), minimized the claim that that states ought to show deference to the executive. Instead, it reiterated that injunctive relief was warranted because Trump's pre-and post-inaugural comments is "evidence [that the] President's anti-Muslim animus was overwhelming and unrebutted" and therefore remains a First Amendment Establishment Clause violation; and, although the president enjoys broad discretion over foreign affairs and immigration matters, the Constitution places firm limits on the exercise of that authority. Furthermore, similar arguments were made in a separate amicus brief from major U.S. cities and counties with large immigrant populations, including Los Angeles, Chicago, and New York (notably, sanctuary cities), who also observed that EO-2 would have the counter-intuitive effect of interfering with fighting the war on terror due to the distrust that the Order created between the immigration and law enforcement communities.[74]

---

71 International Refugee Assistance Project v. Trump, *supra* note 46.
72 International Refugee Assistance Project v. Trump, 857 F.3d 554 (4th Cir. 2017). The different amici interests are collected in Litigation Documents & Resources Related to Trump Executive Order on Immigration, *supra* note 22.
73 The States' brief cited Arizona v. United States, 132 S.Ct. 2492 (2012), a Roberts Court precedent, and Youngstown Sheet & Tube Co. v. Sawyer, 343 U.S. 579 (1952), a landmark case involving the scope and limits of presidential authority, for this principle. BRIEF FOR THE STATES OF TEXAS, ALABAMA, ARIZONA, ARKANSAS, FLORIDA, KANSAS, LOUISIANA, MONTANA, OKLAHOMA, SOUTH CAROLINA, SOUTH DAKOTA, AND WEST VIRGINIA, AND GOVERNOR PHIL BRYANT OF THE STATE OF MISSISSIPPI AS *AMICI CURIAE* IN SUPPORT OF APPELLANTS AND A STAY PENDING APPEAL (in International Refugee Assistance Project v. Trump, U.S. Court of Appeals for the Fourth Circuit, March 27, 2017), 2–4, https://assets. documentcloud.org/documents/3525638/IRAP-CA4-Texas-Et-Al-Amicus-Br.pdf. See also *id.*, 13–20.
74 BRIEF OF CHICAGO, LOS ANGELES, NEW YORK, PHILADELPHIA, AND OTHER MAJOR CITIES AND COUNTIES AS *AMICI CURIAE* IN SUPPORT OF AFFIRMANCE AND IN OPPOSITION TO MOTION OF

In *International Refugee Assistance Project v. Trump*[75] (*IRAP*) a divided Fourth Circuit, sitting en banc and largely split along ideological lines,[76] sided with the lower court and states that urged that the injunction stay in place. Circuit Judge Roger Gregory's majority opinion first reasoned that the individual petitioners and organizations representing refugee interests had established standing due to the personal and economic injuries EO-2 caused. On the merits, the court held that the injunction is valid because they also were likely to succeed on their First Amendment Establishment Clause claim. Trump's campaign and post-election comments revealed a non-secular, anti-Muslim religious animus that undercut any assertion that EO-2 was designed to protect national security. As the court put it, the Constitution "protects [the] Plaintiffs' right to challenge an Executive Order that in text speaks with vague words of national security, but in context drips with religious intolerance, animus, and discrimination."[77] In contrast, in separate dissents Circuit Judges Paul Niemeyer and Dennis Shedd argued that the court overstepped its authority in not affording EO-2 deference on national security grounds, whereas Circuit Judge G. Steven Agee argued that the appellees lacked standing.[78]

Whereas the Fourth Circuit's *IRAP* ruling rested on constitutional grounds, the Ninth Circuit's decision in *Hawaii v. Trump*[79] centered on the statutory issue of whether the Trump travel ban exceeded his delegated powers granted to him by Congress to regulate the nation's borders through immigration action. The federal government filed the appeal after Hawaii district court Judge Derrick K. Watson, an Obama appointee, granted injunctive relief that prevented enforcement of the 90-day entry ban from six predominately Muslim

DEFENDANTS-APPELLANTS FOR A STAY PENDING APPEAL (in International Refugee Assistance Project v. Trump, U.S. Court of Appeals for the Fourth Circuit, April 19, 2017), www.ca4.uscourts.gov/docs/pdfs/17-1351/17-1351-amicusbrief-chicagocitiescounties-corrected.pdf?sfvrsn=2. See also BRIEF *AMICUS CURIAE* OF VIRGINIA, MARYLAND, CALIFORNIA, CONNECTICUT, DELAWARE, ILLINOIS, IOWA, MAINE, MASSACHUSETTS, NEW MEXICO, NEW YORK, NORTH CAROLINA, OREGON, RHODE ISLAND, VERMONT, WASHINGTON, AND THE DISTRICT OF COLUMBIA IN SUPPORT OF APPELLEES' OPPOSITION TO STAY PENDING APPEAL (in International Refugee Assistance Project v. Trump, U.S. Court of Appeals for the Fourth Circuit, March 31, 2017), 8, 20, www.clearinghouse.net/chDocs/public/IM-MD-0004-0074.pdf.

75 International Refugee Assistance Project v. Trump, 857 F.3d 554 (4th Cir. 2017).
76 The 10–3 vote is divided between Republican and Democratic presidential appointments. G.W. Bush re-nominated Gregory for the circuit judgeship after Clinton gave him a recess appointment. The remaining judges in the majority (Diana Motz, Robert King, James Wynn, Albert Diaz, Henry Floyd, Pamela Harris, William Traxler, and Stephanie Thacker) are Clinton or Obama appointees. Of the majority, Motz, King, Wynn, Diaz, Floyd, and Harris joined Gregory's opinion in full, whereas Traxler concurred in the judgment, and Keenan and Thacker concurred in part and in the judgment. Judges Paul Niemeyer, Dennis Shedd, and G. Steven Agee each registered separate dissents. See *id.*, and Federal Judicial Center, BIOGRAPHICAL DIRECTORY OF FEDERAL JUDGES, www.fjc.gov/history/judges/search/glossary-search/y.
77 International Refugee Assistance Project v. Trump, *supra* note 73, 4. Judge Gregory reasoned that the anti-Muslim animus is an "affirmative showing" and allegation of "sufficient particularity" of "bad faith" by the executive, which empowers the courts to reject the principle of deference that ordinarily applies to uphold the "facially legitimate" decisions of the political branches that are made for "bona fide" national security reasons. *Id.*, 51–52. See Kerry v. Din, 125 Ct. 2128 (2015) (an "affirmative showing of bad faith" that is "plausibly alleged with sufficient particularity" will negate judicial deference, quoting J. Kennedy's concurring opinion at *id.*, 2141); Kleindienst v. Mandel, 408 U.S. 753, 769 (1972) (courts will defer to executive action in immigration visa denial cases if that are for "facially legitimate" and "*bona fide* reason").
78 International Refugee Assistance Project v. Trump, *supra* note 75, at 148–205.
79 Hawaii v. Trump, 2017 WL 2529640 (June 12, 2017).

countries and the 120-day refugee suspension/50,000 refugee cap. There, after finding that the affected individuals had standing, Judge Watson issued a temporary restraining order[80] and then a preliminary injunction[81] on the grounds that they would likely prevail in showing that EO-2 violated the First Amendment's Establishment Clause. In the ensuing appeal, however, a three-judge panel of the Ninth Circuit rested its opinion on statutory instead of constitutional grounds.[82]

In *Hawaii v. Trump*,[83] in a *per curiam* opinion Circuit Court Judges Michael Hawkins, Ronald Gould, and Richard Paez (all Clinton appointees) first deemed the case justiciable, holding that EO-2 created cognizable injuries to the State of Hawaii's proprietary and sovereign interests and to Dr. Ismail Elshikh, an American citizen whose Syrian mother-in-law had not been able to come into United States. Next, the court stated that although the President invoked the broad authority delegated to him by Congress under Section 1182(f) of the Immigration and Nationality Act (INA) to restrict border entry, he did so without making explicit findings that excluding aliens on the basis of their nationality was necessary to protect the security of the nation. For that reason, the President overstepped his delegated authority because, in the court's words, "National security is not a 'talismanic incantation' that, once invoked, can support any and all exercise of executive power under § 1182(f)."[84] Based on this reasoning, and since the INA placed important constraints on the exercise the President's constitutional authority,[85] EO-2 could not validly impose a 90-day travel ban on foreign nationals from the designated Muslim countries, suspend refugee access for 120 days, or restrict the total number of refugees to 50,000.[86]

Significantly, the court reached its conclusions after receiving input from nearly fifty amicus briefs, including two from the States led by their respective Republican and Democratic attorney generals, and one from the City of Chicago that argued that the travel

---

80 Hawaii v. Trump, *supra* note 47.

81 Hawaii v. Trump, *supra* note 48.

82 The circuit court did so after observing that the lower court decided the case on constitutional grounds even though it was more appropriate to consider the statutory claims first under the doctrine of constitutional avoidance. Hawaii v. Trump, *supra* note 50, 14–15.

83 *Id.*

84 *Id.*, 43, citing to United States v. Robel, 389 U.S. 258, 263–64 (1967) and Korematsu v. United States, 323 U.S. 214, 235 (1944) (Murphy, J., dissenting).

85 The panel reasoned that the President's constitutional powers to issue EO-2 were at its "lowest ebb" under the tripartite analytical framework established by *Youngstown Sheet & Tube Co. v. Sawyer*, 343 U.S. 579, 635–638 (1952)(Jackson, J., concurring), since his actions were incompatible with three INA statutory restrictions (U.S.C. §1152(a)(1)(A) [banning discriminating on the basis of nationality in making visa decisions]; 8 U.S.C. § 1157 [requiring President to follow codified procedures in setting the number of refugee admissions per fiscal year]; and, 8 U.S.C. § 1182(a)(3)(B) [outlining specific criteria for establishing inadmissibility based on terrorism-related reasons] that limited executive power over to control immigration. *Id.*, 61–62.

86 §§3 and 6 of EO-2 were thus invalidly invoked by the President, thus allowing the court to grant injunctive relief because the plaintiffs were likely to prevail on their statutory claims. Hawaii v. Trump, 2017 WL 2529640 9th Cir (June 12. 2017), 47–48. Additionally, the court ruled that EO-2 conflicted with two other INA provisions: 8 U.S.C. §1152(a)(1)(A) (banning discriminating on the basis of nationality in making visa decisions); and 8 U.S.C. § 1157 (requiring the President to follow codified procedures in setting the number of refugee admissions per fiscal year). *Id.*, 55–56, 60. The court, however, did not rule on the issue of whether EO-2 conflicted with 8 U.S.C. § 1182(a)(3)(B) (outlining specific criteria for establishing inadmissibility based on terrorism-related reasons). *Id.*, 60–61.

ban caused irreparable injuries to its residents.[87] In weighing the opposing arguments, the court did not make any reference to the brief authored by the Republican-led AGs, but it did cite those representing the views of the Democratic-led AG's to support its conclusion that EO-2 caused adversely affected the States' and municipalities' proprietary and sovereign interests, namely by disrupting their residents' lives and impairing the operation (and underlying economies) of state universities, medical institutions, refugee programs, tourism, and community-based law enforcement collaborations.[88]

Presidential proclamation (September 24, 2017)

On September 24, 2017, in a presidential proclamation, President Trump announced new travel restrictions that indefinitely banned most travel to the United States from eight countries, including most of those that were the subject of the March 6 executive order and ban.[89] The travel restrictions were declared on the same day that the temporary 90-day ban pertaining to foreign nationals from six mostly Muslim-populated countries was set to expire. Under the proclamation, which was issued after Trump officials performed a comprehensive global review of immigration security measures, nationals from Iran, Libya, Syria, Yemen, and Somalia (identified under the March 6 order), plus those from Chad, North Korea and Venezuela (not subject to the March 6 order), were subject to travel restrictions or more rigorous screenings. Perhaps to undercut the argument that the President's actions are not a religiously based "Muslim ban," two of the countries, North Korea and Venezuela, are not Muslim-dominated regions. Notably, the proclamation dropped Sudan from the list of countries previously affected by the travel ban; and it did not affect or address the refugee suspension component of the March 6 order. For the affected countries, though, the

---

87 These briefs largely mirrored the arguments made by most of the same *amici* before the Fourth Circuit in International Refugee Assistance Project v. Trump, see *supra* notes 74 and 75. See also Brief for the States of Texas, Alabama, Arizona, Arkansas, Florida, Kansas, Louisiana, Montana, North Dakota, Oklahoma, South Carolina, South Dakota, Tennessee, and West Virginia, and Governor Phil Bryant of the State of Mississippi as Amici Curiae in Support of Appellants and a Stay Pending Appeal (in Hawaii v. Trump, U.S. Court of Appeals for the Ninth Circuit, April 10, 2017), http://cdn.ca9.uscourts.gov/datastore/general/2017/04/11/17-15589%20States'%20 amicus%20brief.pdf.; Brief of Chicago, Los Angeles, New York, Philadelphia, and Other Major Cities and Counties as *Amici Curiae* in Support of Affirmance and in Opposition to Motion of Defendants-Appellants for a Stay Pending Appeal (in Hawaii v. Trump, U.S. Court of Appeals for the Ninth Circuit, April 21, 2017), http://cdn.ca9.uscourts.gov/datastore/general/ 2017/04/21/17-15589%20City%20of%20Chicago%20Amicus.pdf.; and, Brief of the States Of Illinois, California, Connecticut, Delaware, Iowa, Maine, Maryland, Massachusetts, New Mexico, New York, North Carolina, Oregon, Rhode Island, Vermont, Virginia, and Washington, and the District of Columbia as *Amicus Curiae* in Support of Plaintiffs-Appellees (in Hawaii v. Trump, U.S. Court of Appeals for the Ninth Circuit, April 20, 2017), http:// cdn.ca9.uscourts.gov/datastore/general/2017/04/20/17-15589%20States%20Illinios%20et%20al%20 amicus.pdf.
88 Hawaii v. Trump, *supra* note 50.
89 Pres. Proclamation No. 89, Presidential Proclamation Enhancing Vetting Capabilities and Processes for Detecting Attempted Entry Into the United States by Terrorists or Other Public-Safety Threats, (Sept. 24, 2017). www.whitehouse.gov/the-press-office/2017/09/24/ enhancing-vetting-capabilities-and-processes-detecting-attempted-entry

restrictions, which vary country by country, were set to begin on October 18, as set forth by the terms and conditions identified in the proclamation.[90]

In light of the presidential proclamation, on the following day the Supreme Court removed *Trump v. International Refugee Assistance Project* from its October 2017 calendar, "pending further order of the Court."[91] In its order, it instructed the parties to brief the legal question of whether the challenges to the travel ban have been mooted by the announcement of the proclamation and the impending expiration of the 120-day refugee suspension on October 24.[92] Until (and if) the justices weigh in on the justiciability questions, the merits of the case will not be heard which, of course, is a course of action that would allow the justices to sidestep deciding the principal constitutional issues of the travel ban litigation.

Conclusions

As in the political fight over Obamacare and health care policy,[93] state attorney generals have become influential litigants in shaping the contours of judicial precedents affecting anti-terrorism initiatives such as the Trump travel ban. At least in some respects, the competing legal arguments made by them in the underlying Fourth and Ninth Circuit litigation that was originally set to be reviewed by the Supreme Court in *Trump v. International Refugee Assistance Project* in October 2017 share a resemblance to the new federalism rhetoric that seeks to prevent the federal government from impinging on state sovereignty interests and rights. Most predominately, the Democratic coalition of state attorney generals that are resisting the travel ban have claimed that the president and the federal government are limited in their actions by the Tenth Amendment or prohibitions imposed under the Supreme Court's anti-commandeering precedents. In contrast, the Republican coalition of state attorney generals defend the travel ban because they assert that the President is empowered to ban entry under the Constitution's Article II provisions, or by authority of the powers delegated to him under statute to impose the ban because of national security concerns. Not surprisingly, these political divisions over how to interpret the law by and large are match the configuration of red and blue states in the 2016 national political map.[94] Not only do the opposing arguments underscore how far the states will go in making their claims of deference or resistance in the face of the impact that the ban has on state residents, public universities, medical facilities, and tourism industries, they also register that

90　See generally, Amy Howe, *Trump issues new order on travel.* SCOTUSBLOG (2017), www.scotusblog.com/2017/09/trump-issues-new-order-travel/.

91　Amy Howe, *Justices take travel ban cases off October argument calendar.* SCOTUSBLOG (2017), www.scotusblog.com/2017/09/justices-take-travel-ban-cases-off-october-argument-calendar/.

92　Order in Pending Cases (Trump v. International Refugee Assistance Project; and, Trump v. Hawaii, 16–1436; 16–1540, September 25 2017), www.supremecourt.gov/orders/courtorders/092517zr_jiel.pdf.

93　In August, 2017, sixteen Democratic-led state attorney generals successfully intervened in a U.S. Court of Appeals for the District of Columbia appeal on the grounds that their presence was necessary to protect States' interests in preserving Obamacare subsidies in the aftermath litigation challenging them and in light of the Republicans failure to repeal and replace Obamacare. Amy Goldstein, *Court ruling could help keep Obamacare subsidies,* WASHINGTON POST, August 1, 2017, www.washingtonpost.com/national/health-science/court-ruling-could-help-keep-obamacare-subsidies/2017/08/01/85b3ab66-7727-11e7-9eac-d56bd5568db8_story.html?utm_term=.b62b4a3b7f19.

94　Katherine Schulten, *Red and Blue Map, 2016,* NEW YORK TIMES, November 9, 2016, www.nytimes.com/2016/11/09/learning/red-and-blue-map-2016.html?_r=0.

challengers to the ban perceive their institutions to have a growing global profile that needs to be protected from federal government incursions on matters of immigration and foreign policy.[95]

As indicated earlier, the underlying litigation leading up to *Trump v. International Refugee Assistance Project* raised justiciability questions that pertain to new federalism principles and Roberts Court decisions relative to the standing of states to challenge federal incursions. To illustrate, the parties debated whether individuals and organizations that were adversely affected by the executive order had a "personal stake" in the case under the well-established three-prong standing doctrine test of showing injury-in-fact, traceability, and redressability[96] or if the States could challenge the edict because they were entitled to a "special solicitude" as sovereigns under *Massachusetts v. EPA* (2006).[97] In *Massachusetts*, states affected by climate change were deemed to have standing to challenge the EPA's decision not to regulate the emissions of greenhouse gases under the Clean Air Act. After observing that "States are not normal litigants for the purposes of invoking federal jurisdiction," the Court reasoned that Massachusetts had an independent stake in protecting its territorial quasi-sovereign interests against the threat of climate change. Alternatively, as the Ninth Circuit ruled in *Washington v. Trump* (2017), a case brought in response to Trump's first (January 27) executive order, the states argued under that they were entitled to bring the lawsuit the doctrine of third party standing because the injuries they suffered are "inextricably bound up with the activity the litigant wishes to pursue." In *Washington*, the Ninth Circuit reasoned that the travel ban's disruptive effects on state universities gave the states the legal capacity to sue for the harms suffered by students and faculty.[98] An analogous claim to establishing standing is to assert that the states can protect their own proprietary interests or safeguard their residents' well-being in exercising its *paren patriae* role. Notably, both of these latter arguments were used in Washington and Minnesota's brief at the district court level in *Washington v. Trump* (2017).

Moreover, especially in light of the September presidential proclamation, a mootness issue is most relevant in the travel ban litigation. Before the Proclamation's issuance, the mootness doctrine was in play because of the vagueness of the executive order's effective date, a legal issue raised by President Trump's decision to change it in a what acting U.S. Solicitor General Jeffrey Wall called a "clarifying memorandum" that the White House issued to relevant national security and law enforcement officials on June 14, 2017.[99] The memo was issued in fear of the chance that the Section 2(c) 90-day ban and the Section 6(a) 120-day refugee suspension would expire because the executive order's original effective date was March 16, 2017 (which meant that the § 2(c) suspension of entry expired after 90 days, on June 14, 2017 which moots the dispute over the 90-day ban; and, the 120-day refugee suspension would also lapse accordingly). Thus, the memo declared that the relevant portions of Sections 2 and 6 have an effective date of "72 hours after all applicable injunctions are

95 See Banks and Blakeman, *supra* note 37.
96 Lujan v. Defenders of Wildlife, 504 U.S. 555 (1992).
97 Massachuetts v. EPA, 549 U.S. 497.
98 Washington v. Trump, *supra* note 45.
99 Greg Stohr, *Trump Modifies Travel Ban to Address Possible Expiration*, Bloomberg Politics, June 14, 2017, www.bloomberg.com/news/articles/2017-06-14/trump-amends-travel-ban-to-address-possible-expiration-date.

lifted or stayed."[100] For some court watchers, if that memo is given legal effect, the memo would have been successful in changing the effective date to whenever the order is permitted to go into effect by the courts, which could be June 26, 2017, the date of the Court's ruling in *Trump v. International Refugee Assistance Project*. If it is not given legal effect, the date of mootness may be earlier, especially since the federal government argued that it needed more time to review existing screening and vetting procedures under the ban's time frame.[101]

Beyond threshold justiciability challenges, the key issues the Supreme Court might ultimately address on the merits relate to whether the President exceeded his constitutional or statutory authority in issuing the travel ban. Relative to the constitutional issue, the justices are likely to examine the president's action in light of *Youngstown Sheet & Tube Co. v. Sawyer* (1952),[102] a landmark precedent that examines if the President acted independently, or with or against congressional authority, in issuing the ban. The controlling opinion, written by Justice Robert Jackson, explains that the President's powers vary in accordance with types of action he takes. In Justice Jackson's words:

1) When the President acts pursuant to an express or implied authorization of Congress, his authority is at its maximum, for it includes all that he possesses in his own right plus all that Congress can delegate . . .;
2) When the President acts in absence of either a congressional grant or denial of authority, he can only rely upon his own independent powers, but there is a zone of twilight in which he and Congress may have concurrent authority, or in which its distribution is uncertain. . . .; or,
3) When the President takes measures incompatible with the expressed or implied will of Congress, his power is at its lowest ebb, for then he can rely only upon his own constitutional powers minus any constitutional powers of Congress over the matter.[103]

For Jackson, Truman's claim to power was at its "lowest ebb," or in the third category, because Congress had enacted the Taft-Hartley Act, which specifically prohibited the seizure of private property in labor disputes. In this light, the Court reasoned that the President did not have a constitutional or statutory basis to take control of the steel mills, thus nullifying his order.[104]

Accordingly, as Congress has delegated to the President Section 1182(f) powers under the INA to bar the entry of foreign nationals whenever he finds that their entry is "detrimental to the interests of the United States," the constitutional validity of the ban is likely to be significantly determined by whether the Roberts Court finds that the President acted at the apex of his powers (the first prong) or at its nadir (the third prong). Whereas Trump

---

100 Donald J. Trump, PRESIDENTIAL MEMORANDUM FOR THE SECRETARY OF STATE, THE ATTORNEY GENERAL, THE SECRETARY OF HOMELAND SECURITY, AND THE DIRECTOR OF NATIONAL INTELLIGENCE (2017), www.whitehouse.gov/the-press-office/2017/06/14/presidential-memorandum-secretary-state-attorney-general-secretary.
101 Litman, *supra* note 53.
102 Youngstown Sheet & Tube Co. v. Sawyer, 343 U.S. 579 (1952).
103 *Id.*, 635–37.
104 See John Contrubis, *Executive Orders and Proclamations*, CRS REP. CONGR. CRS WEB (1999), https://fas.org/sgp/crs/misc/95-772.pdf.

administration lawyers assert that the President's ban falls under the first prong because it is race-neutral and consistent with the policy aim of protecting national security, the attorneys challenging the ban claim that the President's powers were at its lowest point since the executive order is incompatible with three INA statutory restrictions (U.S.C. §1152(a)(1) (A) [banning discriminating on the basis of nationality in making visa decisions]; 8 U.S.C. § 1157 [requiring President to follow codified procedures in setting the number of refugee admissions per fiscal year]; and, 8 U.S.C. § 1182(a)(3)(B) [outlining specific criteria for establishing inadmissibility based on terrorism-related reasons]) that limited executive power over to control immigration.[105]

Another constitutional issue regarding the First Amendment's Establishment Clause is germane. Specifically, in deciding Section 2(c)'s constitutionality the justices will have interpret how two key Supreme Court precedents relate to each other. Both precedents generally pertain to the legal question of whether the law provides an exception to the doctrine of consular non-reviewability, a principle that prevents courts from reviewing the visa decisions of consular officers as a matter of deference to the political branches.[106] To illustrate, in *IRAP v. Trump*, the Fourth Circuit deemed the travel ban violated the First Amendment's prohibition that forbids government from taking action that favors one religion over another. From the government's perspective, the 90-day travel ban did not have a religious purpose since it is based on a "facially legitimate and bona fide" justification of safeguarding national security pursuant to *Kleindienst v. Mandel* (1972).[107] But, to the challengers, Justice Anthony's concurring opinion in *Kerry v. Din* (2015)[108] vitiated that reason because President Trump's campaign and post-election comments about the ban demonstrate that his order was done in "bad faith."[109] Thus, the Supreme Court might decide if the Fourth Circuit ruling in *IRAP v. Trump* was correct in reasoning that Trump's anti-Muslim animus fits *Kerry's* requirements of being an "affirmative showing" and an allegation of "sufficient particularity" of "bad faith" by the executive, which gives the judiciary the power to "look behind" and reject *Mandel's* principle of deference that ordinarily applies to uphold the "facially legitimate" decisions of the political branches that are made for "bona fide" national security reasons. In interpreting the interplay between *Mandel* and *Din*, a key factor will be if the Supreme Court determines that Trump's comments as a politician is relevant evidence of racial hatred and bad faith, something that divided the majority and dissenting justices in the Fourth Circuit *International Refugee Assistance Project v. Trump*.

---

105 Notably, the Ninth Circuit panel reached this conclusion in *Hawaii v. Trump* (2017). See *supra* notes 82–86.

106 The consular non-reviewability doctrine is related to an analogous (and infamous) deference plenary powers doctrine that originated from the Chinese Exclusion case, *Chae Chan Ping v. United States*. Kevin Johnson, *Argument preview: The doctrine of consular non-reviewability—historical relic or good law?*, SCOTUSBLOG (2015), www.scotusblog.com/2015/02/argument-preview-the-doctrine-of-consular-non-reviewability-historical-relic-or-good-law/. *See also* Margo Schlanger, *Symposium: Could this be the end of plenary power?*, SCOTUSBLOG (2017), www.scotusblog.com/2017/07/symposium-end-plenary-power/.

107 Kleindienst v. Mandel, *supra* note 77.

108 Kerry v. Din, *supra* note 77.

109 In International Refugee Assistance Project v. Trump (2017), the Fourth Circuit determined that Justice Kennedy's concurrence was *Kerry's* controlling opinion, a judgment also made by the Ninth Circuit. International Refugee Assistance Project v. Trump, *supra* note 72, 49–50.

Regardless of the outcome, the Trump travel ban litigation remains important because it directly implicates federalism as well as basic constitutional principles relating to the judicial lines that will be drawn in ascertaining the proper boundaries of government authority that separate the legislative and executive branches. The legal divisions reveal that partisan politics is a growing characteristic of federalism disputes, a trend that is embedded in today's culture wars and increasingly affecting the realm of foreign affairs. These developments are consistent with movements in the states to practice a form of "uncooperative federalism"[110] or "partisan federalism"[111] whenever the interests therein believe they must resist federal policies[112] (Bulman-Pozen and Gerken 2009). The fact that trends are increasingly conspicious across the political landscape is underscored by the prevalance of federalism arguments appearing in areas of constitutional law that traditionally affords the federal government great leeway in regulating foreign affairs and national security policies.[113] Whether the Roberts Court relies upon the new federalism principles that gained more prominence in the Rehnquist Court era, however, remains an open question until (and whether) the Supreme Court opts to decide the travel ban case.

110 Jessica Bulman-Pozen & Heather K. Gerken, *Uncooperative Federalism*, 118 YALE LAW J. 1256 (2009).
111 Jessica Bulman-Pozen, *Partisan Federalism*, 127 HARV. LAW REV. 1077 (2014).
112 Bulman-Pozen & Gerken, *supra* note 110.
113 GLENNON & SLOANE, *supra* note 35.

4 Capital punishment and federalism

International obligations and domestic standards

Mary Welek Atwell

In the latter half of the twentieth century, when most liberal democracies and other modernized countries abolished the death penalty at the national level, in the United States capital punishment persisted within, and to a great extent because of, a federalist political structure. After the Supreme Court of the United States found the death penalty as applied unconstitutional in *Furman v. Georgia*, states immediately began rewriting their capital statutes to meet constitutional standards.[1] States resisted what they perceived as an intrusion by the federal judiciary into their criminal justice systems and the majority of states set about reasserting control over their own punishment regimes. Franklin Zimring describes this particular approach as "negative federalism," a commitment to states' rights as a way to limit national power.[2] As David Garland notes, in the post-*Furman* era, capital punishment became a symbolic part of a struggle between federal courts and state legislatures carried on in an atmosphere of "law and order" politics.[3] Both Zimring and Garland find the last generation of skirmishes over the death penalty to be inseparable from other cultural conflicts and inseparable from America's racial history. It is a sanction about which Americans disagree profoundly, yet it survives in the law of thirty-one states and is carried out under the supervision of federal courts and within the parameters of constitutional law. Capital punishment is, in many ways, a paradigm of federalism in the United States, a contested site of debates over how to balance state versus national interests.

Part of the federalist revolution associated with the Rehnquist and Roberts Courts involved what Chief Justice William Rehnquist described in *United States v. Morrison* (2000) as the constitutionally required separation of what is truly national from what is truly local.[4] One area the Court identified as "truly local" is ordinary criminal law. Yet the dividing line there is not so clear. A significant area of contention comprises situations where international agreements, such as the Vienna Convention on Consular Rights, conflict with the application of American criminal law.[5] Another example relates to the traditional yardstick for measuring Eighth Amendment violations. When does a criminal sanction violate the prohibition against "cruel and unusual punishment"? A number of Supreme Court opinions have looked to

---

1 Furman v. Georgia, 408 U.S. 238 (1972).
2 Franklin E. Zimring, Contradictions of American Capital Punishment 14 (2003).
3 David Garland, Peculiar Institution: America's Death Penalty in an Age of Abolition 284 (2010).
4 United States v. Morrison, 529 U.S. 598, 618 (2000).
5 Vienna Convention on Consular Relations, April 24, 1963, 21 U.S.T. 77, T.I.A.S. No.6820, (hereinafter cited as Consular Convention).

"evolving standards of decency."[6] These decisions have been based upon a perceived consensus among states with regard to the application of capital punishment. Yet defining those standards has been a source of debate among the Justices. Not only do members of the Court differ about how to count the states forming a consensus (should the count include states that prohibit capital punishment all together?), but the Justices also differ widely on the subject of how much weight to give an individual state's capital regime as a product of the local democratic process. Although the "evolving standards of decency" approach has prevailed in a number of important cases such as *Atkins v. Virginia*,[7] *Roper v. Simmons*,[8] and *Kennedy v. Louisiana*,[9] the more conservative members of the Court have issued powerful dissents against what they believed to be examples of the Court imposing its beliefs and preferences on the states.[10]

The Roberts Court has addressed the intersection of international law with state criminal procedure in several cases, most notably in *Sanchez-Llamas v. Oregon*,[11], *Medellin v. Texas,* [12] and *Leal Garcia v. Texas*.[13] In all three cases, the Court found that state procedural default laws trumped the rights of foreign nationals as provided in the Vienna Convention. Although the International Court of Justice had directed the United States to find a judicial remedy for the violation to the right to consular notification, the Supreme Court refused to require the states to comply. Article VI, the Supremacy Cause of the U.S. Constitution, states that "All Treaties made, or which shall be made, under the Authority of the United States, shall be the Supreme Law of the Land; and the Judges of every State shall be bound thereby, any Thing in the Constitution of laws of any State to the Contrary notwithstanding."[14] Nonetheless, members of the Court have disagreed vigorously among themselves regarding whether treaties and international law should have any influence at all on American death penalty jurisprudence. Accordingly, the first part of this chapter examines the cases in which the Court considered the arguments stemming from a conflict between international obligations and state criminal procedure. This is a significant issue because the Rehnquist and Roberts Courts have taken the position that adherence to an international treaty and the rulings of an international court are merely optional when such provisions conflict with criminal procedures prescribed by laws of individual states. The effort to reconcile such rulings with the Supremacy Clause was revealing of the Court's definition of federalism.

In addition, the effort to apply the Eighth Amendment prohibition against cruel and unusual punishment, an attempt to find a national consensus about capital punishment, often runs up against federalist arguments regarding the "truly local" nature of criminal law. In his dissent in *Glossip v. Gross*, Justice Stephen Breyer called for a thorough review of the constitutionality of capital punishment.[15] Among his criticisms of the current system was its

---

6 Trop v. Dulles, 356 U.S. 86, 101 (1958).
7 Atkins v. Virginia, 536 U.S. 304 (2002).
8 Roper v. Simmons, 543 U.S. 551 (2005).
9 Kennedy v. Louisiana, 554 U.S. 407 (2008).
10 For example, in *Roper v. Simmons,* Justice Scalia wrote that the Court should only "identify a moral consensus of the American people. By what conceivable warrant can nine lawyers presume to be the authoritative conscience of the Nation?"
11 Sanchez-Llamas v. Oregon, 548 U.S. 331 (2006).
12 Medellin v. Texas, 552 U.S. 491 (2008).
13 Leal Garcia v. Texas, 564 U.S. 490 (2011).
14 U.S. CONST. Art. VI.
15 Glossip v. Gross, 135 S.Ct. 2726 (2015)

arbitrariness, or the lack of "reasonable consistency" in the application of the death penalty.[16] Such inconsistency may be an inevitable price to pay for administering the ultimate punishment in a federal system; yet, the criticism underscores the significance of the search for a consistent interpretation of the Eighth Amendment while deferring to the states' sovereignty in the area of criminal law. As a result, the second section of this chapter considers how the Rehnquist and Roberts Courts have applied the evolving standards of decency standard in capital cases. The chapter concludes with a brief discussion of Breyer's analysis of the status of capital punishment in light of decisions handed down during the Court's current term.

International law versus capital punishment

In order to understand the ways in which the Court has dealt with the conflict between state police powers and treaty obligations in recent decades, one must look to two foundational texts—the Vienna Convention on Consular Rights (VCCR)[17] and the decision in *Coleman v. Thompson*.[18] The United States is in many ways an outlier among modern democratic nations in maintaining capital punishment as a legal option. All the nations of the European Union, as well as most in Latin America and the former British Commonwealth, have abolished the use of the death penalty because it is considered a violation of human rights. In contrast, in the United States the sanction is treated merely as a matter of criminal justice policy, as determined by state law. In addition to continuing to execute American citizens, since the VCCR's ratification in 1969, American states have put thirty-two foreign nationals to death in violation of international treaty obligations.[19] The VCCR binds signatory nations to notify the appropriate consulate as soon as one of their citizens is charged with a crime. The critical clause of the convention is Article 36. It states that when a foreign national is detained by law enforcement, the authorities must inform him of the right to contact the consul of his home nation "without delay."[20] The consul could "converse and correspond with him . . . and arrange for his legal representation."[21] According to the treaty, the rights of the foreign national "shall be exercised in conformity with the laws and regulations of the receiving State, subject to the proviso, however, that the said laws and regulations must enable full effect to be given to the purposes for which the rights accorded under this Article are intended."[22] Since most criminal cases in the U.S. fall within the jurisdiction of individual states, the challenge in applying the Vienna Convention is how to assure that state and local authorities comply. If a foreign national is taken into custody by a local police agency and the arresting officer fails to notify him of his right to contact the consul of his native country, the VCCR does not specify the consequences of such a violation. For a variety of reasons, ranging from ignorance to defiance, local and state agencies may

---

16 *Id.* at 2760.
17 See Consular Convention *supra* note 5.
18 Coleman v. Thompson, 501 U.S. 722 (1991).
19 Mark Warren, *Confirmed Foreign Nationals Executed Since* 1976, DEATH PENALTY INFORMATION CENTER, deathpenaltyinfo.org (last visited June 30, 2017).
20 See Consular Convention *supra* note 5.
21 *Id.*
22 MICHAEL JOHN GARCIA. VIENNA CONVENTION ON CONSULAR RELATIONS: OVERVIEW OF U.S. IMPLEMENTATION AND INTERNATIONAL COURT OF JUSTICE INTERPRETATION OF CONSULAR NOTIFICATION REQUIREMENTS 3 (2004).

not comply and the consequences to a foreign national may be serious. The foreign national may have little knowledge of English or of American legal procedures, deficiencies that the consul could help to remedy. Foreign nationals often face more severe penalties in the U.S. than they would at home. Specifically, they may be charged with a crime that could result in a death sentence. In such a trial, the consul's assistance could be invaluable. The consul may be able to produce mitigating evidence during the sentencing phase by uncovering appropriate records in the home country. Such access might not be available to an American lawyer.[23] In addition, the presence of the consul may encourage the local government agencies to follow the rules and to refrain from discriminating against the foreign national. So, although detained foreign nationals have the right to have contact with their consulate "without delay," and although this is a right Americans arrested abroad would consider a vital protection, and although the International Court of Justice has held the U.S. accountable for failing to respect this right, the Supreme Court has allowed states to violate the Vienna Convention with impunity. In several cases where defendants raised the issue of VCCR violations on appeal, the courts have rejected their petitions based on the doctrine of procedural default. The 1991 decision in *Coleman v. Thompson*, discussed next, provides the basis for the rule that determined the fate of many whose rights under the Vienna Convention were disregarded.[24]

Justice Sandra Day O'Connor famously began the majority opinion in *Coleman v. Thompson* with the phrase, "This is a case about federalism."[25] Roger Coleman had been convicted in Virginia for the rape and murder of his sister-in-law. He was sentenced to death. For him, clearly the case was about something other than the structure of government. His lawyers had failed to meet a filing deadline established in state law and had thus missed the opportunity to raise several constitutional claims. The Virginia Supreme Court denied his appeal, as did federal appeals courts, including the U.S. Supreme Court. Justice O'Connor's opinion noted that Coleman's plea had been denied based on "independent and adequate state grounds"[26] and the Supreme Court deferred to that decision. According to Virginia law, a prisoner had thirty days to file a notice of appeal. Coleman's notice had reached the federal court on the thirty-third day. As O'Connor saw it, if Coleman were permitted to file a habeas petition three days late, he and others like him would be allowed "an end run around the limits of the Court's jurisdiction and a means to undermine the State's interest in enforcing its laws."[27] The opinion refers several times to the concern that without procedural default, the state would not have the opportunity to address and correct violations of a prisoner's rights. As in other cases that deferred to a state's criminal laws and procedures, the holding referred to comity and finality as principles vindicated by respect for procedural default. As the Court flatly put it, "We now recognize the important interest in finality served by state procedural rules and the significant harm to the states that results from the failure of federal courts to respect them."[28] O'Connor added emphasis by specifying the rule, "We now make it explicit: in all cases in which a state prisoner has defaulted his federal claims in state court pursuant to an independent and adequate state procedural rule,

23 *Id.*
24 Coleman v. Thompson, *supra* note 18.
25 *Id* at 727.
26 *Id.* at 730.
27 *Id.* at 732.
28 *Id.* at 751.

federal habeas review of the claims is barred unless the prisoner can demonstrate cause for the default and actual prejudice as a result of the alleged violation of federal law, or demonstrate that the failure to consider the claims will result in a fundamental miscarriage of justice."[29]

The Court also addressed an obvious question: suppose that the reason a claim was not raised earlier was because the defense attorney failed to raise it, either through ignorance or neglect? The *Coleman* Court cited *Strickland v. Washington*, a landmark case relating to so-called ineffective assistance of counsel claims under the Sixth Amendment.[30] As long as a lawyer met the *Strickland* test, (his performance was not constitutionally ineffective), the defendant was required to "bear the risk of an attorney error that results in procedural default."[31] All of the cases of foreign nationals which reached the Supreme Court involved situations where their lawyers were uninformed about the Vienna Convention and therefore neglected to raise the issue at trial. All their claims would be rejected as procedurally defaulted.

The dissent in *Coleman*, written by Justice Harry Blackmun and joined by Justices Thurgood Marshall and John Paul Stevens, offers an alternative view of federalism. According to Blackmun, federalism has "no inherent normative value."[32] Its purpose is to "secure to citizens the liberties that derive from the diffusion of sovereign power."[33] He disagreed with his colleagues that federal habeas review of state judgements is an invasion of state sovereignty. Rather, federal habeas reflects "the Supremacy Clause of the Constitution where federal law is higher than State law."[34] For foreign nationals, Justice Blackmun's words were especially meaningful (even if ineffectual) because their claims under the Vienna Convention, a treaty signed by the United States government, were rejected on account of state procedural rules.

The dissent also addressed the issue of attorney failure or incompetence as a cause of procedural default. In Blackmun's words, "To permit a procedural default caused by an attorney error egregious enough to constitute ineffective assistance of counsel to preclude federal habeas review of a state prisoner's federal claims in no way serves the State's interest in preserving the integrity of its rules and proceedings. The interest in finality, standing alone, cannot provide a sufficient reason for a federal court to compromise its protection of constitutional rights."[35] The justices in the minority in *Coleman* anticipated that the majority were on a "crusade to erect petty procedural barriers" to habeas review by "creating a Byzantine morass of arbitrary, unnecessary, and unjustifiable impediments to the vindication of federal rights."[36] The trend Blackmun identified in *Coleman* characterized a great many other cases about federalism particularly those involving foreign nationals and their rights under the Vienna Convention. Some of those cases are discussed next.

29 *Id.*
30 Strickland v. Washington, 466 U.S. 668 (1984).
31 Coleman v. Thompson, *supra* note 18, at 753.
32 *Id.* at 760.
33 *Id.*
34 *Id.* at 761.
35 *Id.* at 774.
36 *Id.* at 760.

Sanchez-Llamas v. Oregon

By the time *Sanchez-Llamas v. Oregon*[37] reached the Supreme Court in 2005, the International Court of Justice (ICJ) had issued a ruling in response to a charge from Mexico that the United States was in violation of the Vienna Convention when it sentenced foreign nationals to death without informing them of their rights under the treaty. In that case, known as *Avena*, Mexico cited the 54 Mexican citizens who sat on death rows in a number of American states.[38] The ICJ ruled that although the United States was both free to provide for capital punishment in its laws and free to assert the doctrine of procedural default, the latter could not be invoked to preclude defense attorneys from raising violations of the Vienna Convention on appeal if those issues had not been mentioned at the initial trial.[39] The heart of the ICJ's ruling was that the United States must provide a judicial remedy for that failure if foreign nationals had not been informed of their consular rights at the time of their detention. There must be review and reconsideration of the conviction and sentence by American courts "with a view to ascertaining whether in each case the violation . . . committed by the competent authorities caused actual prejudice to the defendant."[40] The remedy the United States had offered, the possibility of executive clemency, did not satisfy the ICJ who insisted that Vienna Convention violations required a judicial resolution.

Neither of the two defendants whose appeals were combined in *Sanchez-Llamas* was among the *Avena* petitioners; neither had been sentenced to death. However, the case raised similar issues as those before the ICJ. Moises Sanchez-Llamas, a Mexican national, was arrested in Oregon for attempted murder and given the Miranda warnings, but was not told of his rights under the Vienna Convention. He made incriminating statements during interrogation, but moved to suppress those statements at trial because the authorities had not complied with the VCCR. His plea was denied by Oregon courts, including the state supreme court, which held that the Vienna Convention did not create individual rights that are enforceable in a judicial proceeding. At the Supreme Court, Sanchez-Llamas' case was combined with that of Mario Bustillo, a Honduran national. Bustillo was charged with murder in Virginia. He only raised the issue of denial of his right to consular notification in state habeas proceedings. His claim was rejected as procedurally defaulted.[41]

The Supreme Court addressed three questions in their opinion, written by Chief Justice John Roberts and joined by Justices Antonin Scalia, Anthony Kennedy, Clarence Thomas, and Samuel Alito. They considered the following issues: 1) Did the Vienna Convention create individual rights that are enforceable in American courts?; 2) If a defendant is not notified of the right to consular notification, is suppression of his confession the appropriate remedy?; and 3) May states invoke procedural default to bar subsequent claims under the Vienna Convention?[42]

---

37 Sanchez-Llamas v. Oregon, *supra* note 11.
38 Case Concerning Avena and Other Mexican Nationals (Mexico v. United States of America), 2004 I.C.J. 128 (March 31).
39 ALAN W. CLARKE AND LAURELYN WHITT, THE BITTER FRUIT OF AMERICAN JUSTICE: INTERNATIONAL AND DOMESTIC RESISTANCE TO THE DEATH PENALTY 60–61 (2007).
40 *Id.*
41 Sanchez-Llamas v. Oregon, *supra* note 11, 340–41
42 *Id.* at 338.

As for the individual rights' issue, the Court "assumed, without deciding, that Article 36 does grant Bustillo and Sanchez-Llamas such rights."[43] Regarding whether applying the exclusionary rule to Sanchez-Llamas' statements was the appropriate remedy, they decided in the negative. Suppression would be an extreme remedy, they stated, to be used only for "wrongs of constitutional dimension," such as breaches of the Fourth or Fifth Amendment.[44] As for whether in Bustillo's case, state procedural default rules prevented raising VCCR claims in habeas proceedings, the Court determined that they did. Allowing that the ICJ's ruling concerning the problems with procedural default deserved "respectful consideration," the Court asserted its primacy over the international court in interpreting American constitutional matters. Chief Justice Roberts' opinion quoted Chief Justice John Marshall in *Marbury v. Madison*, pointing out that the judicial power extended to the interpretation of treaties and recalling that such decisions are "emphatically the province of the judicial department" headed by the "one Supreme Court."[45] By contrast, the ICJ's ruling in *Avena* applied only to that particular case and had no relevance to Bastillo's claims. The Court further raised the fear that if Vienna Convention violations could override these procedural default rules, the VCCR might be invoked to claim to override other procedural rules such as statutes of limitations or prohibitions against filing successive habeas petitions. These cases could be the first steps on the proverbial slippery slope.[46] Ultimately the Court determined that even though they would not disparage the importance of the Vienna Convention, that treaty nonetheless provided that rights "shall be exercised in conformity with the laws and regulations of the receiving state" and these cases "in many ways turn on established principles of domestic law."[47]

Justice Stephen Breyer wrote the dissenting opinion, joined by Justices Stevens and David Souter, and in part by Justice Ruth Bader Ginsburg. First, the dissent argued that the Vienna Convention allowed a defendant to raise a claim in state court. The justices contended that the Court should not make a blanket rule against suppression or upholding procedural default. Rather, they considered that suppression could *sometimes* be an appropriate remedy for a VCCR violation and that procedural default rules could *sometimes* be set aside. If the U.S. was to make a serious effort to give full effect to the rights of foreign nationals, then there must be judicial remedies for violations of treaty rights. Breyer's opinion went on to state that because the Vienna Convention was a self-executing treaty, and "one that operates of itself without the aid of any legislative provision" under its stipulations that foreign nationals had individual rights. If those rights are breached by the government, the foreign national could seek "redress in a judicial proceeding."[48] Therefore, in light of this analysis, if the rights existed and if the defendant was entitled to a remedy, what about procedural default? Breyer and the other dissenters answered that question based on whose fault it was that the consular rights were neglected. If the state was responsible for failing to inform the foreign national of his rights and if the state did not provide any other way to raise the issue, then procedural default would not apply.[49] The majority's opinion in

43 *Id.* at 344.
44 *Id.* at 350.
45 *Id.* at 354, quoting C.J. Marshall in Marbury v. Madison, 5 U.S. 137.
46 *Id.* at 358.
47 *Id.* at 361.
48 *Id.* at 373.
49 *Id.* at 393.

Sanchez-Llamas foreshadowed how the Court would rule in the most significant of the Vienna Convention cases, *Medellin v. Texas*.[50]

Medellin v. Texas

Even as the Court considered the *Sanchez-Llamas* case, the more diplomatically sensitive case of Jose Medellin was wending its way through the American judicial system. Medellin was one of the fifty-one Mexican nationals named in the International Court of Justice's 2004 *Avena* ruling. Along with four other young men, Medellin was tried and convicted of capital murder in 1994 for the gang rape and murder of two teenaged girls near Houston, Texas. At the time of his arrest, he informed the police that he had been born in Mexico and that he was not an American citizen. However, he was not informed of his right to seek assistance from the Mexican consulate.[51] While he was on death row and after his initial round of appeals, Medellin wrote to the Mexican consular authorities who subsequently assisted him in the appeals process. He raised the issue of his rights under Vienna Convention when he filed for state habeas relief. The Texas courts rejected the claim on the grounds of procedural default. In 2003, he filed a petition for habeas corpus in federal court.[52] While Medellin's case was making its way through the federal system, the ICJ handed down the *Avena* decision requiring that American courts provide a judicial remedy for violations of consular notification rights.[53] Before the Supreme Court could hear Medellin's case, President George W. Bush issued a memorandum stating his administration's response to the *Avena* ruling.[54]

Bush's memorandum to Attorney General Alberto Gonzales, issued on February 28, 2005, stated "I have determined pursuant to the authority vested in me as President by the Constitution and laws of the United States of America, that the United States will discharge its international obligations under the decision of the International Court of Justice in [*Avena*], by having State courts give effect to the decision in accordance with the general principles of comity in cases filed by the fifty-one Mexican nationals addressed in that decision."[55] Bush's memorandum seemed to require states to find a way to consider the claims brought by defendants such as Medellin. It asserted the authority of the president to override state procedural rules in matters of foreign policy. If Bush's directive took effect, the Texas courts would have to review and reconsider Medellin's appeal. At that point, the Supreme Court opted to send the case back to the Texas courts, who reconsidered it in light of the presidential memo. It would return to the high court in 2007. By that time, the justices had ruled in *Sanchez-Llamas,* articulating a position that would have a bearing on the outcome in *Medellin*.[56] In addition, the make-up of the Court had changed. Chief Justice Rehnquist and Justice O'Connor had been replaced by Chief Justice Roberts and Justice Alito. Both of the latter were strongly committed to their version of federalism which

---

50 Medellin v. Texas, *supra* note 12.
51 *Id*. at 502.
52 *Id*. at 503.
53 *Id*.
54 *Id*. at 504.
55 *Id*.
56 Sanchez-Llamas v. Oregon, *supra* note 11.

involved protecting states' rights to determine their criminal justice systems and skepticism about applying the rulings of the international court.[57]

When the Court granted certiorari in *Medellin*, they addressed two questions: Was the *Avena* judgement directly enforceable as domestic law in state courts?[58] Also, did the President's memorandum independently require that state courts provide review and a reconsideration of *Avena* claims, despite state procedural default rules?[59] In essence, the Court held that the federal government was powerless to require the states to comply with the order of the ICJ. Writing for the majority, Chief Justice Roberts was joined by Justices Scalia, Kennedy, Thomas, and Alito. Justice Stevens concurred in the judgment. As they had held in *Sanchez-Llamas*, the Court reaffirmed that the Vienna Convention did not preclude the application of state procedural default rules. As the state of Texas had argued, they held that the VCCR was not "self-executing," and because Congress had not passed enabling legislation, it did not become part of domestic law and could not displace state procedural default rules.[60] They further held that the President did not have the authority to enforce the *Avena* ruling in state court. As the Court put it, "When the President asserts the power to 'enforce' a non-self-executing treaty by unilaterally creating domestic law, he acts in conflict with the implicit understanding of the ratifying Senate. . . . He may not rely on a non-self-executing treaty to 'establish binding rules of decision that preempt contrary state law'."[61] The ruling—a triumph for state sovereignty—is both a rebuff to the president's authority to direct foreign policy and a challenge to the application of the Supremacy Clause of the Constitution. Such is the position of the dissenting opinion by Justice Breyer, joined by Justices Souter and Ginsburg.

Justice Breyer offered a different sense of federalism than the majority. He noted that the Supremacy Clause of the Constitution meant that a treaty, such as the Vienna Convention, when signed by the United States, constituted/became its domestic law; therefore, it was binding on the states and their courts.[62] The U.S. had accepted the jurisdiction of the International Court of Justice and therefore had an obligation to abide by its rulings. In this case, that meant that the *Avena* judgment required judicial review and reconsideration of the cases cited by Mexico where its nationals had been denied their rights under the VCCR. The obligation to abide by the ICJ's decision meant that the subdivisions of the United States, in this case Texas, required compliance and the court must revisit Medellin's claims to determine whether he had been prejudiced by the violation.[63] Without directly addressing the matter of the president's authority to supersede state law, Breyer found the majority's position strange. It seemed to suggest that under Article II of the Constitution that the president *never* had the authority to set aside state legislation. If that were an accurate

---

57 See, e.g., S. Ernie Walton, *The Judicial Philosophy of Justice John Roberts: An Analysis Through the Eyes of International Law*, 30 EMORY INT'L. L.REV. 39 (2016); Christopher Banks and John Blakeman, *Chief Justice Roberts, Justice Alito and the New Federalism*, 38 PUBLIUS: THE JOURNAL OF FEDERALISM 576 (2008).
58 Medellin v. Texas, *supra* note 12, at 506.
59 *Id*. at 524.
60 *Id*. at 523–24.
61 *Id*. at 531.
62 *Id*. at 539.
63 *Id*. at 541.

reading of the Constitution, he reasoned, the president's ability to carry out foreign policy would be severely compromised.[64]

Medellin appeared to vindicate the views of Texas Solicitor General Ted Cruz who had argued the case before the Court. Cruz described the holding as "a significant victory for U.S. sovereignty, for separation of powers, and for federalism."[65] In addition, Cruz set out the apocalyptic consequences had the Court ruled differently. As he opined in a law review he published, "The President could overturn any law at any time in the name of enforcing any vague, aspirational obligation the United States might have ratified."[66] Others, though, might argue that the Supremacy Clause provides just such primacy of treaties and federal laws over state laws. But in the view of Cruz and those who agreed with him, the sovereignty of the states was at stake in *Medellin*. Notably, the decision recognized that the states are not "mere political subdivisions" and that the federal government could not "commandeer the machinery of state government to implement federal policy." Rather, properly interpreted, the Constitution "recognizes and preserves the autonomy and independence of the States."[67]

As for Medellin, he was executed in Texas on August 5, 2008. Governor Rick Perry ignored numerous domestic and international pleas to postpone the execution. Perry's spokesman was quoted in the *New York Times* that the State was asserting its right to carry out the death sentence despite requests from President Bush, the attorney general, the secretary of state, members of Congress, and the government of Mexico. As Cruz's surrogate argued, the pleas on Medellin's behalf "[didn't] change anything. This is an individual who brutally gang raped two teen age women. We don't really care where you are from; you can't do that to our citizens."[68]

In its decision, the Supreme Court had ruled that in accordance with *Coleman's* "independent and adequate state procedural rule" the defendant had defaulted the right to have his case reviewed, despite rights provided under an international treaty and the judgment of an international court. For law scholar Benjamin Beiter, *Medellin* was an ideal case to determine whether the Court adhered to "an emerging federalism limit on the treaty power." The conflict between state procedural default rules and international obligations involved Medellin, but it also implicated the executive branch's ability to enforce an international agreement in domestic law.[69] The decision made it clear that the Roberts Court would not see state law preempted by international obligation. Also, it would assume that treaties were not self-executing unless explicitly provided by Congress. The "default position was that state law prevails over contradictory treaty obligations,"[70] a clearly innovative interpretation of the Supremacy Clause and a "federalism limit on the treaty power."[71] The Court would revisit the issue one more time in the case of Humberto Leal Garcia.

64 *Id.* at 565.
65 Ted Cruz, *Defending U.S. Sovereignty, Separation of Powers, and Federalism in Medellin v. Texas*, 33 HARV. J.L. & PUB. POL'Y 25, 35 (Winter 2010).
66 *Id.* at 32.
67 *Id.* at 33–34.
68 Quoted in James C. McKinley Jr., *Texas Executes Mexican Despite Objections from Bush and International Court*, NEW YORK TIMES, August 6, 2008, www.nytimes.com/2008/08/06/us/06execute.html.
69 Benjamin Beiter, *Beyond Medellin: Reconsidering Federalism Limits on the Treaty Power*, 85 NOTRE DAME L. REV. 1163, 1182 (2009–2010).
70 *Id.* at 1184.
71 *Id.*

Leal Garcia v. Texas

The case of Mexican national Humberto Leal Garcia (sentenced to death for rape and murder), which concerned a defendant that was not informed of his consular rights under the Vienna Convention, picked up where *Medellin* left off. Like Medellin, Leal was a named petitioner in the *Avena* judgment.[72] Although his first appeal to the Supreme Court in 1998 was denied on the basis of procedural default, he appealed again for a stay of execution in 2011. His last appeal, though, was supported by the Obama administration which maintained that Leal should not be put to death while Congress was considering legislation to implement the Vienna Convention.[73]

Leal's attorneys argued that the prospect for congressional action had greatly improved as a bill had been introduced in the Senate by Senator Patrick Leahy, who chaired the Senate Judiciary Committee and had the backing of the President. Leahy's proposal would authorize the federal courts to evaluate the merits of a Vienna Convention claim. Even with procedural default rules, a petitioner would have access to the federal courts. Nor would such a petition be barred by provisions of the Antiterrorism and Effective Death Penalty Act (AEDPA)[74] that frequently prevented habeas appeals in federal court.[75] Leal also cited the damage to America's international reputation and its foreign policy interests if the United States continued to defy rulings of the international court. Furthermore, there were potential threats to American citizens abroad if consular access could be denied by nations who had agreed to honor the VCCR.[76]

However, the Supreme Court ruled against Leal in a 5–4 decision on July 7, 2011. They reiterated the major points found in *Medellin* and rejected the suggestion that they should order a postponement of the execution while Congress considered legislation to implement the VCCR. As the Court stated, "Our task is to rule on what the law is, not what it might eventually be."[77] Besides denying that Leal's execution would have serious international consequences, they seemed skeptical that a Vienna Convention claim would have any prospect of success.[78] But here lies a conundrum. No one knows whether the lack of respect for his consular rights harmed Leal or any of the others whose VCCR rights were ignored because their claims were never considered.

Justice Breyer again wrote the dissent, which was joined by Justices Ginsburg, Sonia Sotomayor, and Elena Kagan—the latter two were new Obama appointees that replaced Justices Souter and Stevens in the Roberts Court. He saw no harm in a stay of execution. It would prevent an "irreparable breach" of international obligations and provide a chance for Leal's case to receive the judicial review and reconsideration ordered by the *Avena* ruling.[79] The Court, he opined, could wait until the new term began in September and give full consideration to the matter. Such a delay would also give Congress an incentive to act on the Leahy bill.[80] Finally, Breyer noted that the Court usually gave "significant weight"

72 Leal Garcia v. Texas, *supra* note 13.
73 *Id*. at 945.
74 Pub.L.No.104–132, 110 Stat.1214
75 Leal Garcia v. Texas, *supra* note 13.
76 *Id*. at 946.
77 *Id*. at 940.
78 *Id*. at 942–43.
79 *Id*. at 946.
80 *Id*. at 947.

and deference to a president's position in matters of foreign affairs; but here they seemed to find that Texas' interest in putting Leal to death without delay outweighed the other considerations that could be served by a postponement.[81] As he wrote, "[it] is difficult to see how the State's interest in the immediate execution of an individual convicted of capital murder 16 years ago can outweigh the considerations that support additional delay, perhaps only until the end of the summer."[82]

But Breyer's caution did not prevail and only an hour after the Court's decision was announced, Texas executed Humberto Leal Garcia. Andrew Cohen found that the Court went "out of its way" to let Texas proceed with the execution, even though there would have been no real harm in waiting weeks or months to carry it out. Despite arguments from the other two branches of government that emphasized international obligations, the Supreme Court chose to be more attentive to a definition of federalism that emphasized comity "the respectful recognition of judgments from other [state] tribunals," as well as finality, "the efficient execution of sentences."[83] But as law professor Rebecca Sklar warns, comity and finality may not be the highest values. The history of American law demonstrates "the notion that concerns for the constitutionality of convictions and detentions should supersede principles of finality."[84] One might add that adherence to long standing and reciprocal treaty obligations might also supersede those values.

Likewise, political scientists Christopher Banks and John Blakeman find that the Vienna Convention cases showed that the Roberts Court would not accept foreign policy concerns as justification to interfere with state criminal justice policies.[85] After decades when the Supreme Court had protected federal authority over foreign affairs from state policies, *Medellin* and its progeny reflected a more state-centered version of federalism, one that may have been related to a political climate that distrusted the federal government while placing more trust in the states.[86]

Evolving standards of decency

Other manifestations of federalism in capital cases have to do with eligibility for the death penalty and methods of execution. Since *Trop v. Dulles*,[87] the Court has often addressed the constitutionality of capital laws by invoking the concept of "evolving standards of decency" in order to determine whether a state law violated the Eighth Amendment prohibition of cruel and unusual punishment.[88] The notion of proportionality is implicit in these decisions, as the Court considers whether death is a proportionate response to the crime and the criminal, according to contemporary principles of appropriate punishment. The search for evolving standards of decency involves the Supreme Court in trying to determine a national

81 *Id.* at 946.
82 *Id.* at 947.
83 Andrew Cohen, *Humberto Leal Garcia: The Supreme Court Makes a Bad Situation Worse*, THE ATLANTIC (July 8, 2011), www.theatlantic.com/politics/archive2011.
84 Rebecca R. Sklar, *Executing Equity: The Broad Judicial Discretion to Stay the Execution of Death Sentences*, 40 HOFSTRA L. REV. 770, 801 (2011–2012).
85 CHRISTOPHER P. BANKS AND JOHN C. BLAKEMAN, THE U.S. SUPREME COURT AND THE NEW FEDERALISM: FROM THE REHNQUIST TO THE ROBERTS COURT 244 (2012).
86 *Id.* at 192.
87 Trop v. Dulles, *supra* note 6.
88 *Id.* at 101.

consensus about the application of the death penalty. They do this by tallying state laws and jury verdicts along with the Justices' own understanding of the Constitution. They look for a national consensus that, when it reaches a critical point, overrides and absorbs state policy choices. The stauncher federalists among the justices are usually skeptical about finding an evolution in the meaning of the Eighth Amendment. Conservative justices, such as Scalia, argue for an originalist interpretation of the Constitution, the idea that standards of decency would evolve suggests a living Constitution. These jurists tend to be skeptical of the very idea of a developing consensus and uncertain about when it is reached. Therefore, they are more inclined to leave it up to the individual states whether they should execute persons with mental disabilities or juveniles or whether a method of execution meets contemporary standards. Examining decisions of both the Rehnquist and the Roberts Courts in *Atkins v. Virginia*,[89] *Roper v. Simmons*,[90] *Hall v. Florida*,[91] *Kansas v. Marsh*,[92] *Baze v. Rees*,[93] and *Glossip v. Gross*[94] will provide a discussion of how federalism concerns played into the analysis of evolving standards.

Atkins v. Virginia

Justice John Paul Stevens wrote the 6–3 opinion of the Court in *Atkins*. He based the ruling that the death penalty for mentally disabled persons violated contemporary standards and was disproportionate by citing the states which prohibited such sentences. He especially noted the "direction of change"[95]—the fact that most of those prohibitions had been recently enacted—as evidence that "today our society views mentally retarded offenders as categorically less culpable than the average criminal."[96] Furthermore, states that had laws permitting such executions seldom carried them out. "The practice, therefore, has become truly unusual, and it is fair to say that a national consensus has developed against it."[97] However, Stevens' opinion allowed for differences among the states in determining which offenders met the criteria for "mental retardation." In an acknowledgement of the federal system, he wrote, "We leave to the States the task of developing appropriate ways to enforce the constitutional restriction upon its execution of sentences."[98]

Not surprisingly, Chief Justice Rehnquist wrote a strong dissent in which he was joined by Justices Scalia and Thomas. He was particularly incensed that the majority had cited foreign laws, the views of mental health professionals, the positions of religious organizations, and opinion polls as evidence of consensus. "The Court's suggestion that these sources are relevant to the constitutional question finds little support in our precedents and, in my view, is antithetical to considerations of federalism, which instruct that any "permanent prohibition upon the democratic government must [be apparent] in the operative acts . . . that the

89 Atkins v. Virginia, *supra* note 7.
90 Roper v. Simmons, *supra* note 8.
91 Hall v. Florida, 134 S. Ct. 1986 (2014).
92 Kansas v. Marsh, 548 U.S. 163 (2006).
93 Baze v. Rees, 553 U.S. 35 (2008).
94 Glossip v. Gross, *supra* note 15.
95 Atkins v. Virginia, *supra* note 7 at 315.
96 *Id.* at 316.
97 *Id.*
98 *Id* at 317.

people have approved."[99] In other words, a ruling claiming to be based on evolving standards as the rationale for overriding state criminal justice policy should only take into consideration "laws passed by legislatures and the practices of sentencing juries."[100]

A second dissent written by Justice Scalia and joined by Chief Justice Rehnquist and Justice Thomas raised doubts that a consensus on the question existed. Scalia accused the majority of "thrashing about for evidence of consensus,"[101] and of "fabricating a national consensus."[102] In this case, as in others, he objected to counting the states which had abolished the death penalty altogether among those who had rejected its use for the mentally disabled. Apparently, to the dissenters, the fact that certain states had rejected capital punishment for everyone but did not specify that they would not executed the mentally disabled did not serve as objective evidence of evolving standards of decency. To Scalia, *Atkins* was just the most recent in a long line of cases where the Court had exercised its "assumed power to invent a death-is-different jurisprudence" and substitute its own view for both the original meaning of the Eighth Amendment and the policies of the states which maintained the death penalty.[103] Implicit in this criticism is the notion that the states should be free to impose any punishment on any offender except for the "always and everywhere 'cruel' punishments such as the rack and the thumbscrew."[104] If capital punishment is permissible, "the Eighth Amendment is not a ratchet, whereby a temporary consensus on leniency for a particular crime fixes a permanent constitutional maximum, disabling the States from giving effect to altered beliefs and responding to changed social conditions."[105] This opinion would seem to hold that as long as the death penalty is constitutional (about which Scalia and his colleagues had no doubt), individual states should be free to impose it on whomever and for whatever crimes their legislatures decide.

Roper v. Simmons

A similar difference of opinion marked the Court's ruling in *Roper v. Simmons.* There also the majority found evidence of evolving standards of decency prohibiting the execution of juveniles, while the dissenters again objected that no such national consensus existed.[106] Justice Kennedy, who wrote the decision, listed the states that forbade the death penalty for those under 18 years of age. He also noted the direction of change and the infrequency with which juveniles were sentenced to death. "A majority of States have rejected the imposition of the death penalty on juvenile offenders under 18, and we now hold this is required by the Eighth Amendment."[107] The opinion referred to international law and opinion that almost universally condemned the execution of juveniles.[108] Justices Stevens and Ginsburg wrote a concurrence reaffirming their commitment to the evolving standards

---

99   *Id.* at 322.
100 *Id.* at 328.
101 *Id.* at 346.
102 *Id.* at 370.
103 *Id.* at 352–53.
104 *Id.* at 349.
105 *Id.*
106 Roper v. Simmons, *supra* note 8.
107 *Id.* at 568.
108 *Id.* at 575–76.

of decency standard, a rejection of the dissenters' position that called the principle into question.[109]

Justice Scalia again wrote the dissent, which was signed by the Chief Justice Rehnquist and Justice Thomas. As in *Atkins*, the dissent objected to counting non-death penalty states among those which reject the execution of juveniles. The dissenters found that the Court majority "says in so many words that what our people's laws say about the issue does not, in the last analysis matter. . . . The Court proclaims itself sole arbiter of our Nation's moral standards—and in the course of discharging that awesome responsibility purports to take guidance from the views of foreign courts and legislatures."[110] The "people's laws," those enacted by state legislatures, should be the only way to measure a consensus interpreting the Eighth Amendment. Otherwise, in the dissenters' view, the Constitution's meaning Constitution [would] "be determined by the subjective views of five Members of the Court and like-minded foreigners."[111] It would constitute judicial interference in powers reserved to the states, the "truly local" power to determine the provisions of the criminal justice system.

Hall v. Florida

In *Hall v. Florida* the Roberts Court had the opportunity to follow up on the *Atkins* decision.[112] *Atkins* had left the decision of how mental disability would be determined up to the states. Florida depended exclusively on an IQ score of above 70 in deciding whether an individual could be considered mentally disabled and therefore ineligible for the death penalty. Justice Kennedy wrote the 5–4 decision in *Hall* noting a "consistency of the trend" to reject a strict IQ score of 70 as a cutoff in the vast majority of states.[113] He stated that *Atkins* did not give States "unfettered discretion" in determining mental disability. If that were the case, *Atkins* would be a nullity and the Eighth Amendment protection of human dignity would not be a reality.[114] The dissent, written by Justice Alito, joined by Chief Justice Roberts, Justice Scalia, and Justice Thomas, reiterated that *Atkins* had left the decision about how to calculate mental disability to the States. They accused the majority of finding a consensus in the wrong place. Rather than using acts passed by state legislatures, Alito contended that the holding relied on the findings of mental health professionals to find a consensus.[115] The old argument about whether to count abolitionist states resurfaced again in *Hall* as the conservative dissenters argued there was no information on how those states would determine mental disability. Once more it seems that the disagreement is really about whether trying to identify evolving standards of decency is the proper way to apply the Eighth Amendment or whether states do have virtually unfettered discretion to carry out their criminal laws.

109 *Id.* at 587.
110 *Id* at 608.
111 *Id.*
112 Hall v. Florida, *supra* note 91.
113 *Id.* at 1997.
114 *Id.* at 1998.
115 *Id.* at 2002.

Kansas v. Marsh

Further debate about capital sentencing in a federal structure characterized the Roberts Court's 5–4 decision in *Kansas v. Marsh*.[116] Kansas law allowed for a death sentence if a jury found that aggravating and mitigating factors were in balance with each other.[117] The Kansas Supreme Court found the practice unconstitutional.[118] Justice Thomas wrote the opinion, joined by Chief Justice Roberts and Justices Scalia, Kennedy, and Alito. They reversed the state court decision and held that as long as a state system narrows the range of death penalty eligible crimes and allowed juries discretion to make individual sentencing decisions, the State enjoys "a range of discretion in imposing the death penalty, including the manner in which aggravating and mitigating circumstances may be weighed."[119] The U.S. Supreme Court did not have the moral authority or the power to "chip away at the State's prerogatives."[120] To the majority, the prerogatives involved the power of the legislature to set up criminal procedures, but not the power of the state courts to find them unacceptable.

However, a further debate about federalism emerged in a concurrence written by Justice Scalia and a dissent by Justice Stevens. The latter would have upheld the decision by the Kansas Supreme Court finding that the sentencing law was unconstitutional. Stevens found that the decision did no harm to the administration of justice.[121] In other words, deference to the state court judgement was consistent with federalism. As he observed, "Nothing more than an interest in facilitating the imposition of the death penalty in [Kansas] justified this court's exercise of its discretion to review the judgment of the [Kansas]Supreme Court."[122] Scalia took the opposing side. He stated that the Supreme Court's main responsibility, the main reason the Constitution allows the Court to review state court decisions is to "insure the integrity and uniformity of federal law."[123] Stevens' idea of federalism was misguided. If a state court erroneously invalidates the actions taken by the people of the state because they think the federal Constitution requires it, in reviewing that decision the Supreme Court is not undermining state authority but vindicating it. In his words, "When we correct a state court's federal errors, we return the power to a State and to its people."[124]

Baze v. Rees

Two cases before the Roberts Court, *Baze v. Rees* and *Glossip v. Gross*, concerned whether the prevalent method of execution, lethal injection, violated the Eighth Amendment and constituted cruel and unusual punishment.[125] In *Baze v. Rees*, the Court considered the Kentucky execution protocol and found that it met constitutional requirements.[126]

---

116 Kansas v. Marsh, *supra* note 92.
117 *Id*. at 166.
118 *Id*. at 167.
119 *Id*. at 174.
120 *Id*. at 181.
121 *Id* at 200–201.
122 *Id*. at 201.
123 *Id*. at 183.
124 *Id*. at 184.
125 Baze v. Rees, *supra* note 93; Glossip v. Gross, *supra* note 15.
126 Baze v. Rees, *supra* note 93 at 41.

The decision was 7–2 but the justification for finding in favor of Kentucky was fragmented, with no opinion supported by a majority of the Court. The plurality opinion, written by Chief Justice Roberts and joined by Justices Kennedy and Alito, noted that the Supreme Court had never found a state's method of execution unconstitutional. Historically it had deferred to the states and approved firing squads and electrocution.[127] As for lethal injection, Roberts applied an "evolving standards of decency" test. He noted that 36 states did not find the practice "objectively intolerable" but chose to use it as their default method of execution.[128]

The various concurring and dissenting opinions reflected the Court's inability to find a clear position regarding an unanswerable question. How much pain does an individual experience when he is injected with the lethal drugs, and how much pain is permissible under the Constitution? Justices Thomas and Scalia wrote that the only criterion to consider was the "intention" to inflict gratuitous pain. Absent the intention, the method must be acceptable.[129] Justices Ginsburg and Souter would inquire whether the state's protocol was careful enough to avoid unnecessary pain.[130] Justice Stevens wrote that he could not find the method of death unconstitutional but he had concluded that capital punishment itself "represents the pointless and needless extinction of life with only marginal contributions to any discernable public purpose."[131] Justice Scalia felt the need to respond to Stevens, pointing out in a statement of extreme judicial restraint, that under the Constitution, only democratically elected legislatures rather than courts . . . decide what makes significant contribution to social or public purposes."[132]

Glossip v. Gross

In 2015 the Court ruled on another question of the method of execution. In *Glossip v. Gross* the issue concerned Oklahoma's use of the drug midazolam as part of the three drug protocol in executions.[133] The matter seemed particularly timely as there had been several botched executions—in Ohio, Arizona, and Oklahoma—before the ruling was handed down. [134] By 2015, states were scrambling to find drugs for use in executions. The manufacturers of most of the preparations formerly in use would no longer sell them to states to put people to death. Some states had begun to buy drugs from compounding pharmacies which brewed up the mixtures without FDA scrutiny. Other states, such as Oklahoma, used existing preparations, but without any way of measuring their effectiveness as pain suppressants. Thus the question in *Glossip* was whether using an untested method, such as a massive dose of midazolam, risked unnecessary pain and suffering that would be inconsistent with the Eighth Amendment.[135] Justice Alito wrote the opinion for the Court, joined by Chief Justice Roberts and Justices Scalia, Kennedy, and Thomas. The holding is based on a strong sense

127 *Id.* at 48.
128 *Id.* at 52.
129 *Id.* at 102.
130 *Id.* at 114.
131 *Id.* at 83.
132 *Id.* at 87.
133 Glossip v. Gross, *supra* note 15.
134 Michael L. Radelet, *Examples of Post-Furman Botched Executions*, DEATH PENALTY INFORMATION CENTER, deathpenaltyinfo.org (December 8, 2016).
135 Glossip v. Gross, *supra* note 15 at 2731.

of deference to the state regarding the method used to put offenders to death. "Because capital punishment is constitutional, there must be a constitutional method of carrying it out," the majority declared.[136] The choice of method is the business of the states. The opinion notes again that the Court has never rejected any execution method it has reviewed, but had sanctioned the firing squad, the electric chair, and lethal injection, despite previous challenges. Each of these procedures was approved by state law and therefore its constitutionality was assumed.[137] Alito wrote that when a method of execution was approved by state law, anyone who claimed that the method violated the Eighth Amendment must show that it created "an unacceptable risk of pain."[138] The opinion further required a petitioner who challenged the state's method to propose an alternative means of execution—a massive hurdle for any challenger to overcome.[139]

Justice Sotomayor, who wrote a dissent joined by Justices Ginsburg, Breyer, and Kagan, challenged that requirement as not reflective of the Court's holding in *Baze v. Rees*.[140] The dissent believed that instead "the Court [was] motivated by a desire to preserve the State's ability to conduct executions in the face of changing circumstances."[141] States which hastily devised protocols using untested drugs were more likely to fail the cruel and unusual punishment test. If the drugs such as midazolam currently in use were safe, the states would have chosen them initially.[142] Instead, eager to carry out executions, Oklahoma was improvising. According to the Sotomayor dissent, the Court's review of executions should be more searching, not less, when the States were apparently involved in "human experimentation."[143] The key differences in the opinions of the majority and the dissenters in *Glossip* reflect the two sides of the federalism argument as it plays out in capital punishment cases. The majority considered the states as the major decision makers in the area of criminal justice and deferred to their policies. The dissenters were more reluctant to accept Oklahoma's assurances that the determination of how a condemned person should die had been made with proper care. They saw the Court's role as guardian of the offender against a cruel death. The majority saw their responsibility as facilitating the state's implementation of its police powers.

When the *Glossip* decision was handed down, a dissent by Justices Breyer and Ginsburg received a great deal of public attention. Dismissed by Justice Scalia as "gobbledygook,"[144] Breyer's argument is that the entire issue of capital punishment, not just the means of execution, deserves a full hearing before the Court.[145] He wrote that in finding that capital punishment was constitutional in *Gregg v. Georgia*, the Court had assumed that states would find ways to protect against constitutional problems in its administration.[146] Breyer argues that the states have not succeeded. The death penalty is characterized by unreliability (innocent people may be sentenced to death), arbitrariness in its application, long delays between conviction and execution, a decline in public support, and failure to achieve any

---

136 *Id.* at 2732–33.
137 *Id.* at 2732.
138 *Id.* at 2737.
139 *Id.*
140 *Id.* at 2793.
141 *Id.* at 2795–96.
142 *Id.* at 2796.
143 *Id.*
144 *Id.* at 2747.
145 *Id.* at 2755.
146 Gregg v. Georgia, 428 U.S. 153 (1976).

penological purpose.[147] After noting in *Furman v. Georgia* Justice Byron White wrote that the death penalty was "wantonly and freakishly imposed,"[148] Breyer argued that it was still being imposed without the "reasonable consistency" necessary to meet constitutional requirements.[149] According to Breyer, whether one looked at the presence of improper factors, such as race, gender, geography, or resources—or the absence of proper factors, such as egregiousness—one must conclude that the application of the death penalty was arbitrary. He believed that arbitrariness reflected deeply rooted community biases.[150] It was for this very reason, because its application was "arbitrary and capricious," that the Supreme Court in *Furman* found the death penalty as applied was unconstitutional. The brunt of Breyer's argument is that similar problems remain and deserve another review by the Court. State legislatures have not fixed the problems with reliability, arbitrariness, long delays, and the lack of a clear penological purpose. Those judicial matters require a judicial solution.[151]

Breyer's call for a review by the Supreme Court was a far cry from the position of the more conservative members of the Court who seemed generally satisfied with the way the death penalty was being administered in the states. The addition of Justice Neil Gorsuch to the Court in 2017 is unlikely to bring an ally to Breyer's point of view.

The 2016 term

During the 2016 term the Court heard several death penalty appeals. Most had to do with errors in specific cases; and there were some victories for defendants, including further clarification of the standard for intellectual disability.[152] In the cases where Justice Gorsuch voted, he was allied with Justices Thomas and Alito, the two members of the Court most likely to defer to the states and to uphold death sentences.[153] According to law professors Carol Streiker and Jordan Streiker, "the Court's disinclination to interfere with state prerogatives absent egregious legal error" was most obvious in their willingness to allow Arkansas to proceed with several of its planned executions.[154] To use its lethal drugs before they reached their expiration date, Arkansas scheduled eight executions in eleven days. After the Supreme Court lifted a stay, the state was able to carry out four of them. No particular pattern characterized the cases where the executions went ahead from those where they were postponed. To many, the Arkansas events were further evidence of the arbitrariness in the application of the death penalty outlawed in *Furman* and discussed in Justice Breyer's recent dissents.[155]

147 Glossip v. Gross, *supra* note 15 at 2756.
148 Quoted in *id*. at 2756.
149 *Id*. at 2760.
150 *Id*. at 2762.
151 *Id*.
152 Moore v. Texas, 581 U.S. ___ (2017).
153 Stephen McAllister, *Death Penalty Symposium: A court increasingly uncomfortable with the death penalty*, SCOTUSBLOG (June 29, 2017) scotusblog.com/category/special-features/symposium-on-october-term-2016s-death-penalty-decisions.
154 Carol Streiker and Jordan Streiker, *Death Penalty Symposium: Incremental victories for capital defendants but no sweeping change*, SCOTUSBLOG, (June 28, 1027) scotusblog.com/category/special-features/symposium-on-october-term-2016s-death-penalty-decisions.
155 See for example, Mark Berman, *Fourth Arkansas Execution in Eight Days Prompts Questions about Inmate's Movements*, WASHINGTON POST, April 28, 2017.

It is likely that the current Court will see capital punishment through the same lens of federalism as its predecessors. Justice Gorsuch will probably be allied with Justices Thomas and Alito, treating capital cases as a "truly local" matter and deferring to the states. Justice Breyer, with the frequent support of Justice Ginsburg may be expected to continue and expand his critique of the arbitrariness of the death penalty. But his calls for a full review of the issue will not be successful without the votes of Justice Sotomayor, Kagan, and most critically Kennedy. Unless there are further resignations, the Court may be expected to rule for some individual capital defendants if the constitutional problems are sufficiently egregious. Otherwise they will almost certainly allow the executing states to persist.

5 The Supreme Court and the Affordable Care Act

The consequences of the *NFIB v. Sebelius* decision for health care policy

John Dinan

Few U.S. Supreme Court decisions in recent decades were as highly anticipated as a 2012 ruling, *NFIB v. Sebelius*,[1] featuring several challenges to the constitutionality of the Affordable Care Act of 2010 (ACA).[2] Generally viewed as the signature domestic-policy legislation of President Barack Obama's administration, the ACA made various changes to the U.S. health care system. Most important in terms of its contribution to reducing the number of uninsured persons, the ACA directed states to make all non-elderly persons below a certain income level eligible to enroll in the joint federal-state Medicaid program or the states would risk losing all their existing Medicaid funding. The ACA also mandated that nearly all persons purchase health insurance or pay a fine. States are also required to establish exchanges (marketplaces), or permit the federal government to operate an exchange in their state, where individuals can shop for insurance and (depending on their income) qualify for federal subsidies. The ACA also imposed numerous regulations on insurance companies in terms of which plans can be offered, how much can be charged for premiums, and who can be denied coverage.[3]

After more than half of the state governments, along with several private plaintiffs and groups, challenged the constitutionality of the ACA's individual-mandate and Medicaid-expansion provisions and enjoyed some success in federal district and appellate courts, the Supreme Court held three days of oral argument in March 2012 and issued a decision on June 28, 2012.[4] The Court concluded that "the Affordable Care Act is constitutional in part and unconstitutional in part."[5] The Court upheld the individual mandate, based on Chief Justice John Roberts' determination that it was not a legitimate exercise of Congress's commerce power but could be deemed legitimate under Congress's tax power.[6] However, the Court found fault with the Medicaid expansion, concluding that Congress exceeded the

1 567 U.S. 519 (2012).
2 Pub. L. No. 111–148, 124 Stat. 119.
3 These various components of the Affordable Care Act are discussed in John Dinan, *Shaping Health Reform: State Government Influence in the Patient Protection and Affordable Care Act*, 41 PUBLIUS: J. FEDERALISM 395, 395–396 (2011).
4 For a brief history of the lawsuit, see Nathaniel Persily, Gillian E. Metzger, and Trevor W. Morrison, *Introduction, in* THE HEALTH CARE CASE: THE SUPREME COURT'S DECISION AND ITS IMPLICATIONS 1, 2–3 (Nathaniel Persily, Gillian E. Metzger, and Trevor W. Morrison, eds., 2013).
5 *NFIB*, 567 U.S. at 588 (2012).
6 *Id*. at 574.

confines of the spending power and improperly coerced states by threatening to withhold all existing Medicaid funding for states failing to expand Medicaid.[7]

In the years since *NFIB*, the Supreme Court has issued other rulings regarding the ACA. Most notably, in *King v. Burwell* (2015), a ruling seen as critical for enabling the law to continue functioning, the Court held that federal subsidies could be given to persons purchasing insurance not only through a state-established exchange (as is clear from the statute) but also through a federally operated exchange (despite conflicting and unclear language in the ACA).[8] The Supreme Court also considered the legitimacy of regulations promulgated by the U.S. Department of Health and Human Services (HHS) pursuant to implementation of the ACA, especially HHS regulations regarding birth control coverage under the law. In *Burwell v. Hobby Lobby Stores, Inc.* (2014) the Court relied on the federal Religious Freedom Restoration Act in ruling that closely held for-profit businesses cannot be required to make contraceptive coverage available to their employees when doing so would conflict with business-owners' religious beliefs.[9] In a subsequent ruling, in *Zubik v. Burwell* (2016), the Court vacated and remanded for further consideration various circuit court decisions dealing with the question of whether various religious non-profit groups could obtain exemptions from this HHS regulation.[10] In still another case that has not yet advanced beyond federal district court, D.C. District Court Judge Rosemary Collyer ruled in *U.S. House of Representatives v. Burwell* (2016) that the Obama administration could not continue to make cost-sharing reduction payments to insurance companies to compensate them for the high costs of covering low-income persons purchasing insurance through the ACA exchanges. Judge Collyer determined that Congress in passing the ACA had *authorized* these payments, but Congress had not *appropriated* the funds, as is constitutionally required before money can be spent.[11]

In short, although the Supreme Court and other federal courts have issued other rulings concerning the ACA,[12] the 2012 *NFIB* ruling is the lone Supreme Court decision to invalidate an ACA provision, rather than an agency regulation promulgated pursuant to the law. Therefore, *NFIB* is the focus of this essay.

In analyzing the effects of the *NFIB* ruling shortly after it was issued, some scholars focused on the doctrinal consequences.[13] Would the ruling put at risk other policies regarding education and environmental protection? Because this was the first time the Supreme Court resolved a spending-power challenge by holding that a federal act unduly coerced states, scholars and practitioners had a keen interest in gaining clarity about the principle that would apply in future cases. Was the Medicaid-expansion directive a *sui generis* case? Or would state

7 *Id.* at 585.
8 135 S.Ct. 2480 (2015).
9 134 S.Ct. 2751 (2014).
10 578 U.S. __ (2016).
11 No. 1:14-cv-01967 (D.D.C. May 12, 2016).
12 For a review of leading U.S. Supreme Court rulings regarding the ACA, see Christopher P. Banks, *Of White Whales, Obamacare, and the Roberts Court: The Republican Attempts to Harpoon Obama's Presidential Legacy*, 50 PS: POL SCI. & POL. 40–43 (2017).
13 Samuel R. Bagenstos, *The Anti-leveraging Principle and the Spending Clause after* NFIB, 101 GEO L. J. 861 (2013); Eloise Pasachoff, *Conditional Spending after* NFIB v. Sebelius: *The Example of Federal Education Law*, 62 AM U. L. REV. 577 (2013); Lynn A. Baker, *The Spending Power after* NFIB v. Sebelius, 37 HARV. J. L. & PUB. POL'Y 71 (2013).

officials and private plaintiffs rely successfully on the *NFIB* precedent to challenge various other policies?

Meanwhile, some scholars who analyzed the *NFIB* decision soon after it was issued focused on assessing the practical consequences for negotiations between federal and state officials regarding implementation of policies.[14] As Samuel R. Bagenstos wrote in a 2013 article,

> The most significant effect of *NFIB*'s Spending Clause holding is unlikely to appear in judicial decisions at all. That is the effect of the decision in creating a more state-friendly context for bargaining between state and federal officials in the day-to-day administration of cooperative spending programs.[15]

My purpose is to contribute to this second line of inquiry. I analyze the consequences of *NFIB* for the ACA's implementation and focus on the extent to which the ruling has influenced state-federal bargaining over the design and administration of the Medicaid expansion in the half-decade since the ruling. Several studies have analyzed negotiations between state and federal officials regarding the Medicaid expansion in one or more states.[16] Now that a half decade has passed, the time is ripe to take stock of the full set of consequences of the ruling for the ACA's Medicaid-expansion provision.

To preview my conclusions, developments in the five years since the *NFIB* decision demonstrate that states gained significant leverage from the ruling and in several key respects. First, the decision enabled states preferring not to expand Medicaid to maintain this position, even as federal officials sought to induce officials in some of these states to sign on to the expansion. Second, officials in some states who were open to expanding Medicaid but preferred to do so on their own terms won some important concessions from federal officials in gaining significant flexibility in designing their Medicaid programs. State officials have not secured all their objectives in these negotiations with federal officials. Nevertheless, the ruling changed the bargaining power of state officials in these negotiations and produced important changes in the way that Medicaid expansion has been implemented across the country.

---

14 Theodore W. Ruger, *Health Policy Devolution and the Institutional Hydraulics of the Affordable Care Act*, in THE HEALTH CARE CASE: THE SUPREME COURT'S DECISION AND ITS IMPLICATIONS 359, 369–371 (Nathaniel Persily, Gillian E. Metzger, and Trevor W. Morrison, eds. 2013); Samuel R. Bagenstos, *Federalism by Waiver after the Health Care Case*, in THE HEALTH CARE CASE: THE SUPREME COURT'S DECISION AND ITS IMPLICATIONS 227–244 (Nathaniel Persily, Gillian E. Metzger, and Trevor W. Morrison, eds. 2013); Erin Ryan, *The Spending Power and Environmental Law after* Sebelius, 85 U. COLO. L. REV. 1003 (2014).

15 Bagenstos, *supra* note 13, at 921.

16 John Dinan, *Implementing Health Reform: Intergovernmental Bargaining and the Affordable Care Act*, 44 PUBLIUS: J. FEDERALISM 399 (2014); Frank J. Thompson and Michael R. Gusmano, *The Administrative Presidency and Fractious Federalism: The Case of Obamacare*, 44 PUBLIUS: J. FEDERALISM 426 (2014); Shanna Rose, *Opting In, Opting Out: The Politics of State Medicaid Expansion*, 13 FORUM 63 (2015); DANIEL BELAND, PHILIP ROCCO & ALEX WADDAN, OBAMACARE WARS: FEDERALISM, STATE POLITICS, AND THE AFFORDABLE CARE ACT 118–122 (2016); GREG M. SHAW, THE DYSFUNCTIONAL POLITICS OF THE AFFORDABLE CARE ACT 88–96 (2017); Carol S. Weissert, Benjamin Pollack, & Richard P. Nathan, *Intergovernmental Negotiation in Medicaid: Arkansas and the Premium Assistance Waiver*, 47 PUBLIUS: J. FEDERALISM 445 (2017).

This analysis also has broader implications for understanding the consequences of other Supreme Court federalism decisions. The general lesson to be drawn from analyzing the effects of this particular ruling is that Supreme Court decisions limiting federal power are generally influential not because they impose an insurmountable barrier to achieving federal objectives; rather, their principal effect is to supply leverage to state officials or other critics of federal policies in ways that force federal officials to accomplish their objectives in alternative ways that are more accommodating to state officials or other critics of proposed policies. This has been the main consequence of the Supreme Court's federalism decisions issued in recent decades regarding the Commerce Power,[17] Tenth Amendment,[18] Eleventh Amendment,[19] and Enforcement Clause of the Fourteenth Amendment.[20] Analyzing the consequences of the *NFIB* decision makes clear that this lesson applies with particular force in Spending Power cases, where Court decisions are likely to be particularly influential in shaping the bargaining power of state and federal officials in negotiations about the design and administration of federal programs.

The *NFIB v. Sebelius* case

The *NFIB v. Sebelius* ruling originated in a lawsuit filed in the U.S. District Court for the Northern District of Florida by Florida attorney general Bill McCollum and twelve other state attorneys general (AGs) on March 23, 2010, the day that President Obama signed the ACA.[21] This lawsuit, eventually joined by 26 states, several individual plaintiffs, and the National Federation of Independent Business (NFIB), was not the only anti-ACA lawsuit filed that day. Virginia attorney general Ken Cuccinelli filed a separate suit in the U.S. District Court for the Eastern District of Virginia that raised similar but not identical constitutional challenges. During the next several years, additional challenges were filed by other plaintiffs.[22]

These lawsuits challenged various aspects of the ACA, but two provisions attracted the most attention and were central to the Supreme Court's *NFIB* ruling: the individual mandate

---

17 The Court found that the Commerce Power could not support passage of the Gun-Free School Zones Act, in *U.S. v. Lopez*, 514 U.S. 549 (1995) or the civil-remedy provision of the Violence Against Women Act, in *U.S. v. Morrison*, 529 U.S. 528 (2000).

18 The Court invoked the Tenth Amendment in invalidating a provision of the Low-Level Radioactive Waste Policy Amendments Act, in *New York v. U.S.*, 505 U.S. 144 (1992) and the background-check provision in the Brady Handgun Violence Prevention Act, in *Printz v. U.S.*, 521 U.S. 898 (1997).

19 The Court invoked the Eleventh Amendment in limiting congressional power to abrogate state sovereign immunity in the case of the Indian Gaming Regulatory Act, in *Seminole Tribe v. Florida*, 517 U.S. 44 (1996), federal patent and trademark statutes, in *Florida Prepaid v. College Savings Bank*, 527 U.S. 628 (1999), and *College Savings Bank v. Florida Prepaid*, 527 U.S. 666 (1999), the Fair Labor Standards Act, in *Alden v. Maine*, 527 U.S. 706 (1999), the Age Discrimination in Employment Act, in *Kimel v. Florida*, 528 U.S. 62 (2000), and Title I of the Americans with Disability Act, in *Alabama v. Garrett*, 531 U.S. 356 (2001).

20 In *Boerne v. Flores*, 521 U.S. 507 (1997), the Court ruled that the Section Five of the Fourteenth Amendment could not encompass enforcement of the Religious Freedom Restoration Act against state governments.

21 Discussed in *NFIB*, 567 U.S. at 540.

22 This includes, among other lawsuits, *Thomas More Law Ctr. v. Obama*, filed in U.S. District Court for the Eastern District of Michigan and appealed to the U.S. Court of Appeals for the Sixth Circuit, *Thomas More Law Ctr. v. Obama*, 631 F.3d 529 (6th Cir. 2011), and *Liberty University v. Geithner*, filed in U.S. District Court for the Western District of Virginia and appealed to the U.S. Court of Appeals for the Fourth Circuit, *Liberty University v. Geithner*, 671 F.3d 391 (4th Cir. 2011).

and Medicaid expansion. The challenge to the individual mandate attracted the most attention. In the midst of the congressional debate surrounding the drafting and passage of the ACA in 2009 and early 2010, several law professors, senators, and state attorneys general argued that Congress lacked the power to require individuals to purchase health insurance and urged members of Congress not to include such a provision in the health care law.[23] As a July 2009 Congressional Research Service report concluded, "despite the breadth of powers that have been exercised under the Commerce Clause, it is unclear whether that clause would provide a solid constitutional foundation for legislation containing a require-ment to have health insurance."[24] Moreover, scholars and public officials who doubted the legitimacy of the individual mandate contended that it could not be authorized by other constitutional powers, whether the tax power or necessary and proper clause, even as many other scholars and officials pushed back against these claims and cited numerous precedents that could be understood as authorizing the individual mandate.[25] Once it became clear in early 2010 that the ACA would likely pass and include an individual mandate, state attorneys general began to draft lawsuits challenging this provision and were prepared to file these suits on the day the ACA was signed.

Although these anti-ACA lawsuits focused primarily on challenging the individual mandate, the Florida lawsuit also challenged the law's Medicaid expansion. The Medicaid-expansion provision attracted particular attention in December 2009, as the bill was nearing passage in the Senate and Democratic leaders were led to make significant concessions to several wavering Senators in order to gain their support for the bill. At that time, Democrats held 60 Senate seats, just enough to invoke cloture and move to a vote on the bill; a single Democratic defection would have doomed the bill's prospects. One concession that was included in the Senate bill emerged out of negotiations with the final Democratic hold-out, Nebraska senator Ben Nelson. Dubbed the "Cornhusker Kickback," this provision offered more generous federal funding for Medicaid expansion in Nebraska than for any other state. At the suggestion of several Republican senators, a number of Republican state attorneys general, including Florida AG McCollum and South Carolina AG Henry McMaster, formed the Cornhusker Kickback Working Group and began considering various ways that this differential treatment for Nebraska might be challenged.[26] No such suit was filed because this provision was removed from the final version of the law that passed Congress in March 2010. But discussions among members of this working group also focused on constitutional challenges to the Medicaid expansion as a general proposition, along with other provisions of the law.[27] When Florida and 12 other state AGs, mostly drawn from this working group, filed a lawsuit challenging the ACA, the suit included a claim that the Medicaid expansion encroached on state sovereignty.[28]

23 Josh Blackman, Unprecedented: The Constitutional Challenge to Obamacare 35–58 (2013); Andrew Koppelman, The Tough Luck Constitution and the Assault on Health Care Reform 72–80 (2013).

24 Jennifer Staman & Cynthia Brougher, Cong. Research Serv., R40725, Requiring Individuals To Obtain Health Insurance: A Constitutional Analysis 3 (July 24, 2009).

25 The debates among members of Congress about the constitutionality of the Affordable Care Act are discussed in Rebecca E. Zietlow, *Democratic Constitutionalism and the Affordable Care Act*, 72 Ohio St. L. J. 1367, 1395–1401 (2011).

26 Dinan, *supra* note 3, at 405.

27 Blackman, *supra* note 23, at 59–61.

28 *Id.* at 82.

No federal district or circuit court found the arguments challenging the Medicaid expansion persuasive; but the arguments against the individual mandate enjoyed more success and ultimately brought the case to the Supreme Court. The district court judges that heard the Virginia and Florida lawsuits both sided with plaintiffs' claims that the individual mandate was unconstitutional. In the Virginia case, Judge Henry Hudson issued his decision in December 2010 and held that this provision was unconstitutional but severable from the remainder of the law.[29] But in issuing his decision in the Florida case in January 2011, Judge Roger Vinson went further and held that the individual mandate was unconstitutional and not severable; therefore, the entire law was flawed.[30] Judge Hudson's ruling in the Virginia case was reversed by the U.S. Court of Appeals for the Fourth Circuit, where a unanimous three-judge panel ruled in September 2011 that Virginia lacked standing to challenge the individual mandate. The Fourth Circuit panel rejected the argument that the state could gain standing by virtue of having enacted a state law seeking to insulate state residents from the mandate, in contravention of federal law.[31] But the U.S. Court of Appeals for the Eleventh Circuit, in a two-one ruling in August 2011, upheld Judge Vinson's ruling in the Florida lawsuit that the individual mandate was unconstitutional, even as the panel determined that the individual mandate was severable from the remainder of the law. The Eleventh Circuit panel rejected challenges to the Medicaid expansion.[32] The U.S. Supreme Court granted certiorari to multiple parties—to NFIB, Florida and 25 other states, and HHS—each of whom sought to appeal the Eleventh Circuit's ruling on various grounds.

The Supreme Court's decision in *NFIB* was surprising for various reasons, not least because of the reasoning relied on by the Court, and in particular the Chief Justice, in upholding the individual mandate. Four conservative Justices—Antonin Scalia, Anthony Kennedy, Clarence Thomas, and Samuel Alito—deemed the individual mandate illegitimate.[33] Four liberal justices—Stephen Breyer, Ruth Bader Ginsburg, Sonia Sotomayor, and Elena Kagan—would have upheld the individual mandate as a legitimate exercise of the commerce power.[34] Chief Justice Roberts concluded that the commerce power could not be read as authorizing the individual mandate, and in this sense, he sided with the conservative justices. But he joined with the four liberal justices in upholding the individual mandate, albeit on an alternative basis. Although Roberts acknowledged that the individual mandate was not initially enacted as a tax, he argued that the Court had a duty to view laws in the most favorable way when considering whether to invalidate them. In this case, Roberts concluded that the individual mandate could be saved by viewed the mandate as an exercise of Congress's tax power.[35]

Even more surprising was the Court's invalidation of the Medicaid-expansion provision, specifically the penalty for states declining to expand Medicaid. Although the Court devoted one of the three days of oral arguments to considering the legitimacy of Medicaid expansion, challenges to the Medicaid-expansion provision had not prevailed in any of the lower court decisions and attracted far less attention during the litigation than challenges to the individual

---

29 Virginia v. Sebelius, 728 F.Supp. 2d 768 (E.D. Va. 2010).
30 Florida v. HHS, 780 F.Supp. 2d 1256 (N.D. Fla. 2011).
31 Virginia ex rel. Cuccinelli v. Sebelius, 656 F.3d 253 (4th Cir. 2011).
32 Florida v. HHS, 648 F.3d 1235 (11th Cir. 2011).
33 *NFIB*, 567 U.S. at 618.
34 *Id*. at 657.
35 *Id*. at 563.

mandate.[36] Chief Justice Roberts again played a crucial role in a complex and diverse set of coalitions and explanations for the Medicaid-expansion portion of the ruling. Seven justices (the four conservative justices who would have also struck down the individual mandate, along with the Chief Justice and Justices Breyer and Kagan) ruled that the Medicaid expansion provision was not a legitimate exercise of Congress's spending power.[37] But then came the question of whether to invalidate the entire Medicaid expansion or to invalidate merely the penalty for non-expansion set out in the statute, by which states could lose the entirety of their existing Medicaid funding. The four conservative justices would have invalidated the entire Medicaid expansion.[38] But the Chief Justice, joined by the four liberal justices, determined that the constitutional violation could be addressed simply by precluding the federal government from withholding existing Medicaid funding for non-expanding states.[39]

The Court's ruling in *NFIB* regarding the Medicaid expansion was particularly notable in that it marked the first time that the Supreme Court held that an act of Congress adopted pursuant to the Spending Power was invalid because it coerced states into participating in the program. The Court had in prior cases identified factors that could render a spending-clause program coercive, as in *South Dakota v. Dole* (1987) while upholding a uniform drinking-age law that threatened non-compliant states with a loss of 5 percent of federal transportation funding.[40] The Court had also in prior years invalidated certain acts passed pursuant to the spending clause, as in *Arlington Central School District Board of Education v. Murphy* (2006), albeit not because the law was coercive but because states had not been given clear notice of the conditions attached to receipt of federal funds.[41]

This aspect of the *NFIB* ruling was all the more notable because during the prior two decades the Supreme Court invalidated a number of congressional acts on federalism grounds by relying on other constitutional clauses and doctrines but without invoking the coercion doctrine.[42] The Court struck down several laws passed pursuant to the Commerce Power[43]

---

36 BLACKMAN, *supra* note 23, at 257.

37 *NFIB*, 567 U.S. at 575–585

38 *Id*. at 690–691.

39 *Id*. at 585–588.

40 483 U.S. 203 (1987). In his Opinion for the Court, Chief Justice William Rehnquist acknowledged that "in some circumstances, the financial inducement offered by Congress might be so coercive as to pass the point at which 'pressure turns into compulsion,'" but he stressed that in this case "all South Dakota would lose if she adheres to her chosen course as to a suitable minimum drinking age is 5% of the funds otherwise obtainable under specified highway grant programs," and therefore the drinking-age statute "offered relatively mild encouragement to the States," while ensuring that "the enactment of such laws remains the prerogative of the States not merely in theory, but in fact." *Id*. at 211–212. Justice Sandra Day O'Connor dissented; but her dissent did not rest on a claim that the drinking-age law was coercive. Rather, she argued that "establishment of a minimum drinking age of 21 is not sufficiently related to interstate highway construction to justify so conditioning funds appropriated for that purpose." *Id*. at 213–214.

41 548 U.S. 291 (2006).

42 The federalism decisions issued during the Rehnquist Court and the Roberts Court, along with the absence of any decisions invoking the coercion doctrine to invalidate congressional legislation, are discussed in John Dinan, *The Rehnquist Court's Federalism Decisions in Perspective*, 15 J. L. & POL. 127 (1999); John Dinan, *The Rehnquist Court's Federalism Decisions (review essay)*, 41 PUBLIUS: J. FEDERALISM 158 (2011); CHRISTOPHER P. BANKS & JOHN C. BLAKEMAN, THE U.S. SUPREME COURT AND NEW FEDERALISM: FROM THE REHNQUIST COURT TO THE ROBERTS COURT (2012); Ilya Somin, *Federalism and the Roberts Court*, 46 PUBLIUS: J. FEDERALISM 441 (2016).

43 See *supra* note 17 and accompanying text.

and various other laws passed pursuant to the enforcement clauses of the Fourteenth or Fifteenth Amendment.[44] The Tenth Amendment was invoked to prevent Congress from commandeering state and local officials.[45] Additionally, the Court relied on the Eleventh Amendment in a number of cases to prevent Congress from abrogating state sovereign immunity in federal (and in one case state) litigation.[46] As the Court was issuing these various decisions, especially in the later years of the Rehnquist Court, commentators noted the absence of any Spending Power decisions grounded in the coercion doctrine. In fact, some scholars remarked that such rulings were conspicuous by their absence in what was otherwise a wide-ranging revival of federalism clauses and doctrines.[47] In this and other respects, the Court's reliance on the coercion doctrine in *NFIB* was notable and attracted significant attention, with one scholar concluding that "The Court's invalidation of the mandatory Medicaid expansion is probably the most important ruling invalidating a federal statute on federalism grounds since the New Deal."[48]

Consequences of the *NFIB v. Sebelius* ruling

In assessing the consequences of the *NFIB* ruling, many analysts sought to determine whether the Court's invalidation of the penalty for states declining to expand Medicaid would place in legal jeopardy various federal policies.[49] For various reasons, however, including the distinctive nature of the Medicaid program and the lack of subsequent Supreme Court decisions applying the coercion test invoked in *NFIB*, it is not possible to offer definitive conclusions about the ruling's doctrinal effects. Nevertheless, it is worth taking stock, briefly, of what can be said about the doctrinal effects for other policies before turning to assess the practical effects for the ACA's implementation, something that can be assessed with more confidence.

Doctrinal consequences

One difficulty in assessing the ruling's doctrinal influence is that the Court's reasoning regarding the coercion test has to be pieced together from the joint dissenting opinion of Justices Scalia, Kennedy, Thomas, and Alito on one hand, and the majority opinion of the Chief Justice, who was joined in this respect by Justices Breyer and Kagan. In concluding that the Medicaid-expansion provision was coercive, the joint dissent stressed the amount of federal money that states risked losing if they declined to participate. Noting that federal Medicaid funding prior to the ACA's passage comprised 22 percent of all state expenditures across the country, the dissent concluded that the threat of losing so much federal funding and the burden of replacing it meant that states did not in practice face a meaningful choice.[50] In his opinion, the Chief Justice also highlighted the amount of funds states were at risk of losing, in a way that he said amounted to the federal government placing "a gun to the head"

---

44 See *supra* note 20 and accompanying text.
45 See *supra* note 18 and accompanying text.
46 See *supra* note 19 and accompanying text.
47 Samuel R. Bagenstos, *Spending Clause Litigation in the Roberts Court*, 58 DUKE L. J. 345, 348 (2008).
48 Somin, *supra* note 42, at 447.
49 See *supra* note 13 and accompanying text.
50 *NFIB*, 567 U.S. at 682.

of state officials.[51] But the Chief Justice went on to stress that the ACA's Medicaid expansion was not merely a modification to an existing program, as was the case with prior changes to the Medicaid program; rather, it was "a shift in kind, not merely degree" and in a way that "transformed" the program.[52] A good deal of scholarship in *NFIB*'s immediate aftermath sought, albeit with difficulty, to identify guidelines from these separate opinions about how to draw a clear line between permissible encouragement and illegitimate coercion.[53]

Another challenge in making predictions about the impact of the coercion test going forward stems from the distinctive nature of the Medicaid program and the ACA's Medicaid-expansion directive. Federal funding for K-12 education is substantial. But as the joint dissenting opinion noted, the amount of federal education funding is less than half of the level of federal Medicaid funding in most states and even less than that in many states.[54] Other federal programs and policies provide even smaller amounts of funding to states. In short, the Supreme Court in *NFIB* reaffirmed its 1987 holding in *Dole* that it was not coercive for Congress to withhold 5 percent of federal transportation funding for a state refusing to raise the drinking age, even as it held that it would be coercive to withhold the entirety of a state's existing Medicaid funding for declining to sign on to the ACA's Medicaid expansion. But it is not clear how to apply the principles set out in *NFIB* in circumstances falling in the broad space between these cases, especially given that there are no other cases comparable to the Medicaid program and Medicaid-expansion directive.

Further adding to the difficulty of advancing conclusions about the doctrinal effects of *NFIB* coercion test is the lack of any Supreme Court decisions applying this test in the half decade since the 2012 decision. Litigants have invoked *NFIB* in challenging federal programs and directives. And federal district and circuit court judges have occasionally relied on *NFIB*. Most recently, Judge William Orrick III of the U.S. District Court for the Northern District of California issued an April 2017 ruling enjoining enforcement of President Donald Trump's executive order threatening sanctuary cities and counties with a loss of various federal funds for not assisting federal officials in enforcing federal immigration directives.[55] After quoting the portion of the Supreme Court's *NFIB* ruling where the Chief Justice concluded that the ACA's threatened denial of Medicaid funds for states not participating in the expansion "was unconstitutionally coercive and represented a 'gun to the head,'" Judge Orrick wrote that the Trump executive order "threatens to deny sanctuary jurisdictions all federal grants, hundreds of millions of dollars on which the Counties rely. The threat is unconstitutionally coercive."[56] But the U.S. Supreme Court has not provided any additional guidance in interpreting and applying the coercion test.

Consequences for the ACA's implementation

When we turn from assessing *NFIB*'s doctrinal effects for other federal programs to consider the practical effects for the ACA's implementation, it becomes possible to advance conclusions more confidently, given the extensive record of state actions and state-federal negotiations

51 *Id.* at 581.
52 *Id.* at 583.
53 See, e.g., Bagenstos, *supra* note 13; Pasachoff, *supra* note 13.
54 *NFIB*, 567 U.S. at 683–684.
55 County of Santa Clara v. Trump, 17-cv-00574 (N.D. Cal. April 25, 2017)
56 *Id.* at 39.

regarding Medicaid in the half decade after the ruling. One clear effect has been to give states a meaningful choice about whether to sign on to the ACA's Medicaid expansion. As of July 2017, nineteen states continue to resist Medicaid expansion,[57] an outcome unforeseeable in the absence of the *NFIB* ruling. The decision also strengthened the bargaining position of state officials in negotiations with federal officials about the terms of the Medicaid expansion. Seven of the thirty-one states that expanded Medicaid have done so via waivers approved by HHS that authorize alternative means of designing the expansion and delivering Medicaid services to the expansion population.[58] Medicaid waivers have been granted on a regular basis well before the ACA's passage and *NFIB*'s issuance. Without the benefit of the *NFIB* ruling, however, state officials would almost certainly have been rebuffed in their efforts to secure some of the waivers they received in the five years after the decision.

The Medicaid program and the ACA's Medicaid expansion

Congress established the Medicaid program in 1965 to provide health care for certain needy persons, at the same time that it created the Medicare program to provide health care for senior citizens.[59] Medicare is a purely federal program, along the lines of Social Security's retirement program. But Medicaid is a federal-state program funded and administered jointly by the federal and state governments. The federal government pays between 50 and 75 percent of the costs of covering most Medicaid recipients. The precise federal share is determined by a state's income level, with the federal government covering 50 percent of the costs of coverage in the wealthiest states and covering up to a maximum of 83 percent of the costs in the poorest state. In the most recent fiscal year, the federal share ranged from 50 percent to 75 percent. States opting to participate in Medicaid—and participation is optional and only became universal once Arizona opted to participate in 1982—must follow federal rules, which require that states cover the blind, disabled, pregnant women, families of dependent children, and low-income elderly persons. But states can also choose to cover other persons and provide additional services beyond what is mandated by federal law.

The main change wrought by the ACA was to require states to cover all non-elderly persons making less than 138 percent of the federal poverty level, which currently amounts to just above $16,000 annual income for a single person. Some states had already chosen to cover some childless adults even before the ACA's passage. But for the first time, all states would be required to do so and to extend this coverage up to 138 percent of the poverty level, under pain of losing all of their existing federal Medicaid funding. Due in part to the influence of state officials and intergovernmental organizations in the drafting of the ACA, Congress provided for a much more generous federal contribution to the costs of covering the Medicaid expansion population as opposed to persons already covered by Medicaid. The ACA committed the federal government to paying 100 percent of the costs of covering newly eligible Medicaid recipients, during the first three years of the program (from 2014 to 2016). Beginning in 2017, the federal match gradually declines until it remains at 90 percent from 2020 onward.

---

57 Greg Goelzhauser and Shanna Rose, *The State of American Federalism 2016–2017: Policy Reversals and Partisan Perspectives on Intergovernmental Relations*, 47 PUBLIUS: J. FEDERALISM 285, 291 (2017).
58 Weissert, et al., *supra* note 16, at 446.
59 The description of the Medicaid program in this paragraph and the next paragraph draws on *id.* at 448–449.

Proponents of Medicaid expansion

In considering the reactions of state officials to the Medicaid-expansion directive and the way that the *NFIB* ruling altered these calculations, one group of states was always prepared to sign on to the expansion and was generally unaffected by the Court's ruling. In most states where Democrats controlled the legislature and governorship—and also in some states with Republican governors—Medicaid expansion was viewed as an attractive proposition, especially because the federal government would cover the full costs of covering newly eligible Medicaid enrollees for the first three years.[60] A number of states therefore declared their intent to expand Medicaid in the aftermath of the ACA's passage and saw no reason to change course after the *NFIB* ruling.[61] Meanwhile, some states that had not yet signed on to the Medicaid expansion, including several states with Republican governors, agreed to expand Medicaid soon after the issuance of the decision.[62]

Opponents of Medicaid expansion

A second group of state officials, including many Republican legislators and governors, were strongly opposed to expanding Medicaid and, by virtue of the *NFIB* ruling, were able to withstand pressure from federal officials to sign on to the expansion. During the twenty-seven months between the ACA's passage and the Supreme Court's ruling, a few state officials discussed the possibility of declining the Medicaid expansion.[63] But few state officials seriously entertained the prospect, in view of the tremendous financial penalty that their states could suffer, in terms of losing the entirety of their existing Medicaid funding and having to make up the difference through additional state revenue. In short, prior to *NFIB*, these states technically had the option of declining the Medicaid expansion, but in practice state officials did not view the choice as a meaningful one.

One effect of the *NFIB* ruling was to make the choice to expand Medicaid voluntary not only in a technical sense but also in a meaningful way. Nineteen states have concluded that the costs of expansion outweigh the benefits and have therefore taken advantage of the path set out in *NFIB* whereby they can decline to expand Medicaid but continue their existing Medicaid program and without losing their existing federal Medicaid funding. Officials in these states have reached this decision for various reasons and based on a range of concerns.[64] Some state officials were concerned about the added costs to state budgets of expanding Medicaid once the federal share dropped to 95 percent (after three years) and then eventually to 90 percent. Moreover, some state officials doubted that the federal government would maintain its contributions at this level in future years, thereby leaving states to foot the bill for more of the costs of expansion down the road. Regardless of the motivation and reasoning, prior to the *NFIB* decision, officials in states who objected to the expansion did not perceive that they could decline participation, but after the decision they were prepared to do so.

---

60 Dinan, *supra* note 16, at 409.
61 For an illustrative discussion concerning California, see BELAND, *supra* note 16, at 106–108.
62 For a discussion of the decisions to expand Medicaid in Nevada and Arizona, see Rose, *supra* note 16, at 71–73.
63 SHANNA ROSE, FINANCING MEDICAID: FEDERALISM AND THE GROWTH OF AMERICA'S HEALTH SAFETY NET 241–243 (2013).
64 See Dinan, *supra* note 16, at 410; BELAND, *supra* note 16, at 111–114.

Moreover, the *NFIB* ruling has enabled officials in some of the 19 non-expansion states to resist what they perceived to be undue pressure on the part of federal officials to expand Medicaid or forego other benefits. Although in one sense the *NFIB* ruling only eliminated the ability of federal officials to withhold a state's existing Medicaid funding as a penalty for non-expansion, in another sense, some state officials have relied on the anti-coercion principle expressed in the ruling to push back against federal officials who have sought to link participation in Medicaid expansion with other benefits.

Reliance on the anti-coercion principle in *NFIB* to resist expansion was on most prominent display in Florida in 2015, where Republican Governor Rick Scott charged that the Obama administration was trying to coerce the state to expand Medicaid by threatening not to renew funding for a Low Income Pool program that compensated hospitals for treating the uninsured. This dispute between Florida officials and federal officials is complex and stems from a waiver Florida secured a decade earlier as part of a plan to cover Medicaid recipients through managed care organizations. The original waiver, along with the Low Income Pool funding stream, had to be renewed periodically. In 2014 federal officials renewed the waiver for three years but only extended the Low Income Pool funding for one year. In early 2015, as the Low Income Pool funding was up for renewal, federal officials signaled they were not prepared to extend the funding at the same rate and under the same conditions.[65] When Governor Scott went public with his complaints about what he viewed as efforts in these negotiations to pressure the state of expand Medicaid, federal officials maintained that the decision about whether to renew the Low Income Pool funding would be made separately from the state's decision about whether to expand Medicaid.[66] But the governor pointed to various comments by federal officials during state-federal negotiations indicating that the Obama administration was trying to put pressure on the state to join the Medicaid expansion.[67]

In an effort to prevent the Obama administration from doing so, Governor Scott filed a lawsuit that relied heavily on the anti-coercion principle in *NFIB*. The lawsuit charged that federal officials were trying "to do precisely what the Supreme Court held just three years ago that the Constitution prohibits it from doing—namely, coerce states into dramatically expanding their Medicaid programs by threatening to cut off federal funding for unrelated programs unless they 'agree' to do so."[68] When the governor withdrew his lawsuit two months later, he claimed victory, arguing: "Florida saw a tremendous win for low income families this week when the Obama Administration finally agreed to continue funding part

65 For background, see Jessica Schubel and Judith Solomon, *Understanding the Issues Surrounding Florida's Low-Income Pool* (Center on Budget and Policy Priorities, April 27, 2015), www.cbpp.org/research/health/understanding-the-issues-surrounding-floridas-low-income-pool.

66 Peter Sullivan, *Florida Governor Confronts HHS in ObamaCare Fight*, THE HILL, May 6, 2015, http://thehill.com/policy/healthcare/241218-fla-governor-demands-feds-respond-on-health-funds-right-now.

67 See, e.g., the comments reported in Marc Caputo and Rachana Pradhan, *Florida to Sue over Obamacare Medicaid Expansion*, POLITICO, April 16, 2015, www.politico.com/story/2015/04/florida-lawsuit-sue-obamacare-medicaid-rick-scott-117051; Kathleen McGrory and Steve Bousquet, *Gov. Rick Scott Sues Feds Over healthcare money, Medicaid expansion*, MIAMI HERALD, April 16, 2015, www.miamiherald.com/news/politics-government/state-politics/article18676365.html.

68 Complaint for Injunctive and Declaratory Relief at 1, Scott v. Burwell, No. 3:15-cv-00193-RS-CJK (N.D. Fla. Apr. 28, 2015), available at www.flgov.com/wp-content/uploads/2015/04/001-Complaint-Filed.pdf.

of Florida's Low Income Pool program even though our state did not expand Obamacare. Because of this great victory, we have decided to dismiss our lawsuit against the Obama Administration for attempting to coerce Florida into expanding Obamacare. It is unfortunate it took a lawsuit to make the right thing happen."[69]

State officials' ambivalence about Medicaid expansion

If one effect of the *NFIB* ruling was to enable some states to resist federal pressure and decline to expand Medicaid, another was to give leverage to officials in other states who were open to expanding Medicaid but only in exchange for federal officials' willingness to afford them flexibility to tailor the program to distinctive state circumstances and interests. Officials in this final group of states were conflicted about whether to sign on to the Medicaid expansion. On one hand, Medicaid expansion would bring a lot of federal funds to the state. The lure of federal money was especially prized by hospitals that were a principal beneficiary of this funding and whose lobbyists exerted a good amount of influence on state officials to sign on to the expansion. At the same time, state officials had long complained about various conditions imposed on states by congressional statutes and by federal officials who administered the Medicaid program and thereby limited states' flexibility to tailor the delivery of Medicaid services in distinctive ways. Some state officials concluded that expanding Medicaid without gaining flexibility in the design of the program would be inadvisable; but if some flexibility could be obtained then expansion might be more attractive.[70]

Obama administration officials were eager to expand Medicaid into as many states as possible. Therefore, they were willing to entertain requests from these state officials for waivers from various program requirements. Waivers, which are available under Section 1115 of the Social Security Act (as amended), had been a longstanding feature of Medicaid policy-making well before the ACA. Through the years, states had requested and occasionally gained from Republican and Democratic presidential administrations significant flexibility to experiment with alternative means of delivering Medicaid services, such as through managed-care organizations, or covering additional groups or providing additional services.[71] However, after the ACA's passage, federal officials in the Obama White House and in HHS were anxious to boost the number of persons covered by the president's signature domestic policy, especially in a situation where state officials' decisions about expanding Medicaid would go a long way to determining the extent of coverage gains under the law. As a result, once the *NFIB* ruling made clear that states would have a meaningful choice about whether to expand Medicaid, Obama administration officials expressed a willingness to consider state waiver requests that had not been seriously entertained prior to the Court's decision, especially because the political dynamics within state governments often meant that the only

---

69 Quoted in Gray Rohrer, *Gov. Scott drops Medicaid lawsuit with federal government*, ORLANDO SENTINEL, June 25, 2015, www.orlandosentinel.com/news/politics/political-pulse/os-gov-scott-drops-medicaid-lawsuit-with-federal-government-20150625-post.html.

70 See Dinan, *supra* note 16, at 410–411.

71 Frank J. Thompson and Courtney Burke, *Executive Federalism and Medicaid Demonstration Waivers: Implications for Policy and Democratic Process*, 32 J. HEALTH POL. POL'Y & L. 971 (2007); Carol S. Weissert and William G. Weissert, *Medicaid Waivers: License to Shape the Future of Fiscal Federalism*, in INTERGOVERNMENTAL MANAGEMENT FOR THE 21ST CENTURY 157–175 (Timothy J. Conlan and Paul L. Posner eds. 2014).

way to overcome Republican legislators' resistance to expansion was to permit an alternative arrangement for doing so.[72]

In February 2013, Arkansas was the first state to negotiate a deal with HHS that led to a waiver allowing Medicaid expansion to proceed in a different way than envisioned by the ACA. As Carol S. Weissert, Benjamin Pollack, and Richard P. Nathan have detailed in a rich account of the state-federal bargaining that produced the Arkansas waiver, HHS Secretary Kathleen Sebelius was generally eager for states to expand Medicaid and especially eager for southern states to do so, given their general reluctance on this issue.[73] Arkansas's Democratic governor, Mike Beebe, also favored expansion. But members of the Republican-controlled Arkansas legislature were unwilling to simply sign on to expansion in its traditional form. Republican legislators preferred various alternative approaches and were particularly interested in relying on what they viewed as a market-based approach to covering currently uninsured persons.[74]

These negotiations were "not one-sided," as Weissert and her co-authors observed.[75]

Federal officials were eager to strike a deal; but they were unwilling to approve some of Arkansas officials' proposals. After extensive negotiation, state officials were able to secure an agreement in principle whereby HHS would allow Arkansas to expand Medicaid in a way not foreseen by the ACA's drafters. Governor Beebe summarized these negotiations and the influence wielded by state officials when he remarked in an interview several days before the deal was finalized in February 2013:

> I had a productive meeting Friday afternoon with Secretary Sebelius. I presented her with the ideas raised by our legislators, particularly the option that at least some of the potential Arkansas expansion population would be able to obtain private insurance coverage through our exchange. The Secretary has given me feedback, which I will share with legislators, concerning the choices available to Arkansans as our state moves forward. I am always cautious in my optimism, but I feel good about Arkansas's options coming out of this meeting."[76]

In what has been alternatively labeled a private-option plan or a premium-assistance plan, the deal that state officials worked out with HHS allows Arkansas to use Medicaid funding to purchase private health insurance plans, through a federally operated ACA exchange, for persons who would have become eligible for traditional Medicaid coverage under the ACA by virtue of their income level.[77] Arkansas was not the first state to adopt a premium-assistance plan that subsidized the purchase of private health insurance. Some states were

72 On this point, see Rose, *supra* note 16, at 75.
73 Weissert, et al., *supra* note 16.
74 *Id.* at 452–453.
75 *Id.* at 453.
76 Quoted *id.* at. 454.
77 Described in Jane B. Wishner, John Holahan, Divvy Upadhyay, and Megan McGrath, *Medicaid Expansion, The Private Option and Personal Responsibility Requirements: The Use of Section 1115 Waivers to Implement Medicaid Expansion under the ACA* 5–8 (Urban Institute, May 27, 2015), www.urban.org/sites/default/files/publication/53236/2000235-Medicaid-Expansion-The-Private-Option-and-Personal-Responsibility-Requirements.pdf.

operating such plans on a much smaller scale. But the Arkansas plan went much further than any plan in existence at that point.[78]

Although Arkansas's Medicaid-expansion plan is the most dramatic deviation from the ACA's original design, a half-dozen other states secured federal waivers authorizing them to participate in the ACA's Medicaid expansion in innovative ways: Arizona, Iowa, Indiana, Michigan, Montana, New Hampshire. Still another state, Pennsylvania, also secured a Medicaid-expansion waiver, as a result of negotiations between Republican Governor Tom Corbett and HHS officials. But after defeating Corbett in the 2014 election and assuming the governor's office, Democrat Tom Wolf decided to proceed via a traditional Medicaid expansion and without making use of the flexibility secured through the waiver.[79] As of summer 2017, therefore, seven states are operating Medicaid-expansion plans authorized via Section 1115 waivers.

These Medicaid-expansion waivers vary in the type and extent of flexibility that states sought and received from federal officials.[80] A few states, including Iowa, reached agreements with federal officials allowing them to rely on an Arkansas-style private-option plan to purchase insurance for some portion of the persons who would have otherwise been eligible for traditional Medicaid coverage under the ACA.[81] Other states, including Michigan, agreed to expand Medicaid on the condition that federal officials allow the state to charge a portion of Medicaid recipients a monthly premium or co-payments to defray some of the costs of their Medicaid coverage.[82] Indiana's plan goes the furthest of any state operating a ACA Medicaid-expansion waiver. Among other elements in what has been described as a plan that is "more complex than others approved to date,"[83] the Indiana plan provides for cutting off coverage and preventing re-enrollment for a period of time for Medicaid recipients above the poverty line who fail to make premium payments.[84] In these and other respects, state officials pressed federal officials for flexibility in the design and delivery of Medicaid services and were able to secure authorization to deviate from statutory requirements in ways that would likely not have been forthcoming in the absence of the leverage that states gained by virtue of the Court's *NFIB* ruling.

State officials' influence in these negotiations was not unlimited. Federal officials pushed back against a number of proposals seeking additional flexibility in the terms of the Medicaid expansion. When some state officials expressed interest in undertaking a partial expansion that would only cover persons making up to the poverty level, federal officials made clear early in the process, in December 2012, that this would not be permissible. States choosing to expand Medicaid would have to cover persons in some fashion up through 138 percent of the poverty level.[85] Federal officials also refused to approve waiver requests calling for

78 Dinan, *supra* note 16, at 414–415.
79 Kaiser Family Foundation, *Medicaid Expansion in Pennsylvania: Transition from Waiver to Traditional Coverage* (April 3, 2015), http://kff.org/medicaid/fact-sheet/medicaid-expansion-in-pennsylvania/.
80 For a chart identifying and comparing the various features of these seven states' Medicaid-expansion waivers, *see* Elizabeth Hinton, Robin Rudowitz, & MaryBeth Musumeci, *3 Key Questions: Section 1115 Medicaid Demonstration Waivers* 4 (Kaiser Family Foundation, February 2017).
81 Wishner et al., *supra* note 77, at 8–10.
82 *Id.* at 11–12.
83 Kaiser Family Foundation, *Medicaid Expansion in Indiana* (Feb. 3, 2015), http://kff.org/medicaid/fact-sheet/medicaid-expansion-in-indiana/.
84 *Id.*
85 Thompson and Gusmano, *supra* note 16, at 430.

Medicaid recipients to pay more than nominal premiums or co-payments.[86] State officials were also rebuffed in their efforts to require Medicaid recipients to meet various work-search requirements as a condition of continuing to receive Medicaid benefits.[87] Federal officials' reluctance to grant state officials all of the flexibility they were seeking led some states to pull out of these negotiations and decline the Medicaid expansion. However, in other cases, beginning with Arkansas in early 2013 and most recently with Montana in late 2015, state and federal officials have been successful in negotiating waivers permitting Medicaid expansion in innovative ways.

Donald Trump's victory in the 2016 presidential election and his appointment of Tom Price as health and human services secretary has emboldened still other states, especially Republican-controlled states, to request waivers and press for additional flexibility in designing their Medicaid programs. In some cases, as in Kentucky and Indiana, states had already expanded Medicaid, with or without a waiver, and were seeking greater flexibility to deviate from federal requirements.[88] In other cases, as in Maine and Wisconsin, states had not expanded Medicaid but sought to restructure their existing programs, generally by imposing work requirements or other requirements on beneficiaries.[89] Trump administration officials were already more disposed than their predecessors to entertain Medicaid waiver requests of this particular sort; therefore, the *NFIB* ruling is likely to be less important in empowering states to gain flexibility during the Trump presidency than during the Obama presidency.[90]

The effect of *NFIB* during the Trump presidency is likely to be diminished further if congressional Republicans are able to revise the ACA and explicitly grant states more flexibility in designing Medicaid programs. In that case, state officials would have less need to benefit from the leverage gained from the *NFIB* ruling in securing more flexibility from federal officials, because this flexibility would be provided by statute. The prospects of Congress passing major changes to the ACA dimmed considerably, however, when in a July 2017 vote the Senate rejected, by a 51–49 margin, a bill making several narrow changes to the ACA.[91] As a result, negotiations between state and federal officials over Medicaid-expansion plans under the ACA are likely to continue, with state officials continuing to benefit in these negotiations from the leverage gained by virtue of the *NFIB* ruling.

Conclusion

My purpose has been to assess the consequences of the Supreme Court's 2012 *NFIB v. Sebelius* ruling for implementation of the Affordable Care Act, focusing particularly on the consequences for the ACA's Medicaid expansion, which was arguably the most important component of the law but was altered in significant ways by the Court's ruling. Shortly after

86 Wishner et al., *supra* note 77, at 5.

87 *Id.*

88 Virgil Dickson, *Indiana adds Medicaid work requirement to waiver request*, MODERN HEALTHCARE May 25, 2017, www.modernhealthcare.com/article/20170525/NEWS/170529942.

89 Amy Goldstein and Juliet Eilperin, "At Trump's urging, states try to tilt Medicaid in conservative directions," WASHINGTON POST (May 25, 2017).

90 *Id.*

91 Robert Pear and Thomas Kaplan, *Senate Rejects Slim-downed Obamacare repeal as McCain Votes No*, NEW YORK TIMES, July 27, 2017, www.nytimes.com/2017/07/27/us/politics/obamacare-partial-repeal-senate-republicans-revolt.html.

the decision was handed down some scholars predicted that the main effect would be to increase state officials' leverage in bargaining about the design and implementation of the ACA, among other policies. In subsequent years, scholars have analyzed negotiations between state and federal officials over Medicaid-expansion plans in particular states. My intent has been to take stock of the effects of *NFIB* on state-federal bargaining over Medicaid expansion in the five years after the decision and with an eye to examining the full range of state actions and state-federal negotiations and specifying the particular consequences in these respects.

Developments in the half-decade after *NFIB* demonstrate that the ruling has had two main consequences in terms of strengthening states' leverage in bargaining with federal officials. First, the ruling has enabled state officials who oppose the ACA's Medicaid expansion to resist signing on, even in the face of efforts by federal officials to pressure them to do so. Prior to the decision, all or nearly all states were expected to agree to the expansion. But after the Supreme Court ruled in *NFIB* that Congress could not penalize non-expansion states by withholding their existing Medicaid funding, nineteen states chose not to expand. Moreover, when officials in some states perceived that federal officials were trying to link the decision to expand Medicaid with renewal of other health programs, these state officials relied on the *NFIB* precedent to resist this type of pressure and maintain their non-expansion stance while still securing federal approval for other funding streams or programs.

A second effect of the *NFIB* ruling is to enable state officials who were open to expanding Medicaid to secure concessions from federal officials regarding the design of the program in exchange for agreeing to the expansion. State and federal officials have engaged for decades in negotiations about waivers allowing states to undertake alternative ways of structuring Medicaid programs and delivering Medicaid services. But once the *NFIB* ruling made state participation in the ACA's Medicaid expansion truly optional, this enhanced states' leverage in these negotiations and led federal officials to approve waivers permitting innovations that would likely not have been offered in the absence of the Court ruling. In some cases, states were able to win approval to structure their Medicaid-expansion plans in ways that deviated from federal statutory requirements in notable ways.

This analysis of the consequences of the Court's *NFIB* decision, and particularly the focus on ways the decision increased the leverage of state officials in negotiations with federal officials, also has broader lessons for understanding the consequences of the Court's federalism decisions more generally. As shown in several studies published in the early 2000s, the Court's federalism decisions have rarely erected insurmountable constitutional barriers to the exercise of federal power, whether by blocking re-passage of invalidated statutes[92] or preventing passage of subsequent legislation.[93] Rather, the principal consequences have been to enhance the leverage of opponents of federal policies, whether state officials, members of Congress, or interest groups, in their efforts to alter the design of these policies and occasionally prevent their enactment in the political process.[94]

---

92 John Dinan, *Congressional Responses to the Rehnquist Court's Federalism Decisions*, 32 PUBLIUS: J. FEDERALISM 1 (2002).

93 John Dinan, *Consequences of the Rehnquist Court's Federalism Decisions for Congressional Lawmaking*, 34 PUBLIUS: J. FEDERALISM 39 (2004).

94 J. Mitchell Pickerill, *Leveraging Federalism: The Real Meaning of the Rehnquist Court's Federalism Jurisprudence for States*, 66 ALB. L. REV. 823 (2003); J. MITCHELL PICKERILL, CONSTITUTIONAL DELIBERATION IN CONGRESS: THE IMPACT OF JUDICIAL REVIEW IN A SEPARATED SYSTEM (2004).

This was particularly evident when considering the consequences of the Rehnquist Court's federalism decisions. From the early 1990s to the early 2000s, the Rehnquist Court invalidated the Gun Free School Zones Act, the applicability of the Religious Freedom Restoration Act to state governments, and a provision of the Violence Against Women Act, all on the grounds that they exceeded the boundaries of congressional power. During this time, the Court also struck down the Low-level Radioactive Waste Policy Amendments Act and a temporary background-check provision of the Brady Handgun Violence Prevention Act for improperly commandeering state officials. In other cases, the Court held that Congress violated states' sovereignty when it enacted legislation providing that state governments could be sued without their consent. These rulings were consequential, but not because they imposed insurmountable barriers to reenactment of the invalidated statutes. As I concluded in a prior study of congressional efforts to respond to each of these decisions and re-enact the invalidated measures, "the Court's decisions have altered the balance of power within Congress, in that they have forced supporters of these measures to build and hold coalitions for the reenactment of these measures and have given opponents another opportunity to prevent this from occurring."[95] A similar lesson emerged from an analysis of the consequences of the Rehnquist Court's federalism decisions for congressional efforts to pass other policies aside from the invalidated measures. In fact, "the principal effects of judicial decisions may lie not so much in their capacity to erect constitutional barriers to various policies but rather in their ability to empower opponents of these policies by providing them with additional arguments and support for their positions."[96]

The Roberts Court's *NFIB* decision might be viewed in a similar fashion and as having comparable consequences, albeit not by empowering congressional critics of federal policies but rather by increasing the leverage of state officials who opposed or were ambivalent about the ACA's Medicaid expansion. The *NFIB* decision therefore serves as a useful reminder of the benefits of assessing the consequences of Supreme Court decisions in terms of their political effects and their capacity to strengthen the bargaining position of various actors in the political system, whether federal officials or state officials or interest groups.[97] Federalism scholars have long conceived of intergovernmental relations as an opportunity for bargaining between federal and state officials. Legal scholars concerned with studying the consequences of judicial rulings would benefit from approaching the Supreme Court's federalism decisions in such a fashion.

95 Dinan, *supra* note 92, at 3.
96 Dinan, *supra* note 93, at 67.
97 This argument is advanced most notably in ERIN RYAN, FEDERALISM AND THE TUG OF WAR WITHIN (2012).

6 Federalism, marriage equality, and LGBT rights

Nancy J. Knauer

This chapter explores the role federalism has played in shaping the trajectory of LGBT rights in the United States, specifically in the context of marriage equality. Since the late 1970s, LGBT rights advocates and their opponents have engaged in a sophisticated practice of strategic institutional choice.[1] They have waged their struggle over LGBT rights at the federal, state, and local levels through court cases, legislative initiatives, executive action, and popular referenda. Rather than wait for uniform federal reforms, LGBT advocates have often pursued partial, but attainable, goals at the state and local levels. These simultaneous and overlapping advocacy efforts have resulted in wide variation on the state and local levels that was most pronounced in the case of marriage equality, but continues today with respect to non-discrimination protections and religious exemptions. The high degree of state-level variation brings to mind Justice Brandeis' optimistic vision of federalism where "a single courageous state may, if its citizens choose, serve as a laboratory; and try novel social and economic experiments without risk to the rest of the country."[2] But the lived experience of trying to navigate a confusing patchwork of favorable laws and hostile prohibitions has exacted a heavy toll on the LGBT community.

At its core, federalism represents an institutional choice. It calibrates the balance of power between the state and national governments largely through court-made doctrine that attempts to flesh out the framework of institutional authority outlined in the U.S. Constitution. Although it answers the all-important question of who should decide a particular issue, it does not provide an answer to the underlying substantive question. For example, federalism may reject a federal definition of marriage because the regulation of marriage has traditionally been the province of the states, but it remains agnostic as to the substance of that state regulation. Accordingly, federalism can facilitate either a progressive or a conservative impulse. The mantle of federalism has been used to justify some of this country's most shameful and immoral regimes, such as the Jim Crow laws and the "massive resistance" segregationist movement, but it has also served as the foundation for progressive era reforms, such as state workmen's compensation laws. Today, progressive advocates invoke federalist principles to support state level innovations with respect to the legalization of marijuana, right-to-die initiatives, climate change measures, and health care reform. Conservative advocates also employ federalism to support socially conservative causes, including broad religious exemption laws and restrictive abortion laws.

---

1 NEIL KOMESAR, LAW'S LIMITS: THE RULE OF LAW AND THE SUPPLY AND DEMAND OF RIGHTS 174–82 (2001) (explaining strategic institutional choice).
2 New State Ice Co. v. Liebmann, 285 U.S. 262, 311 (1932) (Brandeis, J., dissenting).

In the case of marriage equality, both sides marshaled appeals to federalism and states' rights to further their view of the social good, only to abandon them when federalism no longer served their purposes. Beginning with the 1993 Supreme Court of Hawai'i decision in *Baehr. v. Lewin*,[3] LGBT advocates secured significant victories based on state constitutional claims. These claims remained the primary basis of pro-marriage litigation until 2009 and reflected an express strategic decision to build positive case law at the state level before mounting federal challenges.[4] Despite periodic victories, the vast majority of the states rejected marriage equality and took steps to block same-sex marriage through legislative action and state constitutional amendments. To this end, anti-marriage groups organized many successful citizens' initiatives and excelled in the use of direct democracy to blunt the potential impact of favorable court rulings or legislative action. But they were also willing to put their commitment to states' rights aside and support the federal Defense of Marriage Act (DOMA),[5] which imposed a restrictive national definition of marriage in an area historically reserved to the states.[6] The advocates of marriage equality also eventually turned away from state level reforms to focus instead on federal constitutional claims—first to defeat DOMA and then to mandate nationwide marriage equality.[7]

This strategic and wholeheartedly political use of federalism is completely appropriate and unremarkable behavior for advocates who are attempting to effect social change or reform. Their intense institutional jockeying demonstrated not only the vertical interplay of state and federal authority, but also the horizontal balance of power existing among the co-equal branches at each level of government. At times the fight for marriage equality resembled a high stakes game of "rock, scissors, paper" where one gain was met with yet another challenge—a favorable court decision was mooted by legislation only to be invalidated by a court case that was then overturned by a citizens' initiative.[8] As judges, legislators, and voters all scrambled to weigh in on the future of equal marriage rights, the central question remained "who decides?"

This tumultuous process produced a perplexing array of innovative state-level marriage laws, some of which recognized same-sex marriage or a lesser status, such as domestic partnership, and some of which prohibited not only same-sex marriage, but also any recognition of same-sex relationships. DOMA added a second layer of complexity by mandating that for all federal purposes marriage was a union between one man and one woman, which meant that a couple could be married under state law, but still considered unmarried for the purposes of all federal benefits. The result was an increasing lack of uniformity that, when combined with our highly mobile society, placed an untenable burden on same-sex couples. Marriages could disappear as a couple crossed the state line and prove meaningless at tax time.

---

3 Baehr v. Lewin, 852 P.2d 44 (Haw. 1993).
4 David J. Garrow, *Toward a More Perfect Union*, N.Y. TIMES MAG., May 9, 2004, at 52 (describing evolution of coordinated same-sex marriage litigation).
5 Defense of Marriage Act, Pub. L. No. 104–199, 110 Stat. 2419 (1996) (codified as amended at 1 U.S.C. § 7 (1997), 28 U.S.C. § 1738C (1997)), invalidated by U.S. v. Windsor, 133 S. Ct. 2675 (2013).
6 See, e.g., Sosna v. Iowa, 419 U.S. 393, 404 (1975) (identifying domestic relations as "an area that has long been regarded as a virtually exclusive province of the States").
7 U.S. v. Windsor, 133 S.Ct. 2675 (2013) (invalidating DOMA); Obergefell v. Hodges, 135 S.Ct. 2584 (2015) (invalidating restrictive state marriage prohibitions).
8 Nancy J. Knauer, *The Recognition of Same-Sex Relationships: Comparative Institutional Analysis, Contested Social Goals, and Strategic Institutional Choice*, 28 U. HAW. L. REV. 23, 76 (2006).

The question of marriage equality was finally resolved at the federal level in two landmark U.S. Supreme Court cases. In 2013, *U.S. v. Windsor* invalidated the restrictive federal definition of marriage under DOMA.[9] Two years later, *Obergefell v. Hodges* put an end to the confusing patchwork of state level marriage laws by invalidating state laws that restricted marriage to the union of one man and one woman.[10] Both decisions are considered historic civil rights cases, but each case seemed to strike a different balance between the powers of the state and national governments. *Windsor* affirmed the primacy of a state's definition of marriage, but then two years later the very same Justices voted in *Obergefell* to invalidate restrictive state definitions of marriage.

The Court's apparent love-hate relationship with federalism in the context of marriage equality has invited speculation that the rulings represented yet another example of politicized decision-making where Justices act more like advocates than impartial arbiters.[11] An institutional view of federalism, however, can help clarify that the visions of federalism expressed by the majority opinions in *Windsor* and *Obergefell* are not necessarily at odds. Deference to the states represents an institutional choice, but, as with any institution, federalism has both specific competencies and limitations. Even the most innovative state "experiment" must comport with the constitutional safeguards of the Fourteenth Amendment. Although *Windsor* may have affirmed that states retain the authority to define and regulate marriage, *Obergerfell* reminds us that such authority is necessarily constrained by the federal constitutional guarantees of liberty and equal protection. Accordingly, *Obergefell* remains true to the template of federalism sketched out by the Tenth Amendment, which refers to not only the powers delegated to the national government, but also the powers prohibited to the States by the Constitution: "The powers not delegated to the United States by the Constitution, *nor prohibited by it to the States*, are reserved to the States respectively, or to the people.[12]

This chapter examines the role of federalism in the struggle for marriage equality with respect to both the choices made by advocates and the decisions made by judges. The first two sections of this chapter examine the legal strategy that ultimately led to marriage equality, as well as the confounding range of relationship recognition laws and prohibitions that emerged during the two decades leading up to *Windsor* and *Obergefell*. The third section provides an overview of both *Windsor* and *Obergefell*, with a particular emphasis on their corresponding visions of federalism. A brief conclusion closes with the observation that federalism has proven to be a pragmatic, but also imperfect, institutional choice for LGBT rights advocates because state level civil rights protections are generally not portable, and they remain especially vulnerable to majoritarian measures such as citizens' initiatives. As explained below, this observation has particular salience for both our understanding of federalism and the future of LGBT advocacy.

---

9 U.S. v. Windsor, 133 S.Ct. 2675 (2013).
10 Obergefell v. Hodges, 135 S.Ct. 2584 (2015).
11 See, e.g., Megan Garber, *The U.S. Supreme Court Is Acting Like Congress*, THE ATLANTIC, June 27, 2015, www.theatlantic.com/politics/archive/2015/06/9-angry-judges/396989/.
12 U.S. CONST. Amend. X [emphasis added].

The demand for marriage equality and relationship recognition

Although a handful of same-sex marriage cases were brought in the 1970s during the early days of the Gay Liberation movement,[13] the concerted push for marriage equality did not start until the mid-1990s when a series of positive decisions from the Hawai'i state courts in *Baehr v. Lewin* and *Baehr v. Miike* signaled that same-sex couples could secure the right to marry under state constitutions.[14] For LGBT advocates, the decision to focus on state constitutional law was a pragmatic and strategic one. The 1986 U.S. Supreme Court decision in *Bowers v. Hardwick*[15] had upheld the constitutionality of criminal sodomy laws, making it highly unlikely that the Court would recognize a fundamental right to marry for same-sex couples based on *Loving v. Virginia*.[16] In addition, the U.S. Supreme Court had dismissed one of the early marriage cases, *Baker v. Nelson*,[17] for want of a federal question in 1972. *Bowers v. Hardwick* was not overruled until *Lawrence v. Texas* in 2003[18]—the same year that the Supreme Court of Massachusetts mandated marriage equality.[19]

The demand for marriage equality was in many ways a natural extension of the broader goals of equality and individual freedom espoused by the gay rights movement, but it was never a universally shared goal within the LGBT community.[20] The initial wave of the HIV/ AIDS epidemic in the 1980s had highlighted the disadvantages faced by same-sex couples because they were not able to marry or otherwise formalize their relationships. As the gay community was being devastated by an unrelenting disease, same-sex partners were refused hospital visitation rights, disregarded in medical decision making, evicted from apartments, and denied the property rights typically extended to surviving spouses or other family members. These experiences brought into sharper focus the human costs involved in the lack of relationship recognition. Regardless of the length or quality of their relationship, same-sex partners were considered legal strangers. Against this backdrop, it became clear to the burgeoning gay rights movement that it was essential to secure some form of legal recognition for same-sex relationships in order to safeguard one's loved ones. The only question for debate was what form that recognition should take. Whereas some advocates championed full marriage equality,[21] others favored different forms of nonmarital recognition that could provide legal protections without the traditional trappings of marriage.[22]

In response to the demand for legal recognition, state and local legislatures began to craft a number of mechanisms to address the glaring inequities experienced by same-sex

---

13 Jones v. Hallahan, 501 S.W.2d 588 (Ky. 1973); Singer v. Hara, 522 P.2d 1187 (Wash. App. 1974); Baker v. Nelson, 191 N.W.2d 185 (Minn. 1971).

14 Baehr v. Lewin, 852 P.2d 44 (Haw. 1993); Baehr v. Miike, No. 91–1394, 1996 WL 694235, at *21 (Haw. Cir. Ct. 1996), *aff'd* 950 P.2d 1234 (Haw. 1997).

15 Bowers v. Hardwick, 478 U.S. 186 (upholding constitutionality of criminal sodomy law).

16 Loving v. Virginia, 388 U.S. 1, 12 (1967) (recognizing a fundamental right to marry).

17 Baker v. Nelson, 191 N.W.2d 185 (Minn. 1971), *appeal dismissed*, 409 U.S. 810 (1972).

18 Lawrence v. Texas, 539 U.S. 558 (2003).

19 Goodridge v. Dep't of Pub. Health, 798 N.E.2d 941 (Mass. 2003) (holding that limiting access to protections and benefits of civil marriage violates state constitution).

20 Paula L. Ettelbrick, *Since When is Marriage a Path to Liberation?*, OUT/LOOK: NAT'L GAY & LESBIAN Q., Fall 1989, at 9, 14–17.

21 Thomas B. Stoddard, *Why Gay People Should Seek the Right to Marry*, OUT/LOOK: NAT'L GAY & LESBIAN Q., Fall 1989, at 9, 9–13.

22 NANCY POLIKOFF, BEYOND GAY AND STRAIGHT MARRIAGE: VALUING ALL FAMILIES UNDER THE LAW (2008).

couples, especially surviving same-sex partners. The legislative reforms provided varying levels of legal recognition and protection, ranging from the limited grant of domestic partner employee benefits to laws that created a parallel status that extend all the rights and obligations of marriage. Often the legislative reforms were enacted following a favorable decision by the state's highest court and were designed specially to forestall a full grant of marriage equality.

The first tangible gains were on the local or municipal level. The earliest ordinances were enacted in the 1980s and extended spousal benefits, specifically health insurance, to the same-sex partners of city employees.[23] These benefits became to be known as domestic partner benefits. At the same time, major employers also began to offer domestic partnership benefits to their employees. Later, more comprehensive ordinances established domestic partnership registries, extended full spousal rights to domestic partners, and, in some instances, required city contractors to provide domestic partner benefits.[24] Many of these ordinances were largely symbolic and granted few substantive rights because they could only extend to same-sex couples the rights that were within the power of the city or municipality to grant, such as municipal spousal tax benefits, and the ability to transfer certain municipal licenses to a same-sex partner.[25]

When marriage advocates turned their attention to state constitutions, they focused on states with gender-neutral marriage laws and Equal Rights Amendments.[26] After favorable court rulings were nullified by citizens' initiatives, it also became clear that it was important to focus on states with constitutional structures that were difficult to amend through appeals to direct democracy. The long-term strategy was to build sufficient support among the states before bringing a federal claim.[27] During this period, plaintiffs were actively discouraged from initiating federal claims in order to avoid the creation of negative precedent at the federal level.[28] It was not until 2009 that advocates began to bring federal challenges to restrictive marriage laws.[29]

The first state-wide legal recognition for same-sex couples was enacted in 1997 when Hawai'i approved the Reciprocal Beneficiaries Act (the "Act") in response to ongoing marriage litigation.[30] The legislation was an attempt to take the steam out of the push for marriage equality by addressing some particular areas where same-sex couples were disadvantaged, such as inheritance rights and medical decision making. Under the Act, the legislature created the status of "reciprocal beneficiary," and extended approximately sixty rights and responsibilities commonly associated with marriage to individuals who registered as "reciprocal beneficiaries."[31] The Act was not expressly limited to same-sex couples in order

---

23 Nancy J. Knauer, *Domestic Partnership and Same-Sex Relationships: A Marketplace Innovation and a Less than Perfect Institutional Choice*, 7 TEMP. POL. & CIV. RTS. L. REV. 337, 348 (1998).

24 S.D. Myers, Inc. v. City and County of San Francisco, 253 F.3d 461, 467–76 (9th Cir. 2001) (upholding San Francisco ordinance requiring city contractors to offer domestic partnership benefits equal to those provided for spouses).

25 Knauer, *supra* note 23 at 340–41 (describing scope of benefits available).

26 Garrow, *supra* note 4 (discussing coordinated litigation strategy).

27 *Id.*

28 *Id.*

29 Jo Becker, *A Conservative's Road to Same-Sex Marriage Advocacy*, NEW YORK TIMES, Aug. 18, 2009.

30 HAW. REV. STAT. ANN. §§ 572C-1 to -3 (2007).

31 See e.g. HAW. REV. STAT. ANN. § 560:2–102 (2015) (inheritance rights).

to appease the opponents of same-sex marriage who saw the legislation as validation of what they pejoratively referred to as the "homosexual lifestyle."[32]

Three years later, Vermont became the second state to adopt state-wide relationship recognition. As was the case in Hawaii, the Vermont legislature enacted legislation to provide recognition that was short of marriage in response to a favorable court ruling. In 1999, the Vermont Supreme Court ruled in *Baker v. Vermont* that same-sex couples were entitled to the same rights and privileges afforded to married couples under the Vermont Constitution.[33] The decision did not mandate same-sex marriage. Instead, it suspended the issuance of marriage licenses to same-sex couples until the state legislature could remedy the situation. A year later, the Vermont legislature created civil unions for same-sex couples that provided all the rights and privileges of marriage.[34] The Vermont civil union legislation represented the first time a state created a parallel status for same-sex couples that was the legal equivalent to marriage.

As the states continued to grapple with the question of relationship recognition, they developed a range of statutory schemes that varied considerably in terms of scope and went by different names, such as reciprocal beneficiaries, domestic partnerships, and civil unions. During this time, there developed a clear inverse relationship between innovation and uniformity. As innovation and complexity increased, uniformity and consistency decreased. Some of the statutory schemes were restricted to same-sex couples, whereas others were also open to different sex-couples. Some states created an alternative status to marriage that provided a lesser quantum of rights, whereas other states created a statutory category that granted same-sex couples all of the rights and obligations of marriage, but withheld the formal designation of marriage. The states that created a marriage equivalent status did so in order to maintain marriage as a special status reserved for different-sex couples, thereby raising equal protection concerns.[35] All of the states that extended some form of recognition for same-sex relationships later adopted marriage equality in advance of *Obergefell v. Hodges*.

In 2004 Massachusetts became the first state to issue marriage licenses to same-sex couples. A year earlier, the Massachusetts Supreme Court held in *Goodridge v. Department of Public Health* that the Massachusetts Constitution required equal treatment of same-sex couples with respect to marriage.[36] In an advisory opinion, the majority of the justices of the Massachusetts Supreme Court concluded that Vermont-style civil union legislation would not cure the constitutional infirmity.[37] Although aggrieved voters mobilized around a state constitutional amendment, they were not able to overcome procedural hurdles unique to the Massachusetts amendment process.[38]

As more states joined Massachusetts and embraced marriage equality, the confusion over relationship recognition intensified. Despite gains, the majority of states continued to ban same-sex marriage and refused to recognize same-sex marriages performed in other

---

32 HAW. REV. STAT. ANN. § 572C–4 (2015).

33 Baker v. Vermont, 744 A.2d 864 (Vt. 1999).

34 VT. STAT. ANN. tit. 15, §§ 1201–1207 (2016).

35 See, e.g., Susan K. Livio, *Commission Says New Jersey Should Allow Gay Marriage*, STAR LEDGER, Dec. 10, 2008 (summarizing report of New Jersey Civil Union Review Commission).

36 Goodridge v. Dep't of Pub. Health, 798 N.E.2d 941 (Mass. 2003).

37 Opinion of the Justices to the Senate, 802 N.E.2d 565, 570 (Mass. 2004).

38 Pam Belluck, Massachusetts Plans to Revisit Amendment on Gay Marriage, NEW YORK TIMES, May 10, 2005, at A13.

jurisdictions. Depending on where a couple lived and worked, they could be considered legal strangers, spouses, or something in between. Regardless of their status under state law, DOMA ensured that they would be considered unmarried for federal purposes, including taxes, social security, and veterans' benefits. The lack of reciprocity among the states meant that a couple would lose their legally recognized status if they ventured into a non-recognition jurisdiction. The complex and transitory nature of relationship recognition was a source of considerable emotional and economic stress for same-sex couples, who quickly realized that they had to travel at their own risk. In 2004, both the American Psychiatric Association and the American Psychological Association passed resolutions in support of marriage equality, specifically citing the extreme stress experienced by same-sex couples due to the lack of uniform relationship recognition.[39]

The emergence of marriage prohibitions

The restrictive marriage laws that were invalidated by *Windsor* and *Obergefell* were relatively new developments. When the Hawai'i litigation began in the 1990s, the majority of marriage statutes in the United States were actually gender-neutral.[40] The definitional view of a marriage as a union between one man and one woman was so strong that there was no perceived need to limit marriage to different-sex couples. Indeed, the early gay liberation marriage cases had been decided solely on definitional grounds and often in a cursory fashion. The courts simply ruled that marriage, by definition, could only be a union between a man and a woman—end of discussion.[41] In 1972 the U.S. Supreme Court dismissed an appeal of one of these cases, *Baker v. Nelson*, for want of a federal question.[42] Over forty years later, this definitional approach to marriage continued to have judicial adherents, and it figured prominently in the dissenting opinions in both *Windsor* and *Obergefell*.[43]

State level prohibitions

The definitional certainty with which courts had addressed marriage claims was upended in 1993 when the Supreme Court of Hawai'i held in *Baehr v. Lewin* that the denial of marriage licenses to same-sex couples presumptively violated the Equal Rights Amendment to the Hawai'i Constitution.[44] The court reasoned that the denial constituted discrimination based on gender because the plaintiff would have been granted a marriage license to marry a woman if she had been a man. The Supreme Court of Hawai'i remanded the case to the trial court to determine whether the prohibition against same-sex marriage could be justified by a compelling state interest. After extensive fact-finding and hearings, the trial court ruled in 1996 that the state had failed to meet its burden of proof.[45] In 1998, while

---

39 Nancy J. Knauer, Gay and Lesbian Elders: History, Law, and Identity Politics in the United States 91 (2011) (describing resolutions).
40 George Chauncey, Why Marriage? The History Shaping Today's Debate Over Gay Equality 91(2004).
41 See, e.g., Jones v. Hallahan, 501 S.W.2d 588 (Ky. 1973).
42 Baker v. Nelson, 191 N.W.2d 185 (Minn. 1971), *appeal dismissed*, 409 U.S. 810 (1972).
43 See, e.g., Obergefell v. Hodges, 135 S.Ct. 2584, 2619 (Roberts, C.J., dissenting)
44 Baehr v. Lewin, 852 P.2d 44 (Haw. 1993);
45 Baehr v. Miike, No. 91–1394, 1996 WL 694235, at *21 (Haw. Cir. Ct. 1996), *aff'd* 950 P.2d 1234 (Haw. 1997).

the case was still being appealed to the state supreme court, the voters approved the first state constitutional amendment designed to prohibit same-sex marriage.[46] They amended the Hawai'i state constitution to provide that the definition of marriage could only be changed by legislative action.[47] The Supreme Court of Hawai'i eventually affirmed the trial court decision in favor of marriage equality, but by then the constitutional amendment had rendered the court's decision moot because it no longer had the power to alter the definition of marriage.[48]

The Hawai'i marriage litigation and the specter of marriage equality sent shockwaves across the country. It provoked a fierce backlash orchestrated by advocacy organizations that quickly adopted the label "pro-family." Losing no time, Congress enacted DOMA in 1996 while the litigation was still pending in Hawai'i and, for the first time, created a federal definition of marriage.[49] At the state level, "pro-family" forces organized highly successful campaigns to amend state constitutions to prohibit same-sex marriage even when there was no threat of a pending court case. Unlike the constitutional amendment in Hawai'i, this next round of amendments enshrined the restrictive definition of marriage directly in the state constitution, rather than leave the question to the legislature. This constitutional approach eliminated the power of the courts to use state constitutional protections to compel same-sex marriage. It also left legislatures without the power to enact marriage equality and, in many cases, to enact any form of relationship recognition.

By 2006, 44 states had anti-marriage laws that were known as mini-DOMAs or constitutional amendments that restricted marriage to a union of one man and one woman.[50] Just for good measure, a number of states had both statutes and constitutional amendments.[51] Nineteen states eventually passed especially expansive state constitutional amendments that prohibited not just same-sex marriage, but also the grant of any of the "incidents of marriage" to same-sex couples.[52] These broader amendments were in reaction to the state-level experimentation that had occurred with respect to relationship recognition that fell short of marriage equality. They prohibited *any* form of relationship recognition, including civil unions, domestic partnerships, municipal registries, and the grant of domestic partner employee benefits to public employees.[53] In 2004 a Federal Marriage Amendment was introduced in Congress.[54] It would have in placed a restrictive definition of marriage as a

46 CNN.com, *Hawaii Gives Legislature Power to Ban Same-Sex Marriage*, Nov. 8, 1998, *available at* www.cnn.com/ALLPOLITICS/stories/1998/11/04/same.sex.ballot/.
47 HAW. CONST. art. I § 23 ("The legislature shall have the power to reserve marriage to opposite-sex couples."
48 Baehr v. Miike, No. 20371, 1999 Haw. LEXIS 391 (Haw. Dec. 9, 1999) (ruling constitutional amendment rendered lower court decision moot).
49 See, e.g., 142 CONG. REC. at S4870 (statement of Sen. Nickles) (citing court challenges as a driving force behind the need for a definition of marriage).
50 Nancy J. Knauer, *The Recognition of Same-Sex Relationships: Comparative Institutional Analysis, Contested Social Goals, and Strategic Institutional Choice*, 28 U. HAW. L. REV. 23, n. 231 (2006).
51 *Id.*
52 See, e.g., OKLA. CONST. art. II, § 35A (2007) ("Neither this Constitution nor any other provision of law shall be construed to require that marital status or the legal incidents thereof be conferred upon unmarried couples or groups.").
53 See, e.g., Nat'l Pride at Work, Inc. v. Governor of Mich., 748 N.W.2d 524 (Mich. 2008) (prohibiting the grant of domestic partner benefits to public employees).
54 Federal Marriage Amendment, H.R.J. Res. 56, 108th Cong. (2003).

union between one man and one woman in the U.S. Constitution, but it ultimately failed to receive sufficient congressional support.[55]

The federal Defense of Marriage Act

As noted above, DOMA was enacted while the Hawai'i marriage litigation was pending and was designed to stop the potential spread of same-sex marriage throughout the nation. *Baehr v. Lewin* had shown that states could require same-sex marriage as a matter of state constitutional law. The recognition of same-sex marriage by even a single state would have had repercussions on the federal level and potentially created a domino effect among the states. Prior to DOMA, there was no federal definition of marriage because it was traditionally governed by state law. In questions involving federal law, such as taxes or federal benefits, the validity of a marriage was generally determined by reference to the definition of marriage in the state where the couple lived unless there was a specific direction to the contrary in the statute. Without DOMA, the federal government would have been required to recognize all same-sex marriages that were valid under state law. Moreover, the Full Faith and Credit Clause of the U.S. Constitution could have required states to recognize same-sex marriages performed in other jurisdictions.[56] DOMA addressed both of these eventualities head on through two substantive provisions: it adopted a restrictive definition of marriage for all federal purposes[57] and purported to authorize states to refuse to recognize out-of-state same-sex marriages.[58]

DOMA passed both chambers of Congress with overwhelming bipartisan support. Introduced and passed in the months leading up to the 1996 presidential election, both presidential candidates supported the legislation. Republican presidential candidate Senator Bob Dole (R-KS) introduced DOMA in the Senate in May of 1996 where it passed by a vote of 85 to 14.[59] DOMA passed the House of Representatives by a vote of 342 to 67.[60] With veto-proof majorities in both houses of Congress, President Bill Clinton, who was running for reelection, signed DOMA into law in September of that year, well ahead of the November election.[61]

The Report of the U.S. House of Representatives Judiciary Committee explained that DOMA advanced four government interests: (a) defending and nurturing the institution of traditional marriage, (b) defending traditional notions of morality, (c) protecting states'

---

55 Sheryl Gay Stolberg, *Same Sex Marriage Amendment Fails in the House*, NEW YORK TIMES, Oct. 1, 2004, at A14 (noting vote was 227 to 186 in favor of the amendment, but short of two-thirds majority needed).
56 See, e.g., 42 U.S.C. § 416 h(1)(A)(i) (2016) (defining "spouse" for social security purposes by reference to law of domicile).
57 DOMA, Pub. L. No. 104–199, 110 Stat. 2419 (1996), *codified at* 1 U.S.C. § 7 (1997), *invalidated by* U.S. v. Windsor, 133 S. Ct. 2675 (2013).
58 Defense of Marriage Act, Pub. L. No. 104–199, 110 Stat. 2419 (1996), *codified at* 28 U.S.C. § 1738C (1997), *invalidated by* Obergefell v. Hodges, 135 S. Ct. 2584 (2015).
59 H.R. 3396 (104th): Defense of Marriage Act—Final Votes for Roll Call 316 (Jul. 12, 1996) http://clerk.house.gov/evs/1996/roll316.xml.
60 Roll Call Vote 104th Congress—2d Session (Sept. 10, 1996) www.senate.gov/legislative/LIS/roll_call_lists/roll_call_vote_cfm.cfm?congress=104&session=2&vote=00280.
61 Richard Socarides, *Why Clinton Signed the Defense of Marriage Act*, NEW YORKER, Mar. 8, 2013 available at www.newyorker.com/news/news-desk/why-bill-clinton-signed-the-defense-of-marriage-act.

sovereignty and democratic self-governance, and (d) preserving scarce government resources.[62] Focusing primarily on morality, the testimony in the congressional record reflected the heated rhetoric of the time. In support of the legislation, members of Congress invoked Biblical verses, the fall of ancient Rome, and harsh moral condemnation.[63] Both the tone and the vocabulary of the discussion is shocking when measured against present day sensibilities, but it demonstrates how much the public discourse regarding over LGBT has evolved in just a little over two decades.

In many ways, DOMA was a solution in search of a problem. It took eight years before the first state began to issue marriage licenses to same-sex couples.[64] Once same-sex couples could legally marry under state law, DOMA refused to recognize those marriages for all federal purposes. For example, a same-sex couple who was legally married and lived in Massachusetts could file their state income taxes jointly, but had to file their federal taxes as if they were unmarried. They would also not qualify as married for purposes of the 1,138 federal statutory provisions under which marital status is a factor in determining or receiving benefits, rights, and privileges that had been identified by the United States General Accountability Office.[65] These provisions include favorable joint tax rates, Social Security spousal benefits, veterans' benefits, and pension rights.

The federal cases

Beginning in 2009, the focus of the marriage litigation shifted from the state level to the federal level, as litigants argued that same-sex marriage was protected under the U.S. Constitution in the much-anticipated case of *Perry v. Hollingsworth*.[66] *Perry* challenged a California ballot proposition, known as Proposition 8, that amended the California state constitution to prohibit same-sex marriage and block the impact of a state supreme court decision mandating marriage equality. The decision to bring *Perry* was controversial within the LGBT advocacy community and was met with objections that it was too soon to bring a federal challenge.[67] The state-level efforts had produced impressive results. A total of sixteen states and the District of Columbia eventually embraced marriage equality. Ten states and the District of Columbia adopted marriage equality through legislation.[68] The highest courts of five states mandated marriage equality,[69] and one state, Maine, approved

62 House Report 104-664—Defense of Marriage Act, July 9, 1996, www.gpo.gov/fdsys/pkg/CRPT-104hrpt664/html/CRPT-104hrpt664.htm.
63 See, e.g., Complaint, Massachusetts v. HHS, 9–10 (July 8, 2009), www.slideshare.net/LegalDocs/findlaw-mass-sues-over-federal-defense-of-marriage-act.
64 Goodridge v. Dep't of Pub. Health, 798 N.E.2d 941 (Mass. 2003).
65 U.S. GENERAL ACCOUNTING OFFICE, gao-04-353r, DEFENSE OF MARRIAGE ACT: UPDATE TO PRIOR REPORT 1 (Jan. 23, 2004), available at www.gao.gov/new.items/d04353r.pdf.
66 Perry v. Hollingsworth, 133 S. Ct. 2652 (2013).
67 Michael A. Lindenberger, *A Gay-Marriage Lawsuit Dares to Make Its Case*, TIME, Jan. 05, 2010, available at http://content.time.com/time/nation/article/0,8599,1951520,00.html.
68 Delaware (2013); District of Columbia (2010); Hawaii (2013); Illinois (2014): Maryland (2013); Minnesota (2013); New Hampshire (2010); New York (2011); Rhode Island (2013); Vermont (2009); Washington (2012).
69 Goodridge v. Dep't of Pub. Health, 798 N.E.2d 941 (Mass. 2003); In re Marriage Cases, 183 P.3d 384 (Cal. 2008) *overturned by* Proposition 8; Kerrigan v. Commissioner of Public Health, 289 Conn. 135 (Conn. 2008); Varnum v. Brien, 763 N.W.2d 862 (Iowa 2009); Griego v. Oliver, 316 P.3d 865 (N.M. 2013).

same-sex marriage in a citizens' referenda.[70] The remaining states held on to their prohibitions and restrictive definitions of marriage, many of which had been written into their state constitutions. Only a ruling by the U.S. Supreme Court could provide the type of security same-sex couples desired by mandating uniform rules and overcoming the state constitutional amendments.

Although the U.S. Supreme Court granted certiorari, it dismissed *Perry* for lack of standing because the state of California had declined to defend Proposition 8.[71] The result left a favorable lower court decision in place, but carried little precedential weight. The same day that the Court dismissed *Perry*, it decided *U.S. v. Windsor* and invalidated section 3 of DOMA. After *Windsor*, the federal litigation intensified and challenges were brought throughout the country. By the time the Supreme Court decided *Obergefell v. Hodges* in June 2015, lower federal courts had invalidated many state-level marriage prohibitions, and they continued in effect in only fourteen states. *Obergefell* invalidated these remaining state level marriage bans and mandated nationwide marriage equality.

The DOMA litigation

Although DOMA was enacted in 1996, same-sex couples were not able to marry legally until 2004 when Massachusetts became the first state to issue marriage licenses. Once states began to adopt marriage equality, the inequities created by DOMA became clear. Couples who were legally married under state law were considered unmarried for federal purposes and denied access to a wide range of significant federal benefits. By 2013, three major cases had worked their way through the federal courts and were on appeal to the Supreme Court: *Gill v. U.S. Office of Personnel Management*,[72] *Massachusetts v. HHS*,[73] and *United States v. Windsor*.[74]

The U.S. Department of Justice (DOJ) had initially defended DOMA in the federal court challenges, while clearly stating that the Obama "Administration believes the Defense of Marriage Act ('DOMA') is discriminatory and should be repealed."[75] During the course of the DOMA litigation, the U.S. attorney general, Eric Holder, announced that the U.S. Department of Justice would no longer defend DOMA because he had determined that DOMA violated the U.S. Constitution.[76] Specifically, Holder had concluded that sexual orientation was entitled to heightened scrutiny and that the government could not carry its burden under that level of review.[77] Congressional interests intervened, and the U.S.

---

70 Ben Brumfield, *Voters Approve Same-Sex Marriage for the First Time*, CNN, Nov. 7, 2012, www.cnn. com/2012/11/07/politics/pol-same-sex-marriage/.

71 Hollingsworth v. Perry, 133 S.Ct. 2652 (2013).

72 Gill v. Office of Personnel Management, 682 F.3d 1 (1st Cir. 2012), *cert. denied* 133 S. Ct. 2884 (2013).

73 Massachusetts v. HHS, 682 F.3d 1(1st Cir. 2012), *cert. denied*, 129 S.Ct. 2887 (2013).

74 United States v. Windsor, 133 S. Ct. 2675 (2013).

75 Josh Gerstein, *Obama Softens Gov't Tone in Gay-Marriage Suit*, POLITICO, Aug. 17, 2009, www.politico. com/blogs/under-the-radar/2009/08/obama-softens-govt-tone-in-gay-marriage-suit-020693 (quoting brief).

76 Eric H. Holder, Jr., U.S. Att'y Gen., Statement of the Attorney General on Litigation Involving the Defense of Marriage Act, OFF. ATT'Y GEN. (Feb. 23, 2011), https://web.archive.org/web/20110309162048/www.justice.gov/opa/pr/2011/February/11-ag-222.html.

77 *Id.*

House of Representatives Bipartisan Legal Advisory Group (BLAG) continued the defense of the statute in federal court.[78]

All of the DOMA challenges had been successful in the lower courts, but they presented different arguments. *Gill v. OPM* and *U.S. v. Windsor* rested their objection to DOMA on the Due Process Clause and the equal protection guarantees of the Fifth Amendment. *Massachusetts v. HHS* based its objection to DOMA on federalism, relying on the Tenth Amendment and the Spending Clause to argue that Congress had overstepped its authority.[79] The Court dismissed the petitions for certiorari in *Massachusetts v. HHS*, along with *Gill v. OPM*, the day after it decided *Windsor*. However, this section includes a discussion of the arguments presented in *Massachusetts v. HHS* because they provide an opportunity to examine the federalism claims in greater depth. It then turns to *U.S. v. Windsor* and the executive action that was designed to resolve the choice of law issues left unanswered by *Windsor*.

Massachusetts v. HHS—*Federalism*

Many of the marriage cases grew out of compelling personal narratives of bereavement and loss that was then compounded by demeaning treatment under restrictive marriage laws. In *Massachusetts v. HHS*, however, the plaintiff was the Commonwealth of Massachusetts and the core issue presented was federalism or states' rights, not individual rights. Massachusetts argued that DOMA represented an attack on its sovereignty by an overreaching federal government. It contended that DOMA violated the Tenth Amendment and the Spending Clause of Article I of the U.S. Constitution. Massachusetts argued that its retained powers included the authority to regulate and define marriage for its citizens under the Tenth Amendment. DOMA, it claimed, "trespasse[d] on a core area of state sovereignty by creating two separate and distinct categories of married persons."[80]

In addition, Massachusetts asserted that DOMA impermissibly interfered with its distribution of Medicare and Medicaid funds and its management of certain cemeteries that were funded by the U.S. Department of Veterans' Administration. The Spending Clause limits the power of Congress to attach conditions to the receipt of federal funds.[81] It prohibits Congress from exercising its spending power in a manner that makes a state violate the constitutional rights of its citizens.[82] Massachusetts argued that DOMA required the Commonwealth to violate the Equal Protection Clause of the Fourteenth Amendment by treating married individuals in same-sex relationships and married individuals in different-sex relationships differently for purposes of determining eligibility for Medicaid benefits and access to VA cemeteries that it manages.[83]

---

78 Matthew I. Hall, *How Congress Could Defend DOMA in Court (and Why the BLAG Cannot)*, 65 STAN. L. REV. ONLINE 92 (2013) (discussing BLAG's intervention).
79 U.S. CONST. Amend. X; U.S. CONST. Art. I, § 8, cl. 1.
80 Complaint, *Massachusetts v. HHS*, 11 (July 8, 2009), www.slideshare.net/LegalDocs/findlaw-mass-sues-over-federal-defense-of-marriage-act.
81 *Id.*
82 *Id.*
83 *Id.*

The plaintiffs also argued that "DOMA was enacted to codify animus against gay and lesbian people"[84] and, therefore failed to satisfy the rational basis test. In 1996, the Supreme Court in *Romer v. Evans* had ruled that animus was not a legitimate state interest.[85] Citing *Romer*, Massachusetts contended that DOMA was not rationally related to a legitimate state interest because it was based on animus. In support of this claim, Massachusetts cited the following excerpts from the Congressional Record:

> [N]o society that has lived through the transition to homosexuality and the perversion which it lives and what it brought forth." H.R. REP. NO. 104-664, at 15-16; 142 CONG. REC. H7444 (daily ed. July 11, 1996) (statement of Rep. Tom Coburn). "The very foundations of our society are in danger of being burned. The flames of hedonism, the flames of narcissism, the flames of self-centered morality are licking at the very foundations of our society. . . ." 142 CONG. REC. H7482 (daily ed. July 12, 1996) (statement of Rep. Bob Barr). DOMA "will safeguard the sacred institutions of marriage and the family from those who seek to destroy them and who are willing to tear apart America's moral fabric in the process." 142 CONG. REC. S10068 (daily ed. Sept. 9, 1996) (statement of Sen. Jesse Helms).[86]

The trial court decided *Massachusetts v. HHS* on the same day as *Gill v. OPM*. The U.S. District Court for the District of Massachusetts ruled that Section 3 of DOMA violated the Tenth Amendment and fell outside Congress' authority under the Spending Clause.[87] A unanimous decision by the U.S. Court of Appeals for the First Circuit affirmed the lower court decision and declared Section 3 of DOMA unconstitutional but based its decision on the Due Process Clause and equal protection guarantees of the Fifth Amendment.[88] With *Gill v. OPM*, BLAG appealed to the U.S. Supreme Court, but the Court dismissed both petitions for certiorari the day after it decided *U.S. v. Windsor*, thereby foregoing the opportunity to rule expressly on the Tenth Amendment implications of DOMA.[89]

United States v. Windsor

The U.S. Supreme Court considered the petition for certiorari in *U.S. v Windsor* when the petitions in *Massachusetts v. HHS* and *Gill v. OPM* were pending. The attorneys in *Windsor* had taken the unusual step of filing the petition for certiorari while the case was still before the Second Circuit, which is known as a petition for a writ of certiorari before judgment.[90] The Court chose to hear *Windsor* over the consolidated Massachusetts cases. It was widely reported that the Court had deferred action on the Massachusetts cases because

84 *Id*. at 9.
85 Romer v. Evans, 517 U.S. 620.
86 Complaint, *Massachusetts v. HHS*, 9–10 (July 8, 2009), www.slideshare.net/LegalDocs/findlaw-mass-sues-over-federal-defense-of-marriage-act.
87 Massachusetts v. HHS, 698 F.Supp.2d 234 (D.Mass. 2010).
88 Massachusetts v. HHS, 682 F.3d 1 (1st Cir. 2012).
89 Gill v. Office of Personnel Management, 682 F.3d 1 (1st Cir. 2012), *cert. denied* 133 S. Ct. 2884 (2013); Massachusetts v. HHS, 682 F.3d 1 (1st Cir. 2012), *cert. denied*, 129 S.Ct. 2887 (2013).
90 U.S. v. Windsor, No. 2012–307, Petition for Writ of Certiorari Before Judgment, http://sblog.s3.amazonaws.com/wp-content/uploads/2012/10/12-307-Petition.pdf.

Justice Elena Kagan had expressed her intention to recuse herself due to the fact that she had worked on the cases while she was Solicitor General.[91]

Windsor was decided on June 26, 2013, which was ten years to the day that the Court decided *Lawrence v. Texas*. The decision invalidated Section 3 of DOMA and the federal definition of marriage as a union between one man and one woman.[92] The 5–4 ruling opened the door for the first legal recognition of same-sex marriage on the federal level. Justice Anthony Kennedy authored the majority opinion that was joined by Justices Ruth Bader Ginsburg, Stephen Breyer, Sonja Sotomayor, and Elena Kagan. Despite Justice Kennedy's attempt to limit his holding to the constitutionality of the federal statute, his rationale for striking down DOMA quickly served as the basis for numerous federal court decisions invalidating state marriage prohibitions. Just as the dissents in *Windsor* had predicted,[93] the case ultimately helped to pave the way for nationwide marriage equality and *Obergefell v. Hodges*.[94]

The plaintiff was Edie Windsor, an eighty-three-year-old widow. She and her wife, Thea Spryer, had been together for over forty years before they were legally married in Canada in 2007. Their marriage was recognized under the law of the state of New York where they lived at the time of Spryer's death, but it was not recognized on the federal level due to DOMA. When Spryer died, Windsor was presented with a federal estate tax bill of over $363,000 because they were not entitled to the unlimited marital deduction; a relief provision that is designed to maximize the assets available for a surviving spouse. The clear command of DOMA limited the deduction to different-sex married couples. Windsor remarked on the restrictive statute, saying that if Thea's name had been "Theo" everything would have been different.[95]

Unlike *Massachusetts v. HHS*, Windsor argued that Section 3 of DOMA violated her individual rights, specifically those protected by the Due Process Clause and equal protection guarantees of the Fifth Amendment of the U.S. Constitution.[96] DOMA claims arose under the Fifth Amendment rather than the Fourteenth Amendment because DOMA was a federal statute. The Fifth Amendment protects individuals from overreaching federal action, whereas the Fourteenth Amendment protects individuals from state action, such as Proposition 8.[97] Windsor also argued that heightened scrutiny was the appropriate level of review for state action that involved matters of sexual orientation.

In 2011, the District Court for the Southern District of New York held that Section 3 of DOMA did not pass the rational basis test and violated Windsor's equal protection guarantees under the Due Process Clause of the Fifth Amendment.[98] The decision ordered the federal government to refund Windsor the tax that she had paid. The following year, the

91 Lyle Denniston, Kagan, *DOMA, and Recusal*, SCOUTUSBLOG, (Nov. 2, 2012) www.scotusblog.com/2012/11/kagan-doma-and-recusal/.
92 United States v. Windsor, 133 S. Ct. 2675 (2013).
93 See. e.g., *id.*, at 2709–10 (Scalia, J., dissenting).
94 Obergefell v. Hodges, 135 S.Ct. 2584 (2015).
95 Nina Totenberg, *Meet the 83-Year-Old Taking on the U.S. over Same-Sex Marriage*, NPR, Mar. 21, 2013, www.npr.org/2013/03/21/174944430/meet-the-83-year-old-taking-on-the-u-s-over-same-sex-marriage.
96 U.S. v. Windsor, No. 2012-307, Petition for Writ of Certiorari Before Judgment, http://sblog.s3.amazonaws.com/wp-content/uploads/2012/10/12-307-Petition.pdf.
97 Bollinger v. Sharpe, 347 U.S. 497 (1954).
98 Windsor v. United States, 833 F. Supp. 2d 394 (S.D.N.Y. 2012).

Second Circuit of the U.S. Court of Appeals affirmed the district court opinion on the same grounds, but also held that heightened judicial scrutiny was the appropriate level of review.[99] It was the first federal appellate court opinion that adopted the standard of heightened scrutiny for cases involving sexual orientation.[100] This represented a major accomplishment for LGBT advocates who had urged that heightened scrutiny was the appropriate standard of review for decades.[101] It also conformed to the 2011 statement issued by Attorney General Eric Holder concluding that distinctions based on sexual orientation warranted heightened judicial review.[102]

Justice Kennedy's majority opinion spoke in sweeping and sympathetic terms about the disabilities that DOMA imposed on married same-sex couples, asserting that Section 3 of DOMA "demean[ed] the couple, whose moral and sexual choices the Constitution protects."[103] Although the proponents of marriage equality applauded the majority's strong language, its opponents sharply criticized the opinion for its lack of focus and doctrinal rigor.[104] Justice Kennedy concluded that DOMA violated the equal protection guarantees of the Fifth Amendment because the statute did not serve a legitimate purpose, indicating that he applied a rational basis test, rather than heightened scrutiny. Of course, there is no need to reach the question of whether sexual orientation should trigger heightened scrutiny, if that statute fails the lowest level of constitutional scrutiny. Justice Kennedy wrote:

> The federal statute is invalid, for no legitimate purpose overcomes the purpose and effect to disparage and to injure those whom the State, by its marriage laws, sought to protect in personhood and dignity. By seeking to displace this protection and treating those persons as living in marriages less respected than others, the federal statute is in violation of the Fifth Amendment.[105]

Despite his reliance on Fifth Amendment individual protections and guarantees, federalism issues were not absent from Justice Kennedy's opinion. Before turning to his discussion of individual rights, he devoted many pages to a detailed discussion of how DOMA offended the principles of federalism, noting that "[b]y history and tradition the definition and regulation of marriage . . . has been treated as being within the authority and realm of the separate States."[106] After making a forceful argument that the federal government has long deferred to the states in matters of domestic relations, Justice Kennedy nonetheless found that it was not necessary to rule on whether DOMA was a valid "federal intrusion on

99 Windsor v. United States, 833 F. Supp. 2d 394 (S.D.N.Y. 2012); *aff'd*, 699 F.3d 169 (2d Cir. 2012).
100 David Kemp, *The End of an Unjust Law: The Second Circuit Strikes Down DOMA and Sets the Stage for Supreme Court Review*, JUSTIA, October 22, 2012, https://verdict.justia.com/2012/10/22/the-end-of-an-unjust-law.
101 High Tech Gays v. Defense Indus. Sec. Clearance Office, 895 F.2d 563, 571 (9th Cir. 1990) (sexual orientation neither a suspect nor quasi-suspect classification);
102 Eric H. Holder, Jr., *U.S. Att'y Gen., Statement of the Attorney General on Litigation Involving the Defense of Marriage Act*, OFF. ATT'Y GEN. (Feb. 23, 2011), https://web.archive.org/web/20110309162048/www.justice.gov/opa/pr/2011/February/11-ag-222.html.
103 U.S. v. Windsor, 133 S.Ct. 2675, 2694 (2013).
104 See, e.g., *id.*, at 2697–2711 (Scalia, J., dissenting)
105 Windsor, 133 S.Ct. at 2696.
106 *Id.* at 2680.

state power."[107] Instead, Justice Kennedy used the intrusive and extraordinary nature of the legislation to support his conclusion that DOMA did not further a legitimate state purpose, but rather was intended to harm and demean same-sex couples.

Chief Justice John Roberts and Justices Antonin Scalia and Samuel Alito authored dissenting opinions that were joined by Justice Clarence Thomas. Chief Justice Roberts' dissent had the most extensive and explicit discussion of federalism. He rejected the federalism concerns outlined in the majority opinion and argued that intervention in this traditional area of state authority was justified to further the federal government's interest in uniformity and stability. However, he also went to great pains to underscore the central role that respect for states' rights played in Justice Kennedy's opinion, asserting that federalism was "the dominant theme of the majority's holding." In a clear attempt to cabin in the majority's reasoning and limit its influence in future cases challenging state marriage laws, Chief Justice Roberts declared that "it is undeniable that its judgment is based on federalism."[108]

Justice Scalia's dissent was largely taken up with jurisdictional issues, but he strongly seconded Chief Justice Roberts' concern that *Windsor* would be used, improperly in his view, to overturn state marriage prohibitions. As noted above, the concerns of the dissenters proved to be well founded. *Windsor* quickly served as the justification for a rash of federal court decisions from all over the country invalidating restrictive marriage laws. At first glance it might appear paradoxical that a decision invalidating a federal intrusion on state power to define marriage would then serve as the basis for invalidating state definitions of marriage. However, Justice Kennedy's discussion of federalism contained an important proviso. He acknowledged that states have the authority to regulate in the field of domestic relations, but also warned that the regulation had to "respect the constitutional rights of persons."[109] In so doing, Justice Kennedy had set the stage for the invalidation of restrictive state marriage laws provided the courts recognized that same-sex couples had a fundamental right to marry. Lower federal courts lost no time connecting the dots.

Unanswered questions and executive action

Once *Windsor* invalidated Section 3 of DOMA, legally married same-sex couples were considered married for all federal purposes and eligible to receive federal spousal benefits, but the majority's decision had left a few important questions unanswered. It did not address Section 2 of DOMA that purported to give states the authority to refuse to recognize same-sex marriages performed in sister states, contrary to the historical practice that states recognize as valid marriages from other states.[110] Most importantly, *Windsor* did not address what law would control to determine when a same-sex couple would be considered legally married for federal purposes. Justice Scalia specifically raised this concern in his dissent in *Windsor*, noting that the majority decision left unanswered "difficult choice-of-law issues."[111] Although it was clear that a married same-sex couple who resided in a state that recognized same-sex marriage would be considered married for both state and federal purposes, it was

---

107 *Id*. at 2679.
108 *Id*. at 2697.
109 *Id*. at 2691.
110 Larry Kramer, *Same-Sex Marriage, Conflict of Laws, and the Unconstitutional Public Policy Exception*, 106 YALE L.J. 1965 (1997) (discussing Full Faith and Credit concerns raised by Section 2 of DOMA).
111 *Windsor*, 133 S. Ct. at 2708 (Scalia, J., dissenting).

not clear what would happen in the case of a legally married same-sex couple who lived in a state that did not recognize same-sex marriage. Many couples found themselves in this latter situation because they had traveled out of state or to Canada to marry. It also affected couples who had legally married in their state of residence but then later moved to a non-recognition state.

The answer to this "difficult-choice-of-law issue" hinged on whether the federal government would apply a state-of-celebration test that recognized all marriages that were valid where performed or a state-of-residence test that would only recognize those marriage considered valid by the couples' state of residence. Speaking immediately after the *Windsor* decision, President Obama indicated that his administration would apply an expansive interpretation of who counts as married.[112] However, it was not possible to apply a blanket state-of-celebration rule because certain statutory schemes, such as social security,[113] specifically referenced the law of the couples' state of domicile. In the majority of instances, however, the federal government was able to take the position that a couple would be considered married for federal purposes, provided their marriage was valid in the jurisdiction where it was performed.

Although *Windsor* resolved one type of discrepancy between federal and state law, the state-of-celebration rule created yet another. The expansive state-of-celebration rule meant that some couples would be considered married for federal purposes, but unmarried for state purposes. *Obergefell v. Hodges* resolved this disparity in 2015 when it mandated nationwide marriage equality and invalidated Section 2 of DOMA.

Obergefell v. Hodges—Marriage Equality

In *Obergefell v. Hodges*, the U.S. Supreme Court ruled in a 5–4 decision that same-sex couples have a fundamental right to marry guaranteed under the Due Process Clause and the Equal Protection Clause of the Fourteenth Amendment to the U.S. Constitution.

It invalidated state laws prohibiting same-sex marriage and further held that no state had the right to refuse to recognize a same-sex marriage performed in another state. *Obergefell* put an end to the uncertain status of same-sex marriage once and for all by imposing a nationwide rule. Married same-sex couples could now travel from state to state without fear that their relationship would be nullified when they crossed state lines. They were also entitled to federal benefits regardless of their state of residence.

The *Obergefell* decision involved six consolidated cases from four different states: Kentucky, Michigan, Ohio, and Tennessee. The plaintiffs included sixteen same-sex couples, seven of their children, a surviving same-sex spouse, an adoption agency, and a funeral director. All of the cases presented essentially the same question of law. The plaintiffs argued that the state marriage prohibitions violated the U.S. Constitution. In each case, the state either refused to grant a same-sex couple a marriage license or refused to recognize a marriage

---

112 See Lisa Rein & Steve Vogel, *Administration Says It Will Press to Provide Marriage Benefits in All States,* WASH. POST, June 27, 2013, www.washingtonpost.com/politics/administration-says-it-will-press-to-provide-marriage-benefits-in-all-states/2013/06/27/2f84d8e6-df5f-11e2-963a-72d740e88c12_story.html.

113 See, e.g., 42 U.S.C. § 416 h(1)(A)(i) (2014) (defining "spouse"); *RS 00207.001 Widow(er)'s Benefits Definitions and Requirements, POMS,* SOC. SECURITY ADMIN. (May 14, 2013), https://secure.ssa.gov/poms.nsf/lnx/0300207001.

performed in another state. The plaintiffs all prevailed at the trial court level. The different federal district courts that heard the cases all ruled in favor of the plaintiffs and invalidated the applicable state law prohibitions on same-sex marriage.[114]

The plaintiff in the lead case, Jim Obergefell, became the public face of marriage equality while the case was pending before the Court. As a widower, he had a particularly poignant story to share. When Obergfell's partner of many years, John Arthur, was diagnosed with amyotrophic lateral sclerosis (ALS), they travelled from Ohio, where they lived, to Maryland, where they could legally marry. By that time, Arthur was extremely frail and had to travel on a medical transport plane. On July 11, 2013, Obergefell and Arthur were married in Baltimore on the tarmac at the airport. Arthur died three months later, and the state of Ohio refused to list Obergefell as his spouse on Arthur's death certificate. Obergefell sued to be included as surviving spouse on his husband's death certificate and to have his husband's status at death recorded as "married."

The lower court victories came at a time when a growing number of federal courts had begun to rule in favor of marriage equality on the heels of the *Windsor* decision.[115] The *Obergefell* cases were appealed in 2014 to the U.S. Court of Appeals for the Sixth Circuit, which has jurisdiction over Kentucky, Michigan, Ohio, and Tennessee. The Sixth Circuit decision broke ranks with four other federal courts of appeal that had earlier that year found in favor of marriage equality. On November 6, 2014, a three-judge panel of the Sixth Circuit ruled 2–1 to uphold the state law marriage prohibitions.[116] The majority opinion concluded that "[n]ot one of the plaintiffs' theories . . . makes the case for consti-tutionalizing the definition of marriage and for removing the issue from the place it has been since the founding: in the hands of state voters."[117] Writing for the two-judge majority, Judge Sutton framed his opinion in terms of federalism. He identified the central question as "Who decides?" and asked, "Is this a matter that the National Constitution commits to resolution by the federal courts or leaves to the less expedient, but usually reliable, work of the state democratic processes?"[118] In particular, Judge Sutton rejected using *Windsor's* reasoning as support for marriage equality. Instead, as the Chief Justice had urged in his dissent in *Windsor*, Judge Sutton asserted that *Windsor* was principally a case about federal-ism, stating "Why was DOMA anomalous? Only federalism can supply the answer."[119] The Sixth Circuit decision provided the circuit split that commentators had suggested was necessary to get the Supreme Court to grant certiorari to a case challenging state marriage restrictions.

On June 26, 2015, two years to the day after the *Windsor* decision, the Supreme Court ruled in favor of marriage equality. Justice Kennedy again authored the majority opinion, which again was joined by Justices Ginsburg, Breyer, Sotomayor, and Kagan. Justice Kennedy's opinion cited as precedent the 1967 Supreme Court case *Loving v. Virginia*,

---

114 Obergefell v. Wymyslo, 962 F. Supp. 2d 968 (SD Ohio 2013); Bourke v. Beshear, 996 F. Supp. 2d 542 (WD Ky. 2014); Love v. Beshear, 989 F. Supp. 2d 536 (WD Ky. 2014); Henry v. Himes, 14 F. Supp. 3d 1036 (SD Ohio 2014); Tanco v. Haslam, 7 F. Supp. 3d 759 (MD Tenn. 2014); DeBoer v. Snyder, 973 F. Supp. 2d 757 (ED Mich. 2014).
115 Obergefell v. Hodges, 135 S.Ct. 2584, 2597.
116 DeBoer v. Snyder, 772 F. 3d 388 (2014).
117 *Id*. at 402–03.
118 *Id*. at 396.
119 *Id*. at 414.

which had overturned criminal anti-miscegenation laws.[120] *Obergefell* affirmed that marriage is a fundamental right guaranteed under the Due Process Clause of the Fourteenth Amendment. It then found that restrictive state marriage laws violated the Equal Protection Clause of the Fourteenth Amendment. The Court rejected the argument that the decision of whether to permit same-sex couples to marry should be left to the states, as well as the argument that allowing same-sex couples to marry would harm the institution of marriage. The majority concluded:

> No union is more profound than marriage, for it embodies the highest ideals of love, fidelity, devotion, sacrifice, and family. In forming a marital union, two people become something greater than once they were. As some of the petitioners in these cases demonstrate, marriage embodies a love that may endure even past death. It would misunderstand these men and women to say they disrespect the idea of marriage. Their plea is that they do respect it, respect it so deeply that they seek to find its fulfillment for themselves. Their hope is not to be condemned to live in loneliness, excluded from one of civilization's oldest institutions. They ask for equal dignity in the eyes of the law. The Constitution grants them that right.[121]

Chief Justice Roberts and Justices Scalia, Thomas, and Alito all authored separate dissenting opinions. Chief Justice Roberts's dissent was joined by Justices Scalia and Thomas. Not surprisingly, the Chief Justice disagreed with the majority's Due Process and Equal Protection analysis, but his dissent is most notable for its claim that the Court had overstepped its constitutional authority. According to Chief Justice Roberts, the question of marriage equality should have been left to the political process rather than decided by the Court. He also warned that the majority's opinion would have negative consequences for religious liberty and said that Justice Kennedy had unfairly maligned the opponents of marriage equality.

Central to his argument, was a strong definitional view of marriage that recalled the early marriage cases. In fact, Chief Justice Roberts' opinion discussed *Baker v. Nelson* in some detail. His primary critique, however, was based on what he perceived to be the majority's judicial activism: "By deciding this question under the Constitution, the Court removes it from the realm of democratic decision."[122] He objected strenuously to the Court's answer to the age-old question of "Who decides?", instead asserting that the political process would be the best arbiter. Specifically, with regard to federalism, Justice Roberts claimed that "The fundamental right to marry does not include a right to make a State change its definition of marriage."[123] He distinguished *Loving* with a finely parsed discussion of marriage and how same-sex marriage changes the "core definition of marriage" whereas *Loving* left that definition in place.[124]

Justice Scalia's dissent minced no words and called the majority's decision a "threat to American democracy" because it usurped the power of the people to define marriage.[125]

---

120 Loving v. Virginia, 388 U.S. 1 (1967).
121 Obergefell v. Hodges, 135 S.Ct. 2584, 2608 (2015).
122 *Id.* at 2625 (Roberts, C.J., dissenting).
123 *Id.* at 2611 (Roberts, C.J., dissenting).
124 *Id.* at 2622 (Roberts, C.J., dissenting).
125 *Id.* at 2626 (Scalia, J., dissenting).

Although the major target of his dissent was substantive due process, he discussed also federalism. Justice Scalia reminded the majority that only two years earlier they had asserted in *Windsor* that marriage was "a virtually exclusive province of the States" and the federal government had long "deferred to state law policy decision with respect to domestic relations."[126]

Justice Alito's dissent also expressly discussed federalism. After concluding that the Constitution does not answer the question of whether same-sex couples should be permitted to marry, Justice Alito praised the innovation and experimentation that is the hallmark of robust federalism. He expressed his regret that the majority chose to make a blanket determination for the entire country, noting that "The system of federalism established by our Constitution provides a way for people with different beliefs to live together in a single nation."[127] Justice Alito had a strong preference for state level variation where some states allow same-sex marriage and others prohibit it. Of course, it was exactly that type of state-level variation that placed an untenable burden on same-sex couple across this nation.

Conclusion

Marriage equality was facilitated by federalism and a strong respect for state and local variation. The early gains on the state and local level helped normalize the legal recognition of same-sex relationships while also providing meaningful protection for couples covered by the laws. These protections, however, were limited and in many respects fragile because they were not portable and were especially vulnerable to being overturned through majoritarian measures such as citizens' initiatives. They represented an imperfect, but pragmatic, institutional alternative on the road to nationwide marriage equality.

With the advent of marriage equality, the LGBT movement leapfrogged over certain important legal milestones, most notably comprehensive non-discrimination protections. In more than half of the states, individuals can be fired or evicted from their apartments or refused service at a place of public accommodation because of their sexual orientation or gender identity. Where protections are in place, opponents of LGBT rights have lobbied for the adoption of expansive religious exemptions. The next chapter in LGBT advocacy will address the lack of universal non-discrimination protections and push for broad religious exemptions. Central to this pursuit will be the question: Who decides?

The 2016 presidential election upended the expectations of many commentators regarding the direction of the country and the future of LGBT rights. Although same-sex marriage may be the settled law of the land, it remains to be seen whether the promise of marriage *equality* will be realized. The Trump administration has rolled back many of the administrative advancements in LGBT rights and has pledged support for strong religious exemptions.[128] Despite 241 original co-sponsors, the Equality Act has little chance of moving forward in the 115th Congress.[129] Many of President Trump's appointees and judicial

126 *Id.* at 2627 (Scalia, J., dissenting).
127 *Id.* at 2643 (Alito, J., dissenting).
128 See Michael D. Shear and Charlie Savage, *In One Day, Trump Administration Lands 3 Punches Against Gay Rights*, July 27, 2017.www.nytimes.com/2017/07/27/us/politics/white-house-lgbt-rights-military-civil-rights-act.html?mcubz=0&_r=0.
129 Human Rights Campaign, *The Equality Act*, May 2, 2017, www.hrc.org/resources/the-equality-act.

nominees have anti-LGBT records.[130] Justice Neil Gorsuch, who replaced Justice Antonin Scalia, has already expressed his skepticism about the scope and breadth of *Obergefell* in a dissent to a per curiam opinion involving the parental rights of same-sex married couples.[131] His appointment has not changed the balance of the Court on this issue, but his vote could become pivotal if there are other vacancies. At the federal level, these developments may delay the evolution of LGBT rights, but they cannot completely stop progress because public opinion remains decidedly in favor of strong non-discrimination protections and marriage equality.[132] And, ultimately, it is the people who decide.

130 See, e.g., Andrew Kaczynski and Paul LeBlanc, *Trump Nominee Sam Clovis: 'As Far as We Know' Homosexuality's a Choice, 'Logical' LGBT Protections Could Lead to Legalization of Pedophilia*, CNN, Aug. 21, 2017, www.cnn.com/2017/08/21/politics/kfile-sam-clovis-lgbt-comments/index.html.
131 Pavan v. Smith, 582 U. S. ____ (2017) (Gorsuch, J., dissenting).
132 GALLUP, *Gay and Lesbian Rights*, www.gallup.com/poll/1651/gay-lesbian-rights.aspx.

7 The legalization of marijuana and the interplay of federal and state laws

Sam Kamin

Marijuana regulation occupies a unique place in our federalism. Marijuana is the only substance or activity that, while entirely forbidden by federal law, is increasingly authorized, regulated, and taxed by state governments. This division of authority means that neither the state authorizing marijuana nor the federal government prohibiting it is fully able to achieve its policy preferences. The federal government can prohibit all marijuana conduct throughout the country; but, as a practical matter, it cannot prevent the states from legalizing and regulating the substance themselves. On the other hand, states experimenting with marijuana law reform remain frustrated by the continuing federal prohibition of the drug. First, states can do nothing to protect their citizens from the criminal and civil enforcement of federal law; those acting in compliance with state marijuana laws remain under constant threat of federal law enforcement. Second, even in the absence of active federal law enforcement, states' marijuana law reform is impeded by the collateral consequences of federal prohibition. In law reform states, marijuana businesses have great trouble obtaining banking, legal, and other crucial services; marijuana patients and users risk losing their jobs, parental rights, and other benefits for engaging in conduct that is authorized under state law. These collateral consequences render the status quo unstable; the states cannot fully implement marijuana law reform so long as the federal government continues to prohibit the drug.

A solution to the current marijuana regulatory standoff will require the federal and state governments to share authority cooperatively. In this discussion, Canada offers the United States a positive example. In April of 2017, Canada's Liberal government proposed a law that would legalize and regulate the drug at the federal level on July 1, 2018. The proposal would make Canada the first nation in North America and only the second in the world to legalize marijuana for all adults.[1] Under the proposed Canadian legislation, the federal government in Ottawa sets the floor for many important regulatory issues—minimum age for purchase, maximum purchase amount, etc.—while leaving the provinces free to create their own policies within that framework. The provinces can impose more stringent regulations or can, presumably, prohibit marijuana sales entirely. This model of shared responsibility provides the United States with a path out of the current stalemate over marijuana policy—if adopted in the United States, such a policy of shared governance would permit sensible experimentation with marijuana law reform in a way that will satisfy both state and federal interests.

---

1 Uruguay legalized marijuana in 2013. See John Walsh and Geoff Ramsey, *Uruguay's Drug Policy: Major Innovations, Major Challenges*, BROOKINGS INSTITUTION (2016).

The unique legal status of marijuana in the United States

The Federal Controlled Substances Act

A reaction against the perceived libertine excesses of the 1960s,[2] the federal Controlled Substances Act created a list of drugs whose recreational use was prohibited.[3] Controlled substances were divided into five categories or Schedules; while the CSA set forth rules regulating the production and sale of Schedule II through V, drugs in the most serious Schedule I were treated quite differently. These drugs, which Congress found to have no approved medical use and a high probability for abuse, were prohibited entirely under the law—they were thus illegal for all purposes whether medical or recreational.[4] Schedule I drugs cannot be prescribed by federally licensed physicians and anyone found producing or selling them is subject to harsh criminal penalties under the law.[5] Congress listed marijuana as a Schedule I drug alongside substances such as heroin and LSD while other, arguably less dangerous drugs, such as cocaine and methamphetamines are listed in Schedule II, permitting their medical use under careful supervision.[6] Although both the CSA itself[7] and marijuana's inclusion in Schedule I[8] have been repeatedly challenged in court over the years, both endure to this day.

In passing the Controlled Substances Act, Congress did not forbid the states from regulating controlled substances as well. Quite the opposite, in fact. The federal government welcomed the states to set up their own laws punishing the recreational production and sale of controlled substances. Given the vast size differences between state and federal law enforcement budgets, the enforcement of drug laws at the state and local level, rather than federal enforcement of the CSA, makes up the vast majority of drug law enforcement in the United States.[9] In the years following the passage of the CSA, the states were witting partners

---

2 As John Erlichman told a reporter, the War on Drugs was an integral part of the Nixon campaign's greater war on the American left:

> The Nixon campaign in 1968, and the Nixon White House after that, had two enemies: the antiwar left and black people. You understand what I'm saying? We knew we couldn't make it illegal to be either against the war or black, but by getting the public to associate the hippies with marijuana and blacks with heroin, and then criminalizing both heavily, we could disrupt those communities. We could arrest their leaders, raid their homes, break up their meetings, and vilify them night after night on the evening news. Did we know we were lying about the drugs? Of course we did.

Dan Baum, *Legalize It All: How to Win the War on Drugs*, HARPERS MAGAZINE, 22, April, 2016.

3 21 U.S.C. § 801, et. seq.
4 21 U.S.C. § 812(b)(2).
5 Anyone cultivating more than 1,000 plants—a not unusual number in a state that has legalized marijuana—is subject to a term of imprisonment of between 10 years and life. 21 U.S.C. § 841(b)(1)(A)(vii).
6 21 U.S.C. § 812(c).
7 See, e.g, Gonzales v. Raich, 545 U.S. 1 (2005) (rejecting a Commerce Clause challenge to the regulation of marijuana grown at home for personal use).
8 See, e.g., Americans for Safe Access v. DEA, 706 F.3d 438 (2013) (rejecting, under the deferential "arbitrary and capricious" standard a challenge to the classification of marijuana as a Schedule I drug.).
9 See, e.g., Alex Kreit, *Beyond the Prohibition Debate: Thoughts on Federal Drug Laws in an Age of State Reforms*, 13 CHAPMAN L. REV. 555 (2010) ("In 2008 there were a total of only 626 simple marijuana possession cases disposed of in federal court. To put this number in perspective, there were approximately 754,233 arrests for marijuana possession nationwide in 2008.").

in the prohibition of marijuana, with every state passing a marijuana provision forbidding the production and sale of the drug for any purpose. Over time, however, public opinion moved away from prohibition[10] and many state and local governments lowered criminal penalties for marijuana and chose to deprioritize marijuana law enforcement.[11]

The reasons for the growing unhappiness with marijuana prohibition is difficult to pinpoint precisely.[12] However, one important motivator was surely a disconnect in the minds of many between the formal classification of marijuana as a heavily addictive drug without medical benefits and the perception many had of marijuana as a relatively benign substance that provided pain relief and appetite stimulation for critically ill patients. In addition, the costs of marijuana law enforcement were high and often born unequally, with historically underrepresented groups suffering far more arrest, conviction, and imprisonment even though studies consistently showed that they were no more likely to use the drug than were whites.[13]

These trends came together in a push in several states to authorize the use of marijuana for medical purposes. In 1996, California passed Proposition 215, becoming the first state in the country to implement a medical marijuana law. Under Proposition 215, doctors could recommend marijuana for the treatment of certain enumerated conditions or for "for any other illness for which marijuana provides relief" and medical marijuana patients and their caregivers were exempted from the state's laws prohibiting the cultivation or possession of the drug.[14] However, it is important to understand that Proposition 215 did not legalize marijuana under state law, even for patients and caregivers. Marijuana production and sale remained criminal under in California, but medical patients and their designated caregivers had an affirmative defense that could be asserted at trial. Furthermore, and more fundamentally, federal law continued to prohibit all marijuana conduct regardless of state law to the contrary. The United States Supreme Court made clear that compliance with state medical marijuana laws was not a defense in a *federal* prosecution under the Controlled Substances Act.[15] Thus, while Proposition 215 provided some protection under state law for marijuana patients and caregivers, it provided no protections whatsoever vis-à-vis federal law.

Despite the half-loaf that medical marijuana offered those unhappy with state marijuana prohibition—keeping marijuana criminal for most adults while providing only an affirmative defense to those who could assert a medical need—it gained popularity in the years that followed, principally in those states in the American West that used the voter-initiative

10 Support for the legalization of marijuana moved from just 12% at the time of the Controlled Substances Act to 60% today. Gallup Polling, Support for Legal Marijuana Use Up to 60% in US, October 19, 2016, www.gallup.com/poll/196550/support-legal-marijuana.aspx

11 See, e.g., Dana Graham, *Decriminalization of Marijuana: An Analysis of the Laws of the United States and the Netherlands*, 23 LOYOLA L.A. INT'L & COMP. L. Rev. 229, 322–23 (2001) (describing decriminalization efforts in the United States).

12 *Id*. at 308–20 (discussion the rationales supporting and opposing marijuana prohibition).

13 See, ACLU, MARIJUANA IN BLACK AND WHITE 4 (2013) (Reporting that "on average, a Black person is 3.73 times moer likely to be arrested for marijuana possession than a white person, even though Blacks and whites use marijuana at similar rates.").

14 Because marijuana remained illegal under federal law, doctors could still not *prescribe* marijuana. The Ninth Circuit in *Conant v. Walters*, 309 F. 3d 629 (2002) held a prohibition on a doctor recommending a treatment to her patient would run afoul of the first amendment.

15 US v. Oakland Cannabis Buyers' Cooperative, 532 U.S. 483 (2001) (holding that there is no medical necessity exception to the Controlled Substances Act).

process. By 2000, a handful of states had followed California's example and exempted medical patients and caregivers from their state marijuana prohibitions, all of enacting their medical marijuana provisions through voter initiatives.[16] Because marijuana remained illegal under federal law, however, caregivers generally kept a low profile, helping a few patients at a time grow marijuana to treat their illnesses.[17]

Beginning late in the first decade of the 2000s, however, entrepreneurs in California, Colorado and elsewhere became bolder, pushing the definition of caregiving to its logical limits (and perhaps beyond). Medical marijuana "dispensaries" came out of the shadows and establishing storefront shops and advertising in the local press their willingness to provide medical marijuana to anyone with a doctor's recommendation.[18] Larger dispensaries started serving hundreds or even thousands of patients with little oversight from state or local authorities.[19] Legalization opponents and law enforcement officials objected that such commercial activity was inconsistent with the limited nature of state medical marijuana provisions; most laws implementing medical marijuana did not explicitly authorize any form of commercial distribution.[20]

With marijuana remaining illegal under federal law, and with little textual support for their actions, what emboldened these marijuana entrepreneurs to make clear to the public (and law enforcement) that they were selling drugs in clear violation of federal law? Their newfound courage was largely a result of signals from the Obama administration that it would be taking a less punitive approach to marijuana than previous administrations. As a presidential candidate in 2008, Senator Barack Obama hinted that the enforcement of federal marijuana laws would not be a major priority of his administration and early indications from his administration seemed to make good on this promise. In October of 2009, Deputy Attorney General David Ogden released a memorandum directed to United States Attorneys around the country advising them how to enforce federal marijuana law in those states that had authorized marijuana for medical purposes. Although the Ogden Memo was careful to point out that marijuana remained illegal throughout the country,

---

16 Alaska, Colorado, Hawaii, Maine, Nevada, Oregon, and Washington State all followed California's example. For a complete timeline of marijuana law reform in the United States, see NORML, *Marijuana Map*, http://norml.org/states, last visited August 15, 2017.

17 See, e.g., William Breathes, *The History of Cannabis in Colorado . . . Or How the State Went to Pot*, WESTWORD, November 1, 2012, www.westword.com/news/the-history-of-cannabis-in-coloradoor-how-the-state-went-to-pot-5118475. ("For nearly a decade after the passage of Amendment 20, the medical marijuana program in this state was small, mostly underground, and run by a few pioneering caregivers.").

18 See, e.g., Jeff Miron, *Marijuana Policy in Colorado*, CATO INSTITUTE WORKING PAPER (2014), https://object.cato.org/sites/cato.org/files/pubs/pdf/working-paper-24_2.pdf ("In early 2009, Colorado . . . witnessed an explosion of new medical marijuana patient applications and the emergence of over 250 medical marijuana dispensaries, which were legally permitted to operate as 'caregivers.' One dispensary claimed to be a primary caregiver for 1,200 patients. The state had few ways of responding to this development and took little action against the commercial operations. By the end of 2009, new patient applications had soared from around 6,000 across the first seven years to an additional 38,000 in just one year."

19 Kate McLean, *The Legal but Largely Unregulated World of Pot Merchants Thrives*, NEW YORK TIMES, June 5, 2010 ("Harborside Health Center in Oakland is the largest medical marijuana store in the world—it shares 52,000 registered members with a sister location in San Jose.").

20 See, e.g., Tim Hoover, *AG Suthers Says Colorado Can Tax Medical Marijuana*, DENVER POST, November 16, 2009 (quoting Colorado Attorney General John Suthers as stating that there is an argument that Colorado's Amendment XX did not authorize medical-marijuana dispensaries).

it informed U.S. Attorneys that the pursuit of federal enforcement "priorities should not focus federal resources in your States on individuals whose actions are in clear and unambiguous compliance with existing state laws providing for the medical use of marijuana."[21] Despite its cautionary language,[22] the Ogden memo was taken by activists and cannabis entrepreneurs alike as the promised major shift in federal policy away from marijuana law enforcement. Although a subsequent memo issued two years later reiterated the cautionary tone of the Ogden memo,[23] commercial activity in medical marijuana states continued to flourish.[24] In some states, like Colorado, extensive rules were put in place to regulate the nascent industry; in others, like California, regulation was left to the local level creating a more anarchic market.

As the number of states adopting medical marijuana initiatives continued to grow, some contemplated the next logical step in marijuana law reform: a push to make marijuana legal for all adults, not just those who could demonstrate a medical need. In 2010, such a measure narrowly failed in California in the face of significant federal opposition.[25] However, with more carefully drafted initiatives and a more favorable presidential year electorate, Colorado and Washington State passed initiatives in 2012 legalizing the possession of small amounts of marijuana for all adults (so-called adult-use or recreational marijuana legalization).[26] Although adult-use initiatives follow on the heels of and build on the successes of medical marijuana initiatives, they are structurally quite different. Adult-use laws made legal the possession of small amounts of marijuana by adults as well as, in most states, the home production of small amounts of marijuana. States adopting adult-use laws also charged their legislatures with developing a regulatory regime to license and tax the commercial production and sale of marijuana for adults.

This promise of a tightly regulated and taxed marijuana market became an important part of the appeal to voters of recreational legalization. While the medical marijuana movement had been driven largely by compassion for those ill-served by traditional medicine, other

21 David W. Ogden, *Memorandum for Selected United States Attorneys Re: Investigations and Prosecutions in States Authorizing the Medical Use of Marijuana*, October 19, 2009, www.justice.gov/archives/opa/blog/memorandum-selected-united-state-attorneys-investigations-and-prosecutions-states.

22 *Id.*, at 2 ("[T]his memorandum does not alter in any way the Department's authority to enforce federal law, including laws prohibiting the manufacture, production, distribution, possession, or use of marijuana on federal property. This guidance regarding resource allocation does not "legalize" marijuana or provide a legal defense to a violation of federal law, nor is it intended to create any privileges, benefits, or rights, substantive or procedural, enforceable by any individual, party or witness in any administrative, civil, or criminal matter. Nor does clear and unambiguous compliance with state law or the absence of one or all of the above factors create a legal defense to a violation of the Controlled Substances Act.").

23 James Cole, *Memorandum for United States Attorneys Re: Guidance Regarding the Ogden Memo in Jurisdictions Seeking to Authorize Marijuana for Medical Use*, June 29, 2011, www.justice.gov/sites/default/files/oip/legacy/2014/07/23/dag-guidance-2011-for-medical-marijuana-use.pdf ("The Ogden Memorandum was never intended to shield such activities from federal enforcement action and prosecution, even where those activities purport to comply with state law. Persons who are in the business of cultivating, selling or distributing marijuana, and those who knowingly facilitate such activities, are in violation of the Controlled Substances Act, regardless of state law.").

24 It was widely reported in early 2010 that Denver had more marijuana dispensaries than Starbucks. See Christopher N. Osher, *As Dispensaries Pop Up, Denver May Be Pot Capital, USA*, DENVER POST, January 2, 2010.

25 See, e.g., John Hoeffel, Youth Vote Falters, Prop. 19 Falls Short, LA Times, November 3, 2010.

26 See, e.g, Jack Healy, *Voters Ease Marijuana Laws in 2 States, but Legal Questions Remain*, NEW YORK TIMES, November 7, 2012.

public policy outcomes soon came to the fore as the emphasis shifted to adult use. In addition to arguing that marijuana was a safer alternative to alcohol and should be regulated as such,[27] adult use advocates often emphasized the failure of decades of marijuana prohibition to extinguish demand for the drug, a demand that was then being satisfied entirely by criminal gangs and international drug cartels. Creating regulated markets for the production and distribution of marijuana thus promised voters a double fiscal win: On the one hand, less money would be spent on law enforcement to imprison people for conduct that many saw as relatively benign. On the other hand, legalization would produce revenue by taxing an industry that had traditionally operated entirely outside the law. In other words, legalization promised that both that less money would be spent and that more revenue would be generated.

Given the Obama administration's warnings regarding the limited scope of federal acquiescence, however, there remained great uncertainty regarding whether these new regulatory regimes would be allowed to proceed without federal interference. The federal government had grudgingly accepted *medical* marijuana laws in the states; there was justifiable concern on the part of state regulators and would-be licensees that the Obama Administration would take steps to prevent the states from implementing the taxation and regulation regimes that were now a necessary part of adult use legalization. After a long period of uncertainty and anticipation, the federal government eventually acquiesced to rapidly changing events on the ground, taking an explicit hands-off policy with regard to all manner of marijuana law reform in the states. A third enforcement memorandum issued by the Justice Department, the so-called Cole Memo, stated that so long as the states regulated marijuana in a way that comported with eight federal enforcement priorities, the states would be allowed to exercise this leadership through regulation rather than prohibition:

> In jurisdictions that have enacted laws legalizing marijuana in some form and that have also implemented strong and effective regulatory and enforcement systems to control the cultivation, distribution, sale, and possession of marijuana, conduct in compliance with those laws and regulations is less likely to threaten the federal priorities set forth above. Indeed, a robust system may affirmatively address those priorities by, for example, implementing effective measures to prevent diversion of marijuana outside of the regulated system and to other states, prohibiting access to marijuana by minors, and replacing an illicit marijuana trade that funds criminal enterprises with a tightly regulated market in which revenues are tracked and accounted for. In those circumstances, consistent with the traditional allocation of federal-state efforts in this area, enforcement of state law by state and local law enforcement and regulatory bodies should remain the primary means of addressing marijuana—related activity.[28]

Buoyed by this newfound clarity in federal enforcement policy, Colorado and Washington State rolled out their adult-use regulatory regimes in 2014 and for the first time adults could buy marijuana from a state-licensed store without a doctor's recommendation. That same

---

27 Both Amendment 64 in Colorado and Proposition 64 in Colorado were pitched to voters as initiatives to regulate marijuana like alcohol.

28 James M. Cole, *Memorandum for All United States Attorneys Re: Guidance Regarding Marijuana Enforcement*, August 29, 2013, www.justice.gov/iso/opa/resources/3052013829132756857467.pdf.

year, the states of Oregon and Alaska as well as the District of Columbia[29] adopted adult-use laws based on the Colorado and Washington model; four more states—California, Nevada, Maine, and Massachusetts followed in 2016. In addition, a total of 29 states plus the District of Columbia have approved medical marijuana laws. Marijuana is thus available in one form or another in more than half the states and to a super-majority of the nation's population.

As more and more states develop regimes to tax and regulate marijuana for adults, marijuana production and sale has become big business. Washington and Colorado, the first two states to implement adult-use regulations both sold over $1 billion in marijuana products in 2016[30] and with the massive state of California—with its huge population and 50-year tradition of cannabis growing—coming online in early 2018, the size of the industry will make another quantum leap. As promised, state revenues attributable to marijuana have also increased: Marijuana activists trumpeted in July 2017 the fact that Colorado had passed more than $500 million in state tax revenue.[31]

An untenable compromise

Despite all of marijuana law reform's advances over the last twenty years, there remains a fundamental limit to the states' experimentation with alternatives to marijuana prohibition. So long as marijuana remains illegal under federal law, a state's desire to engage in marijuana law reform necessarily remains unrealized. This is so because while a state can remove its own marijuana prohibitions and, as I will explain more fully below, can refuse to participate in the enforcement of federal marijuana prohibition, it can do very little to prevent the enforcement of that same federal prohibition within its borders. Federal law remains the supreme law of the land and all of those throughout the country, even those complying with state law authorizing marijuana conduct, remain subject to the CSA's terms.[32] Thus, the decision of the Obama administration not to contest the states' decisions to implement marijuana law reform is best seen as a truce between the state and federal government rather than as a permanent, forward-going solution.

Like any statement of prosecutorial intent, the Ogden and Cole Memoranda that issued from the Obama Justice Department are nothing more than statements of prosecutorial grace; they are valid only until they are amended or withdrawn by the Justice Department. We can see this most clearly in the fact that the Obama Justice Department announced

---

29 Interestingly, the District of Columbia, which approved adult use legalization in 2014, has been blocked by federal legislation from instituting a regulatory regime. Congress, which controls the city's budget, has precluded it from spending money to implement a regulatory regime for medical marijuana. Section 809 of the Consolidated and Further Continuing Appropriations Act of 2015, Pub. L 113–235 (Dec. 16, 2014) ("None of the Federal funds contained in this Act may be used to enact or carry out any law, rule, or regulation to legalize or otherwise reduce penalties associated with the possession, use, or distribution of any schedule I substance under the Controlled Substances Act (21 U.S.C.§ 801 et seq.) or any tetrahydrocannabinols derivative.").

30 See, e.g., Reid Wilson, *Legal Pot Sales Top $1 Billion in 2016*, THE HILL, February 10, 2017, http://thehill.com/homenews/state-watch/318976-legal-pot-sales-top-1-billion-in-2-states (stating that Colorado exceeded $1.3 billion in 2016 and that Washington State had sold $984 million with several months left in the fiscal year).

31 Katelyn Newman, *Milestoned: Colorado Pot Tax Revenue Surpasses $500M*, US NEWS, July 20, 2017.

32 See Oakland Cannabis Buyers' Cooperative, *supra* note 15. But see McIntosh, *infra* note 34.

three different positions (or clarifications of positions) with regard to marijuana in just four years. Obviously now that the Obama administration has left office, there is nothing to stop the Trump Justice Department from repealing those memoranda and replacing them with another, more punitive one.

Aware of that possibility, Congress has taken action to try to give the Obama administration's hands-off enforcement policy the power of law. A rider to a spending bill, the so-called Rohrbacher-Farr Amendment, first passed in 2014, prohibits the Department of Justice from using money allocated to it to "prevent" with medical marijuana states from implementing their laws.[33] Although the language of the amendment is ambiguous, at least one federal court has read it as forbidding the department from prosecuting those acting in compliance with state medical marijuana rules.[34] However, this amendment has passed Congress only as a rider to an appropriations bill that must be renewed each year; it has not been written into law in a way that grants predictability to the states.[35] Furthermore, it applies only to medical marijuana laws; even under Rohrbacher-Farr, the eight states adopting adult-use marijuana laws continue to exist solely at the whims of federal prosecutors.

More fundamentally, however, it is important to see that even if the Rohrbacher-Farr Amendment or the Cole Memo were written into law, even if the federal government made an enforceable promise not to enforce federal law against those in compliance with state marijuana regulations, not even *that* would free the states' hands to develop their own marijuana policies. That is because, so long as marijuana remains illegal under federal law, everyone who engages in any marijuana conduct puts themselves at risk *even if federal marijuana laws are never enforced at all*.

To see why, consider the case of Brandon Coats in Colorado. Coats was an employee at Dish Network and a quadriplegic who used medical marijuana to control seizures.[36] Although there was no allegation that Coats was ever impaired at work, he was fired when he tested positive for the drug as part of Dish's drug testing policy. Coats objected that he was acting in compliance with state law and that he was therefore protected by a state statute which precludes termination for engaging in lawful off-duty conduct; no allegation was ever made that his use of medical marijuana violated Colorado law. However, the Colorado Supreme Court unanimously concluded that he was not protected by the lawful off-duty conduct statute because his conduct was not "lawful":

> Nothing in the language of the statute limits the term "lawful" to state law. Instead, the term is used in its general, unrestricted sense, indicating that a "lawful" activity is that

---

33 Consolidated and Further Continuing Appropriations Act, 2015 § 538, 128 Stat. 2130 (2014) ("None of the funds made available in this Act to the Department of Justice may be used, with respect to [enumerated medical marijuana states] to prevent such States from implementing their own State laws that authorize the use, distribution, possession, or cultivation of medical marijuana.").

34 US v. McIntosh, 833 F.3d 1163, 1179 (9th Cir. 2016) (determining that under the Amendment, the government must prove that the defendants' "conduct was completely authorized by state law, by which we mean that they strictly complied with all relevant conditions imposed by state law on the use, distribution, possession, and cultivation of medical marijuana.").

35 The rider passed the Senate on July 27, 2017 but it is still unclear whether it will be approved by the House. See Jacob Sullum, *Rejecting Sessions' Plea, Senate Panel Votes to Protect Medical Marijuana*, Reason.com, July 27, 2017, http://reason.com/blog/2017/07/27/rejecting-sessions-plea-senate-panel-vot.

36 Coats v. Dish Network, 350 P.2d 849, 850 (Col. 2015).

which complies with applicable "law," including state and federal law. We therefore decline Coats's invitation to engraft a state law limitation onto the statutory language.[37]

Thus, even though every enforcement statement issued by the Department of Justice would have insulated Coats' marijuana use from federal prosecution, even though there was never any thought that he might be arrested for using marijuana to treat his symptoms, he was subject to termination for using marijuana as permitted by state law.

Other consequences for marijuana consumers can be just as profound. For example, using marijuana, even in compliance with state and local law, can put one's parental rights at risk.[38] Because marijuana use is still criminal activity, even if authorized by state law, courts have terminated or otherwise curtailed parental rights when it was demonstrated that one or more of the parents were using marijuana for medical purposes. Marijuana use can also impact one's immigration status or ability to travel to the United States. Consider the case of "Claudia."[39] Attempting to travel to the U.S. from her native Chile to meet her American boyfriend, Claudia was asked by customs agents where she had traveled on a previous trip to the United States. When she listed Colorado among other states, her phone was taken from her and the agents discovered photographs of a marijuana store. When she admitted she had sampled marijuana on that visit, she was detained for twelve hours and ultimately placed on a return flight to Santiago; she can no longer enter the United States. Though she was never charged with any crime, her admission to conduct that she considered legal may have permanently lost her right to visit the United States.[40]

For marijuana businesses (and their state regulators) the consequences are less drastic but no less profound. The most obvious example is banking. Because banks are regulated at the federal level, they are often reluctant to do business with the marijuana industry; as a result, businesses must either work entirely in cash or else engage in subterfuges to obtain banking services. This is far more than an inconvenience for a few marijuana businesses. Forcing a billion-dollar industry to operate nearly entirely in cash is bad public policy. It makes businesses and their employees ready targets of crime as robbers understand that they are likely to discover large volumes of cash. But the problem runs deeper still. State government officials are charged with regulating and taxing marijuana businesses and this task is made significantly more difficult by the inability of licensed businesses to obtain even the most basic of banking services. Given that several of the federal enforcement priorities set forth in the Cole Memo deal with the close supervision of marijuana businesses—preventing organized crime from infiltrating licensed businesses, preventing the diversion of marijuana out of state, etc.—the fact that marijuana remains a cash business creates a proverbial

37 *Id.* at 852.
38 See, e.g., Marka B. Fleming and Gwendolyn McFadden-Wade, *The Unthinkable Choice: The Constitutional Due Process Right to Parent or the Legal Right to Legal Right to Use Medical Marijuana*, 25 B.U. PUB. INT. L.J. 299 (2015) (giving examples and concluding: "qualified parents have been forced to choose between parenting without the use and medical benefits of medical marijuana and potentially losing custody of their children if they are found using the drug.").
39 Joel Warner, *Marijuana Is Legal in Colorado—But Only If You're a US Citizen*, WESTWORD, September 13, 2016, www.westword.com/news/marijuana-is-legal-in-colorado-but-only-if-youre-a-us-citizen-8304837.
40 For a more detailed discussion of the ancillary consequences of marijuana's federal prohibition see Chemerinsky, et al., *Cooperative Federalism and Marijuana Regulation*, infra note 70 at 97–100.

catch-22. Federal law makes banking impossible which makes compliance with federal priorities far more difficult.[41]

These are just two examples, but many others could be cited. The important takeaway is that there is something fundamentally unstable in the fact that the states continue to license (and draw revenue from) conduct that is completely prohibited under federal law. Although a truce currently exists between the state and federal governments, it does not offer a permanent solution to the current standoff. As the states seem unlikely to throw up their hands and abandon marijuana law reform any time soon, the question arises what if anything the federal government might do to break the impasse.

What happens next?

Many in the marijuana law reform movement were looking forward to 2016 as the year in which policy tipped irretrievably away from prohibition at the federal level. With the passage of referenda on November 8, 2016, marijuana became legal for adults in four new states, bringing to eight the number of states allowing marijuana possession by all adults. In addition, by early 2017, initiatives and legislative enactments created a majority of 29 states permitting marijuana to be obtained with a doctor's recommendation.[42] In the face of such building momentum, it seemed only a matter of time before marijuana's classification as a Schedule I drug came to an end.

Of course, this enthusiasm was significantly dampened by what happened at the top of the ticket on election night 2016. Although Hillary Clinton was hardly perceived as a friend of the burgeoning marijuana industry, Donald Trump's election has been seen as a significant setback to law reform. His selection of 2016 of Jeff Sessions to be his attorney general confirmed law reformers' worst fears. Sessions is an unreconstructed drug warrior with a long-standing antagonism toward marijuana and its use.[43] Early indications from the new Department of Justice hinted at a major policy change in how federal marijuana law is enforced.[44] Yet six months into the new administration no change in policy has yet manifested;

---

41 As I have documented elsewhere, there are a number of other significant hurdles facing the industry. See, e.g., Sam Kamin and Eli Wald, *Medical Marijuana Lawyers: Outlaws or Crusaders*, 91 OREGON L. REV. 869 (2013) (detailing the difficulty marijuana businesses have in obtaining legal counsel); Sam Kamin and Viva Moffat, *Trademark Laundering, Useless Patents, and Other IP Challenges for the Marijuana Industry*, 73 WASH. & LEE L, REV. 217 (2016) (detailing the difficulty marijuana businesses have in enforcing intellectual property rights).

42 See, e.g., Governing, *State Marijuana Laws in 2017 Map*, www.governing.com/gov-data/state-marijuana-laws-map-medical-recreational.html.

43 See, e.g., James Higdon, *Jeff Sessions' Coming War on Legal Marijuana*, POLITICO MAGAZINE, December 5, 2016, www.politico.com/magazine/story/2016/12/jeff-sessions-coming-war-on-legal-marijuana-214501 ("By nominating Senator Jefferson Beauregard Sessions III for attorney general, President-elect Donald J. Trump is about to put into the nation's top law enforcement job a man with a long and antagonistic attitude toward marijuana. As a U.S. Attorney in Alabama in the 1980s, Sessions said he thought the KKK 'were OK until I found out they smoked pot.' In April, he said, 'Good people don't smoke marijuana,' and that it was a 'very real danger' that is not the kind of thing that ought to be legalized.'").

44 See, e.g., Lydia Wheeler, *Trump's DOJ Gears up for a Crackdown on Marijuana*, THE HILL, July 23, 2017, http://thehill.com/regulation/administration/343218-trumps-doj-gears-up-for-a-crackdown-on-marijuana ("The Trump administration is readying for a crackdown on marijuana users under Attorney General Jeff Sessions. President Trump's Task Force on Crime Reduction and Public Safety, led by

while other Obama executive orders were reversed in the early days of the Trump administration, no sweeping policy pronouncement has yet issued with regard to marijuana. As of August 1, 2017, the Cole Memorandum remains the latest word from the federal government regarding federal enforcement priorities.

While we cannot know for sure why the Trump administration has not (yet) sought to undo marijuana law reform in the states, at least part of the explanation must be the practical and legal limitations on the federal power to do so. The most obvious practical consideration is that marijuana law reform enjoys significant support throughout the United States. This manifests in many ways. First, public opinion polls continue to show strong support marijuana law reform: 60 percent of Americans now support full legalization, a number that sat at just 12 percent when the CSA was passed.[45] Even larger majorities support medical marijuana laws—more than four in five adults nationwide favor legalizing marijuana for medical use, up from three out of four in 2011.[46] What is more, the generational divide on marijuana legalization indicates that things should only improve for marijuana law reformers: The younger the group surveyed, the more likely they are to support marijuana law reform.[47]

Furthermore, marijuana legalization is no longer simply a Western, initiative-driven movement. Legislatures in Ohio, Pennsylvania, and New Jersey and elsewhere have adopted medical marijuana by statute. Marijuana law reform has taken hold throughout the Northeast and even now into the Deep South. What is more, medical marijuana is now authorized in nearly every swing state in the nation; of the ten most closely contested states in the 2016 presidential election (Michigan, New Hampshire, Wisconsin, Pennsylvania, Florida, Minnesota, Nevada, Maine, North Carolina, and Arizona)[48] only Wisconsin and North Carolina lack laws permitting medical marijuana. In a world of scarce enforcement resources, taking on an issue that has tremendous national support and that has been passed in nearly all of the states that President Trump would need to win in order to obtain reelection would seem like a poor strategic choice. Governors in marijuana law reform states, particularly those deriving significant revenue from taxed adult sales, are likely to push back hard against any federal policy that takes that revenue off the books.

But if the Trump/Sessions administration were to move against the marijuana law reform in the states despite all of these political concerns, how would it do so? One of the easiest ways—which would involve no cooperation with coordinate branches of government— would be to simply begin enforcing federal marijuana laws against those violating it in the states. While this might be the most straight-forward option, it is not without its practical problems as well. As we have seen, the share of drug law enforcement carried out by the

Sessions, is expected to release a report next week that criminal justice reform advocates fear will link marijuana to violent crime and recommend tougher sentences for those caught growing, selling and smoking the plant.").

45 Gallup Poll, *Support for Legal Marijuana Use up to 60%*, October 19, 2016, www.gallup.com/poll/196550/support-legal-marijuana.aspx.

46 Harris Poll, *Increasing Percentages of Americans Are Ready for Legal Marijuana*, May 7, 2015, www.theharrispoll.com/health-and-life/Americans-Ready-for-Legal-Marijuana.html.

47 See Gallup, *supra* note 10 (showing that while only 45% of those 55 and older support marijuana legalization, 61% of those between 35 and 54 support such action and 77% of adults under 35 do).

48 David Catanese, *The 10 Closest States in the 2016 Election*, US News & World Report, November 14, 2016.

federal government is tiny. Thus, it is unrealistic to assume that the DEA and the Department of Justice would be able to arrest, prosecute, and imprison all or even many of those acting in violation of federal law in the states. Colorado, for example, has more than 100,000 people on its medical marijuana rolls,[49] more than 1,000 marijuana stores, and nearly 1,500 marijuana cultivation facilities.[50] By contrast, in 2012 there were just 6,963 marijuana arrests made by the DEA *in the entire country*.[51] Arresting even a small fraction of those violating federal marijuana laws in a single state, therefore, would require a vast expansion of the enforcement resources of the federal government.

Of course, the arrest, prosecution, and incarceration of the entire marijuana industry (or even of a substantial number of its customers) would not be necessary to break the back of the nascent industry. A few strategic, high profile enforcement actions might well be enough to encourage the rest of the industry to close up shop. In the same way that the federal government cannot conceivably remove the estimated 11 million individuals in the country without authorization, the federal government cannot prosecute all of those in the 28 states permitting marijuana for some adults. But, as with immigration, full enforcement is not needed to achieve federal goals; a well-settled fear of enforcement can prove an effective deterrent sufficient to change the conduct of vulnerable groups.[52]

Given resource scarcity, the government might choose to employ an enforcement strategy based on the forfeiture of assets traceable to violations of the Controlled Substances Act.[53] Attorney General Sessions has expressed an increased willingness to use asset forfeiture to achieve the goals of the Department of Justice.[54] An asset forfeiture proceeding is far easier and less resource-intensive for the government than is a prosecution—it requires only proof to a preponderance of the evidence that the property was used in or derived from illegal conduct. In the case of warehouses filled with marijuana, that would be a very easy showing for the government to make. As with criminal prosecutions, the government would not need to target all or even most marijuana businesses in order to have a significant impact on behaviors.

But there is an even less costly, and less overtly confrontational, means for the federal government to shut down state-licensed marijuana businesses. Before ultimately settling on a non-interference policy, the Obama Justice Department sent cease and desist letters to

49 Colorado Department of Public Health and the Environment, *Medical Marijuana Registry Program Statistics*, June 2017, www.colorado.gov/pacific/sites/default/files/CHED_MMR_Monthly_Report-JUNE_2017.pdf.

50 Colorado Department of Revenue, *Marijuana Enforcement Division Licensed Medical and Retail Marijuana Business* as of July 3, 2017, www.colorado.gov/pacific/enforcement/med-licensed-facilities.

51 US Dept. of Justice, Bureau of Justice Statistics, *Federal Justice Statistics, 2011–12* (2015).

52 For more on the parallels between immigration and marijuana enforcement, see Sam Kamin, *Prosecutorial Discretion in the Context of Immigration and Marijuana Law Reform: The Search for a Limiting Principle*, 14 OHIO ST. J. CRIM. L. 183 (2016).

53 The civil forfeiture provisions of the Controlled Substances Act are extraordinarily broad. The CSA permits the forfeiture of any property used to violate the CSA or ay property "constituting, derived from, or traceable to, any proceeds obtained directly or indirectly" from a violation of the CSA. 18 USC § 981.

54 See Department of Justice, Office of Public Affairs, *Attorney General Sessions Issues Policy and Guidelines on Federal Adoptions of Assets Seized by State or Local Law Enforcement*, July 19, 2017, www.justice.gov/opa/pr/attorney-general-sessions-issues-policy-and-guidelines-federal-adoptions-assets-seized-state.

several marijuana businesses in Colorado[55] and Washington State[56] indicating that they were operating within a thousand feet of a school and had to shut down. What is more, the letters went both to dispensaries and to their property owners. In this way, the dispensaries' landlords were essentially converted into attorneys general, incentivized to remove offending drug dealers from their properties through the threat of asset forfeiture. It is easy to see the appeal of such letters; compared to formal enforcement actions, such warning letters can prove an incredibly cost-effective way of inducing compliance with federal law. Sessions' Justice Department might utilize such letters as an efficient means of bringing the marijuana industry to heel.

All of these approaches—criminal enforcement, civil asset forfeiture, cease and desist letters—are means of targeting the marijuana industry that has arisen in law reform states. But what if the federal government wanted to strike deeper at marijuana law reform? Is there a way for the federal government to undo not just the marijuana industry that has sprung up under state law, but the underlying state laws themselves? That is, could a Justice Department bent on rolling back the clock of law reform, challenge both the regulations under which states are licensing violations of the CSA and even state marijuana legalization laws? Here, the picture becomes considerably murkier.

What is clear, however, is that the administration cannot force the states to participate in marijuana prohibition if they choose not to do so. While *Gonzales v. Raich* affirmed the power of the federal government to prohibit marijuana,[57] the anti-commandeering principle implicit in the Tenth Amendment to the Constitution prevents the feds from mandating action by an apparatus of state government.[58] For example, the Supreme Court has struck down a federal statute that required state law enforcement officials to run background checks on those seeking to purchase handguns.[59] Although Congress is authorized under the Commerce Clause to regulate the sale of handguns,[60] and may presumably require federal agents to conduct background checks on those seeking to purchase them, it cannot require the states to do that work on the federal government's behalf. Similarly, the federal government cannot require the state legislatures to enact (or fail to enact) a statute prohibiting marijuana or to regulate marijuana in a particular way.[61]

55 On January 12, 2012, United States Attorney John Walsh sent letters to 23 Colorado dispensaries indicating that they were operating within 1,000 feet of school property and that their assets were subject to forfeiture unless they desisted operations within 45 days. Heath Urie, *Feds Threaten to Shut Down 23 Colorado Marijuana Shops near Schools*, DENVER POST, January 12, 2012; *Letter from John F. Walsh, United States Attorney*, dated January 12, 2012, http://extras.mnginteractive.com/live/media/site21/2012/0112/20120112_023542_01-12-12%20dispensary%20redacted.pdf

56 See Levi Pulkkinen, *DEA Targets Marijuana Dispensaries in School Zones*, SEATTLE POST INTELLIGENCER, August 23, 2012.

57 See note 7, *supra*.

58 See generally, Robert A. Mikos, *On the Limits of Supremacy: Medical Marijuana and the States' Overlooked Power to Legalize Federal Crime*, 62 VAND. L. REV. 1421 (2009).

59 Printz v. United States, 521 U.S. 898 (1997).

60 At least so long as there is a demonstrated nexus to interstate commerce. See, e.g., Lopez v. United States, 514 U.S. 549 (1995) (upholding a Commerce Clause challenge to the federal gun free school zone statute on the basis that Congress had failed to demonstrate a sufficient nexus between gun possession at schools and interstate commerce.).

61 See New York v. United States, 505 US 144 (1992) (holding that the federal government was not permitted to impose on the states a requirement that they either set up a regulatory regime for low-level radioactive waste or else take title to the waste themselves.). An issue raised, but not decided by New York,

Even though the federal government may not require the states to enact prohibition, or presumably, to reinstate marijuana prohibitions where they have been overturned, it may seek to invalidate a state marijuana provision on the basis that the state law is preempted by the CSA. The federal government may choose, in any area where it can legislate, to prohibit the states from acting in that area, rendering any state legislation in that area a nullity.[62] For example, the federal government has preempted the field of patent law; only the federal government may issue patents and any patent legislation passed by the states (even if it is identical in all respects to federal law) is preempted by the federal law.

The question of preemption is entirely one of congressional intent; so long as Congress is authorized to legislate in a particular policy arena, it is free to determine how much, if any, of that authority to share with the states. Courts generally require an explicit manifestation of congressional intent before finding a desire to preempt the field, and in the area of marijuana regulation, such intent is clearly absent. Rather, Congress preempted only those state laws that are so inconsistent with the CSA that the two "cannot be read together."[63] The dynamics of drug enforcement in the United States set forth above make clear why this should be so. The federal government has never wished to be the sole regulator of marijuana law in the United States. Rather, because of limited federal law enforcement resources, the federal government wants to—indeed it must—have the states take an active role in marijuana regulation.

The question remains, however, whether any state's marijuana laws are so inconsistent with federal law that the two cannot be read together. The most obvious example of inconsistency between state and federal law would be the situation in which it is impossible to comply with both state and federal law. This would be the case, for example, if the state were to require conduct that the federal government had forbidden. It should be apparent at the outset that the legalization of marijuana at the state level does not (without more) create such a conflict. All one need do to comply with both state and federal law is to abstain from all marijuana conduct. Courts have also read the preemption language of the CSA to preempt state laws that stand as an impermissible obstacle to the enforcement of federal law.[64] It is true that state legalization initiatives do make the accomplishment of a federal goal—the

---

whether the federal government may prohibit the states from passing certain legislation, has been taken up by the Supreme Court next term in *Christie v. NCAA*, 2017 WL 2742859 (2017). The case considers the Constitutionality of the Professional and Amateur Sports Protection Act which forbade any states from adopting legislation legalizing sports gambling after a particular date. The Court will have to decide whether there is a meaningful distinction between requiring legization of a state legislature and prohibiting it. If *Christie* upholds PASPA, that might have the effect of permitting a ban on future marijuana regulation but New York seems to preclude a commandment that the states undo their previous marijuana law reform.

62 See, e.g., Stephen Gardbaum, *Congress's Power to Preempt the States*, 33 PEPPERDINE L. REV. 39, 45 (2005) ("It is undoubtedly true that if Congress exercises its power of preemption, then state laws in conflict with this exercise are trumped under the Supremacy Clause. So, for example, if Congress chooses to enact a law that deprives the states of all regulatory authority in the field of automobile safety standards, then any particular state automobile standard relied on by a plaintiff in a lawsuit will be in conflict with the federal law and trumped by the automatic operation of the Supremacy Clause.")

63 Congress has stated that the CSA preempts inconsistent state laws only where "there is a positive conflict between [a] provision of this subchapter and that State law so that the two cannot consistently stand together" 21 U.S.C. § 903.

64 See, e.g., Robert A. Mikos, *Preemption Under the Controlled Substances Act*, 16 J. HEALTH CARE L. & POL'Y., 5, 8 (2013) ("Under the test now employed by courts and commentators, state marijuana reforms

elimination of all marijuana conduct—more difficult to achieve. However, as we have seen, the states cannot be compelled to facilitate such a goal without their consent. They cannot put obstacles in the path of a federal goal, but they are not required to work on behalf of the federal government to achieve its goals.

A closer case would be presented by a preemption challenge to a state's tax and regulatory regime for marijuana rather than simply to its legalization laws. After all, a regulatory scheme not only permits violations of state law, it literally licenses them. Furthermore, the state profits from violations of federal law by imposing a tax on such conduct.[65] This was the theory espoused by the states of Oklahoma and Nebraska when they sued Colorado before the United States Supreme Court, claiming that Colorado's regulatory regime was preempted by the Controlled Substances Act.[66] The states admitted that Colorado was free to legalize marijuana but contested its ability to regulate and tax such violations of federal law. The problem with such a suit, however, is that it cannot put the states (or any other plaintiff) in a better position than they were in before their lawsuit was filed. Were Oklahoma and Nebraska to prevail on their claims, marijuana would be legal but unregulated in Colorado. Given that the injury alleged by the Oklahoma and Nebraska was that Colorado marijuana was flowing into their territories, it is difficult to see why that circumstance would be improved (rather than significantly worsened) by a ruling that removed all state regulation of marijuana. The same conundrum would be present in a preemption suit brought by the federal government—if the harm alleged is that regulations in Colorado and elsewhere were disrupting the federal prohibition effort, the Justice Department would have difficulty explaining why that effort would be aided by a ruling that would leave marijuana legal but unregulated in adult-use states.

> If these problems with a preemption suit proved prohibitive, a final approach available to the federal government would be to use the power of the purse to convince the states to return to prohibition. That is, the federal government could attempt to do through the spending power what it cannot do by force—to convince marijuana states to undo their legalization and regulatory rules—by threatening to withhold key federal funding if they did not. Even here, however, it is far from clear whether their efforts would be successful. In *NFIB v. Sebelius*,[67] the Supreme Court upheld the Affordable Care Act to a challenge under the Spending Power, but it noted that the federal government's ability to achieve through the spending power what it cannot through decree is limited. The founders, the Court wrote, meant to create two separate sovereigns. "That insight has led this Court to strike down federal legislation that commandeers a State's legislative or administrative apparatus for federal purposes. It has also led us to

---

are preempted if they require someone to violate federal law, or—more controversially—if they simply pose an obstacle to some ill-specified congressional objective.").

65 It should be noted, however, that the federal government benefits in the same way. Federal law requires that those who violate the controlled substances act pay federal income tax on their revenues and denies such taxpayers to deduct their expenses. 26 U.S.C. §280E ("No deduction or credit shall be allowed for any amount paid or incurred during the taxable year in carrying on any trade or business if such trade or business (or the activities which comprise such trade or business) consists of trafficking in controlled substances. . . ."). For a thorough discussion of the implications of 280E, see Edward J. Roche, Jr., *Federal Income Taxation of Medical Marijuana Businesses*, 66 TAX LAWYER 13 (2013).

66 Nebraska, et al., v. Colorado, 136 S.Ct. 1034 (2016).

67 132 S.Ct. 2566 (2012). See also, South Dakota v. Dole, 483 U.S. 203 (1987).

scrutinize Spending Clause legislation to ensure that Congress is not using financial inducements to exert a 'power akin to undue influence.' Congress may use its spending power to create incentives for States to act in accordance with federal policies. But when 'pressure turns into compulsion,' the legislation runs contrary to our system of federalism. '[T]he Constitution simply does not give Congress the authority to require the States to regulate.'"[68]

While we do not know exactly where the line between pressure and coercion lies, the *Sebellius* court made clear that it is scrutinizing the Congress to make sure that it was not attempting to do by withholding funds what it was forbidden to do expressly. What is more, an attempt by the Trump administration to withhold funding from so-called sanctuary cities was recently enjoined as an impermissible exercise of the spending power. The trial court was skeptical about many aspects of the executive order[69]—the nexus between the federal spending and the city policy, the power of the executive to exercise the spending power, and the degree of coercion inherent in the federal action. Were the Trump administration to move single-handedly to cut off certain federal funds to adult-use marijuana states, we could expect an immediate lawsuit seeking to enjoin that action on these same grounds.

So, we can see that at least part of the reason that the Justice Department has been slow to crack down on marijuana law reform in the states is that its lacks a good option for doing so. Thus, the status quo persists, as frustrating as that might be to the states and federal government alike.

Conclusion

So what then is the way forward? I have written elsewhere that one possibility is an explicit cooperative federalism arrangement between the state and federal governments to share power over marijuana regulation.[70] Under this arrangement, the federal marijuana prohibition would remain in effect as the law of the land, but the states could petition the federal government to have their own rules, rather than federal law, govern marijuana conduct within their territory.

Amending the CSA to include a cooperative federalism framework for marijuana laws would give the federal government influence over the enforcement and regulatory priorities of those states that choose to ease prohibitions on marijuana. By requiring opt-out states to comply with specific federal marijuana enforcement and regulatory priorities, such an approach would incentivize states—which have much greater drug enforcement resources than the federal government—to use local law enforcement resources to help achieve federal priorities. Simply stated, the federal government can incentivize state marijuana enforcement and regulatory priorities by requiring opt-out states to comply with enumerated guidelines in order to avoid CSA oversight within their borders.[71]

---

68 FSIB v. Sebelius at 2574. (citing Printz and New York).
69 See County of Santa Clara v. Trump, 2017 WL 1459081 (issuing a preliminary injunction against enforcement of Executive Order 13768 on a number of bases including the Spending Power).
70 Erwin Chemerinsky, Jolene Forman, Allen Hopper, and Sam Kamin, *Cooperative Federalism and Marijuana Regulation*, 62 UCLA L. Rev. 74 (2015).
71 *Id.* at 119.

130 *Sam Kamin*

Under a cooperative federalism approach, the federal government could thus establish criteria for determining whether a state had sufficiently robust rules in place—these might look like the eight criteria the Cole Memorandum set forth for determining whether to use scarce resources against those in violation of federal marijuana laws.[72] The states would then have a free hand to determine whether the best way to achieve those goals would be through enforcing their own prohibitions or seeking a waiver to experiment with regulation instead.

While this model would be more respectful of the states' traditional role in drug enforcement than any of the federal options described above, it would also have the advantage of making marijuana legal in those states that are allowed to opt out of the CSA. Because the only law governing marijuana in opt-out states would be stat law, those acting in compliance with state laws and regulations would be acting lawfully. Thus, the collateral consequences of marijuana conduct that are currently such an obstacle to the implementation of true marijuana law reform in the states would vanish. The states could then fully implement their preferred policies and we would finally be able to determine which regulations produced the most beneficial outcomes. Another possible solution to the current marijuana impasse is the example currently being set by Canada. In Canada, the Liberal government announced that it would be implementing national marijuana legalization effective July 1, 2018.[73] However, the proposal reads much more like a shared governance arrangement than like a top-down pronouncement to the provinces. As the government explained on its website:

> The federal, provincial and territorial governments would share responsibility for overseeing the new system.
> The federal government's responsibilities would be to:
>
> • set strict requirements for producers who grow and manufacture cannabis
> • set industry-wide rules and standards, including:
>
>   o the types of cannabis products that will be allowed for sale
>   o packaging and labelling requirements for products
>   o standardized serving sizes and potency

---

72 Those criteria are:

• Preventing the distribution of marijuana to minors;
• Preventing revenue from the sale of marijuana from going to criminal enterprises, gangs, and cartels;
• Preventing the diversion of marijuana from states where it is legal under state law in some form to other states;
• Preventing state-authorized marijuana activity from being used as a cover or pretext for the trafficking of other illegal drugs or other activity;
• Preventing violence and the use of firearms in the cultivation and distribution of marijuana;
• Preventing drugged driving and the exacerbation of other adverse public health consequences associated with marijuana use;
• Preventing the growing of marijuana on public lands and the attendant public safety and environmental dangers posed by marijuana production on public lands; and
• Preventing marijuana possession or use on federal property.

Id. at 1–2. If there is a criticism of the Cole Memo, though it is that neither federal prosecutors nor the states knew how to evaluate the success of marijuana regulation.

73 Alan Freeman, *Canada Announces Plans to Legalize Marijuana by July 2018*, WASHINGTON POST, April 13, 2017.

o prohibiting the use of certain ingredients
o good production practices
o tracking of cannabis from seed to sale to prevent diversion to the illicit market
o restrictions on promotional activities

The provinces and territories would license and oversee the distribution and sale of cannabis, subject to federal conditions. They could also:

- increase the minimum age in their province or territory (but not lower it)
- lower the personal possession limit in their jurisdiction
- create additional rules for growing cannabis at home, such as lowering the number of plants per residence
- restrict where adults can consume cannabis, such as in public or in vehicles.[74]

The Canadian government is quite explicit that it wishes to share regulatory responsibility with the provincial governments. On many important questions the federal law will create a regulatory floor, setting standards for how marijuana is to be produced, what products may be available, and so forth. The provincial and local governments will be able to raise this floor within their jurisdiction; and, they will be able to place additional limits not inconsistent with the federal rules. Such a system obviously has great applicability to the United States. The federal government could determine what its bare requirements for a valid regulatory regime for marijuana might be. For example, it could prohibit for-profit distribution, certain products, or sale to those under 25. The states would then be free to operate within this regime, banning sales outright, or even, conceivably, criminalizing marijuana within their own territory. Unlike under the current system where the states are precluded from fully implementing their desired policy preferences, a shared governance model could truly allow the states to become the laboratories of democracy of which Justice Louis Brandeis spoke nearly a century ago.[75]

---

74 Government of Canada, Legalizing and Strictly Regulating Canada: The Facts, www.canada.ca/en/services/health/campaigns/legalizing-strictly-regulating-cannabis-facts.html, last visited August 15, 2017.
75 New State Ice Co. v. Liebmann, 285 U.S. 286, 311 (1935) (Brandeis J., dissenting) ("Denial of the right to experiment may be fraught with serious consequences to the Nation. It is one of the happy incidents of the federal system that a single courageous State may, if its citizens choose, serve as a laboratory; and try novel social and economic experiments without risk to the rest of the country.")

8 The firm constitutional foundation and shaky political future of environmental cooperative federalism

Robert L. Glicksman

Environmental regulation in the United States is based on a cooperative federalism foundation, which splits authority and responsibility for adopting, implementing, and enforcing environmental protection standards between the federal and state governments. Early attacks in court on this framework based on alleged limits on the federal government's regulatory authority failed. The Rehnquist Court's recognition of limits on federal power under the Commerce Clause of the Constitution[1] prompted a second wave of litigation seeking to impose constraints on regulatory authority. These ventures, too, largely met a hostile judicial reception, at least as a matter of constitutional law.

The Rehnquist and Roberts Courts were more receptive to claims that federal regulation exceeded statutory limits. It relied on the Constitution's federalism structure to interpret narrowly the intended scope of delegated federal regulatory power. This federalism dynamic surfaced most prominently in cases construing the scope of regulatory jurisdiction under the federal Clean Water Act (CWA), although the issue has also arisen under the Clean Air Act (CAA). More recently, the Roberts Court recognized limits on federal power under the Spending Clause[2] that have the potential to rein in federal environmental regulatory authority, albeit probably only at the margins. On the other hand, the courts have recognized limits on state regulatory power under the Supremacy[3] and dormant Commerce Clauses.

The cooperative federalism structure built into the nation's key environmental statutes[4] has largely withstood the test of time, nearly fifty years after Congress kicked off the "environmental decade" by adopting the CAA in 1970. Federal power to protect the environment has emerged relatively unscathed. The Roberts Court may chip away at that power at the margins, through its interpretations of the Commerce Clause, the Spending Clause, and the Tenth Amendment,[5] but there is little indication that its current lineup is prepared to sharply constrain that power.

The environmental cooperative federalism venture that has served the nation so well is nevertheless under attack. The Trump administration is committed to sharply curtailing the

---

1 U.S. CONST. Art. I, § 8, cl. 3.
2 *Id*. Art. I, § 8, cl. 1.
3 *Id*. Art. VI, cl. 2.
4 Unless otherwise indicated, environmental statutes refer to those aimed at controlling pollution, not those governing natural resource management. The latter implicate additional constitutional provisions, such as the Property Clause, *id*. Art. IV, § 3, cl. 2, which vests in Congress the power to adopt "needful Rules and Regulations" for management of federally owned lands and resources.
5 *Id*. Amend. X.

scope of federal environmental regulatory action as a matter of regulatory policy if not constitutional law. The President and his top environmental appointees have professed a commitment to federalism and protection of state sovereignty. This commitment seems disturbingly one-sided, however. Although the administration favors limitations on federal environmental regulatory authority, its willingness to acknowledge and support state authority in this area appears to be limited to state efforts to remove regulatory constraints and free up development. The administration has sought to slash federal funding that traditionally has allowed the states to play a vital role in environmental cooperative federalism. Without it, the state role will necessarily weaken. Further, the administration has raised the prospect that it may support preemption of state efforts to impose environmental constraints more stringent than federal regulation provides. This asymmetric approach to state power fuels the perception that the Trump administration's devotion to federalism is a thinly veiled mask for its fervor to ravage environmental protection regulatory authority at both the federal and state levels.

This chapter begins by exploring the structure of and rationale for traditional cooperative federalism. It then surveys the constitutional parameters of both federal and state environmental regulatory power, emphasizing decisions by the Rehnquist and Roberts Courts that bear on the scope of each sovereign's powers. The chapter concludes by analyzing the threats to environmental cooperative federalism posed by the Trump administration's policies.

Traditional environmental cooperative federalism

Cooperative federalism structures to achieve public policy goals are not confined to environmental law and policy, as the chapters in this book attest. Environmental regulation, however, has been a prominent arena in which Congress has relied on this model of governance. One member of the Supreme Court has described cooperative federalism as an approach in which Congress invites state and local authorities to make decisions subject to minimum federal standards instead of preempting state authority in pursuit of a nationally uniform approach to problem solving.[6] In an early environmental case, the Court described a "program of cooperative federalism" as one "that allows the States, within limits established by federal minimum standards, to enact and administer their own regulatory programs, structured to meet their own particular needs."[7] In another case, it used that term to describe instances in which, although "Congress has the authority to regulate private activity under the Commerce Clause," it has chosen "to offer States the choice of regulating that activity according to federal standards or having state law pre-empted by federal regulation."[8] Cooperative federalism statutes thus anticipate "a partnership between the States and the Federal Government, animated by a shared objective" and employ "permissible method[s] of encouraging a State to conform to federal policy choices."[9]

In a nutshell, cooperative federalism in environmental regulation promotes "shared governmental responsibilities for regulating private activity."[10] Environmental statutes in the

---

6 City of Rancho Palo Verdes, California v. Abrams, 544 U.S. 113, 127–28 (2005) (Breyer, J., concurring).
7 Hodel v. Virginia Surface Mining & Reclamation Ass'n, 452 U.S. 264, 289 (1981).
8 New York v. United States, 505 U.S. 144, 167 (1992).
9 *Id.*
10 1 GEORGE CAMERON COGGINS & ROBERT L. GLICKSMAN, PUBLIC NATURAL RESOURCES LAW § 5:3 (2d ed. 2007) (citing Susan Rose-Ackerman, *Cooperative Federalism and Co-Optation*, 92 YALE L.J. 1344 (1983)).

cooperative federalism mold assign important roles to both levels of government. Under legislation such as the CAA and CWA, the federal government, acting through authority delegated to the Environmental Protection Agency (EPA), is responsible for adopting standards that provide a minimum level of protection throughout the country.[11] Under these laws, Congress has carved out a significant role for the states to implement federal standards, subject to EPA's approval. According to J.B. Ruhl, environmental cooperative federalism statutes provide "opportunities for states to implement national goals and standards through state-run programs that satisfy certain delegation criteria regarding equivalency to the federal regime and adequacy of enforcement, in exchange for which the federal government takes a back seat in the particular delegated state."[12] States need not respond to these invitations to craft policies that suit their economic and environmental needs,[13] but if they do not, EPA will step into the breach.[14]

Under most federal environmental statutes, states may apply to EPA for authorization to administer the permit programs that provide the principal means of applying emission standards or other regulatory obligations (such as monitoring, recordkeeping, and reporting) to individual regulated entities.[15] Individual permits are typically subject to EPA veto.[16] A state choosing not to seek permitting authority forfeits to EPA the power to administer the permit program for regulated sources within the state. The environmental statutes typically divide authority to enforce statutory or regulatory obligations between the federal and state governments, although the statutes differ in the extent to which EPA must await state action before proceeding.[17] EPA retains exclusive authority to enforce some federal standards.[18] Finally, cooperative federalism statutes tend to include "savings clauses" that reserve state authority to adopt controls more stringent than those adopted or required by EPA,[19] with some exceptions.[20] Thus, federal standards usually serve as floors, not ceilings, on regulatory stringency.[21]

---

11 E.g., 33 U.S.C. § 1311(b) (technology-based effluent limitations under the CWA); 42 U.S.C. § 7409(b) (2012) (national ambient air quality standards (NAAQS) under the CAA).

12 J.B. Ruhl, *Cooperative Federalism and the Endangered Species Act — Is There Hope for Something More?*, in STRATEGIES FOR ENVIRONMENTAL SUCCESS IN AN UNCERTAIN JUDICIAL CLIMATE 325, 326 (Michael Allan Wolf ed., 2005). See, e.g., 42 U.S.C. §§ 7407(a), 7410(a) (making states responsible for implementing NAAQS and setting forth minimum requirements for acceptable state implementation plans); see also 33 U.S.C. § 1313(c) (vesting in states the responsibility to adopt and implement water quality standards).

13 The CAA affords each state the "liberty to adopt whatever mix of emission limitations it deems best suited to its particular situation." Train v. Natural Res. Def. Council, Inc., 421 U.S. 60, 79 (1975).

14 E.g., 33 U.S.C. § 1313(c)(4), (d)(2) (CWA); 42 U.S.C. § 7410(c) (CAA).

15 E.g., 33 U.S.C. § 1342(b) (CWA); 42 U.S.C. 6926 (Resource Conservation and Recovery Act (RCRA)); 42 U.S.C. §§ 7661-7661f (CAA).

16 33 U.S.C. § 1342(d)(2) (CWA); 42 U.S.C. § 7661d(b)-(c) (CAA).

17 E.g., 42 U.S.C. § 7413(b) (CAA); see also United States v. Power Engineering Co., 303 F.3d 1232 (10th Cir. 2002); Harmon Indus., Inc. v. Browner, 191 F.3d 894 (8th Cir. 1999) (addressing when the federal government may "overfile" when dissatisfied with a state's enforcement approach).

18 E.g., 42 U.S.C. § 7413(a)(3) (CAA). Cf. 29 U.S.C. § 666 (Occupational Safety and Health Act).

19 E.g., 33 U.S.C. § 1370(1) (CWA); 42 U.S.C. § 6929 (RCRA); 42 U.S.C. § 7416 (CAA).

20 E.g., 7 U.S.C. § 136v(b) (barring states from adopting labeling or packaging requirements different from those required under federal pesticide statute); 42 U.S.C. §§ 7543(a), 7545(c)(4), 7573 (CAA provisions barring adoption of state standards to control motor vehicle emissions, specify permissible fuel additives, and control aircraft emissions).

21 For a summary of cooperative federalism under the CWA, see United States Dep't of Energy v. Ohio, 503 U.S. 607, 633–34 (1992). See also Robert L. Glicksman, *From Cooperative to Inoperative Federalism: The*

The rationale for shared federal and state environmental regulatory authority is well known. One reason to vest standard-setting in the federal government is to assure that every American enjoys a minimum level of protection against public health threats arising from polluting activities, regardless of where they live. If individual states decide to enhance those protections, they are free to do so by adopting more stringent standards.[22] Congress also carved out a predominant federal role to address collective actions problems that experience showed that states were incapable of tackling or unwilling to address. These include addressing transboundary negative externalities, preventing a race to the bottom among the states, facilitating the pooling of resources capable of effectively addressing environmental threats, providing uniformity in areas such as standard-setting for nationally marketed products, and restricting state or local authority to preclude the local siting of socially important but environmentally undesirable uses.[23]

Inviting states to play a significant role in the pursuit of environmental regulatory goals also promotes important values. These include enhancing participatory democracy (because it is usually easier for citizens to access state than federal officials), allowing states to craft regulatory solutions that are responsive to local needs and conditions, taking advantage of the superior expertise that state officials possess on the nature and extent of environmental problems affecting their citizens, and allowing states to experiment with regulatory approaches to gain knowledge that may ultimately benefit other states and federal regulators.[24] Vesting overlapping and concurrent standard-setting and enforcement authority in both levels of government also creates a safety net that protects against inertia by or capture of regulators.[25]

Challenges to the constitutionality of cooperative federalism

Early constitutional challenges

Regulated entities took little time to challenge the constitutionality of environmental cooperative federalism statutes. The lower courts uniformly rejected those attacks, and the Supreme Court soon followed suit. The Court issued its most important early decision

---

Perverse Mutation of Environmental Law and Policy, 41 WAKE FOREST L. REV. 719, 737–47 (2006) (describing environmental statutes reflecting cooperative federalism).

22 See Adam Babich, *Our Federalism, Our Hazardous Waste, and Our Good Fortune*, 54 MD. L. REV. 1516, 1532–33 (1995) (Cooperative federalism "holds the promise of allowing states continued primacy and flexibility in their traditional realms of protecting health and welfare, while ensuring that protections for all citizens meet minimum federal standards").

23 See Robert L. Glicksman & Richard E. Levy, *A Collective Action Perspective on Ceiling Preemption by Federal Environmental Regulation: The Case of Global Climate Change*, 102 N.W. U. L. REV. 579, 591–62 (2008).

24 See Alejandro E. Camacho & Robert L. Glicksman, *Functional Government in 3-D: A Framework for Evaluating Allocations of Government Authority*, 51 HARV. J. ON LEGIS. 21, 39–42 (2014) (summarizing benefits of decentralized governance); see also New State Ice Co. v. Liebmann, 285 U.S. 262, 311 (1932) (Brandeis, J., dissenting) (touting federalism's potential to empower states to act as laboratories by "try[ing] novel social and economic experiments without risk to the rest of the country"); MARTHA DERTHICK, THE INFLUENCE OF FEDERAL GRANTS: PUBLIC ASSISTANCE IN MASSACHUSETTS 220 (1970) (noting that cooperative federalism "enables the cooperating governments to benefit from one another's special capacities while still preserving the value of political pluralism").

25 See Camacho & Glicksman, *supra* note 24, at 52.

in 1981 in *Hodel v. Virginia Surface Mining and Reclamation Association*,[26] rejecting claims by an association of companies engaged in surface coal mining that the Surface Mining Control and Reclamation Act (SMCRA)[27] violated a host of constitutional provisions, including the Commerce Clause and the Tenth Amendment. Like other environmental cooperative federalism statutes, SMCRA authorizes federal performance standards, delegation of permitting authority to willing states, and shared enforcement authority (between the states and the Department of the Interior).[28]

The coal companies argued that SMCRA's regulation of private lands within a single state exceeded the scope of federal regulatory power under the Commerce Clause. The Court stressed the deference courts must afford congressional findings that regulated activities affect interstate commerce, and the "plenary" nature of the authority granted to Congress by the Commerce Clause.[29] It held that Congress rationally determined that regulation of intrastate surface coal mining is necessary to protect interstate commerce from the resulting adverse effects. It found ample constitutional authority for Congress's establishment of uniform national standards to prevent destructive interstate competition among the states to attract coal mining, deeming this effort a "traditional role for congressional action under the Commerce Clause."[30] In doing so, the Court endorsed a series of lower court decisions that had "uniformly found the power conferred by the Commerce Clause broad enough to permit congressional regulation of activities causing air or water pollution, or other environmental hazards that may have effects in more than one State."[31]

The coal producers' Tenth Amendment attacks on SMCRA fared no better. They argued that constraints on surface mining on steep slopes impermissibly interfered with the traditional state and local power to regulate land use. The Court disagreed, reasoning that these constraints applied only to private coal mining operations. SMCRA did not compel states to enforce the standards, to expend any state funds, or to participate in the federal regulatory program in any way; the federal government would take on the burden of implementation and enforcement in any state choosing not to participate. As a result, SMCRA did not "commandeer" state legislative processes "by directly compelling them to enact and enforce a federal regulatory program."[32] Again, the Court approvingly cited lower court decisions upholding other environmental statutes in the face of Tenth Amendment challenges.[33] It ruled that Congress does not invade powers reserved to the states under the Tenth Amendment "simply because it exercises its authority under the Commerce Clause in a manner that displaces the States' exercise of their police powers."[34] The next year, the

---

26 452 U.S. 264 (1981).
27 30 U.S.C. §§ 1201–1328.
28 *Hodel,* 452 U.S. at 268–72.
29 *Id.* at 276.
30 *Id.* at 281–82.
31 Among the cases cited were United States v. Byrd, 609 F.2d 1204 (7th Cir.1979) (CWA); Sierra Club v. EPA, 540 F.2d 1114 (D.C. Cir. 1976) (CAA); District of Columbia v. Train, 521 F.2d 971 (D.C. Cir. 1975) (CAA); United States v. Ashland Oil & Transp. Co., 504 F.2d 1317 (6th Cir. 1974) (CWA); S. Terminal Corp. v. EPA, 504 F.2d 646 (1st Cir. 1974) (CAA).
32 *Hodel,* 452 U.S. at 288.
33 *Id.* (citing Friends of the Earth v. Carey, 552 F.2d 25 [2d Cir. 1977] [CAA]; Sierra Club v. EPA, 540 F.2d 1114 [D.C. Cir. 1976] [CAA]).
34 *Id.* at 291. In another case decided the same day, the Court held that SMCRA's provisions protecting prime farmland violated neither the Commerce Clause nor the Tenth Amendment. Hodel v. Indiana, 452 U.S. 314 (1981).

Court used similar reasoning to turn aside Commerce Clause and Tenth Amendment challenges to another cooperative federalism statute involving energy regulation.[35]

A decade later, the Court identified an environmental statutory provision that ran afoul of the Constitution's federalism provisions. In *New York v. United States*,[36] it upheld surcharges imposed on states for disposal of radioactive waste generated without complying with Low-Level Radioactive Waste Policy Act of 1985 requirements to participate in efforts to site and build new disposal facilities. It also ruled that conditioning the receipt of federal funds on compliance with the statute's schedule for constructing, or participating in an interstate compact that constructed, a disposal site was a valid exercise of the Spending Clause.

The Court concluded, however, that the act's provisions forcing states not complying with the requirements for helping to site new disposal facilities to take title to waste generated within their borders violated the Tenth Amendment. Those provisions purportedly offered the states the "choice" of accepting ownership of low-level waste or regulating disposal according to federal instructions. The Court reasoned, however, that:

> A choice between two unconstitutionally coercive regulatory techniques is no choice at all. Either way, "the Act commandeers the legislative processes of the States by directly compelling them to enact and enforce a federal regulatory program," an outcome that has never been understood to lie within the authority conferred upon Congress by the Constitution.[37]

New York v. United States established that Congress may not offer a state "no option other than that of implementing [federal] legislation. . . ."[38] Congress has not replicated the 1985 act's "take title" provisions in other federal statutes, however, and most efforts to extend that precedent to other pollution control statutes failed.[39] Despite *New York*, little environmental legislation has been vulnerable to Tenth Amendment challenge.

A 2015 decision by the U.S. Court of Appeals for the D.C. Circuit is illustrative.[40] The court rebuffed claims by a group of states and industrial entities that CAA provisions allowing EPA to override state determinations on the appropriate status of air quality control regions (attainment, nonattainment, or unclassifiable) amounted to unconstitutional commandeering. The statute does not compel states to implement a federal regulatory program.

---

35 FERC v. Mississippi, 456 U.S. 742, 767 (1982).
36 505 U.S. 144 (1992).
37 *Id.* at 176 (quoting *Hodel*, 452 U.S. at 288).
38 *Id.* at 177.
39 See, e.g., Nebraska v. EPA, 331 F.3d 995 (D.C. Cir. 2003) (rejecting Tenth Amendment attack on the Safe Drinking Water Act [SDWA]); City of Abilene v. EPA, 325 F.3d 657 (5th Cir. 2003) (upholding conditions on EPA-issued stormwater discharge permits under the CWA); Envtl. Def. Ctr. v. EPA, 319 F.3d 398 (9th Cir. 2003) (same); Virginia v. Browner, 80 F.3d 869 (4th Cir. 1996) (rejecting challenge to CAA provisions authorizing EPA to impose sanctions on states with inadequate permit programs); *cf.* Wyoming v. United States, 279 F.3d 1214 (10th Cir. 2002) (holding that agency's refusal to permit state to vaccinate elk on national wildlife refuge to prevent brucellosis did not violate Tenth Amendment). On rare occasions, Tenth Amendment challenges succeeded. See ACORN v. Edwards, 81 F.3d 1387 (5th Cir. 1996) (holding that SDWA requirement that states establish remedial plans to remove lead-contamination from school and day-care center drinking water facilities impermissibly sought to control state legislative processes).
40 Mississippi Comm'n on Envtl. Quality v. EPA, 790 F.3d 138 (D.C. Cir. 2015).

Instead, it authorizes EPA "to promulgate and administer a federal implementation plan of its own if the State fails to submit an adequate state implementation plan [SIP]," imposing the "full regulatory burden" on the federal government if a state chooses not to submit a SIP.[41] In another CAA case, the same court interpreted Supreme Court precedents as "repeatedly affirm[ing] the constitutionality of federal statutes that allow States to administer federal programs but provide for direct federal administration if a State chooses not to administer it."[42]

More recent constitutional attacks

Twenty-five years after Congress enacted the CAA, the constitutionality of federal environmental legislation seemed secure. With few exceptions, the courts at all levels had turned aside federalism-based challenges to cooperative federalism regimes. In 1995, however, for the first time in decades, the Supreme Court in *United States v. Lopez*[43] concluded that a federal statute exceeded Congress's Commerce Clause authority. Five years later, the Court invalidated another statute on the same ground in *United States v. Morrison*.[44]

Neither of these decisions involved an environmental statute. They nevertheless triggered a new round of constitutional challenges to federal environmental legislation. Those efforts were no more successful than the first wave of constitutional challenges had been, as the courts easily distinguished *Lopez* and *Morrison* in finding solid grounding for the environmental statutes in the Commerce Clause. The lower courts rejected claims that statutory provisions directed at purportedly intrastate, local activities exceeded the scope of federal legislative authority under the Commerce Clause. Among the statutes whose provisions survived these attacks were the SDWA,[45] the CAA,[46] the Comprehensive Environmental Response, Compensation, and Liability Act (CERCLA),[47] and the CWA.[48]

The Roberts Court fortified these decisions in its 2006 *Raich* decision,[49] in which it confirmed the continuing validity of *Wickard v. Filburn*.[50] That 1942 case established that Congress may regulate purely local activities that are part of an economic class of activities that have a substantial effect on interstate commerce. Ten years later, the Roberts Court again ruled in *Taylor v. United States* that Congress may regulate intrastate activities based on their "aggregate effects on interstate commerce."[51] Although neither of these cases addressed an environmental statute, the courts of appeals relied on them in dismissing Commerce Clause challenges to regulation of intrastate activities under statutes such as the Endangered Species Act (ESA). Every appellate court to address the issue, some of which

---

41 *Id.* at 175.
42 Texas v. EPA, 726 F.3d 180, 196–97 (D.C. Cir. 2013) (citing *New York* and *Hodel*).
43 514 U.S. 549 (1995) (invalidating the Gun-Free School Zones Act).
44 529 U.S. 598 (2000) (invalidating the Violence Against Women Act).
45 E.g., Nebraska v. EPA, 331 F.3d 995 (D.C. Cir. 2003).
46 E.g., United States v. Ho, 311 F.3d 589 (5th Cir. 2002); Allied Local & Reg'l Mfrs. Caucus, 215 F.3d 61 (D.C. Cir. 2000).
47 E.g., United States v. Olin Corp. 107 F.3d 1506 (11th Cir. 1997).
48 E.g., United States v. Gerke Excavating, Inc., 412 F.3d 804 (7th Cir. 2005), *vacated on other grounds*, 548 U.S. 901 (2006); United States v. Deaton, 332 F.3d 698 (4th Cir. 2003).
49 Gonzalez v. Raich, 545 U.S. 1 (2006).
50 317 U.S. 111 (1942).
51 Taylor v. United States, 136 S. Ct. 2074, 2079–80 (2016).

predated *Raich*, has held that the ESA's taking prohibition does not violate the Commerce Clause, notwithstanding differences in the rationales for concluding that the ESA's regulatory scheme has a substantial effect on interstate commerce even when the species in question is found only in one state.[52] The ESA is not structured along the lines of a traditional cooperative federalism statute. But the courts' expansive interpretations in ESA cases of the Commerce Clause's application to intrastate economic activities with substantial aggregate effects on interstate commerce are consistent with and have lent force to cases in which recent efforts to convince courts that cooperative federalism statutes such as the CAA outstrip Congress's Commerce Clause power have met a frosty judicial reception.[53]

Constitutional avoidance

Although the Supreme Court has yet to conclude that an environmental statute is not supported by the Commerce Clause, it has relied on constitutional limits on the power to regulate commerce to interpret the scope of one of these statutes, the CWA, narrowly. The Court has long sought to avoid unnecessarily addressing constitutional questions by adopting an interpretation of a statute susceptible to multiple interpretations that eliminates the alleged constitutional deficiency.[54] In the *SWANCC* case,[55] the Army Corps of Engineers, which jointly administers the CWA's dredge and fill permit program with EPA, required a permit for an abandoned sand and gravel pit containing ponds that provided habitat for migratory birds. The Court found it unnecessary to address whether that expansive application of the permit program ran afoul of the Commerce Clause. Instead, it held that the Corps' position conflicted with congressional intent, ruling that the CWA does not extend to ponds that are not adjacent to open water.

The Court reasoned that "[w]here an administrative interpretation of a statute invokes the outer limits of Congress' power, we expect a clear indication that Congress intended that result."[56] It added that its "prudential desire not to needlessly reach constitutional issues . . . is heightened where the administrative interpretation alters the federal-state framework by permitting federal encroachment upon a traditional state power."[57] In the absence of clear congressional intent to cover the affected waters, the Court construed the statute narrowly "to avoid the significant constitutional and federalism questions raised by [the Corps'] interpretation."[58]

---

52 See, e.g., People for the Ethical Treatment of Property Owners v. U.S. Fish and Wildlife Serv., 852 F.3d 990 (10th Cir. 2017); Markle Interests v. United States, 827 F.3d 452 (5th Cir. 2016), *reh'g en banc denied*, 848 F.3d 635 (5th Cir. 2017); San Luis & Delta-Mendota Water Auth. v. Salazar, 638 F.3d 1163 (9th Cir. 2011); Alabama-Tombigbee Rivers Coal. v. Kempthorne, 477 F.3d 1250 (11th Cir. 2007); Rancho Viejo, LLC v. Norton, 323 F.3d 1062 (D.C. Cir. 2003); Gibbs v. Babbitt, 214 F.3d 483 (4th Cir. 2000).

53 See, e.g., Mississippi Comm'n on Envtl. Quality v. EPA, 790 F.3d 138, 181 (D.C. Cir. 2015) ("[T]here is no doubt that the general regulatory scheme of the [CAA] has a substantial relation to interstate commerce.").

54 RICHARD E. LEVY & ROBERT L. GLICKSMAN, STATUTORY ANALYSIS IN THE REGULATORY STATE 156–57 (2014) ("Statutes should be construed to avoid constitutional issues or problems.").

55 Solid Waste Agency of N. Cook County v. U.S. Army Corps of Eng'rs, 531 U.S. 159 (2001) (*SWANCC*).

56 *Id*. at 172.

57 *Id*. at 172–73.

58 *Id*. at 174.

A plurality of the Court relied on similar reasoning five years later in ruling in the *Rapanos* case that the Corps improperly applied the dredge and fill permit program to wetlands based on their indirect connections to tributaries of navigable waters.[59] Lacking a "clear and manifest" statement from Congress, the plurality refused to conclude that Congress intended to "authorize an unprecedented intrusion into traditional state authority" that "presses the envelope of constitutional validity."[60] It concluded that the program applies only to "relatively permanent, standing or flowing bodies of water," not to channels in which water flows intermittently or ephemerally.[61] Justice Anthony Kennedy wrote a concurring opinion advancing a "significant nexus" test that the lower courts have applied in most subsequent cases. In doing so, he asserted that his interpretation of the statute avoided federalism concerns more effectively than the plurality's approach.[62] Some lower courts have relied on *SWANCC* or *Rapanos* to interpret federal environmental legislation narrowly.[63]

The Roberts Court and spending and commerce clause constraints on federal power

To date, the Roberts Court's Commerce Clause and Tenth Amendment jurisprudence has not posed threats to the constitutionality of federal environmental statutes. Its interpretation of the Spending Clause has the potential to do so, however. In 2012, the Court addressed the constitutionality of portions of the Patient Protection and Affordable Care Act of 2010 (ACA) in the *Sebelius* case.[64] Five justices agreed that the federal tax power[65] supported the individual mandate (which penalizes individuals refusing to purchase health insurance). Seven justices in two separate opinions, however, concluded that that the ACA's reliance on the Spending Clause to withhold all federal Medicaid funding from states refusing to expand the program's coverage for the poor was constitutionally problematic. Chief Justice John Roberts characterized the threat to pull back all Medicaid funding to uncooperative states as "a gun to the head" of the states and "economic dragooning" that was impermissibly coercive.[66]

The federal government has long provided financial assistance to help its state partners fulfill their responsibilities under the environmental laws. Even before Congress adopted the CAA, it provided financial and technical assistance to state regulators.[67] EPA provided first grants and then loans to help municipalities meet their CWA water treatment responsibilities.[68] Sometimes, these funds come with strings attached. Indeed, Congress has invoked its power to withdraw funding for other activities if states fail to meet their environmental statutory obligations. The CAA, for example, authorizes EPA to withhold federal funding for highway construction from states that do not comply with their duties to improve air

59 Rapanos v. United States, 547 U.S. 715 (2006).
60 *Id.* at 738.
61 *Id.* at 739.
62 *Id.* at 782–83 (Kennedy, J., concurring in the judgment).
63 E.g., In re Needham, 354 F.3d 340 (5th Cir. 2003); Rice v. Harken Exploration Co., 250 F.3d 264 (5th Cir. 2001).
64 Nat'l Fed'n of Indep. Business v. Sebelius, 567 U.S. 519 (2012).
65 U.S. CONST. art. I, § 8, cl. 1.
66 *Sebelius,* 567 U.S. at 581, 582.
67 See Glicksman & Levy, *supra* note 23, at 596; Glicksman, *supra* note 21, at 730.
68 See 33 U.S.C. §§ 1281–1288.

quality in areas not yet in compliance with the NAAQS.[69] Before *Sebelius*, the Fourth Circuit held that this conditional funding mechanism is not impermissibly coercive and that the conditions on receipt of highway funding are reasonably related to the goal of reducing air pollution. Holding that the highway sanctions are a valid exercise of the spending power, the court concluded that "Congress may ensure that funds it allocates are not used to exacerbate the overall problem of air pollution."[70]

Some scholars have argued that *Sebelius* may dictate a contrary conclusion, having clarified the extent of (or imposed new constraints on) the exercise of the federal spending power.[71] The D.C. Circuit, however, has dismissed the contention that the highway sanctions "impose such a steep price that State officials effectively have no choice but to comply—in contravention of [*Sebelius*]."[72] For several reasons, the court determined that the highway sanctions "are not nearly as coercive as those in the ACA."[73] First, a noncomplying state only risks forfeiture of funding for transportation projects or grants applicable to its non-attainment areas rather than losing all federal funding for an existing program. Second, states risk losing a much lower percentage of their federal funding, either for highway construction or of their overall budget than in *Sebelius*. Third, although imposition of a condition that did not restrict how the affected federal highway funds were to be used might be problematic, the CAA redirects federal highway funds of noncomplying states to Congress' chosen programs, including those that would improve air quality. Fourth, the problematic condition in *Sebelius* was new both because it had been recently enacted at the time of the litigation and because conditions it imposed additional requirements with which states had to comply to continue receiving preexisting federal funding. Neither the CAA's requirement to submit a SIP nor its highway funds sanction was a newly imposed condition. As a result, the states were "not suddenly surprised by dramatically new conditions retroactively imposed after a long period in which the State had accepted and relied upon unconditional federal funding—as was the case in [*Sebelius*]."[74]

Moreover, even if highway sanctions are newly problematic after *Sebelius*, few environmental statutes are likely to be similarly affected. Jonathan Adler and Nathaniel Stewart, who have suggested that the highway sanctions may violate the Spending Clause, conclude that "conditional spending requirements under other federal environmental statutes appear to be far less vulnerable. At present, most other federal environmental statutes simply impose conditions on how funding for state-level environmental programs is to be spent or do no more than threaten conditional preemption."[75]

Sebelius also has potential implications for Commerce Clause jurisprudence. The Court's conclusion that the tax power supported the individual mandate precluded the need to address whether the mandate is a legitimate exercise of Commerce Clause authority. Chief Justice Roberts nevertheless weighed in, albeit arguably in dicta. Justice Antonin Scalia,

69 42 U.S.C. § 7509(b)(1).
70 Virginia v. Browner, 80 F.3d 869, 882 (4th Cir. 1996).
71 Jonathan H. Adler & Nathaniel Stewart, *Is the Clean Air Act Unconstitutional? Coercion, Cooperative Federalism and Conditional Spending After NFIB v. Sebelius*, 43 ECOLOGY L.Q. 671, 701 (2016) (calling EPA withholding of federal highway funds from noncompliant states "vulnerable" after *Sebelius*).
72 Mississippi Comm'n on Envtl. Quality v. EPA, 790 F.3d 138, 175 (D.C. Cir. 2015).
73 *Id*. at 177.
74 *Id*. at 179.
75 Adler & Stewart, *supra* note 71, at 722.

joined by three other justices, also did so in a separate opinion. Neither opinion disputed that health care was imbued with commerce or that individuals' decisions not to obtain health insurance affected insurance markets. They took issue, however, with the federal government's attempt to compel someone not actively in health care markets to buy insurance. Both opinions distinguished *Wickard*'s aggregation of the local effects of an economic class of activities with substantial effects on interstate commerce because the wheat farmers growing for home consumption in that case engaged in affirmative conduct. Roberts concluded that the federal government cannot compel activity under the Commerce Clause "whenever enough [individuals] are not doing something the Government would have them do."[76]

Putting aside that the Roberts and Scalia Commerce Clause analyses were unnecessary to the decision given the agreement of a majority of the Court that the tax power supports the individual mandate, this portion of *Sebelius* is not likely to provide fertile ground for future Commerce Clause attacks on environmental regulation in most cases. Because almost all pollution and other environmental harms result from affirmative economic activity, the compulsion to enter a market involuntarily that troubled Roberts and Scalia is lacking. One context that might be analogous to *Sebelius* involves forcing an individual to address hazardous substances under his or her land under "passive migration" theories derived from federal hazardous waste statutes. Even then, however, the landowner would have acted in acquiring the property (unless title passed by will or intestate succession). It is unclear whether courts would find Commerce Clause concerns in such a case to be cogent, but even if they do, the Commerce Clause reasoning in the Roberts and Scalia opinions in *Sebelius* do not appear to pose a significant threat to the constitutionality of most federal environmental statutory provisions.

Constraints on state power

The flip side of the cooperative federalism coin is the exercise of state regulatory authority in the pursuit of environmental protection goals. The primary constraints on state regulatory power in this context are the Supremacy Clause and dormant Commerce Clause. The former provides that federal law prevails over inconsistent state law. Preemption issues turn on whether Congress intended to preserve or negate state law in particular circumstances. To the extent that the environmental statutes explicitly preserve a role for the states (such as by allowing them to adopt standards more stringent than federal law), preemption is not an issue, although questions concerning the proper interpretation and application of statutory savings clauses and related provisions often arise.[77] The Roberts Court concluded in 2011 that the CAA displaces federal common law public nuisance remedies for harms caused by greenhouse gas (GHG) emissions.[78] That case turned on separation of powers, not federalism considerations. The Court left open whether state common law claims survived.[79] The Sixth

---

76 *Sebelius*, 567 U.S. at 553.
77 See, e.g., Sandi Zellmer, *When Congress Goes Unheard: Savings Clauses' Rocky Judicial Reception*, in PREEMPTION CHOICE: THE THEORY, LAW, AND REALITY OF FEDERALISM'S CORE QUESTION 144 (William W. Buzbee ed., 2009).
78 Am. Elec. Power Co. v. Connecticut, 564 U.S. 410 (2011).
79 *Id*. at 429.

Circuit subsequently held that the CAA preserves claims under more stringent state law, including state common law.[80]

The dormant Commerce Clause restricts the ability of states and localities to control the flow of interstate commerce or discriminate against out-of-state commerce. The Rehnquist Court repeatedly struck down state and local attempts to prohibit the importation of solid waste generated elsewhere or otherwise to control the flow of waste.[81] The Roberts Court distinguished those cases in upholding a flow control ordinance that forced waste haulers to send waste to facilities owned and operated by a state-created public benefit corporation.[82] Finding that the ordinance did not discriminate against interstate commerce, the Court upheld it because any incidental burden it may have had on interstate commerce was outweighed by the public benefits conferred.

None of these cases directly implicated cooperative federalism statutes. Dormant Commerce Clause issues may arise, however, in contexts in which challenged state laws can be regarded as efforts to exercise preserved authority to advance federal environmental goals through more stringent regulation. The Ninth Circuit ruled in 2013 that California's Low Carbon Fuel Standard, which sought to reduce GHGs emitted in the production of transportation fuel, neither improperly discriminated against interstate commerce nor violated the dormant Commerce Clause's prohibition on extraterritorial state regulation.[83] More recently, the Eighth Circuit struck down Minnesota's renewable portfolio standard (RPS),[84] which was also designed to combat climate change.[85] The panel members disagreed on the rationale. One concluded that the standard qualified as improper extraterritorial regulation because, to comply with it, integrated utilities must either unplug from the electric grid or seek approval from Minnesota regulators of transactions that may import electricity into Minnesota. The RPS improperly foisted on surrounding states Minnesota's policy of increasing the cost of electricity by restricting use of the most cost-efficient sources of generating capacity.[86] A second judge concluded that the RPS was preempted because it conflicted with the CAA's cooperative federalism regime by limiting a source state's authority to govern emissions from sources within its own borders. The CAA creates other mechanisms for a state to object to upwind state emissions.[87] That result purports to advance, not frustrate Congress's cooperative federalism goals, but it creates the potential

---

80 Merrick v. Diageo Americas Supply, Inc., 805 F.3d 685 (6th Cir. 2015).

81 See C&A Carbone, Inc. v. Town of Clarkstown, 511 U.S. 383 (1994); Oregon Waste Sys., Inc. v. Oregon Dep't of Envtl. Quality, 511 U.S. 93 (1992); Fort Gratiot Sanitary Landfill, Inc. v. Michigan Dep't of Natural Resources, 504 U.S. 353 (1992); Chem. Waste Mgmt., Inc. v. Hunt, 504 U.S. 334 (1992).

82 United Haulers Ass'n, Inc. v. Oneida-Herkimer Solid Waste Mgmt. Auth., 550 U.S. 330 (2007).

83 Rocky Mountain Farmers Union v. Corey, 730 F.3d 1070 (9th Cir. 2013), *reh'g en banc denied*, 740 F.3d 507 (9th Cir 2014).

84 RPSs require electric utilities to generate at least a minimum amount of power from renewable or other low carbon or carbon-free energy sources. See ROBERT L. GLICKSMAN ET AL., ENVIRONMENTAL PROTECTION: LAW AND POLICY 1247 (7th ed. 2015).

85 North Dakota v. Heydinger, 825 F.3d 912 (8th Cir. 2016).

86 *Id.* at 922.

87 *Id.* at 927–29 (Colloton, J., concurring in the judgment). *Compare* Allco Finance Ltd. v. Klee, 2017 WL 2782856 (2d Cir. 2017) (upholding Connecticut's RPS program, which did not discriminate against out-of-state renewable energy producer).

to block states from supplementing weak or nonexistent implementation of CAA provisions authorizing regulation of GHGs.[88]

Sabotaging environmental cooperative federalism through abdication and asymmetrical devolution

The discussion thus far indicates that, with few exceptions, cooperative federalism statutes stand on strong constitutional footing. The principal current threats to environmental cooperative federalism statutes and the protective goals they embody come from the executive branch, not the courts. The environmental policy decisions advanced during the first six months of the Trump Administration reflect an unprecedented retrenchment from the leadership role that EPA has exercised in this arena, at Congress's direction, for nearly 50 years. At the same time, despite paying lip service to federalism principles, the Administration seems intent on effectively disabling the exercise of meaningful state regulatory power, if not ousting important components of that authority entirely.

Early in the Trump Administration, EPA began repealing or delaying implementation of at least thirty environmental regulations. This was the largest and fastest effort to eliminate regulatory constraints that EPA had ever undertaken, and included delaying CAA rules restricting fugitive methane emissions from the oil and gas industry[89] and preventing explosions and spills at chemical plants.[90] Most prominently, EPA announced it would take steps to repeal an Obama EPA rule defining the jurisdictional boundaries of various CWA programs (the so-called "waters of the United States" or WOTUS rule)[91] and the Clean Power Plan (CPP), EPA's effort to control GHG emissions from existing electric generating units under the CAA.[92] EPA's action on the WOTUS rule came in response to an executive

88 For discussion of whether the federal government's failure to regulate can preempt state regulation, see Robert L. Glicksman, *Nothing Is Real: Protecting the Regulatory Void through Federal Preemption by Inaction*, 26 VA. ENVTL. L.J. 5 (2008) (concluding that preemption by inaction should occur only in limited circumstances).

89 Oil and Natural Gas Sector: Emission Standards for New, Reconstructed, and Modified Sources, 81 Fed. Reg. 35,824 (June 3, 2016). EPA announced in May 2017 that the rule, which had gone into effect nearly a year earlier, would be stayed pending its reconsideration of the rule. The D.C. Circuit blocked the stay, finding it to be arbitrary and procedurally defective, and disagreeing that industry never had an opportunity to comment on the rule. Clean Air Council v. EPA, 2017 WL 2838112 (D.C. Cir. 2017). It temporarily stayed issuance of its order to allow the Administration to seek further review. Clean Air Council v. EPA, No. 17–1145 (D.C. Cir. July 13, 2017).

90 Accidental Release Prevention Requirements: Risk Management Programs Under the Clean Air Act; Further Delay of Effective Date, 82 Fed. Reg. 27,133 (June 14, 2017); Coral Davenport, *E.P.A. Chief Voids Obama-Era Rules in Blazing Start*, NEW YORK TIMES, July 2, 2017; see also Oliver Milman, *Trump's alarming environmental rollback: what's been scrapped so far*, THE GUARDIAN, July 4, 2017, www. theguardian.com/environment/2017/jul/04/trump-emvironmental-rollback-epa-scrap-regulations (The Trump Administration "has proceeded with quiet efficiency in its dismantling of other major environmental policies. The White House, Congress and [EPA] have dovetailed to engineer a dizzying reversal of clean air and water regulations implemented by Barack Obama's administration.").

91 *EPA, U.S. Army Move to Rescind 2015 "Waters of the U.S."*, EPA News Release, June 27, 2017, www.epa. gov/newsreleases/epa-us-army-move-rescind-2015-waters-us.

92 Announcement of Review, 82 Fed. Reg. 16,329 (Apr. 4, 2017) (announcing intent to review, "and, if appropriate, . . . as soon as practicable and consistent with law, initiate proceedings to suspend, revise or rescind" this rule). EPA also withdrew proposed rules to establish a federal implementation plan for states failing to comply with federal regulations. Withdrawal of Proposed Rules: Federal Plan Requirements for

oOrder directing EPA to "publish for notice and comment a proposed rule rescinding or revising the rule, as appropriate and consistent with the law."[93] Retaining this Obama-era rule was apparently not an available option, regardless of the results of EPA's review. The announcement on the CPP came on the heels of President Donald Trump's issuance of an executive order promoting domestic energy production that mandated EPA review of the CPP and other CAA regulations directed at GHG emissions.[94] The same order immediately repealed Obama administration executive orders, memoranda, and reports relating to climate change.[95]

President Trump's orders to EPA to review and, if appropriate, repeal both the WOTUS rule and the CPP invoked federalism concerns. The order directing EPA to review the CPP enunciated a policy of "respecting the proper roles of the Congress and the States concerning these matters in our constitutional republic."[96] Likewise, the order directing EPA to review the WOTUS rule was premised on a policy of "showing due regard for the roles of the Congress and the States under the Constitution" in addressing water pollution,[97] and the order itself was titled "Restoring the Rule of Law, Federalism, and Economic Growth by Reviewing the 'Waters of the United States' Rule."

EPA later issued a press release describing EPA Administrator E. Scott Pruitt's "Back-to-Basics agenda," which included "returning power to the states" and "restoring states' important role in the regulation of local waters by reviewing the WOTUS . . . rule."[98] Pruitt has repeated in other forums that an important focus of his agenda is "cooperative federalism. Partnership,"[99] which he labeled a "great concept" that had not yet proven effective.[100] He provided a different explanation for the agency's whirlwind approach to rescinding or delaying implementation of these and other rules, however, proclaiming in an interview with Breitbart, "We're going to roll it back, those things that were unlawful, we're going to roll back those things that were an overreach, we're going to roll back the steps taken by the previous administration."[101]

Before being confirmed, Pruitt postulated that EPA "was never meant to be our nation's front-line environmental regulator."[102] This demonstrably false statement flies in the face

Greenhouse Gas Emissions from Electric Utility Generating Units Constructed on or Before January 8, 2014; Model Trading Rules; Amendments to Framework Regulations; and Clean Energy Incentive Program Design Details, 82 Fed. Reg. 16,144 (Apr. 3, 2017).

93 Exec. Order No. 13778, § 2(a), 82 Fed. Reg. 12,497 (Feb. 28, 2017).

94 Exec. Order No. 13783, § 4, 82 Fed. Reg. 16,093 (Mar. 28, 2017).

95 *Id.* § 3.

96 *Id.* § 1(d).

97 Exec. Order No. 13778, *supra* note 93, § 1.

98 EPA Launches Back-To-Basics Agenda at Pennsylvania Coal Mine, News Release, Apr. 13, 2017, www.epa.gov/newsreleases/epa-launches-back-basics-agenda-pennsylvania-coal-mine.

99 Kevin Bogardus, *Pruitt talks up partnership with state regulators*, E&ENEWS, Apr. 7, 2017, www.eenews.net/greenwire/stories/1060052820.

100 Niina Heikkenen, *Pruitt wants to give power to states. Not all of them want it*, CLIMATEWIRE, May 22, 2017, www.eenews.net/climatewire/2017/05/22/stories/1060054887.

101 Charlie Spiering, *Exclusive: Scott Pruitt Promises 'EPA Originalism' in Donald Trump Administration*, BREITBART, Mar. 28, 2017, www.breitbart.com/big-government/2017/03/28/exclusive-scott-pruitt-promises-epa-orginalism-in-donald-trump-administration/; see also Milman, *supra* note 90 (quoting Pruitt's promise to roll back regulations "in a very aggressive way," and quoting a characterization of that scale of rollback as unprecedented by President George W. Bush's first EPA administrator).

102 Bridget DiCosmo & David LaRoss, *Pruitt Opponents Target Nominee's Federalism Approach as 'Shell Game,'* ENVTL. POLICY ALERT, Feb. 1, 2017; see also Heikkenen, *supra* note 100 ("Pruitt said Congress

of voluminous evidence that Congress intended EPA to play exactly that role and that demonstrates a willful ignorance of the history of federal environmental regulation that is shocking for an EPA Administrator. Before Congress enacted the foundational cooperative federalism statutes, the federal government's role was more confined than those laws would afford it. The states' previous failures to provide acceptable levels of environmental quality induced Congress to create a more robust federal presence. Congress was also aware of the collective action problems, noted earlier, that make a strong federal presence essential. As I have explained elsewhere, "Congress made EPA the dominant partner because experience convinced it that the states lacked the will or the capacity to achieve air quality protection goals."[103] When Congress amended the CAA in 1977 and 1990, in the face of many states' persistent noncompliance with the NAAQS, it rethought the initial allocation of authority—and chose to rebalance the scales even more heavily in favor of federal power.[104] Congress made similar judgments when enacting the other cooperative federalism statutes,[105] although at least one Supreme Court justice has grossly mischaracterized the resulting cooperative federalism structures.[106] Nevertheless, as attorney general of Oklahoma, Pruitt filed lawsuits challenging EPA's authority in the context in which collective action problems may most clearly call for federal power—interstate pollution.[107]

Pruitt's EPA has made it clear that it will use federalism as a sword to justify federal regulatory retrenchment. In its proposed rescission of the WOTUS rule, EPA cited § 101(b) of the CWA, which enunciates a policy "to recognize, preserve, and protect the primary responsibilities and rights of States to prevent, reduce, and eliminate pollution, [and] to plan the development and use (including restoration, preservation, and enhancement) of land and water resources."[108] The preamble to the proposal indicated that EPA and the Corps of Engineers would "consider[ ] the relationship of the CWA objective and policies, and in particular, the meaning and importance of section 101(b)."[109] EPA asserted that, in promulgating the rule in 2015, the agencies acknowledged § 101(b) but failed to discuss its importance in guiding their choices in defining the scope of the CWA's reach. The agencies would redress that deficiency by "more fully consider[ing]" § 101(b), "including the extent to which states or tribes have protected or may protect waters that are not subject to CWA jurisdiction."[110] Some have suggested that the Trump administration also may be interested

initially intended for states to be a 'primary or active partner' in implementing regulations created under environmental legislation.").

103 Robert L. Glicksman & Jessica A. Wentz, *Debunking Revisionist Understandings of Environmental Cooperative Federalism: Collective Action Responses to Air Pollution*, in THE LAW AND POLICY OF ENVIRONMENTAL FEDERALISM: A COMPARATIVE ANALYSIS 3, 6 (Kalyani Robbins ed., 2015).

104 *Id.*

105 See Glicksman, *supra* note 21, at 740 ("The terminology of state primacy and of federal-state partnerships is misleading, however. The federal pollution control statutes unquestionably put the federal government, acting through authority delegated to EPA, in the driver's seat.").

106 See Glicksman & Wentz, *supra* note 103, at 4–6 (describing Justice Kennedy's misconceptions concerning cooperative federalism under the CAA in his dissent in Alaska Dep't of Envtl. Conservation v. EPA, 540 U.S. 461 [2004]).

107 EME Homer City Generating, L.P. v. EPA, 795 F.3d 118, 121 (D.C. Cir. 2015) (listing Pruitt as an attorney for petitioners challenging the Cross-State Air Pollution Rule).

108 33 U.S.C. § 1251(b).

109 Definition of "Waters of the United States"—Recodification of Pre-existing Rules, 82 Fed. Reg. 34,899, 34,902 (July 27, 2017).

110 *Id.*

in putting the states in charge of remedy selection in hazardous substance cleanups under CERCLA.[111] Congressional Republicans have introduced legislation that would require state approval before federal agencies may list species as endangered or threatened under the ESA.[112]

This withdrawal of the federal government from its historic role in protecting the environment is troublesome. It might be less so if the Trump administration were truly committed to state empowerment and a sufficient number of states were willing and able to step into the breach created by EPA's significantly diminished role, but the administration's professed commitment to the exercise of meaningful state regulatory power is belied by its actions.

As early as his confirmation hearings, Pruitt raised the possibility that he would revoke waivers previously granted by EPA allowing California to enact tailpipe emission standards for GHGs under the CAA that are more stringent than EPA's, notwithstanding the statute's general preemption of state authority to enact or enforce emissions standards for new motor vehicles.[113] Congress chose to allow California to adopt its own, more stringent emission standards because of the severity of auto-related pollution in the southern part of the state resulting from its climate and topography, and the state's leadership role in controlling mobile source pollution.[114] California began restricting vehicle emissions before federal agencies did so. According to California regulators, EPA's effort to block the state's authority to enforce its current standards restricting GHGs or to adopt future restrictions would eviscerate its ability to achieve its target of 40 percent reductions in GHG emissions below 1990 levels by 2030.[115] The effects of revoking California's waiver would extend to other states, several of which have adopted standards equivalent to more stringent California standards approved by EPA.[116]

Pruitt announced in 2017 that he would not revoke California's waiver,[117] declaring that "[c]urrently, the waiver is not under review."[118] But he had previously made it clear that the waiver is "something that is granted on an annual basis."[119] A refusal to renew the waiver at some time down the road cannot be ruled out. Indeed, in litigation concerning the validity of California's standards EPA has stated its intention to review previously granted waivers

111 Brian Dabbs, *Attorneys, Industry Mull Superfund Devolution Under Trump*, 47 ENV'T REP. (BNA) 4137 (Nov. 18, 2016).

112 See S. 935, 115 Cong. (2017–2018), www.congress.gov/bill/115th-congress/senate-bill/935/text.

113 42 U.S.C. §7543(a), (b) (prohibition and waiver provisions); *id.* § 7507 (authorizing other states to adopt California's standards). See Evan Harper, *Trump's Pick Casts Doubt on California's Power to Regulate Auto Emissions*, L.A. TIMES, Jan. 18, 2017, www.latimes.com/nation/la-na-pol-epa-confirmation-20170118-story.html; Doug Obey, *Pruitt Vows to 'Review' California GHG Waiver, Hints at Unprecedented Step*, ENVTL. POLICY ALERT, Feb. 1, 2017, at 18.

114 H.R. REP. NO. 90–278, at 42 (1967).

115 Curt Barry, *CARB Chief Says Trump Blocking Vehicle Rules Would 'Destroy' GHG Plan*, ENVTL. POLICY ALERT, Feb. 1, 2017, at 19.

116 See, e.g., Motor Vehicle Mfrs. Ass'n of U.S., Inc. v. New York State Dep't of Envtl. Conservation, 79 F.3d 1298 (2nd Cir. 1996) (approving New York standards).

117 Dale Kasler, *Is Trump White House blinking on clash over California's clean air rules?*, SACRAMENTO BEE, June 15, 2017, www.sacbee.com/news/local/environment/article156435834.html.

118 See Jennifer A. Dlouhy, *EPA Isn't Reviewing California's Clean Air Waiver: Pruitt*, 48 ENV'T REP. (BNA) 1140 (2017) (emphasis added) (quoting Pruitt's congressional testimony).

119 Obey, *supra* note 113, at 18.

for other air pollutants.[120] This tepid defense of state leadership in combating mobile source pollution that contributes to both climate change and increased ozone concentrations is a far cry from Pruitt's call for EPA to step down so that states can play a heightened role.[121] Further evidence of the administration's willingness to preempt protective state initiatives is its threat to preempt state RPSs.[122]

The budgets the administration presented to Congress demonstrate even more clearly its questionable devotion to fostering vibrant state regulatory activity in an effort to shift the locus of environmental policymaking authority.[123] The administration proposed cutting EPA's budget by about 30 percent in fiscal year 2018.[124] It sought to reduce EPA staffing by about 20 percent to its lowest levels since the mid-1980s.[125] Trump's budget called for reductions in EPA's civil enforcement program by 18 percent, its criminal enforcement program by 16.5 percent, and the forensics support for enforcement by about 44 percent. The administration justified these cuts by characterizing enforcement as a "shared" federal-state effort.[126] According to President Barack Obama's former assistant administrator for the Office of Enforcement and Compliance Assurance, however, the cuts would deal "a death blow to environmental enforcement."[127]

The dramatic cuts sought by the administration would affect the states. Its budget proposal would have slashed EPA's categorical grants to the states by 45 percent.[128] It also would have cut state funding beyond environmental cooperative federalism programs, including funding for coastal restoration, hurricane protection, and wildland fire suppression, all of which tend to be dealt with locally.[129] The budget sought to cut support for states to develop SIPs, the core mechanism for achieving the NAAQS, by 24 percent, and for state and local air quality programs generally by 45 percent.[130] Funding for favored state programs, including cleaning up the Great Lakes, Chesapeake Bay, and Puget Sound, would have been eliminated entirely. Other targets included beach protection, nonpoint source pollution, pollution prevention,

---

120 See Kat Sieniuc, *EPA Sees 9th Circ. Pause Calif. Waiver Case*, Law360, May 11, 2017, www.law360.com/articles/923106/epa-sees-9th-circ-pause-calif-caa-waiver-case.
121 See also Richard Revesz, *According to Scott Pruitt, states only have the right to pollute, not protect their environments*, L.A. Times, Mar. 20, 2017, www.latimes.com/opinion/op-ed/la-oe-revesz-pruitt-epa-federalism-20170320-story.html.
122 See Stuart Caplin, Brian Harms & Emily Prince, Trump Administration Considers Preemption of State Renewable Policies, Renewable Energy Insights, May 24, 2017, www.renewableinsights.com/2017/05/trump-administration-considers-preemption-state-renewable-policies/.
123 EPA, *Fiscal Year 2018: Justification of Appropriation Estimates for the Committee on Appropriations*, EPA-190-K-17-002 (May 2017), www.epa.gov/sites/production/files/2017-05/documents/fy-2018-congressional-justification.pdf.
124 Coral Davenport, *Budget Seeks Cuts at E.P.A. to Regulators and Cleanups*, N.Y. Times, May 20, 2017, www.nytimes.com/2017/05/19/climate/trump-epa-budget-superfund.html?_r=0.
125 Brian Danns, *Budget Calls for 3-Year Low in Staff Levels*, 48 Env't Rep. (BNA) 1014 (2017).
126 Kevin Bogardus, *Trump calls for cutting budget by 30%, slashing 3,200 jobs*, Greenwire, May 23, 2017, www.eenews.net/stories/1060054996.
127 Renee Schoof, *Civil, Criminal Environmental Enforcement Cut in Trump Budget Plan*, 48 Env't Rep. (BNA) 1012 (2017).
128 *Id.*
129 Kellie Lunney, *Trump budget targets land acquisition, conservation programs*, Greenwire, May 23, 2017, www.eenews.net/greenwire/stories/1060054995/.
130 Bogardus, *supra* note 126; Emily Holden & Camille von Kaenel, *Leaked budget shows cuts to Pruitt's stated priorities*, ClimateWire, May 22, 2017, www.eenews.net/climatewire/2017/05/22/stories/1060054888.

radon, and underground storage tanks.[131] Perhaps most transparently, the administration indicated it wants to eliminate or reduce federal spending on state actions that extend beyond EPA's own (weakening) requirements.[132]

Thus, devolution only goes so far. It does not encompass support for state policies and programs that seek more rigorous environmental regulation than the Trump administration sees fit to administer. As the executive director of the National Association of Clean Air Agencies[133] put it, "[w]hile the Trump Administration has been touting its commitment to 'cooperative federalism,' these proposed budget cuts belie that assertion."[134] Similarly, the executive director of the Environmental Council of the States reasoned that "[t]o have cooperative federalism, you have to have financial support. There is a fairly significant disconnect going on."[135]

Congress made it clear that the Trump budget had no chance of being enacted. But money talks. It is hard to interpret the administration's budget requests as anything other than a concerted effort to hollow out environmental regulation at both the federal and state levels. This destructive endeavor is a far cry from the vibrant cooperative federalism venture which is the administration's purported aim.

The Trump administration's aversion to a vibrant and environmentally protective version of cooperative federalism does not sound the death knell of state participation in innovative and effective environmental protection. Progressive states such as California continue to implement programs that extend beyond federal regulatory requirements, including its efforts to reduce GHG emissions[136] and ozone pollution.[137] States and localities took steps to join the 2015 Paris climate accord after President Trump repudiated it.[138] The attorney generals of states that value rather than disdain environmental protection have begun challenging Trump administration efforts, sometimes in concert with one another, to roll back, delay implementation of, or otherwise weaken federal regulatory initiatives under-taken under or demanded by the cooperative federalism statutes.[139] These efforts are being

131 Brian Dabbs, *More Power to States, Funding Cuts Contradictory: Texas Official*, 48 ENV'T REP. (BNA) 681 (2017).

132 Bogardus, *supra* note 126.

133 The National Association of Clean Air Agencies describes itself as "the national, non-partisan, non-profit association of air pollution control agencies in 40 states, the District of Columbia, four territories and 116 metropolitan areas." NACAA, www.4cleanair.org/.

134 Sean Reilly, *Report details sweeping impact of Trump's proposed cuts*, E&ENEWSPM, May 19, 2017, www.eenews.net/eenewspm/2017/05/19/stories/1060054862.

135 Kevin Bogardus, *Budget undercuts Pruitt's promises to states*, GREENWIRE, Apr. 4, 2017, www.eenews.net/greenwire/stories/1060052582.

136 See Jacques Leslie, *In the Face of a Trump Environmental Rollback, California Stands in Defiance*, YALE ENV'T 360, Feb. 21, 2017, http://e360.yale.edu/features/in-the-face-of-trump-environmental-rollback-california-stands-in-defiance; Keith Goldberg, *Trump, Calif. Poised for Energy and Climate War*, LAW360, Apr. 21, 2017, www.law360.com/articles/915197/trump-calif-poised-for-energy-and-climate-policy-war; Ethan Shenkman et al., *9 Things to Know About Trump's Paris Agreement Decision*, LAW360, June 2, 2017, www.law360.com/articles/930728/9-things-to-know-about-trump-s-paris-agreement-decision (describing climate change initiatives in California, New York, and Washington).

137 See Tony Barboza, *As Trump's EPA Delays Smog Rules, California Vows to Forge Ahead*, L.A. TIMES, June 8, 2017, www.latimes.com/local/lanow/la-me-ozone-delay-20170607-story.html.

138 Benjamin Storrow & Emily Holden, *Governors Face Pressure to Distance Themselves from Trump*, E&ENEWS, June 5, 2017, www.scientificamerican.com/article/governors-face-pressure-to-distance-themselves-from-trump-on-climate/.

139 Juan Carlos Rodriquez, *California AG Promises to Battle Trump on Enviro Issues*, LAW360, Mar. 30, 2017, www.law360.com/articles/908179/california-ag-promises-to-battle-trump-on-enviro-issues.

undertaken without the support of and sometimes in direct opposition to federal officials, and state funding cuts would hamper their ability to fill federal regulatory gaps.

Conclusion

The environmental cooperative federalism statutes have survived decades of judicial challenges in which litigants have asserted, with little success, that these statutes contravene constitutional limits on federal or state regulatory authority. Changes in the future composition of the Supreme Court may impose more significant constraints on cooperative federalism ventures than the Court has been willing to recognize to date. In the meantime, the constitutional underpinnings of these environmental statutes, which carve out distinctive roles for EPA and the states, seem solid. Environmental cooperative federalism, however, is facing perhaps its stiffest test in the form of the Trump administration's efforts to reshape environmental law, both in substance and structure. This time, the threat comes from within. The extent to which environmental cooperative federalism is capable of emerging unscathed from this assault is not yet clear.[140] The fate of nearly fifty years of environmental protection advances hangs in the balance.

The Sabin Center for Climate Change Law maintains a database of state attorney general actions "to advance environmental law and policy objectives," including legal actions against the federal government and "defensive actions" supporting federal and state rules. State Attorneys General Environmental Actions, http://columbiaclimatelaw.com/resources/state-ag-environmental-actions/.

140 For discussion of previous coordinated assaults, see Thomas O. McGarity, *EPA at Helm's Deep; Surviving the Fourth Attack on Environmental Law*, 24 FORDHAM ENVTL. L. REV. 205 (2013).

9 Immigration federalism

Pratheepan Gulasekaram

As a concept, and to many, immigration federalism[1] remains an oddity. To those who view immigration policy as solely within the province of the federal government, state and local involvement seems anathema. Courts and elected officials have reaffirmed and re-energized this notion by continually invoking paeans to "exclusive" federal powers of immigration.[2] Yet, despite these talismanic incantations, it has long been true that states and localities play an important role in immigration policymaking. At no time has this been more evident than the present. Since 1996, the Congress has not been able to enact any broad or comprehensive immigration reform, despite several noteworthy, but failed, attempts to address a "broken" immigration system. In this legislative void, presidents from both political parties have implemented administrative policies and executive actions in an attempt to control immigration enforcement and influence congressional lawmaking. Notably, however, the country's chief executive officers have not been the only, or even most important, sources of immigration policymaking. For much of the past two decades, states and localities have also filled the legislative void, enacting an unprecedented volume of policies that affect immigrants and immigration.

Depending on the jurisdiction, these subfederal policies have taken both restrictionist and integrationist bents.[3] Some places, like Arizona and several states and cities across the southern United States, have enacted decidedly restrictionist laws, focusing on immigration

---

1 I use the term "immigration federalism" to mean sub-federal attempts at regulating immigration or aspects of noncitizens' lives. This chapter is based on, and contains excerpts from, prior co-authored work on immigration federalism with S. Karthick Ramakrishnan, Professor of Public Policy, U.C. Riverside). See PRATHEEPAN GULASEKARAM & S. KARTHICK RAMAKRISHNAN, THE NEW IMMIGRATION FEDERALISM (Cambridge Univ. Press 2015). The quantitative and qualitative empirical data reference in this chapter is presented, unabridged and in full detail, in that work. For further reference, pleas also see the following co-authored works with Professor Ramakrishnan: *The President and Immigration Federalism*, 68 FLA. L. REV. 101 (2016); *Immigration Federalism: A Reappraisal*, 88 N.Y.U. L. REV. 2074 (2013); and *The Importance of the Political in Immigration Federalism*, 44 ARIZ. ST. L. J. 1431 (2012).
2 See, e.g., De Canas v. Bica, 424 U.S. 351, 354–55 (1976); Chy Lung v. Freeman, 92 U.S. 275, 280 (1875).
3 See GULASEKARAM & RAMAKRISHNAN, THE NEW IMMIGRATION FEDERALISM at 7 (explaining the usage of "restrictionist" and "integrationist"). Throughout this chapter, I use "restrictionist" to connote a variety of policies that emphasize robust immigration enforcement and are aimed at reducing immigration flows. Most of these policies have, as their focus, undocumented immigrants and unauthorized migration, but may cut broader to express a general distaste for increased levels of both lawful and unlawful migration. I use the term "integrationist" to connote a variety of policies that are generally immigrant-friendly, seeking to accommodate and integrate immigrants into communities regardless of immigration status.

enforcement schemes, penalizing employment of undocumented immigrants, and restricting educational access. Meanwhile, places like California and New York City have done the opposite. These states and localities have limited cooperation with federal authorities, and provided welfare, state licenses and permits, educational access, and education financing for undocumented noncitizens within the bounds of federal law. Litigation in federal courts has curtailed some of these subfederal efforts, headlined by the landmark *Arizona v. United States* case from 2012.[4] But other state and local policies have received the blessing of the Supreme Court, as with state employer sanctions laws in *Whiting vs. U.S. Chamber of Commerce* in 2011.[5] Still other policies have failed to garner high court review, leaving uncertainty and a patchwork of possibilities depending on the jurisdiction. As a result of both this legal breathing room and the highly partisan immigration politics of the United States, the nation is now a landscape of variegated immigration policies.

This chapter summarizes the origins, current state, and future direction of immigration federalism. Focusing on recent political and legal history, the first section details post-1965 changes to federal immigration law and policy that created the demographic, legal, and political conditions for state and local involvement in immigration regulation. Second, the chapter explains how those post-1965 developments were used by key policy activists after 2001 to enact an unprecedented number of state and local immigration laws, both restrictionist and integrationist. Here, the chapter details how these activists were able to take advantage of political polarization and the post-9/11 climate to proliferate restrictionist state and local laws for several years. That trend that was followed by a decidedly integrationist turn in 2012, which in turn was followed by a return to a steady state of proliferation of both types of subfederal responses after the 2016 presidential election. Finally, the third section assesses the political and legal effects of persistent subfederal immigration participation in immigration regulation. Here, the chapter suggests the importance of state and local lawmaking to entrenching and resisting federal policies, and the ways in which the current state of subfederal policymaking changes theoretical and doctrinal approaches to understanding immigration federalism.

Unauthorized migration and the legal foundation for state and local immigration regulation

For the past century and a half, the federal government has been the primary organ of immigration policy. During that time, in assessing various legal challenges to both federal and subfederal laws that pertain to immigration or immigrants, courts have at times suggested that immigration is an exclusively federal responsibility. In its 1875 *Chy Lung v. Freeman* opinion, striking down California's attempt to regulate admission at its ports of entry, the Supreme Court stated "the passage of laws which concern the admission of citizens and subjects of foreign nationals to our shores belongs to Congress, and not to the states.[6]" In 1915, in nullifying an Arizona law that mandated employers hire native-born citizens, the court once again reiterated, "The authority to control immigration . . . is vested solely in the federal government.[7]" Even more recently in 2012, in invalidating several provisions of Arizona's omnibus immigration enforcement scheme, the Court reaffirmed "the Government

---

4 132 S. Ct. 2492 (2012).
5 131 S. Ct. 1968 (2011).
6 92 U.S. at 280.
7 Truax v. Raich, 239 U.S. 33, 42 (1915).

of the United States has broad, undoubted power over the subject of immigration and the status of aliens.[8]"

Yet, despite these incantations, it is equally clear that throughout American history, states and localities have always played a role in regulating immigrants and enacting laws that encourage or discourage the presence of noncitizens within their jurisdictions. Indeed, the first laws regulating migration were state and local laws that controlled the admission of paupers, criminals, or the sick into their respective areas.[9] That era of predominantly state and city-centered migration regulation came to an end after the Civil War, as the federal government robustly entered the policymaking sphere in the late 1800s. But, even after the first major federal immigration laws, and throughout much of the early twentieth century, states and localities continued to enact employment, registration, and land ownership laws intended to regulate the lives of immigrants.[10] Many of these efforts were curtailed by the U.S. Supreme Court as it began to develop its jurisprudence on immigration federalism.[11] Still, up until last decades of the 20th century, immigration federalism was not the primary legal concern of courts or commentators. The high Court issued isolated decisions on the subject, while never clarifying its doctrinal methodology and relying on broad incantations of exclusive spheres of federal authority that had little resonance with emerging on the ground realities.

The modern era of immigration federalism had its roots in a series of developments beginning in 1965 that would galvanize novel and voluminous state and local interventions. Specifically, four post-1965 changes fundamentally altered the demographics, public policy emphasis, and jurisprudential reaction to immigration in the United States, setting the stage for significant state and local involvement to follow. First, in 1964, the United States terminated the Bracero Program with Mexico; thus, starting in 1965, one major avenue for cyclical labor migration was eliminated. Second, the 1965 Amendments to the Immigration and Nationality Act (INA)[12] and later adjustments in the 1970s, restricted western hemisphere immigration, thereby limiting Mexican and Central American immigration into the United States for the first time. Third, courts began simultaneously carving out some room for state and local enactments in some areas of immigration-related regulation. Finally, for the first time, major federal immigration laws enacted after 1965 expressly recognized opportunities for state and local involvement.

For nearly a quarter century, from 1942 to 1964, the federal government maintained a guest worker program with Mexico. The Bracero Program created a system of seasonal Mexican labor migration to help address farming and agricultural shortfalls during wartime and post-war U.S. labor sectors.[13] The program grew from fewer than 100,000 workers

---

8 Arizona v. United States, 132 S. Ct. 2492, 2498 (2012).

9 Gerald Neuman, *The Lost Century of Immigration Law (1776–1875)*, 93 COLUM. L. REV. 1833 (1993).

10 See Hines v. Davidowitz, 312 U.S. 52 (1941) (striking down state alien registration law); Cornelius v. City of Seattle, 123 Wash. 550 (1923) (upholding city prohibition on noncitizens working in sanitation profession); Patsone v. Pennsylvania, 232 U.S. 138 (1914) (upholding state law barring noncitizens from hunting wild game); see also, Luis F.B. Plasencia, et al., *The Decline of Barriers to Immigrant Economic and Political Rights in the American States 1977–2001*, 37 INT'L MIGRATION REV. 5, 7–8 (2003).

11 See, e.g., Hines, 312 U.S. 52; Truax, 239 U.S. 33.

12 See Immigration and Nationality Act Amendments of 1965, Pub. L. No. 89–236, 79 Stats. 911, 89th Cong. (1965).

13 KITTY CALAVITA, INSIDE THE STATE: THE BRACERO PROGRAM, IMMIGRATION, AND THE I.N.S. 19 (Routledge 1992); Ellis W. Hawley, *The Politics of the Mexican Labor Issue 1950–1965*, 40 AGRIC. HIST. 157 (1966).

per year in the 1940s, to more than 400,000 per year in the 1950s.[14] Congress terminated the program in 1964, as federal lawmakers were debating the major INA changes that were to come in the following year. The Bracero Program and its demise are important for immigration federalism because during its lifespan, the program set networks and processes of migration into motion that continued well beyond its termination. The elimination of the program did not abolish the migration patterns that it helped create, and could not eradicate the cross-border familial and financial ties that had been cemented over the past decades. Those connections and related migration patterns continued to exist despite changes to immigration law and policy.

Second, with the 1965 amendments to the INA, Congress removed the explicit racial and national origin barriers to immigration and naturalization that had long been part of federal immigration law. Congress replaced its discriminatory policies with a more open immigration system that, for the most part, allowed admission to immigrants without explicit regard to race or national origin. However, as a tradeoff, the new system also implemented per-country limitations on every migrant-sending country.[15] These caps, while formally equal in the sense that every sending country would have access to the same maximum number of visas, disparately impacted migrants from countries with historically high migration to the United States. Eligible applicants from those countries soon exceeded the allotted yearly quotas, a condition that persists through today.

Most notably, these amendments for the INA imposed, for the first time, hard limits on legal migration from Mexico and Central America. This dramatic change caused a marked shift in the demographics, meaning, and political and legal importance of unlawful migration. After these changes to the INA, once-lawful migrants became unlawful. In short, the cap on lawful migration from Mexico and Central American countries created the new category of the "illegal immigrant."[16]

Just as the category of "illegal immigrant" began to take shape and the unlawfully present population of the U.S. grew, the country went into economic recession in the early 1970s. Not surprisingly, several states began passing the first wave of laws to address these conjoined concerns. State-level laws on employer sanctions, educational access, and public benefits for noncitizens began popping up in several jurisdictions.[17] As these state and local laws emerged, so did the number of federal court cases challenging them. Soon, an equivocating immigration federalism doctrine began to take shape. At times, the Court seemed firmly to view state and local discrimination against noncitizens as violative of noncitizens' individual rights and an intrusion on the exclusive authority of the federal government. For example, in *Graham v. Richardson* (1971),[18] the high Court struck down state welfare laws that discriminated on the basis of citizenship, finding that such policies impermissibly intruded into a field occupied by the federal government. It also held that the legal residents challenging the law constituted a "inherently suspect class" triggering the court's most exacting

---

14 S. Comm. on the Judiciary, 96th Cong., *A Report on Temporary Worker Programs: Background and Issues* 36 (Government Printing Office 1980).

15 8 U.S.C. § 1152(a) & (b).

16 Although I use the term in quotes here, throughout this chapter I use the terms "undocumented immigrant", "unauthorized immigrant", or "unlawfully present person" to refer to the same group colloquially referred to by some as an "illegal immigrant."

17 See GULASEKARAM & RAMAKRISHNAN, THE NEW IMMIGRATION FEDERALISM, 42–49.

18 Graham v. Richardson, 403 U.S. 365 (1971).

scrutiny.[19] In *Plyler v. Doe* (1982), the court relied on the Fourteenth Amendment's equal protection clause to strike down Texas' attempt to exclude undocumented children from its public school system.[20]

On the other hand, other cases allowed room for state and local regulation that affected immigrants. For instance, in *De Canas v. Bica* (1976), the Court paid lip service to its oft-repeated claim that the "power to regulate immigration is unquestionably a federal power."[21] Nevertheless, the Court upheld California's law that penalized the employment of unauthorized workers, stating "but the court has never held that ever state enactment which in any way deals with aliens is a regulation of immigration, and thus per se preempted by this constitutional power, wither latent or exercised."[22] *De Canas'* holding seemed to signal the Court's implicit recognition that certain forms of state and local responses to federal immigration policies were inevitable. And, importantly, it signaled the possibility that states and localities might regulate of aspects of noncitizens lives, even when that regulation could indirectly incentivize or disincentivize migration flows.

Moreover, the contrast between cases like *Graham* or *Plyler*, on the one hand, and *De Canas,* on the other, began to illustrate the paucity of the doctrinal approach taken by older cases. Broad statements that the Constitution created exclusive or dominant spheres of regulatory authority failed to answer the more complicated questions of how exactly that authority should be divided when state and local lawmaking straddled areas of traditional state concern and immigration. As the third section of this chapter argues, this doctrinal conundrum still continues, but the explosion and entrenchment of present-day subfederal immigration policies are forcing commentators—and, possibly courts—to evolve their theoretical approaches to evaluating immigration federalism.

The doctrinal space carved out for some types of state and local regulation led to the fourth critical post-1965 development: Congress began expressly recognizing, and leaving room for, subfederal involvement. Prior to the mid-1980s, federal immigration statutes scarcely, if at all, contemplated the presence of state and local policies that could have a substantial impact on immigration.[23] But, starting with the Immigration Reform and Control Act of 1986,[24] it was clear that Congress had become acutely aware of the complications and possibilities of state and local involvement. Ten years prior to IRCA, *De Canas* had opened up the possibility of state regulation of employers for hiring unauthorized workers. By the mid-1980s, several other states had followed suit and had enacted similar employer sanctions law.[25] In response, as part of IRCA's major immigration overhaul (which included a massive legislative "amnesty" for undocumented immigrants), Congress implemented a federal employer sanctions system.[26] The inclusion of this federal provision immediately preempted the eleven state and local schemes that were then in place. Although the state laws were

---

19 403 U.S. at 375–76.

20 Plyler v. Doe, 457 U.S. 202 (1982).

21 *De Canas,* 424 U.S. at 354–55.

22 *Id.*

23 There were some notable exceptions. Indeed, one of the first federal immigration laws incorporated state commissioners into the process of inspecting disembarking ship passengers. An Act to Regulate Immigration, Sess. I, ch. 376, 22 Stat. 214, 47th Cong. (1882).

24 Pub. L. 99–603, 100 Stat. 3445 (1986).

25 Kitty Calavita, *California's "Employer Sanctions" Legislation: Now You See It, Now You Don't,* 12 POL. & SOC'Y 205 (1983)

26 8 U.S.C. § 1321(a)(h)(2).

thereafter voided, the fact that federal law expressly addressed that state level development showcased the power of state policies in placing the issue on the national agenda and pushing Congress to legislate a federal scheme to address it.

While IRCA's effect on state and local laws was limited to employer sanctions, Congress' next and last major overhaul of immigration law left significant space for subfederal involvement in across of breadth of regulatory areas. The 1996 set of federal laws—which included some or all provisions of the Illegal Immigration Reform and Responsibility Act (IIRIRA),[27] the Personal Responsibility and Work Opportunity Reconciliation Act (PRWORA),[28] and the Antiterrorism and Effective Death Penalty Act (AEDPA)[29]—provided for the possibility of both restrictionist and integrationist subfederal laws. On the enforcement side, provisions like IIRIRA's Section 287(g) allowed states and localities to enter into cooperative agreements with the federal government to help enforce immigration laws.[30] And, other sections allowed for state participation in enforcing specific crimes.[31] In addition, the federal welfare overhaul purported to devolve to states the precise authority the Supreme Court had stripped away two decades earlier in *Graham*: They allowed states to determine whether or not certain categories of noncitizens would be eligible for important public welfare programs.[32] In contrast, other sections of the 1996 overhaul allowed states to take integrative steps. PWORA's devolution of welfare decisions to the states meant that they could choose to be more generous to noncitizens than the floor set by the federal government. In addition, certain IIRIRA provisions were written drafted in such a way as to permit states, with careful drafting, to offer public benefits, professional licenses, and other educational benefits to undocumented immigrants.[33]

Ultimately, these four post-1965 developments—terminating the Bracero program, equalizing all per-country migration despite historical and geographic ties, leaving doctrinal leeway for state and local involvement, and enacting federal statutes that allowed certain state-level policies - set the stage for our current moment of immigration federalism. After 2001, these factors led to states and localities taking advantage of legal and political opportunities to engage in robust immigration policymaking.

State and local policy proliferation in our current immigration federalism

The statutory leeway and doctrinal uncertainty characteristic of the immigration federalism developments after 1965 became the tinder for an explosion of subfederal immigration laws after 2001. This section details this phenomenon and provides an evidence-based explanation for its occurrence. Fundamentally, key political actors—issue entrepreneurs—capitalized on

---

27 Pub. L. No. 104–208, 110 Stat. 3009–546, 104th Cong. (1996) (expanding grounds for removal, reducing judicial review, reducing relief from removal, and expanding list of offenses with mandatory detention).
28 Pub. L. No. 104–193, 110 Stat. 2105, 104th Cong. (1996) (limiting eligibility of noncitizens for federal public benefits, and authorizing states to similarly restrict noncitizen access)
29 Pub. L. N. 104–132, 110 Stat. 1214, 104th Cong. (1996) (requiring mandatory detention of noncitizens convicted of a range of offenses).
30 8 U.S.C. § 1357(g).
31 8 U.S.C. § 1324 (providing state enforcement authority for the crime of smuggling undocumented immigrants).
32 8 U.S.C. § 1601, et. seq.
33 8 U.S.C. §§ 1621(d), 1623(a).

post-2001 party polarization and ethnic nationalism to start a legislative cascade of subfederal immigration laws in receptive jurisdictions. This trend was overwhelmingly restrictionist for the first several years, but turned integrationist as immigrant advocates and pro-immigrant forces began recognizing the value of a state-level strategy and adopting it. After the election of Donald Trump in 2016, both restrictionist and integrationist enactments have become prominent again.

Of course, as the prior section noted, even before 2001, states and localities had been making inroads in immigration regulation. California's and other states' employer sanctions laws had forced Congress to address the issue and include prohibitions on unauthorized employment in federal law. In addition, in the early 1990s, California attempted a more comprehensive enforcement scheme with its infamous Proposition 187.[34] Prop 187 sought to limit access to public services for undocumented persons, barred their enrollment in public schools, and required state and local participation in immigration enforcement.[35] That law garnered some interest in politically like-minded states and had the potential to spread. In the end, however, Prop 187 died in litigation and the copycat efforts elsewhere never came to fruition. In addition to California, other jurisdictions also engaged in immigration and immigrant-related regulation.[36]

While such enactments created headlines and controversy in the 1990s, they were fledgling efforts, lacking the political, financial, and ideological heft to spread as a legislative movement.[37] It was only after 2001, when key policy activists, elected officials, and national party operatives saw the potential of state and local policymaking as a way of influencing the national agenda and instantiating a *de facto* national immigration policy, did subfederal immigration regulation reach unprecedented levels. Thus, the critical difference between efforts like Prop 187 and the post-2001 proliferation was the presence of a networked group of policy activists who recognized the advantages that federalism offered for implementing their legislative vision, and changing the national conversation on immigration. The remainder of this section provides a politicized account of that work, which continues to describe and define immigration federalism today.

After a period of relative subfederal inaction on immigration following the 1996 federal laws, the terrorist attacks of September 11, 2001, reignited immigration federalism. The fact that the 9/11 hijackers were foreign-born noncitizens galvanized legislative responses intended to shore up immigration enforcement.[38] These responses seemed to have little, if any, impact on national security, but would profoundly affect the lives of noncitizens. Soon after 9/11, localities began using § 287(g), which had lay dormant for several years since enactment as part of IIRIRA, to enter into agreements with federal officials to help enforce immigration law. This increase in 287(g) agreements was the beginning of a larger movement. The number of proposed and passed state and local laws began to rapidly increase by 2004, and in the period from 2004 through 2012, states and localities enacted a record number of laws intended to help control immigration and disincentivize unlawful migration.[39]

34 Cal. Prop. 187, 1994 Cal. Legis. Serv. A-78. (Cal. 1994).
35 See LULAC v. Wilson, 908 F. Supp. 755 (C.D. Cal. 1995) (enjoining Prop 187)
36 GULASEKARAM & RAMAKRISHNAN, THE NEW IMMIGRATION FEDERALISM, at 57.
37 *Id.*, at 51–54.
38 GULASEKARAM & RAMAKRISHNAN, THE NEW IMMIGRATION FEDERALISM, at 108.
39 Nat'l Conference of State Legislatures, *A Review of State Immigration Legislation in 2005* (2007), www.ncsl.org/research/immigration/immigrant-policy-project-state-legislation-117.aspx.

The state of Arizona drew the greatest attention with the passage of high-profile laws like the Legal Arizona Workers Act (LAWA)[40] in 2007 and its Support Our Law Enforcement Safe Neighborhoods Act of 2010 (more popularly known as SB 1070).[41] Arizona, however, was not alone in its attempts to target unauthorized immigrants. Localities like San Bernardino, California, began clamoring for a county-level "Illegal Immigration Relief Act."[42] Although that particular proposal never passed, it garnered significant attention, and later, similar ordinances proposed in other places did.[43] Restrictive laws emerged in other states such as Oklahoma, Georgia, Indiana, and North Carolina, where few would have previously identified as immigrant destinations or facing significant problems due to immigration.[44] At the local level, places like Hazleton in Pennsylvania, Farmers Branch in Texas, and Fremont in Nebraska became fixtures on national cable and print media because of their restrictive town ordinances penalizing activities such as work solicitation or renting to undocumented persons.[45]

All told during the period from 2001 through 2012, states and localities enacted restrictionist laws that:

– Required law enforcement to check immigration status of they came into contact with as part of their law enforcement duties;
– Restricted public benefits based on citizenship status;
– Required employers to use the federal E-Verify database and penalized them by revoking business licenses if they failed to comply;
– Penalized landlords for leasing property to undocumented persons;
– Criminalized day laborers and day-labor centers through anti-solicitation laws;
– Restricted higher education access or denied in-state tuition rates at public universities;
– Voided contracts entered into by undocumented persons; and
– Restricted access to identification cards and driver's licenses for unlawfully present persons.[46]

Variations on many of these categories of laws might have existed before the last couple decades. The scope and breadth of these enactments after 2001, however, was striking.[47]

---

40 Arizona House Bill 2779, 48th Leg. 1st Reg. Sess. (Ariz. 2007).
41 Arizona Senate Bill 1070, 49th Leg., 2nd Reg. Sess. (Ariz. 2010).
42 San Bernadino, Cal., [Proposed] Illegal Immigration Relief Act (2006), available at www.ailadownloads. org/advo/SanBernandinoIllegalImmigraitonOrdinance.pdf.
43 See, e.g., Fremont, Neb., Ordinance 5165 (June 21, 2010); Farmers Branch, Tex., Ordinance 2903 (Jan. 22, 2007); Escondido, Cal., Ordinance No. 2006–38R (2006)); Hazelton, Pa., Ordinance 2006–18 (Sept. 21, 2006); Colorado S.B. 90, C.R.S. §§29-29-101 – 103 (2006).
44 See, e.g., Michael McNutt, *Oklahoma House Passes Anti-Illegal Immigrant Bill*, NewsOK, Mar. 11, 2011; Patrick Jonson, *Far from Mexican Border, Georgia Mulls Arizona-Style Immigration Crackdown*, Christian Science Monitor, Apr. 14, 2011.
45 See *supra* nn. 43 and 44.
46 See GULASEKARAM & RAMAKRISHNAN, THE NEW IMMIGRATION FEDERALISM, at 58–67 and accompanying notes; see also, Christina Rodriguez, Muzaffar Chisti, and Kimberly Nortman, *Testing the Limits: A Framework for Assessing the Legality of State and Local Immigration Measures* at pp. 2–3, Migration Policy Institute (2007).
47 See *supra* n. 39. As monitored by the National Conference of State Legislatures and other organizations, in 2005 approximately 300 laws were proposed across the country, with 39 passed into law.

Equally striking was the geography of these new restrictionist laws. At the state level, they popped up in Arizona, but not California or New Mexico. States across the south, like Georgia and Alabama, were also hotbeds of activity. At the local level, these policies were popping up in isolated counties in California, and previously unknown localities like Hazelton, Pennsylvania, or Fremont, Nebraska. Many of these areas were unassociated with high immigrant populations, or the demographic problems that might be connected to massive social upheaval and migration patterns. In other places like Arizona, or select counties in California, migration may have been a notable demographic reality. But even with those historically immigrant-heavy areas, it was not clear why certain states and localities would choose to enact restrictionist laws when jurisdictions of similar size and demographics did not.

Together, the volume and geography of this spike in restrictionist subfederal policy-making begged a pressing question: What accounted for this sudden rise in state and local activity in these disparate locations? If elected officials from enacting jurisdictions were to be believed, the answer would be the severe public policy problems and demographic pressures caused by immigration. Commonly cited in media reports and political rhetoric were factors such as overcrowding, language isolation, economic deprivation, crime, and sudden population changes.[48] In signing Arizona's SB 1070 into law, for example, then-Governor Jan Brewer remarked:

> Senate Bill 1070 represents another tool for our state to use as we work to solve a crisis we did not create and the federal government has refused to fix . . . The crisis caused by illegal immigration and Arizona's porous border. . . .
>
> [D]ecades of federal inaction and misguided policy have created a dangerous and unacceptable situation.[49]

Similarly, then-Mayor of Hazelton (now, Congressman) Lou Bartletta urged, "In Hazelton, illegal immigration is not some abstract debate about walls and amnesty, but it is a tangible, very real problem."[50] As evidenced in these statements, the claims of pressing policy problems were paired with a claim of federal failure; that is, a claim that the federal government had chosen not to address these pressing public policy concerns. Therefore, states and localities were virtually compelled to take matters in their own hands and begin enacting the tough immigration enforcement and immigrant-related laws that the federal government had not.

Undoubtedly, this conventional wisdom had intuitive appeal. It jived with common federalism assumptions that different regions of the country face different demographic pressures, based on their particular circumstances; therefore, solutions are needed that might be different from a one-size-fits-all national policy or more lax policies in other juris-dictions. The plausibility of this narrative was bolstered by Congress' failure to pass federal

48 See, e.g., Ben Casselman, *Immigration is Changing Much More Than the Immigration Debate*, FiveThirtyEight, July 9, 2014; Alex Kotlowitz, *Our Town*, N.Y. TIMES MAGAZINE, Aug. 5, 2007.
49 Statement by Gov. Jan. Brewer on the signing of Senate Bill 1070, Apr. 23, 2010.
50 *Comprehensive Immigration Reform: Examining the Need for a Guest Worker Program*, Hearing before the S. Comm. of the Judiciary, 109th Cong. 11–13 (2006) (Statement of Hon. Louis Barletta, Mayor, City of Hazelton, Pa.).

immigration reform despite several high profile attempts to do so.[51] In addition, immigrants were increasingly moving to "new destinations"[52] that were different than the traditional immigrant gateways to the U.S. The story of public policy necessity also resonated with long-held assumptions that immigrants steal jobs and contribute to wage depression and economic stress. Accordingly, in the absence of careful study, the sudden rise and spread of restrictionist laws from 2004 through 2012 seemed to comport with classic federalism themes of federal failure and region-specific solutions to demographic realities of immigrant settlement.

As it turns out, however, this conventional explanation is misleading and empirically unsupportable. Upon closer scrutiny, restrictive responses by state and local governments to undocumented migration were unrelated to commonly cited and objectively measurable demographic pressures. When viewed systemically across all jurisdictions in the country, commonly cited policy concerns—like recent immigrant population growth, the proportion of Spanish-dominated households, crime, and local and economic stress—were not salient in explaining the proposal and passage of restrictionist state and local laws.[53] In Arizona, for example, restrictionist laws were finding favor despite marked drop in violent crime.[54] Among municipalities that passed restrictive ordinances, new immigrants averaged just a slight amount higher than the average for municipalities across the country.[55] Perhaps more to the point, the overwhelming majority of jurisdictions that shared the same demographic factors as enacting jurisdictions—such as growth in immigrant populations, having a recently arrived immigrant population, or a high proportion of Spanish-speaking immigrants—did not propose, let alone pass, any immigrant-related laws.[56] Further, not only was such demographic change and connected policy problems an insufficient to explain why jurisdictions would enact restrictionist laws, it turns out those were not necessary factors either. Forty-two percent of the municipalities enacting restrictionist laws during this time, had recent immigrant populations below the national average, with a quarter of the cases having recent immigrants only accounting for fewer than 0.5 percent of the city's residents.[57]

If oft-referenced demographic factors and policy concerns failed to explain the rise of state and local restrictionism, what did? The evidence reveals that, after controlling for all other factors, political partisanship had the strongest and most consistent effects on proposal and passage of state and local immigration laws.[58] Hundreds of cities and several states experienced the demographic change identical to, or even more severe than, places that enacted restrictionist state laws. Yet, an exceedingly minute number chose to respond with

51 Rachel Weiner, *How Immigration Reform Failed, Over and Over*, WASHINGTON POST, Jan. 30, 2013 (chronicling attempts to pass federal immigration reform).
52 Audrey Singer, Brookings Inst., *The Rise of New Immigrant Gateways* 2 (February 2004); Paul Vitello, *As Illegal Workers Hit Suburbs, Politicians Scramble to Respond*, NEW YORK TIMES, Oct. 6, 2005.
53 GULASEKARAM & RAMAKRISHNAN, THE NEW IMMIGRATION FEDERALISM, at 75–86 and Appendices A and B.
54 Randal C. Archibold, *On Border Violence, Truth Pales Compared to Ideas*, NEW YORK TIMES, June 19, 2a010; see generally, Ruben G. Rumbaut, et al., Migration Pol'y Inst., *Debunking the Myth of Immigrant Criminality: Imprisonment among First- and Second-Generation Young Men* (June 2006).
55 GULASEKARAM & RAMAKRISHNAN, THE NEW IMMIGRATION FEDERALISM, at 75–86 and Appendices A and B.
56 *Id.*
57 *Id.*
58 *Id.*

enforcement-heavy and immigrant-targeted legislation. The catalytic characteristic common to most enacting jurisdictions is not demographic upheaval; rather, they shared a partisan mix highly receptive to restrictive policies.

But partisanship and polarization were only the fertile groundwork. Seeding that soil during post-2001 period were key policy activists—immigration issue entrepreneurs. These entrepreneurs, unlike in prior eras, were able to exploit dynamics within the Republican Party to proliferate restrictionist policies across several jurisdictions.[59] Immigration issue entrepreneurs were those who did the work of promoting the salience of immigration issues, framing those concerns in particular ways intended to energize voters, and offering solutions for those issues to receptive elected officials and constituencies. The work of spreading immigration restrictionism for the better part of a decade was primarily accomplished through the coordinated work of issue entrepreneurs like Kris Kobach, Tom Tancredo, Lou Dobbs, and the organizations Federation of Americans for Immigration Reform (FAIR) and Numbers USA.[60]

Immigration issue entrepreneurs often created pre-written model laws for states and localities, and shopped them to elected officials and jurisdictions where those proposals would find favor. These entrepreneurs worked together in a network, some to draft legislation and legal justifications, some to lobby and influence elected officials, some to keep relevant issue in media headlines, and some to organize grassroots call-in and letter-writing campaigns. Together, they explicitly and implicitly invoked feelings of ethnic nationalism and cultural threat from immigration to energize voters and legislatures in support of their restrictionist proposals.[61] The post-9/11 rhetoric of restrictionist elected officials and issue entrepreneurs focused on the cultural, economic, and security threat of foreigners. Although the 9/11 attacks involved mostly Saudi nationals, issue entrepreneurs soon conflated the racialized threat of Middle Eastern and Arab foreigners with migration across the southern border of the United States.[62] Purposely confusing terrorism and unauthorized migration, policy activists like Kris Kobach argued that local law enforcement officers were empowered to, and should engage in, immigration enforcement. The resulting rapidity and sequential spread of these state and local laws gave the impression to the public and the media that undocumented migration had become one of the most pressing threats to the economy and national security of the country, and it absolutely required state and local responses.

That cascade of state and local policies, in turn, dynamically influenced federal lawmakers. The federated nature of political parties forced federal lawmakers to take heed of the

---

59 *Id.,* at 95–99.

60 *Id.,* at 99–105. Kris Kobach is a former Department of Justice official who served as a legal officer for FAIR and then as the Kansas Secretary of State. He currently also holds a position with the Trump administration. Tom Tancredo is a former congressman from Colorado who founded the Congressional Immigration Reform Caucus and unsuccessfully ran for the Republican Party presidential nomination in 2008. Lou Dobbs is a media personality and author who for many years hosted a nightly news program on CNN.

61 *Id.,* at 94 and 108–110; see generally, LOUISE CAINKAR, HOMELAND INSECURITY: THE ARAB AMERICAN AND MUSLIM AMERICAN EXPERIENCE AFTER 9/11 (Russell Sage 2009); Media Matters Action Network, *Fear & Loathing in Prime Time: Immigration Myths and the Cable News,* Media Matters for America, May 21, 2008, http://mediamattersaction.org/reports/fearandloathing/online_version.; Jennifer M. Chacon, *Unsecured Borders: Immigration Restrictions, Crime Control, and National Security,* 39 CONN. L. REV. 1827, 1853 (2007).

62 See sources cited, *supra* n. 61.

immigration positions taken by subfederal officials of their own parties. Thus, as state and local officials began supporting highly restrictionist legislation, they were able to anchor the positions of national lawmakers within their own party. An important example is the shift of Senator (and 2008 presidential candidate) John McCain's (R-AZ) position on immigration.[63] In the early and mid-2000s, Senator McCain sponsored and supported several compromise federal legislative efforts, which included a mixture of policies like paths to legalization and increasing visa allocations along with enforcement provisions. However, as state and local officials in his home state began publically supporting Arizona state laws like LAWA and SB 1070, and local sheriffs in Arizona began heavy-handed enforcement efforts, McCain could no longer afford to maintain compromise positions on national immigration proposals. Faced with primary challengers within his party who critiqued his moderate immigration stances, McCain stopped sponsoring compromise federal reform bills and took a hardline, enforcement-heavy stance on immigration.[64] This was a dynamic that replicated itself several times in primary contests during the period of massive restrictionist proliferation. In 2014, then-House Majority Leader Eric Cantor (R-VA) lost his seat for hinting at the need for compromises on immigration policy.[65] As a result, every federal proposal for comprehensive federal immigration reform for over two decades has not passed Congress.

The restrictionist fervor and the work of issue entrepreneurs hit its peak in the late 2000s and into 2011, as Arizona's SB 1070 and Alabama's HB 56 came to represent the paradigmatic state-level restrictionist policies. These were omnibus state laws that contained directives to law enforcement to engage in immigration enforcement, and other sections that effectively barred undocumented children from attending public schools. In 2012, however, that restrictionist momentum hit a roadblock and a new wave of state and local laws with an integrationist bent began to emerge. Similar to the explanation of restrictionist activity, the momentum shift in 2012 towards integrationist subfederal laws was not attributable to any major demographic or migration change. Instead, it was related to political and legal dynamics that weakened restrictionists, while emboldening integrationists.

Three significant developments in 2012 helped turn the tide.[66] First, the United States Supreme Court struck down several provisions of Arizona's SB 1070, dealing it, and laws modeled after it, a serious legal blow. Not only did the decision invalidate the law that had come to represent the restrictionist ideal, but it also allowed immigrant advocacy organizations at the state level to begin shifting resources away from litigation and towards legislation.[67] Second, in that same summer, President Barack Obama announced his Deferred Action for Child Arrivals program (DACA), which allowed undocumented youth to apply for temporary relief from deportation and possibly also gain employment authorization. Although it was a federal administrative program, the program bolstered the cause of immigrant advocates at local, state, and federal levels. For example, maximizing the benefits of the program required state and local policies that facilitated education access or transportation for undocumented persons. Not surprisingly, driver's license access laws rapidly spiked after that, with thirteen states or jurisdictions offering licenses to undocumented persons by the end of 2013. Finally, in November 2012, Obama won re-election with his Republican opponent, Mitt Romney,

---

63 GULASEKARAM & RAMAKRISHNAN, THE NEW IMMIGRATION FEDERALISM at 90–91, 110–111.
64 *Id.*
65 See, e.g., Cameron Joseph, *Cantor Loss Immigration Reform Death Knell*, THE HILL, June 10, 2014.
66 See generally, GULASEKARAM & RAMAKRISHNAN, THE NEW IMMIGRATION FEDERALISM at 12–27.
67 *Id.* at 145–47.

suffering massive losses with Latino and Asian-American voters.[68] With the election loss, the strategy of state-centered immigration enforcement Romney endorsed, suffered at least a temporary political rebuke.

Riding the momentum and opportunities presented by these developments, immigrant advocates began adopting the strategy of subfederal policy proliferation that restrictionists had employed. Looking to states and localities, advocates were able to harness legislative momentum for a set of policies across favorable jurisdictions that:

- Mitigated federal enforcement efforts through non-cooperation and detainer resistance ordinances;
- Provided driver's licenses to all state residents regardless of immigration status;
- Allowed those without legal status to receive municipal identification cards;
- Provided admission to higher education institutions, and facilitated the financing of education through tuition-equity laws or access to scholarships;
- Permitted professional licensing within the state, regardless of immigration status;
- Established local integration agencies, immigrant-resource offices, and "welcoming" initiatives;
- Expanded access to certain state or locally-funded welfare and healthcare programs.[69]

Again, as with the restrictionist trend, partisanship remained a significantly salient factor (as did the size of the Latino electorate in the jurisdiction).[70] Additionally, unlike in the past when much of immigrant advocates' attention, organizational focus, and financial support went only towards national strategies, after 2012, they began capitalizing on opportunities at the state and local level.[71]

In 2016, however, the general trend away from state level restrictionism and towards subfederal integrationism took another turn. During the summer of 2016, President Obama's second deferred action program—the Deferred Action for Parents of Americans (DAPA, which was proposed in late 2014)—was struck down.[72] Prior to its defeat, cities and states with receptive constituencies had been planning public policies to maximize the full potential of DACA and DAPA.[73] While DAPA's defeat was a major blow to immigrant activists, the bigger jolt came a few months later when Donald Trump won the presidency, riding a wave of anti-immigrant, nativist rhetoric.[74]

Although it is still too early to determine whether the Trump era will generate more state-level restrictionism, integrationism, or both, the first several months of 2017 have witnessed

---

68 *President Exit Polls,* New York Times, (2012), http://elections.nytimes.com/212/results/president/exit-polls); Asian American Justice Center, et al., *Behind the Numbers: Post Election Survey of Asian American and Pacific Islander Voters in 2012* (Apr. 2013), www.apiavote.org/sites/apiavote/files/2012research/2012_12_EMBARGOED_Preliminary_Report_AAPI_Voting_FINAL.pdf.

69 See generally, Gulasekaram & Ramakrishnan, The New Immigration Federalism, at 127–41.

70 *Id.,* at 141–43 and Appendix C.

71 *Id.,* at 145–47.

72 United States v. Texas, 809 F.3d 134 (5th Cir. 2015) (enjoining DAPA), *judgment aff'd by an equally divided Court,* 579 U.S. ___ (2016).

73 See generally, Pratheepan Gulasekaram and S. Karthick Ramakrishnan, *The President and Immigration Federalism,* 68 Fla. L. Rev. 101, 172–73 (2016); Cities United for Immigration Action, Mission Statement, www.citiesforaction.us/mission (last visited Aug. 16, 2017); Roque Planas, *Democratic Mayors Rally Support for Obama's Immigration Changes,* Huffington Post, Dec. 8, 2014.

74 Molly Ball, *Donald Trump and the Politics of Fear,* The Atlantic, Sept. 2, 2016; Sarah Posner, *Trump Makes Good on His Nativist Campaign Promises,* Rolling Stone, Jan. 26, 2017.

a continuation of bitter fights over immigration policy being fought at the state and local level, and through state-led litigation in federal courts. True to his campaign promise of heightened immigration enforcement, the fledgling Trump administration has caused immigrant advocates to again redouble defensive efforts intended to mitigate the harshest effects of federal policies. High on Trump's agenda have been the implementation of an immigration ban from nationals of six predominantly Muslim countries and a crackdown on so-called "sanctuary cities" (cities that decline to cooperate with federal authorities on immigration enforcement).[75] Both initiatives showcase the now firmly established power of states and localities in immigration policymaking.

First, Trump's implementation of his executive order creating the "Muslim ban" has been stalled in federal courts that have struck it down on statutory, due process, and first amendment grounds.[76] The Supreme Court is set to hear the case, but it is not clear yet whether it will still be a live issue by then. Regardless of the result, the pushback to the executive orders (EO) is significant because it has been litigated in large part by states. Trump's first attempt at a Muslim ban was stopped in part by a suit by the state of Washington; his second and current attempt enjoined through a suit by the state of Hawaii. In each of those suits, like-minded attorney generals, governors, and mayors of states and localities joined in the litigation as parties or as amicus. Notably, this was not the first prominent use of state-plaintiffs to challenge federal executive actions. Indeed, the Trump immigration ban litigation mirrored the case against Obama's DAPA program. DAPA's defeat in *Texas v. United States* was orchestrated by the attorneys general and governors of twenty-six states— all Republican—using the federal courts as the forum to voice legal and political opposition to a policy they deeply disagreed with.[77]

Second, Trump's executive orders and subsequent actions by administrative agencies under his control have reignited the long simmering debate over the desirability and legality of sanctuary cities and efforts by states and localities to mitigate federal enforcement efforts.[78] In the wake of his election, several jurisdictions reaffirmed their intention to not cooperate with federal immigration enforcement authorities. In addition, other institutions like college campuses and religious centers joined in the movement as well.[79] The Trump administration's subsequent crackdown on those jurisdictions and institutions is currently being litigated in federal court with the Democratic strongholds of San Francisco and Santa Clara counties in California leading the charge.[80] In contrast, restrictionist jurisdictions and officials have

---

75 Exec. Order No. 13780, Protecting the Nation from Foreign Terrorist Entry into the United States, 82 Fed. Reg. 13959 (Mar. 6, 2017) (ordering the cessation of admission of certain nationals from six predominantly Muslim countries); Exec. Order No. 13768, Enhancing Public Safety in the Interior of the United States, 82 Fed. Reg. 8799 (Jan. 25, 2017) (directing a crackdown, through loss of funding, on states and localities that fail to cooperate with the federal government on immigration enforcement).
76 State of Hawaii v. Trump, 1:17-CV-00050 (9th Cir. June 12, 2017) (enjoining EO on statutory grounds); International Refugee Assistance Program v. Trump, 8:17-CV-00361 (4th Cir. May 25, 2017) (enjoining EO on constitutional grounds).
77 Jeffrey Toobin, *An Ideological Scramble on Immigration at the Supreme Court*, THE NEW YORKER, Jan. 19, 2016.
78 GULASEKARAM & RAMAKRISHNAN, THE NEW IMMIGRATION FEDERALISM, at 128–31.
79 Clyde Haberman, *Trump and the Battle Over Sanctuary in America*, NEW YORK TIMES, Mar. 5, 2017.
80 City and Country of San Francisco v. Trump, 3:17-CV-00485-WHO (N.D. Cal. Apr. 25, 2017) (enjoining Executive Order 13768), consolidated with *County of Santa Clara v. Trump*, 3:17-CV-00574 (N.D. Cal. Apr. 25, 2017).

also joined the fray. Some Republican-led states have taken decidedly "anti-sanctuary" stances, enacting state measures that tamp down on the ability of counties, cities, or local law enforcement agencies to resist federal enforcement efforts.[81] These state-level efforts too, are under litigation.[82]

The future and consequences of immigration federalism

Going forward, what does this all this recent legal and political development in immigration federalism portend for the future? How does the partisan nature of subfederal immigration policymaking factor, if at all, into the question whether such laws are constitutional? In what ways are theoretical and doctrinal approaches to subfederal immigration regulation evolving in response to this sustained period of state and local policymaking? These are the questions that this final section takes up. It suggests that immigration federalism for both practical and doctrinal reasons is here to stay. The striking rise of state and local immigration regulation since 2001 and continuing to present day have changed the way in which scholars, courts, and policy analysts might conceive of state and local presence in immigration policymaking. First, immigration federalism is now an indelible and integral feature of our national policy landscape. Second, the dynamics of subfederal immigration proliferation suggest that, although framed as constitutional contests over the proper level of government to handle the issue, debates over the propriety of state and local regulation are battles over competing substantive visions of ideal immigration policy. Finally, because federal legislative efforts on immigration are unlikely to pass for the immediate future, states and localities are likely where policy innovation and resistance to federal efforts will take place. And, as subfederal immigration regulation becomes normalized and integrated into federal schemes, legal doctrine and theoretical descriptions of immigration federalism will also have to conform to this new equilibrium of state and local involvement.

Of course, states and localities do not have carte blanche. Despite congressional inaction, the Supreme Court has established some limits on subfederal action. After 2012, some of the harshest and enforcement-heavy aspects of Arizona's SB 1070 were struck down, sending a message that states could not wholesale create their own omnibus enforcement policies. Yet, the Court also left in place a section of the law that required law enforcement officers to check the immigration status of they have in custody, who they suspect might be unlawfully present.[83] And, the Supreme Court never heard challenges on other aspects of the state law, such as its provision preventing localities from enacting "sanctuary" ordinances to resist federal enforcement. Moreover, it bears remembering that SB 1070 was challenged by a federal administration unfriendly to the idea of a state-level enforcement scheme; with a current federal administration that would likely be friendly to such a state law, it remains

---

81 See, e.g., Texas Senate Bill 4, 85th Leg. (2017) (requiring campus and local police departments to cooperate with federal immigration authorities); Mississippi Senate Bill 2710, 2017 Reg. Sess. (2017) (prohibiting the enactment of sanctuary law).

82 City of El Cenizo, et al. v. State of Texas, 5:17-CV-404 (W.D. Tex. 2017); Jackie Wang, *Border City, County Sue Texas over "Sanctuary" Law*, THE TEXAS TRIBUNE, May 9, 2017.

83 Arizona, 132 S. Ct. at 2509-10. Ultimately, however, the state settled ongoing litigation by civil rights groups over the un-enjoined section (§ 2(b)), with the Arizona attorney general issuing guidelines that took the teeth out of the provision. Michael Kiefer, *Arizona Settles Final Issues of SB 1070*, Az CENTRAL, Sept. 15, 2016.

unclear whether a similar, future effort would meet the same fate.[84] On other matters, the Supreme Court has expressly blessed state-level action. In *Whiting*, the Court upheld a state employer sanctions laws that require the use of E-verify by private employers. Several states, in the wake of that ruling, have enacted some type of employer sanctions law that meets the limitations set by the case.[85] In addition, nothing in recent case law has changed the opportunities provided by the 1996 federal enactments to restrict welfare, or deny undocumented students admission and education financing to undocumented students.

Despite these guidelines and limitations, states and localities are poised to remain important players in immigration policy in a way that they were not positioned to be just a mere twenty, or even fifteen, years ago. In the future, Congress might wish to staunch state-level trends through extensive "field-claiming", or expressly preempting state actions. Congress may also foster state policies through enabling legislation. Finally, it may seek to induce state and local participation in federal schemes, on the terms and bounds set by the federal government. While it is possible Congress could do all of these, none are likely in the immediate future. The deadlock and stalemate on immigration matters is likely to continue even though the Republican Party currently has majorities in both Houses, and occupies the White House. Given the various veto pivots and procedural hurdles to enacting federal legislation, a comprehensive bill that includes expanded visa access and paths to legalization seems unlikely.[86] This extended legislative inaction ensures that states and localities will seek to fill the void, as motivated policy activists and opportunistic party officials push the envelope on policy proliferation. In the absence of a federal legislative response, such policies become ingrained and gather inertia. Unless and until federal courts reject them, such laws galvanize constituencies, anchor policy positions, and become normalized features of the national legislative picture.

Indeed, the next round of federal legislative action, if and when it arrives, will be force to recognize, incorporate, and account for what will then be fairly well established state and local preferences on particular issues. For example, because California has committed itself to providing higher education access and funding to undocumented students, it has effectively forced such issues on to the national agenda if federal lawmakers want to alter that policy outcome. In short, any new federal regime will be shaped by the constraints imposed by current immigration federalism. Integrationist policies in places like California and New York will anchor the federal debate in one direction, while restrictionism in places like Arizona and Texas might pull it the other way. Federal reform is unlikely to wholesale

---

84 On the discretionary power of the president to bring suit, and its impact on the outcome of litigation, see generally, Gulasekaram & Ramakrishnan, *The President and Immigration Federalism*, 68 FLA. L. REV. at 135–143. Of course, several other non-governmental actors also sued against SB 1070. 68 FLA. L. REV. at 136 and n. 191. Although those suits may have led to the same result, it also seems clear that the Court was especially solicitous of the U.S. Solicitor General's view of the conflict between SB 1070 and federal law.

85 National Conference of State Legislatures, *State E-Verify Action*, (Aug. 19, 2015), www.ncsl.org/research/immigration/state-e-verify-action.aspx; National Immigration Law Center, *Policy Resources: E-Verify in the States*, (July 2012), https://www.nilc.org/wp.../2015/.../e-verify-and-states-policyresources-2012-08-13.pdf.

86 GULASEKARAM & RAMAKRISHNAN, THE NEW IMMIGRATION FEDERALISM, at 203. The next round of redisticting after the 2020 census might be an opportunity to shift the voting power of certain districts enough to allow for compromise positions on immigration.

wipe out key features of our current state of subfederal immigration law, given the recent history of state-level policies binding the positions of federal lawmakers from those jurisdictions.

Another reason state-level action is likely to have resonance into the future is that states and localities have become a critical parts administering, entrenching, and resisting federal immigration policies and programs. These actions too have a strongly partisan bent. As noted, coalitions of like-minded states and municipalities have sued to stop executive initiatives of presidents of both parties. Republican-led states initiated the suit that ended up stopping Obama's second major deferred action program (DAPA); Democrat-led states and municipalities are currently litigating (and have won preliminary injunctions) in suits against Trump's Muslim ban and his attempted crackdown on sanctuary cities. But apart from state-led litigation, states and localities are otherwise banding together to facilitate or resist the federal programs. After Obama's announcement of DACA in 2012, states and localities began providing driver's licenses to DACA recipients, and then to the undocumented more generally.[87] This made it easier for those in the program to get to schools or to employment. Mayors of major cities joined together in the trans-local organization, Cities United for Immigration Action, after Obama's announcement of DAPA to consider ways of servicing the population they thought would receive deferred action.[88] And, states began considering ways of making educational more accessible by opening up financing possibilities.

President Trump's immigration initiatives have also received similar state-level support. Some states, including Indiana led by then-Governor, now Vice President, Mike Pence, voiced their objection to housing Syrian refugees, pre-figuring Trump's plans to cut down on refugees, especially those from Muslim countries.[89] And, although Trump's desire to eliminate sanctuary cities has faced resistance in court, some states have used their own legislative processes to tamp down on non-cooperation policies. A recent Texas law prevents law enforcement agencies in the state from declining to participate in federal immigration efforts; similar policies have been enacted in other Republican-led states.[90]

Importantly, these state and local policies are not simply add-ons, afterthoughts, or minor inconveniences to large-scale presidential or congressional actions. In some cases—like driver's licenses or access to state-level benefits—the federal government does not play a significant role, and states and localities are the primary administrators, if not sole providers, of the public good or service. They must act in order to maximize the effectiveness of the federal policy; on the other hand, their inaction or resistance can seriously cripple federal goals. Similarly, city or local law enforcement agency sanctuary policies are effective mostly because local law enforcement is likely to have contact, knowledge, and custody of noncitizens that federal authorities are unlikely to have. The federal government relies on that cooperation to enhance their enforcement efforts, leveraging local officers to stretch federal enforcement capacity. On the flip-side, the state-level action might avoid the constitutional or legal pitfalls

---

87 Gulasekaram & Ramakrishnan, *The President and Immigration Federalism*, 68 FLA. L. REV. at 153–56 and accompanying notes.

88 See *supra* n. 73.

89 Pratheepan Gulasekaram and S. Karthick Ramakrishnan, *States Cannot Reject Syrian Refugees*, WASHINGTON POST, Nov. 19, 2015.

90 See *supra* n. 81; Associated Press, *A Look at State Actions on US "Sanctuary Cities" in 2017*, Voice of America, May 8, 2017 (listing anti-sanctuary proposals).

of federal actions with the same goal. For example, state-level "anti-sanctuary" laws do not face the same federalism-based constitutional challenges that federal efforts must overcome.[91] Thus party officials might advantageously promote the federal agenda through state-level enactments in like-minded states and localities. Because of their complementary nature then, these types of policies are entrenchers of, and critical administrative aids to, any major federal immigration policy.[92]

The persistence, and heavily partisan and politicized proliferation, of state and local policies must also necessarily change our legal and theoretical understanding of immigration federalism. First and foremost, the political factors that underlie present-day immigration federalism necessitate a re-evaluation of the long-held explanations for the need and utility of such policies. At least as it pertains to restrictionist policies, the conventional tropes of region-specific public policy problems caused by changing demographics do not hold. This fact alone does not determine whether such policies are constitutional, but it belies the narrative spun by issue entrepreneurs, elected officials, and even courts in their assessment of these laws. That narrative was (and continues to be) attractive precisely because it plays to classic federalism tropes. The actual empirics of state and local policy proliferation, however, require more forthright and less romantic legal justifications.

By focusing on the role of issue entrepreneurs and political parties, the actual process of state and local immigration policy proliferation is placed in sharper focus. Restrictionist policy activists were successful in generating support for their policies in certain jurisdictions by effectively stoking ethnic nationalism along with exploiting political polarization. In short, issue entrepreneurs were able to harness, and in some cases, exacerbate, racial antipathy and anxiety from national security concerns to generate state and local laws that sought to stem the economic and cultural threats posed by Mexican and other non-white migration. Doctrinally, this evidence matters because it suggests that the conventional structural power frames used to understand state and local immigration federalism—preemption and the Tenth Amendment—might be incomplete or inadequate tools for evaluating the legality of subfederal laws. Indeed, as research and evidence mounts of the use of racial antipathy both in the generation of state and local restrictionist laws,[93] and their possible effects on racially discrete populations, other constitutional principles grounded in equality guarantees and individual rights might prove more appropriate.[94]

In addition, recognizing state and local immigration laws as uncoupled from the conventional federalism narratives about the necessity of meeting local challenges pushes us to view immigration federalism as a nationwide contest over substantive rules, rather than debates over structural power allocation. The politicized account of subfederal policy proliferation shows how local demographic conditions and public policy problems hold

---

91 Cities litigating against the federal government's crackdown on sanctuaries or potential anti-sanctuary legislation may raise Tenth Amendment and federalism-based claims against coercive federal authority. In contrast, a city litigating against the state could not raise those same federal constitutional claims; they may, however, still raise potential due process and first amendment claims, as well as claims based on the state's constitution or laws.

92 Gulasekaram & Ramakrishnan, *The President and Immigration Federalism*, 68 FLA. L. REV. at 169–73.

93 GULASEKARAM & RAMAKRISHNAN, THE NEW IMMIGRATION FEDERALISM, at 192 and nn. 187–194.

94 See generally, *id.*, at 185–94.

little explanatory power over the proposal and passage of immigration laws. The same is true in the recent lawsuits by states against federal executive initiatives, with the suit against Obama's DAPA program joined by states as different (for immigration purposes) as Texas and Alaska. Indeed, little connects various jurisdictions that pass enforcement heavy laws other than their partisan composition, their ripe political conditions, and their political will to do so. In other words, what such jurisdictions are actually doing is demonstrating, through their enactments and policy actions, their vision of a preferred national policy on immigration.

Finally, our current immigration federalism pushes us to a more nuanced theoretical understanding of federalism by forcing us to abandon traditional tropes of exclusive lawmaking domains. Classic conceptions, like those articulated in the old Supreme Court cases, relied on notions of expansive and inherent federal power to the exclusion of state-level involvement.[95] Modern cases eschewed federal exclusivity of all immigration-related matters, but still relied on the idea of zones of policymaking authority.[96] Seen in this light, federalism is purely a structural power dispute over which level of government gets to be the final (or semi-final) decision-maker over immigration matters. A more critical view of the on-the-ground dynamics of present-day immigration federalism, however, showcases the level of entanglement and interdependence of federal and state-level policies.[97] The reason state and local sanctuary or non-cooperation policies have captured the national agenda is because of how critical local law enforcement participation is to broad-scale federal enforcement. State resistance to allowing undocumented persons access to driver's licenses or educational opportunities blunts the effectiveness of federal deferred action programs. These and other instances help illustrate that contemporary immigration federalism is characterized by regulatory overlap and dependence in ways that traditional federalism accounts do not capture. Thus, emerging theoretical work on immigration federalism must, by necessity, remain attentive to federalism in its cooperative and uncooperative varieties, where sovereignty and exclusivity might play diminished roles.[98]

Conclusion

For the majority of the past two decades, concerns over undocumented immigration and a "broken" immigration system have dominated media headlines and political rhetoric from all sides of the political spectrum. Yet, Congress has been unable to vote on or pass any major federal immigration reforms. Instead, in the post-9/11 world, states and localities have become the major source of immigrant-related policymaking. The varied policies from politically disparate jurisdictions reflect the American citizenry's diversity of competing perspectives on this divisive issue, with each enacting state or locality serving as the crucible for national policy battles. Major cases like *United States v. Arizona* or *Texas v. United States* helped define some outer limits to federal, state, and local immigration action, but also showcased the leeway and power of states and localities to influence and change the course

---

95 See, e.g., Chy Lung, 92 U.S. 275; Chae Chan Ping v. United States, 130 U.S. 581 (1889).
96 See *supra* n. 21 and accompanying text.
97 Cf. Heather Gerken, *Federalism All the Way Down*, 124 Harv. L. Rev. 5, 38–44 (2010); Jessica Bulman-Pozen and Heather Gerken, *Uncooperative Federalism*, 118 Yale L. J. 1256, 1265–69.
98 *Id.*

of immigration law and policy. Looking forward, state and local immigration law is certain to play an increasing role in defining the direction of national immigration regulation and its on-the-ground potency. Immigration federalism is thus a form of immigration nationalism.[99] Dozens of cities and states using their legislative and administrative processes to make an argument for, and build policy momentum towards, a new national consensus on immigration with or without the federal government's involvement.

---

99 Cf. Heather Gerken, *Federalism as the New Nationalism: An Overview*, 123 Yale L. J. 1626 (2014).

10 The equal sovereignty principle as federalism sub-doctrine

A reassessment of *Shelby County v. Holder*

Franita Tolson

In the fortieth Congress, which met from 1869 until 1871, African-American suffrage was a central issue on the agenda of congressional Republicans, and in particular, the question of whether additional constitutional protections were necessary to ensure broad enfranchisement among the recently emancipated freedmen. The thirty-ninth Congress previously had passed the Fourteenth Amendment, ratified in 1868, and Section 2 allowed Congress to reduce a state's delegation in the House of Representatives for abridging the right to vote.[1] Some of the debates urging further federal action on voting rights may have seemed downright odd given the recent enactment of this provision. However, Section 2's primary purpose was to minimize the substantial bump in the electoral college and Congress that southern states would enjoy post-emancipation, a bump these states would enjoy even if they disenfranchised a substantial portion of their populations.

Unlike the thirty-ninth Congress, the conversations over suffrage during this period were much more focused on enfranchising African-Americans in the north, a region that had fewer people of color but still suffered from the same virulent racism as states in the deep south. In enacting the Fifteenth Amendment, which barred discrimination in voting on account of race, color, or previous condition of servitude, Congress adopted an enforcement mechanism that was substantively different from Section 2: the former allowed Congress to adopt a broader swath of penalties other than reduced representation, but only on three specified grounds.[2] Essentially, these constitutional provisions were designed to achieve the same goal—broad enfranchisement— but each was targeted towards a specific region of the country. Arguably, differentiation between the states is baked into the Reconstruction amendments, and Congress, through its power to enforce these provisions, can continue to draw distinctions among the states without having to overcome a presumption that such uneven treatment is unconstitutional.[3]

---

1 U.S. CONST. Amend. XIV, § 2.
2 U.S. CONST. Amend. XV, § 1.
3 See Akhil Reed Amar, *The Lawfulness of Section 5—and Thus of Section 5*, 126 HARV. L. REV. F. 109 (2013) (arguing that certain states were forced to adopt the Fourteenth Amendment as a condition of readmission and were thus subject to a certain type of "selective preclearance"). The disparate treatment among states goes beyond the adoption of the Fourteenth Amendment, and, as I argue here, is part of the substantive mandates of the Fourteenth and Fifteenth Amendments. See Thomas B. Colby, *In Defense of the Equal Sovereignty Principle*, 65 DUKE L.J. 1087, 1167–68 (2016) (arguing that "the history supports a claim that Congress should be afforded greater leeway to bend the equal sovereignty principle when acting pursuant to" the Reconstruction Amendments); Part II, *infra* (fleshing out this historical argument).

Recent cases have ignored that differential treatment among the states lies at the heart of those provisions of the Reconstruction Amendments that govern voting and elections, an oversight that can be blamed on the Supreme Court's desire to protect the states' sovereignty over elections at the expense of the federal anti-discrimination laws. As this chapter shows, the Court has become increasingly hostile towards the Voting Rights Act of 1965 (VRA), which, until recently, had been the crown jewel of federal civil rights legislation.[4]

This chapter argues that the Court's increasing focus on federalism, as illustrated by its aggressive use of the equal sovereignty principle in *Shelby County v. Holder*, which held that the VRA's system of selective preclearance violated the structural principle of equal sovereignty, is problematic for three reasons.[5] First, the equal sovereignty principle is what I call "federalism sub-doctrine" that the Court relies on to increase the burdens of legislative fact-finding in order to deter the enactment of federal anti-discrimination legislation. The Court imposes this hurdle based on an erroneous conception of the sovereignty that states retain over elections, which the Court treats as substantially broader than the constitutional text and structure permit.[6] Second, the doctrine is contrary to the text and structure of those provisions of the Fourteenth and Fifteenth Amendments that govern elections, the effects of which the framers intended to be, at least initially, region specific. The selective application of the Reconstruction amendments by congressional Republicans minimized the political risk involved in expanding African-American suffrage to the northern states.

Third, the equal sovereignty principle reflects a broader trend in the case law where the Court treats minority groups, not as historically disenfranchised and subordinated individuals, but as rent-seeking entities like any other special interest group.[7] From the Court's perspective, the Act's 2006 re-authorization was not arrived at organically, or through the legitimate give and take of the legislative process;[8] instead, the process fell victim to

4   Voting Rights Act of 1965, Pub. L. No. 89–110, § 2, 79 Stat. 437, 437 (codified as amended at 52 U.S.C. § 10301 (2012)) [hereinafter "VRA" or "the Act"]. Nine states—mostly in the deep south, along with a few jurisdictions scattered throughout several other states—were covered by section 5.
5   Shelby Cnty. v. Holder, 133 S. Ct. 2612 (2013).
6   *Id.* at 2621–2623. Other cases have diluted the strength of the VRA in the name of state sovereignty. See, e.g., Perry v. Perez, 565 U.S. 388 (2012) (holding that courts, in drawing interim plans, should deter to plans enacted by the state legislature, even if those plans have not been precleared); Northwest Austin Mun. Dist. No. 1 v. Holder, 557 U.S. 193 (2009) [hereinafter NAMUDNO v. Holder] (liberalizing the Act's bailout procedure).
7   While many scholars have ignored this connection, Bertrall Ross is a notable exception and has explored the Court's reliance on public choice theory in the context of the Equal Protection Clause. See Bertrall L. Ross II, *Democracy and Renewed Distrust: Equal Protection and the Evolving Judicial Conception of Politics*, 101 CAL. L. REV. 1565, 1570 (2013). In building on this analysis, the historical discussion in Part II, *infra*, illustrates how problematic the Court's analysis is as a reading of the constitutional text and structure.
8   Notably, Justice Antonin Scalia contended that Section 5 was part of a broader scheme of "racial entitlements" that are very difficult to overturn through the legislative process. See Transcript of Oral Argument at 47, *Shelby Cnty.*, 133 S. Ct. 2612 (2013). Justice Scalia further observed that:

> [T]his is not the kind of question you can leave to Congress. There are certain districts in the House that are black districts by law just about now. And even the Virginia Senators, they have no interest in voting against this. The State government is not their government, and they are going to lose—they are going to lose votes if they do not reenact the Voting Rights Act. Even the name of it is wonderful: The Voting Rights Act. Who is going to vote against that in the future?

Id. at 47–48.

the manipulations of politically savvy minority groups, resulting in legislation that is intrusive of state prerogatives without adequate justification.[9] This view reflects the strong undercurrents of public choice theory in *Shelby County*, where the Court applied a more stringent standard of judicial review in assessing the constitutionality of the Act because it no longer believed that the VRA furthered the public good.[10] Thus, federalism principles could not and should not be subordinated to the minority groups' claim for equal political power.[11]

The equal sovereignty principle as federalism sub-doctrine

Together, sections 4(b) and 5 of the Voting Rights Act suspended all voting related changes in jurisdictions that had a history of engaging in voting related discrimination until those changes were approved by the federal government. *Shelby County v. Holder*, which hobbled this system with its invalidation of the coverage formula, is an extension of the Court's jurisprudential efforts to breathe life into pre-Reconstruction conceptions of the state/federal balance of power over elections.[12] In *Arizona v. Inter Tribal Council of Arizona*,[13] for example, the Court limited Congress's ability to regulate voter qualification standards pursuant to the Elections Clause, which governs the times, places, and manner of federal elections.[14] Similarly, in *Arizona State Legislature v. Arizona Independent Redistricting Commission*,[15] the Court deferred to a state law that delegated the state legislature's redistricting authority over federal elections to an independent commission, deference that was questionable given that the Court was interpreting the scope of a federal constitutional provision—the Elections Clause—in which it had deemed federal power paramount.

Even in cases where the scope of federal power is undeniable, the Court finds an opportunity to reaffirm state authority; the Court's aggressive use of the equal sovereignty principle in *Shelby County* has to be viewed in this context. The Court's critique occurs against the backdrop of its preexisting conception of how our Constitution divides power between the states and the federal government over elections. As the Court observed:

> [T]he framers of the Constitution intended the States to keep for themselves, as provided in the Tenth Amendment, the power to regulate elections. Of course, the Federal Government retains significant control over elections. . . . But States have "broad powers to determine the conditions under which the right of suffrage may be exercised."[16]

---

9 *Id.* at 2624.

10 *Id.* at 2622–24 (noting that "the constitutional equality of the States is essential to the harmonious operation of the Republic," and "the fundamental principle of equal sovereignty remains highly pertinent in assessing subsequent disparate treatment of States").

11 See Guy-Uriel E. Charles and Luis Fuentes-Rohwer, *The Voting Rights Act in Winter: The Death of a Super Statute*, 100 Iowa L. Rev. 1389 (2015).

12 See, e.g., City of Boerne v. Flores, 521 U.S. 507 (1997) (holding that the remedies in congressional legislation enacted under the Fourteenth Amendment must be congruent and proportional to the harm to be addressed).

13 Arizona v. Inter Tribal Council of Ariz., Inc., 133 S. Ct. 2247, 2263 (2013).

14 U.S. Const. Art. I, Sec. 4.

15 Ariz. State Legis. v. Ariz. Indep. Redistricting Comm'n, 135 S.Ct. 2652 (2015).

16 Shelby Cnty. v. Holder, 133 S. Ct. 2612, 2623 (2013) (internal citations omitted).

On this view, the reauthorization of section 4(b) of the VRA is irrational if one assumes, as the Court did, that the Fourteenth and Fifteenth Amendments barely affected state sovereignty over elections and that federal legislation is valid only if evidence of discrimination equals the malevolence of days old.[17] But the Court went even further than simply deeming preclearance to be irrational, instead establishing the equal sovereignty principle for several reasons.

First, with respect to setting the boundaries of congressional power, equal sovereignty was the vehicle through which the Court resolved a tension that had long persisted in its analysis of Congress's enforcement authority under the Reconstruction Amendments since *City of Boerne v. Flores*.[18] In *City of Boerne*, the Court limited Congress's enforcement authority under the Fourteenth Amendment to imposing only those remedies that are "congruent and proportional" to the harm to be addressed based on a review of the legislative record.[19] *Shelby County* narrowed *City of Boerne*'s congruence and proportionality test by decreasing Congress's ability to craft rules that prohibit some constitutional behavior in order to prevent constitutional violations.[20] The decision, through its equal sovereignty holding, also limited Congress's power to enact laws that are jurisdiction specific, even though each state has its own individual body of law that governs the right to vote and therefore makes the substance of the right very different from one jurisdiction to the next.[21]

Under pre-*Shelby County* case law, Congress could regulate constitutional behavior in order to prevent constitutional violations so long as the congruence and proportionality standard was met; this ability was vital to the legitimacy of preclearance, which suspended *all* electoral laws pending federal review.[22] After *Shelby County*, Congress would have to focus on those states with recent voting rights violations, as recent legislative fixes to the VRA have proposed, but this focus necessarily would be under-inclusive and limit the effectiveness of the legislation.[23] Alternatively, Congress could enact more geographically expansive legislation

17 See *id.* at 2616 (arguing that the VRA "requires States to beseech the Federal Government for permission to implement laws that they would otherwise have the right to enact and execute on their own."); *id.* at 2629 (dismissing "second generation barriers" as sufficient to justify the coverage formula). But see Franita Tolson, *The Constitutional Structure of Voting Rights Enforcement*, 89 WASH. L. REV. 379 (2014) (arguing that, in enacting Section 2 of the Fourteenth Amendment, the Framers did not want to completely displace state sovereignty but still intended this provision to radically alter the states' authority over elections).
18 See 521 U.S. 507 (1997) (holding that the Religious Freedom Restoration Act was not a congruent and proportional remedy under Fourteenth Amendment). *See also* Bd. of Trs. v. Garrett, 531 U.S. 356 (2001) (Congress exceeded scope of its powers under Section 5 of the Fourteenth Amendment in abrogating state sovereign immunity under the Americans with Disabilities Act).
19 The Court has oscillated on when Congress has satisfied *City of Boerne*'s congruence and proportionality standard. Compare Kimel v. Fla. Bd. of Regents, 528 U.S. 62 (2000) (Congress could not subject the states to lawsuits under the Age Discrimination in Employment Act because the legislative record did not establish widespread, unconstitutional age discrimination by the states) *with* Nev. Dep't of Human Res. v. Hibbs, 538 U.S. 721 (2003) (Congress can subject states to lawsuits under the Family and Medical Leave Act of 1993 because the legislative record established a pattern of unconstitutional gender discrimination by the states).
20 Shelby Cnty. v. Holder, 133 S. Ct. 2612, 2624 (2013) (criticizing the VRA for suspending "all changes to state election law—however innocuous—until they have been precleared by federal authorities.").
21 *Id.*
22 See *City of Boerne*, 521 U.S. at 525 (pointing to the Voting Rights Act as an example of a congruent and proportional remedy).
23 See Voting Rights Amendment Act of 2014 (initially covering four states). See also Voting Rights Reconstruction Act of 2015.

in order to avoid singling out any particular state, but it would be over-inclusive and potentially run afoul of the fit that the Court now seems to demand of legislation that implicates both the Fourteenth and Fifteenth Amendments.

In other words, the world looks different after *Shelby County.* In the Court's view, the requirement that Congress show a pattern of contemporary constitutional violations before enacting federal voting rights legislation that distinguishes between the states, a difficult endeavor given the absence of clear boundaries, was necessary to preserve the "residual sovereignty" that states retain over elections, derived from the constitutional structure and separate from the Tenth Amendment.[24] The equal sovereignty principle helps the Court to protect this sovereignty without explicitly overruling case law that has allowed Congress to legislate based on some combination of discriminatory intent and effects in the past.[25] For this reason, it does not matter, as Justice Ginsburg points out in dissent, that the states captured by the coverage formula in 1965 "still belonged under the preclearance regime" based on recent records of racial discrimination in voting.[26]

The Court's emphasis on the legislation record is deliberate, which leads to the second point. *Shelby County*'s focus on Congress's process for developing the coverage formula, as opposed to the formula's accuracy in capturing those states that are the worst offenders, is reminiscent of certain federalism doctrines that force Congress to jump through certain procedural hurdles before it can intrude on the state's sovereign authority. Similar to these federalism rules, many of which take the form of clear statement rules, presumptions, and structural inferences,[27] the equal sovereignty principle goes beyond the textual boundaries of the Tenth, Fourteenth, and Fifteenth Amendments, evoking a potentially limitless conception of state sovereignty derived from the Constitution's structure.[28] John Manning has referred to the Court's willingness to police federalism based on general principles not explicit in the constitutional text as a "federalism norm" that reflects the Court's free floating conception of what the Framers intended the state-federal balance of power to be.[29] While *Shelby County* is not a case that falls squarely within the Rehnquist Court's "federalism" revolution,[30] the Roberts Court has continued that Court's reliance on inchoate and

24 Shelby Cnty. v. Holder, 133 S. Ct. 2612, 2623 (2013) ("Not only do states retain sovereignty under the Constitution, there is *also* a 'fundamental principle of equal sovereignty' among the states.") (emphasis added). Leah M. Litman. *Inventing Equal Sovereignty,* 114 MICH. L. REV. 1207, 1212 (2016).

25 See, e.g., Katzenbach v. Morgan, 384 U.S. 641 (1966).

26 Shelby Cnty., 133 S. Ct. at 2651 (Ginsburg, J., dissenting).

27 See, e.g., Alden v. Maine, 527 U.S. 706 (1999) (cementing the idea that state sovereignty extended beyond the boundaries of the Tenth Amendment in finding that Congress cannot subject nonconsenting states to private suit); Bond v. U.S., 131 S. Ct. 2355, 2364 (2011) (observing that the structural component of federalism necessarily creates a source of rights that are directly tied to furthering the goals of our system of government).

28 See Colby, *supra* note 3 (referring to the equal sovereignty principle as structural); Joseph Fishkin, *The Dignity of the South,* 123 YALE L.J. ONLINE 175 (2013) (referring to the equal sovereignty principle as a concept that derives from the "dignity" of the states).

29 See John F. Manning, *Federalism and the Generality Problem in Constitutional Interpretation,* 122 HARV. L. REV. 2003, 2006 (2009) (criticizing the norm as a form of structural inferences that "ascribes to the document as a whole a *general purpose* to preserve a significant element of state sovereignty" based on a less defensible reading of the constitutional text); Franita Tolson, *Reinventing Sovereignty?: Federalism as a Constraint on the Voting Rights Act,* 65 VAND. L. REV. 1195 (2012) (discussing the federalism norm in the context of the VRA).

30 See, e.g., U.S. v. Lopez, 514 U.S. 549 (1995) (invalidating as federal gun control statute as beyond Congress's authority under the Commerce Clause).; Seminole Tribe v. Florida, 517 U.S. 44 (1996)

ephemeral federalism principles, or more aptly federalism "sub-doctrine," in order to reinstate this balance.

For example, in *Gregory v. Ashcroft,* the Court held that Missouri's mandatory retirement age for state judges does not violate the Age Discrimination in Employment Act ("ADEA") because Congress did not clearly express its intention to apply the ADEA to state court judges.[31] The Court required a clear statement because "congressional interference with the Missouri people's decision to establish a qualification for their judges would upset the usual constitutional balance of federal and state powers."[32] It is irrelevant to the Court that older judges experienced discrimination that fell within the ADEA's mandates; rather, the *Gregory* Court stated that its clear statement rule was procedural rather than substantive, or "nothing more than an acknowledgement that the States retain substantial sovereign powers under our constitutional scheme."[33] Similarly, section 4(b) of the Voting Rights Act, despite its accuracy in capturing those states that had, and by some metrics continue to have, the worst voting rights records, was not adopted pursuant to a process that was sufficiently attentive to the state's sovereignty over elections.

Shelby County is also analytical similar to *U.S. v. Morrison,* another federalism decision finding that the theory upon which Congress had based its findings supporting the Violence Against Women Act of 1994—that there was a connection between violence against women and interstate commerce— was legally impermissible. Likewise, the 2006 record underlying the VRA was substantial, but could not salvage Congress's decision to impose the preclearance requirement on the southern states based on forty-year-old data because Congress had a legally insufficient conception of the power that states retain over elections.[34]

For these reasons, some scholars treat the equal sovereignty principle, and the unrealistic expectations that it places on Congress, as doctrine created out of whole cloth with little sanction in the constitutional text, structure, and history.[35] Other commentators have agreed with the Court that the doctrine is not new, but still criticize *Shelby County* on the grounds that its application is novel.[36] All of this criticism has been especially potent, given that the decision stands in stark contrast to the "judicial minimalism" philosophy endorsed by the Roberts Court, where the justices aspire to decide cases on the narrowest grounds possible with few 5–4 decisions.[37]

(Congress's Commerce Clause authority does not extend to abrogating state sovereign immunity in court); New York v. United States, 505 U.S. 144 (1992) (holding that Congress may not commandeer the legislative processes of the states by compelling them to enact and enforce a federal regulatory program).

31 501 U.S. 452 (1991).
32 *Id.* at 463.
33 *Id.* at 461.
34 See *Shelby Cnty.*, 133 S. Ct. at 2636 (Ginsburg, J., dissenting) (noting that the Court rejected a 15,000-page legislative record with 90 witnesses).
35 See Zachary S. Price, *NAMUDNO's Non-Existent Principle of State Equality,* 88 N.Y.U. L. Rev. Online 24 (2013). See also Richard A. Posner, Supreme Court 2013: The Year in Review, SLATE (June 26, 2013), *available at* www.slate.com/articles/news_and_politics/the_breakfast_table/features/2013/supreme_court_2013/the_supreme_court_and_the_voting_rights_act_striking_down_the_law_is_all.html [http://perma.cc/U7PZ-JPPE]. See also, Jeffrey M. Schmitt, *In Defense of Shelby County's Equal State Sovereignty,* 68 OKLA. L. REV. 209 (2016) (tracing the principle to arguments over slavery during the antebellum period).
36 See Colby, *supra* note 3 (tracing the equal sovereignty principle to the doctrine of equal footing).
37 The Chief Justice has tried to cultivate this image of a minimalist court, *see, e.g.,* NAMUDNO v. Holder, 557 U.S.193 (2009) (8–1 decision using the constitutional avoidance canon to avoid resolving the

Whether a new doctrine or an old one, one cannot ignore that the equal sovereignty principle is the Court's attempt to operationalize the specific historical concept that all states enter the Union on equal footing.[38] But, as the next section shows, it is unlikely that this principle of equal footing extends much beyond the point of a state's initial entry.[39] Indeed, the Fourteenth and Fifteenth Amendments suggest that, to the extent that equal sovereignty derives from equal footing, this principle is not a constraint on the federal government's authority to regulate elections.

The Equal Sovereignty Principle as historical anomaly

Shelby County's equal sovereignty principle is contrary to the differential treatment of the states embodied by Section 2 of the Fourteenth Amendment and Section 1 of the Fifteenth Amendment. Despite the decision, however, the equal sovereignty principle is not that controversial, and is arguably consistent with these Amendments, when taken in its most simplistic form: as a doctrine that requires each state to be admitted on equal footing.[40] The concept of equal footing derives from Article IV, Section 3, of the Constitution, which governs the terms upon which a state can be admitted to the Union. This section argues that, while the principle of equal footing survived Reconstruction, the *Shelby County* Court's conception of equal sovereignty was thoroughly debunked by Reconstruction era statutes and constitutional provisions that memorialize Congress's ability to distinguish between the states in protecting the right to vote.[41] Indeed, the Court's case law in the first half of the nineteenth century confirmed that equal footing primarily pertained to a state's initial entry into the Union, making it unlikely that this doctrine justifies the Court's treatment of legislation that distinguishes between the states as presumptively unconstitutional.

In *Pollard v. Hagan*, for example, the Court resolved an ownership dispute over land in Alabama, the title to which depended on whether the United States retained ownership of the contested parcel at the time that Alabama was admitted to the Union. Georgia ceded the land that ultimately became Alabama, including the contested parcel, to the United States, but the parcel was under water when Alabama was admitted to the Union in 1819.[42]

---

constitutionality of section 5 of the Voting Rights Act, even though its interpretation was contrary to the statutory text and congressional intent), but has been unsuccessful. See Nat'l Fed'n of Indep. Bus. v. Sebelius, 567 U.S. 519 (2012) (finding that the Affordable Care Act exceeded the scope of Congress's authority under the Commerce Clause, but sustaining the legislation 5–4 as a valid use of the Tax Power).

38 See Colby, *supra* note 3.

39 See *id.*

40 Article 4, Section 3 provides that, "New states may be admitted by the Congress into this Union; but no new state shall be formed or erected within the jurisdiction of any other state, nor any state be formed by the junction of two or more states or parts of states, without the consent of the legislatures of the states concerned, as well as of Congress." U.S. CONST. ART. IV, SEC. 3.

41 Thomas Colby argues that there is a general structural principle of equality of the states that endures post-admission, but this notion is problematic in much the same way as the general federalism norm—it ignores that specific constitutional provisions have already struck the balance between federal power and equal state sovereignty. See Colby, *supra* note 3. This is especially true in the context of federal elections. See Part II (B), *infra*. In any event, this does not mean that Congress can distinguish between the states at will. The congruence and proportionality test of *City of Boerne v. Flores* is sufficient to protect the sovereignty (and equality) of the states rather than assuming, as the equal sovereignty principle does, that such unequal treatment is presumptively unconstitutional.

42 44 U.S. 212, 220 (1845).

The Court determined that, "When Alabama was admitted into the Union, on an equal footing with the original states, she succeeded to all the rights of sovereignty, jurisdiction, and eminent domain which Georgia possessed at the date of the cession, except so far as this right was diminished by the public lands remaining in the possession and under the control of the United States . . ."[43] Although the land in question was once covered by navigable waters (which had receded by 1823), the "shores of navigable waters" did not become public land such that the United States could grant title over them to a private party in contravention of the rights that Alabama, like Georgia before it, retained over the property.[44]

In the post-Civil War era, the Court continued to rely on the equal footing doctrine, but notably did not extend its scope beyond a state's entry into the Union to resolve substantive issues created by succession. In *Texas v. White*, the underlying controversy was whether the United States had to pay bonds issued by Texas that came due in 1864 after Texas had succeeded from the Union.[45] While part of the confederacy, Texas passed a law that repealed a federal requirement that the governor endorse the notes.[46] The case presented two questions: was Texas a "state" for purposes of filing suit in federal court, and could its reconstructed government stop the U.S. Treasury from issuing payment on notes lacking the governor's endorsement?

The Court held that, since succession was not an act recognized under the Constitution, Texas continued to be a state despite its attempt to succeed from the Union.[47] Thus, the equal footing doctrine comfortably resolved the question of whether Texas could file a lawsuit in federal court because it never lost this basic right that all states enjoy upon entry.[48] But equal footing (and by extension equal sovereignty) was not dispositive of the second (more substantive) question—does the United States have to pay bonds lacking the government's endorsement that came due during the war.[49] Instead, the Court resolved the issue as one of basic contract law, holding that the United States had no obligation to pay the bondholders because they had notice of the deficient title.[50]

Similarly, the doctrine of equal sovereignty is ill suited to resolve the substantive questions surrounding the validity of the Voting Rights Act. *Shelby County* was fundamentally a case about the scope of federal power, or whether sections 4(b) and 5 of the VRA were congruent and proportional remedies to the harm of race discrimination in voting. The Court avoided this question, and refused to decide whether *City of Boerne*'s congruence and proportionality standard applied to legislation enacted pursuant to the Fifteenth Amendment.[51] At issue was not the question of whether Congress was wrong for singling

43 *Id*. at 223.
44 *Id*. at 230.
45 74 U.S. 700, 717 (1869).
46 *Id*. at 732.
47 *Id*. at 725.
48 See Colby, *supra* note 3, at 1166.
49 The Court held true to this position in 1911, when it determined, in *Coyle v. Smith*, 221 U.S. 559 (1911), that a state's decision of where to locate its capitol is outside of the purview of Congress. The *Coyle* plaintiffs argued that the relocation of the capitol from Guthrie to Oklahoma City violated the enabling act that admitted Oklahoma into the Union. Like *Pollard*, *Coyle* dealt with the conditions surrounding a state's admission to the Union, and did not concern conditions imposed on the state post-admission.
50 *White*, 74 U.S. at 737. See also *id*. at 739–40 (Grier, J., dissenting) ("whether we assume the State of Texas to be judicially in the Union (though actually out of it) or not, it will not alter the case").
51 See Shelby Cnty. v. Holder, 133 S. Ct. 2612, 2622 n.1 (2013); NAMUDNO, 557 U.S. 193, 204 (2009).

out the discriminatory behavior of Georgia and Alabama, but not that of Ohio and Michigan. If there is a record supporting Congress's decision to single out the former, then it matters not that Congress had yet to go after the latter.[52]

Given this, what does equality between the states actually require? One plausible reading of *Pollard*, *Texas*, and the other equal footing cases is that equality presumably means that new states have to be admitted "with all of the powers of sovereignty and jurisdiction which pertain to the original States, and that such powers may not be constitutionally diminished, impaired or shorn away by any conditions, compacts or stipulations embraced *in the act under which the new State came into the Union* . . ."[53] Thus, conditions for the admission of new states can vary so long as Congress comports with a baseline of sovereignty established by the original thirteen states.[54] Provided that Congress does not fall below this initial baseline upon admission, however, this principle says very little about Congress's ability to distinguish between the states post-admission when Congress is acting pursuant to its enumerated powers.[55]

The lack of clarity with respect to the scope of equal sovereignty is of especial importance in the context of voting and elections, where federal statutes and constitutional amendments distinguished between the states in both purpose and effect. The Military Reconstruction Act of 1867 is one such example. The act, which "provide[d] for the more efficient Government of the Rebel States," divided the former confederacy into five military districts until a duly elected government could be instituted in each state. Readmission to the Union was contingent upon this new government adopting a state constitution acceptable to Congress, constitutions that endured in some of these states for years. For ten states —Virginia, North and South Carolina, Georgia, Alabama, Florida, Mississippi, Arkansas, Louisiana, and Texas —their "unequal" treatment at the hands of Congress lasted well past the Reconstruction era.

Although a temporary provision, the act created a political framework that congressional Republicans hoped would permanently alter the south. The act also exempted the northern states from its provisions. There was no requirement that the northern states adopt the Fourteenth Amendment as a prerequisite to remaining in the Union, as the Military Reconstruction Act required for the south. Nor did the northern states have to hold constitutional conventions with delegates selected based on something approaching universal suffrage, also a condition imposed on southern states.

More importantly, the Fourteenth Amendment constitutionalized these distinctions between north and south, reflecting the Republicans' fear of retribution from northern states should African-American suffrage be imposed on those jurisdictions and the fact that the enfranchisement of African-Americans was key to Republican political fortunes in the south.[56]

---

52 See Ry. Express Agency v. New York, 336 U.S. 106 (1949) (noting that Congress can legislate in a piecemeal fashion even if such legislation is underinclusive).

53 *Id.* at 573.

54 See United States v. La., 363 U.S. 1 (1960) (conceding that all states enter the union with sovereignty equal to that of the original 13 colonies, but allowing Congress to treat several states differently with respect to maritime boundaries because "rights in the marginal sea are attributes of national rather than state sovereignty").

55 See Litman, *supra* note 24, at 1211 (arguing that the best reading of these cases is that equal sovereignty "only forbids Congress from imposing an admission condition that violates other constitutional rules").

56 DOUGLAS R. EGERTON, THE WARS OF RECONSTRUCTION: THE BRIEF, VIOLENT HISTORY OF AMERICA'S MOST PROGRESSIVE ERA 236 (2014).

Like the Military Reconstruction Act, the framers constructed Section 2 of the Fourteenth Amendment to require southern states to enfranchise their large population of African-Americans, lest they be subject to the penalty of reduced representation, while exempting the northern and western states, with their small minority populations, from this requirement. The north and the west had proven to be especially resistant to any requirement of universal suffrage, and viewed any mandate of suffrage for the Chinese in the west or African-Americans in the north as an unfair penalty on those states that had shown their loyalty during the war.[57]

The election season of 1868 is instructive here. Many Republicans treated Ulysses S. Grant's 1868 election to the presidency as an implicit endorsement of their Reconstruction agenda and, more questionably, as a sign that Republicans should take on voting discrimination in the northern states.[58] These representatives advocated for the enactment of the Fifteenth Amendment believing, erroneously, that African-Americans, although a small percentage of the northern population, would help the party maintain its advantage in future elections.[59]

The push for the Fifteenth Amendment, especially in light of the Fourteenth Amendment's recent ratification, not only pushed away some Republicans, but also further raised the ire of Democrats. During congressional debates over the newly proposed Fifteenth Amendment, supporters often paraded wrongdoing by northern states to justify further congressional action, while detractors expressed concerns over how the Fifteenth Amendment would displace state sovereignty.[60] State delegations, formerly united on the question of the Fourteenth Amendment, stood divided on the propriety of the Fifteenth because that provision gave Congress open-ended authority to address discrimination in voting in the northern states.[61]

In addition, Democrats cautioned Republicans not to view Grant's election as a mandate in support of African-American suffrage in the north because northern voters had almost universally rejected African-American enfranchisement when the question was presented on the ballot.[62] Importantly, as one Democrat observed, Section 2's resolution of the suffrage issue in the south did not make it a foregone conclusion in the north:

> Mr. Chairman, the issues supposed to have been settled by the election of General Grant to the Presidency formed the subject of an elaborate speech by the honorable gentleman from Maine [Mr. Blaine] a few days before the adjournment of Congress for the holidays in December . . . The gentleman lays it down as an inevitable consequence of General Grant's election that negro suffrage must be accepted as a permanent establishment in the southern States, "and at no distant day throughout the entire Union." Yet if negro suffrage, which the very corner-stone of Radical reconstruction, had been divested of all other issues and fairly submitted to the vote of the whole people, what man acquainted with the national sentiment will deny its defeat would have been

57 See MARK WAHLGREEN SUMMERS, THE ORDEAL OF THE REUNION: A NEW HISTORY OF RECONSTRUCTION 81 (2014).
58 Cong. Globe 40th Cong. 3rd Sess. 57–58 (comments of Congressman Blaine).
59 See LaWanda and John H. Cox, *Negro Suffrage and Republican Politics: The Problems of Motivation in Reconstruction*, 33 J. SOUTHERN HIST. 303, 317 (1967) (arguing that Republicans also felt morally obligated to enfranchise African-Americans despite the political risk).
60 See, e.g., 40th Cong, 3rd Sess. 123–124 (exchange between Senators Dixon and Fern of Connecticut).
61 Cox, *supra* note 59, at 309.
62 *Id.*

overwhelming? No other proof is needed to establish this proposition than the decisive vote upon this question when lately presented by itself in several of the great Republican States of the North and the continued exclusion of negroes from the polls in nearly all of them.[63]

Despite these concerns, the Fifteenth Amendment was ratified in 1870. Together, with the Fourteenth Amendment, these provisions left the basic framework of state control over elections in place, but subject to very important caveats that permit differential treatment of the states in order to further the goals of individual equality and broad enfranchisement. This differential treatment was key to the success of the Reconstruction enterprise because African-American suffrage was extremely unpopular in the northern states, requiring piecemeal constitutional and legislative solutions. This dynamic explains Section 2's very unique penalty and the subsequent enactment of the Fifteenth Amendment.[64]

Given this evidence, it is not per se impermissible for the Voting Rights Act, reauthorized under both the Fourteenth and Fifteenth Amendments, to single out the southern states but not equally guilty northern states so long as Congress establishes a record of abridgment or denial of the right to vote sufficient to subject those states to preclearance. Congress has the power to enforce the terms of these Amendments through "appropriate" legislation, and it is difficult to argue, given their structure, that Congress is not permitted to differentiate in enforcement similar to how the Amendments differentiate in terms of substance. As the next section shows, the Court's aggressive use of the equal sovereignty principle stems, not from any constitutional requirement, but from its perception that the primary benefactors of the Act are calculated political actors.

Why equal sovereignty?: The Voting Rights Act as interest group legislation

Shelby County's equal sovereignty principle, as the prior section argues, is problematic both textually and historically; so, this section points to the Court's suspicion of minority political power as one possible explanation for imposing this limitation on Congress's ability to enforce the Reconstruction Amendments. The Court's jurisprudence in various areas—from its Fourteenth Amendment cases to its Voting Rights Act jurisprudence— illustrate the justices' apprehension of minority political power, which often stands in sharp contrast to the Court's admonition to minority voters that they must be politically active rather than litigious in achieving political gains.[65] With underlying tones of public choice theory, recent case law has analyzed the Voting Rights Act from the baseline assumption that minorities have "captured" the political process. In the Court's view, these groups have

---

63 Cong. Globe 40th Cong. 3rd Sess. 269–270 (comments of Congressman Boyer).
64 See Tolson, *supra* note 17.
65 See, e.g., Bartlett v. Strickland, 556 U.S. 1, 15 (2009) ("Section 2 does not impose on those who draw election districts a duty to give minority voters the most potential, or the best potential, to elect a candidate by attracting crossover voters."). See also League of United Latin Am. Citizens v. Perry, 548 U.S. 399 (2006) (determining that African-American voters in an influence district, or a district where they comprise less than a majority, could not bring a claim under the VRA after the district was dismantled because the Court could not determine if their long-term white congressional representative had been their candidate of choice).

been able to use beneficial statutes or legal doctrines to make substantial political gains, so the Court responds by narrowing the relevant statute or doctrine. As this section shows, the Court makes little distinction between gains legitimately achieved in the give and take of the political process and those that are illegitimately achieved by "capturing" the legislative process; rather, the Court's focus is on whether minorities have amassed enough power to disadvantage the majority.

Prominent scholars have relied on public choice theory, which questions the legitimacy of legislation that is the product of advocacy by well-organized interest groups rather than legislators operating in the public interest, to argue for more stringent judicial review of legislation to account for this failure in the political process.[66] Much of this criticism is tied to a deep distrust of the legislature, based on the assumption that elected officials are incapable of acting in the public interest and that judges, especially federal judges with life tenure, are better situated to do so. This argument has some rhetorical force, as James Madison's deep disdain of interest groups and factions led to our system of separation of powers.[67] More recent judicial developments in the campaign finance area also have ushered in an era of unlimited spending, adding to this deep seeded suspicion of elected officials.[68]

Questions remain as to whether all legislation passed through a process that no longer has (and maybe never had) the Madisonian safeguards should be subject to more stringent judicial review. Public choice theory assumes that political actors are economic actors, where the winners "outbid rival seekers of favorable legislation" in exchange for "campaign contributions, votes, implicit promises of future favors, and sometimes outright bribes."[69] This theory presents interest group legislation as redistributivist in nature, where interest groups take resources away from those who do not have the advantage of belonging to the group. Even if all legislation is a product of the self-interested motivations of a few, however, this does not mean that the legislation should be subject to increased judicial scrutiny given that the judicial system—with its elected judges and well-financed litigants—is not necessarily immune from the influence of special interest groups.[70]

The distinct conceptual problems with public choice theory have not prevented some justices, most notably Justice Antonin Scalia, from framing the VRA as self-interested

---

66 See, e.g., William N. Eskridge, Jr. & Philip P. Frickey, *Statutory Interpretation as Practical Reasoning*, 42 STAN. L. REV. 321 (1990); Jonathan R. Macey, *Competing Economic Views of the Constitution*, 56 GEO. WASH. L. REV. 50 (1987); William M. Landes & Richard A. Posner, *The Independent Judiciary in an Interest-Group Perspective*, 18 J.L. & ECON. 875, 877 (1975). But see Frank B. Cross, *The Judiciary and Public Choice*, 50 HASTINGS L.J. 355 (1999). The seminal work in this area is MANCUR OLSON, THE LOGIC OF COLLECTIVE ACTION: PUBLIC GOODS AND THE THEORY OF GROUPS (1965) (explaining how smaller, more cohesive groups are better positioned than larger, more diffuse groups to compete for public goods because they can limit free riding).

67 See THE FEDERALIST NO. 51 (James Madison); see also THE FEDERALIST NO. 10 (James Madison) (arguing that the causes of faction cannot be removed by representative government and geography can control its effects).

68 Citizens United v. FEC, 558 U.S. 310 (2010) (holding that restrictions on the independent expenditures of corporations violate the First Amendment. *See also* McCutcheon v. FEC, 134 S. Ct. 1434 (2014) (invalidating aggregate contribution limits on First Amendment grounds); Emily's List v. FEC, 581 F.3d 1 (D.C. Cir. 2009) (invalidating restrictions on how political action committees spend and raise money).

69 Landes & Posner, *supra* note 66, at 877.

70 See Cross, *supra* note 66, at 360–62 (arguing that richer interest groups benefit in litigation because of the expense involved).

legislation designed to benefit a discrete constituency.[71] But the Act, which was meant to equalize the political arena rather than skew outcomes in favor of minorities, has not had the impact on state authority over elections as it once did.[72] Nevertheless, the assumption underlying *Shelby County*—that minority political power is illegitimate and ill-obtained once it reaches a threshold in which the majority is disadvantaged—has a distinguished pedigree in the Court's caselaw.

In *City of Richmond v. J.A. Croson*, for example, the Court held that strict scrutiny applies to race-based measures aimed at ameliorating the effects of past discrimination, even if such legislation is aimed at helping, rather than harming, racial minorities.[73] In 1983, the majority African-American Richmond City Council adopted a 30 percent minority set-aside plan in order to increase the diversity of its contractors. At the time, the city only awarded 0.67 percent of its contracts to minority-owned firms. The Court struck down the plan, finding that the scope of the state's power to remedy past discrimination is limited to addressing the effects of specific acts of past discrimination.[74]

Notably, much of the Court's decision turned on the power that African-Americans had in Richmond and its perception that the set aside program placed non-minorities at a significant disadvantage. In rejecting the argument that the standard of scrutiny under the Equal Protection Clause should vary "according to the ability of different groups to defend their interests in the representative process," the Court observed that "blacks constitute approximately 50% of the population of the city of Richmond" and "[f]ive of the nine seats on the city council are held by blacks."[75] The Court found these factors dispositive in deciding that strict scrutiny was appropriate because of "the concern that a political majority will more easily act to the disadvantage of a minority based on unwarranted assumptions or incomplete facts."[76] While Richmond is free to address and remedy past discrimination, it has to be fairly traceable to the city and not unduly undermine the rights of the rights of non-minorities—an inquiry that is significantly more probing than if non-minorities are in control of the political process and minorities are subject to their will.[77]

---

71 See footnote 8, *supra*. See also Heather K. Gerken, *Foreword: Federalism All the Way Down*, 124 HARV. L. REV. 4, 60 (2010) (noting that governing bodies dominated by racial minorities are often condemned as segregated); Pamela S. Karlan, *Still Hazy After All These Years: Voting Rights in the Post-*Shaw *Era*, 26 CUMB. L. REV. 287, 293 (1996) ("The Court's repeated references to 'segregation' [in the context of majority–minority districts] obscure the point that the challenged districts are in fact among the most racially diverse districts in the country. Put bluntly, [The Court] accord[s] standing to individuals who claim they are injured by racial integration—or at least racial integration in which whites do not remain the predominant group.").

72 See Bartlett v. Strickland, 556 U.S. 1 (2009) (state has no obligation under the VRA to create influence districts); Riley v. Kennedy, 553 U.S. 406 (2008) (state covered under section 5 does not have to preclear changes required by state supreme court); Georgia v. Ashcroft, 539 U.S. 461, 481 (2003) (citing Johnson v. DeGrandy, 512 U.S. 997, 1020 (1993) (recognizing that the creation of influence districts "creates the risk that the minority group's preferred candidate may lose," but concluding that "minority voters are not immune from the obligation to pull, haul, and trade to find common political ground"); Reno v. Bossier Parish, 528 U.S. 320 (2000) (finding that a redistricting plan enacted with discriminatory intent should be precleared under section 5 if the plan is nonretrogressive).

73 City of Richmond v. J.A. Croson Co., 488 U.S. 469, 485–86 (1989).

74 *Id.* at 490.

75 *Id.* at 495.

76 *Id.* at 495–96.

77 *Cf.* Regents of the Univ. of Cal. v. Bakke, 438 U.S. 265 (1978) (striking down the University of California's plan but endorsing the use of affirmative action overall with no discussion of the racial makeup

The potential disadvantage to the majority was also at issue in *Ricci v. DeStefano*, where the Court held that New Haven violated Title VII of the Civil Rights Act of 1964, a statute that forbids racial discrimination in employment, after the city administered an exam to determine promotions in its fire department and later opted not to rely on the results because the white candidates scored higher on the exam than the minority candidates.[78] The city threw out the test results because it believed that the minority candidates would sue under the disparate impact provisions of Title VII if the test results were used.[79] The Court held that the city's failure to certify the test because of the racial disparity in the results constituted intentional discrimination based on race in violation of Title VII.[80] In particular, the Court noted that, "Many of the candidates had studied for months, at considerable personal and financial expense, and thus the injury caused by the City's reliance on raw racial statistics at the end of the process was all the more severe."[81]

The Court's preoccupation with minimizing the blowback to the politically powerless majority from policies that benefit racial minorities is also evident in its school discrimination cases, which seek to limit the extent to which public schools can rely on race in admissions.[82] In *Parents Involved v. Seattle School District Number One*, the Court invalidated the use of race-conscious criteria in the assignment of pupils, despite the school's claim that it was trying to "achieve the educational benefits" that flow from a racially diverse student body.[83] The Court previously had recognized this diversity interest in *Grutter v. Bollinger*, which sustained the use of race as a plus factor in law school admissions.[84] The Court discounted this interest in diversity in part because the school district's pupil assignment plan resulted in some students being assigned to schools that were not very diverse, in the Court's view, but qualified as "diverse" under the plan.[85] The Court was especially troubled by the fact that the plaintiff, a young white kindergartener, was denied entry into a school less than a mile from his home and assigned to a school ten miles away.[86] The state's interest in racial

of the decisionmakers [here majority white]). See also Gerken, *supra* note 71, at 54 ("The Court routinely dismisses pork and patronage as the usual products of pluralist politics under rational basis review. Yet it was markedly alert to the problem of self-dealing in *Croson* when racial minorities ruled."); Cass R. Sunstein, *Interest Groups in American Public Law*, 38 STAN. L. REV. 29, 49–54 (1985) (arguing that the Court has consistently criticized distribution of resources to certain groups solely because those groups exercised power to obtain government assistance).

78 *Ricci*, 557 U.S. at 557, 574.

79 Civil Rights Act of 1964, 42 U.S.C. § 2000e–2(k) (2006). This provision of Title VII does not require the plaintiff to show that the policy is intentionally discriminatory. *Id.*

80 *Ricci*, 557 U.S. at 592.

81 *Id.* at 593. See also *id.* at 598–608 (Alito, J., concurring) (tracing the city's discriminatory intent to the actions of a "racial powerbroker" and "reverse racist" who lobbied the mayor to discard the results).

82 See Fisher v. Univ. of Texas, 136 S. Ct. 2198, 2208 (2016) ("no deference is owed when determining whether the use of race is narrowly tailored to achieve the university's permissible goals").

83 See Parents Involved in Cmty. Schs. v. Seattle Sch. Dist. No. 1, 551 U.S. 701 (2007).

84 *Id.*; *Grutter v. Bollinger*, 539 U.S. 306, 329 (2003) (upholding the use of race in law school admissions because the state has a compelling interest in diversity).

85 See *Parents Involved*, 551 U.S. at 724 ("[A] school with 50 percent Asian-American students and 50 percent white students but no African-American, Native-American, or Latino students would qualify as balanced, while a school with 30 percent Asian-American, 25 percent African-American, 25 percent Latino, and 20 percent white students would not. It is hard to understand how a plan that could allow these results can be viewed as being concerned with achieving enrollment that is 'broadly diverse.'" [quoting *Grutter*, 539 U.S. at 329]).

86 *Id.* at 717, 759.

integration could not trump the disadvantage to the majority caused by the use of race in this context, a disadvantage that could ensue indefinitely and in a wide variety of contexts.[87] *Parents Involved* ignored, however, that there were still neighborhoods (and therefore schools) in which minorities had failed to make significant inroads because of housing segregation.[88]

Similarly, the companion case to *Parents Involved*—*Meredith v. Jefferson County Board of Education*—involved an area of Kentucky that had recently experienced a significant decrease in minority political power with the merger of Louisville (majority-minority) and surrounding Jefferson County (majority white) in 2000.[89] Instead of the county being subsumed into the city, the opposite occurred in order to transfer the center of power from the city to suburban Jefferson County. Thus, this perception of the majority as the "victims" of racial politics overlooked that the majority had been able to maneuver politically and neutralize minority power.

Given this case law, it is no surprise that the Court has been amenable to efforts by white plaintiffs to combat these types of perceived inequalities in the redistricting context. In *Shaw v. Reno*, the Court created a new cause of action under the Equal Protection Clause of the Fourteenth Amendment to address legislative districts that had been racially gerrymandered. The Court argued that such districting creates impermissible racial stereotypes, even though the state drew at least one of the contested districts to comply with the VRA.[90] *Shaw* has not had the impact on the validity of majority-minority districts as most scholars feared,[91] but the recognition of a new, analytically distinct cause of action under the Equal Protection Clause in order to avoid the "racial balkanization" of majority-minority districting has had serious implications for the Court's views on race and minority power.[92]

In many ways, *Shaw* foreshadowed the trend that would lead to the invalidation of section 4(b) in *Shelby County*: the Court's general suspicion of legislation that disadvantages the majority, even though such governmental actions might have come about in order to

---

87 See Michelle Adams, *Is Integration a Discriminatory Purpose?*, 96 Iowa L. Rev. 837, 841–42 (2011) (noting that Justice Kennedy, who wrote *Ricci* and was the deciding vote in *Parents Involved*, "articulated a view that government can ameliorate the harms of de facto segregation . . . so long as it does not create racial harm," which is "some type of adverse treatment that befalls identifiable individuals because of their race").

88 Quintard Taylor, The Forging of a Black Community: Seattle's Central District from 1870 Through the Civil Rights Era 209–10, 234–40 (1994); *Segregated Seattle*, Seattle Civil Rights & Labor History Project (Dec. 13, 2013), http://depts.washington.edu/civilr/segregated.htm.

89 Meredith v. Jefferson Cnty. Bd. of Educ., 547 U.S. 1178 (2006); *see generally* Aaron M. Renn, *Downsides of Consolidation #2: Cost Increases, Dilution of Urban Interests, Deferred Problems*, Urbanophile (Mar. 7, 2010), www.urbanophile.com/2010/03/07/downsides-of-consolidation-2-cost-increases-dilution-of-urban-interests-deferred-problems/.

90 509 U.S. 630, 654 (1993) (stating that a plan that complies with the VRA can still be unconstitutional).

91 There was no explosion of *Shaw* claims following the decision. Instead, the state's reliance on political, as opposed to racial, factors in crafting districts emerged as a defense to *Shaw* claims. See, e.g., Easley v. Cromartie, 532 U.S. 234, 243–44 (2001) (reversing the district court's finding that race, rather than politics, was a predominant factor in the state legislature's congressional redistricting plan). More recently, minority groups have relied on the *Shaw* claim to challenge racial gerrymanders that pack minority voters in majority-minority districts in the post-2010 round of redistricting. *See* Cooper v. Harris, 137 S. Ct. 1455 (2017); Bethune-Hill v. Va. State Bd. of Elections, 137 S. Ct. 788, 802 (2016).

92 *Shaw*, 509 U.S. at 657 (stating that "racial classifications of any sort pose the risk of lasting harm to our society").

comply with federal anti-discrimination laws (as in *Shaw* and *Ricci*), to promote the diversity in education that is the legacy of *Brown v. Board of Education* (as in *Parents Involved* and *Meredith*), or alternatively as a product of a hard fought political process in which minorities were the victors (as in *Croson*). Arguably, the equal sovereignty principle, used to invalidate a civil rights mandate designed to further similar aims in the context of elections, allows the Court to continue to protect the majority at the expense of minority rights.

Conclusion

Shelby County's equal sovereignty principle is best viewed as federalism sub-doctrine, where the Court places substantial weight on the legislative record in order to protect the states' governing authority over elections. However, the Constitution does not require the special solicitude that the Court has given to the states in this area. The thirty-ninth Congress designed Section 2 of the Fourteenth Amendment to induce the southern states to enfranchise African-Americans; similarly, the fortieth Congress crafted Section 1 of the Fifteenth Amendment to do the same for northern states. The purpose of these Amendments was to achieve the same goal through enforcement mechanisms that had disparate effects among the states, in essence constitutionalizing the unequal treatment that the Court today claims would run afoul of the equal sovereignty principle.

The Court has consistently elevated notions of state sovereignty over any reading of the VRA that would broaden its scope, a view that is driven, at least implicitly, by the sense that the VRA has given minorities a privileged position in the political sphere that is no longer deserved. As this chapter shows, the Court has disregarded the harms that the VRA was designed to target because the Court views the statute's main benefactors as savvy special interest groups who have a legislative advantage over other political actors instead of as victims of systemic and institutional discrimination.

11 Concluding thoughts

Christopher P. Banks

The foregoing essays represent a timely collection of perspectives that unite different academic disciplines for the purpose of exploring the constitutional politics of federalism and its impact of governments and citizens from a public policy standpoint. In doing so, the essays address the criticism that all too frequently federalism scholars "often speak past each other and fail to synthesize a variety of distinct interdisciplinary contributions that potentially could inform law, political science, or public administration studies."[1] In this sense, the essays uniquely address the effect that Supreme Court federalism precedents have in setting the parameters of national law and policies that the states are often bound to respect under constitutional law, including those that relate to the scope and application of gun rights, anti-terrorism initiatives, capital punishment, health care administration, LGBT freedoms, the legalization of marijuana, immigration and environmental regulation, and voting rights. This chapter identifies some of the common themes of the essays and offers a number of conclusions that link the chapters to the larger question about why it is significant to understand the Supreme Court's approach to federalism and policymaking in general.

As Epstein and Kobylka once observed, it is beyond dispute that the Supreme Court "has spoken authoritatively on an increasing number of significant issues of public policy."[2] What is understood less, and certainly more debatable, is whether the Court is or should be a driver of social policy change through its decision-making.[3] In terms of federalism theory and practice, the issue relating to the Court's role has been typically analyzed in "new federalism" scholarship that investigates the impact that the Rehnquist Court had in safeguarding states' rights or sovereignty interests by creating limitations on the exercise of federal power through its structural interpretation of the Commerce or Spending Clauses, the Tenth Amendment, the Eleventh Amendment, or Section Five of the Fourteenth Amendment. That scholarship is important because it implies that the judiciary is willing to assume a leadership role in exercising its authority to curtail affirmatively federal powers whenever they impinge upon traditional state functions in certain areas of public policy, such as education, crime, or economic matters. One closely decided (5–4) pre-Rehnquist

---

1 JOHN D. NUGENT, SAFEGUARDING FEDERALISM: HOW STATES PROTECT THEIR INTERESTS IN NATIONAL POLICYMAKING (2009), at 7.
2 LEE EPSTEIN & JOSEPH F. KOBYLKA, THE SUPREME COURT AND LEGAL CHANGE: ABORTION AND THE DEATH PENALTY (1992), at 1.
3 See CHRISTOPHER P. BANKS & DAVID M. O'BRIEN, THE JUDICIAL PROCESS: LAW, COURTS, AND JUDICIAL POLITICS (2015), 325–328 (surveying the debate among scholars on the issue).

Court era case, *National League of Cities v. Usery* (1976),[4] is illustrative because, in an opinion written by then-Associate Justice William Rehnquist that used a "judicial safeguards" framework, the Court struck down the federal Fair Labor Standards Act on the grounds that foisting minimum wage and maximum hour requirements on state employees interfered with "attributes of sovereignty attaching to every state government," thereby degrading the basic choices the states can make "as States." Dissenting Justice William Brennan's "political safeguards" approach countered that the normal operation of democratic politics, which is embedded in the design of the U.S. Constitution and the way in which States are integrated into electing the president and congressional representatives, automatically (and adequately) protects the States and their interests.

Whether the U.S. Constitution is interpreted as a structural vehicle that enhances judicial powers to protect the States remains a fundamental and ongoing question of new federalism politics. Although *Usery* was later repudiated by the Court in *Garcia v. San Antonio Metropolitan Transit Authority*[5] after Justice Harry Blackmun joined the four *Usery* dissenters in writing the political safeguards approach into constitutional law, the Rehnquist Court had some success in aggressively using its authority to limit federal powers through constitutional interpretation with key decisions such as *New York v. U.S.* (1992),[6] *U.S. v. Lopez* (1995),[7] and *Seminole Tribe of Florida v. Florida* (1996).[8] Moreover, in statutory construction cases, process-based rationales, such as the judicial invocation of clear or plain statement rules, were applied by the high court to block, limit, or constrain federal incursions that adversely affected traditional state regulatory functions related to liquor consumption,[9] political representation,[10] and crime policy,[11] among others. To illustrate, in *Will v. Michigan Dep't of State Police* (1989),[12] a state policeman was barred from asserting a private damages claim against state officials who denied him promotion under a federal civil rights statute because Congress did not make its intention unmistakably clear to allow such an action. Limiting federal powers in the statutory context is thus significant because it permits the Court to impose "hard" or "soft" checks on the political branches in favor of vindicating state sovereignty interests and regulatory policies.[13]

---

4 National League of Cities v. Usery, 426 U.S. 833 (1976).
5 Garcia v. San Antonio Metropolitan Transit Authority, 469 U.S. 528 (1985).
6 New York v. U.S., 488 U.S. 1041 (1992) (nullifing federal law provision that "commanded" states into making policy choices about disposal of low-level radioactive waste as violation of Tenth Amendment).
7 U.S. v. Lopez, 514 U.S. 549 (1995) (invalidating federal law prohibiting gun possession near schools as improper exercise of congressonal commerce authority).
8 Seminole Tribe of Florida v. Florida, 517 U.S. 44 (1996) (Congress could not authorize private lawsuits by Native America tribes against states in federal court under the Eleventh Amendment).
9 South Dakota v. Dole, 483 U.S. 203 (1987) (Congress could condition receipt of federal monies on adoption of minimum age requirements for alcohol consumption through its spending powers if there was clear notice to the states of what the conditions were under law).
10 Gregory v. Ashcroft, 501 U.S. 452 (1991) (Missouri's mandatory retirement for state court judges did not violate the federal Age Discrimination and Employment Act in the absence of a plain statement by Congress that the law was intended to apply to state judicial employees with policymaking functions).
11 Coleman v. Thompson, 501 U.S. 722 (1991) (State court's dismissal of federal habeas appeal upheld because it is based on an independent and adequate ground of procedural default under state court rules imposing a thirty day deadline).
12 Will v. Michigan Dep't of State Police, 491 U.S. 58 (1989).
13 CHRISTOPHER P. BANKS & JOHN C. BLAKEMAN, THE U.S. SUPREME COURT AND NEW FEDERALISM: FROM THE REHNQUIST COURT TO THE ROBERTS COURT (2012), at 108–116.

While scholars are not of one mind whether the Rehnquist Court actually forged a "new federalism revival" that endorses a "dual federalism" model that has also become an established part of Roberts Courts' jurisprudence,[14] a number of essays in the present volume insinuate that while the Supreme Court may be an important catalyst for social and public policy change, it is nonetheless evident that the States and other federalism stakeholders or litigants do not necessarily have to rely upon the judiciary to come to their aid in safeguarding their interests in the constitutional polity. Put differently, the states can protect their prerogatives before or after the Supreme Court establishes a precedent affecting federalism values through litigation testing the limits of constitutional and statutory boundaries. Indeed, the opportunities to shape the law remain fluid and especially robust in a time of growing fluidity, hyper-partisanship, and political dysfunction at the national level. In this context, at least in the short term, it is unclear whether President Donald Trump's new appointment to the Supreme Court, Neil Gorsuch, will have a dramatic impact changing the direction of conservative federalism jurisprudence that seeks to put greater judicial controls on the federal government, ostensibly because his track record on federalism issues while sitting as a Tenth Circuit judge does not clearly indicate if he will align himself with the views of Justice Antonin Scalia, the jurist he replaced on the bench and who was in the coalition of conservative justices supporting state-centric policy outcomes.[15] It is always possible, though, that another Trump appointment may create an impetus for policy change on federalism issues, especially if the new justice fills the vacancy of one of the liberals on the Court. Hence, and in light of the Court's present composition, the malleability of new federalism ideas that are embedded in Supreme Court cases simply remain, so far, the normative basis of legal advocacy or lobbying efforts that seek to gain judicial approval or rejection of progressive or conservative positions in controversial matters of public policy. What effect Supreme Court precedent will have in respect to future advocacy and litigation is an unknown until, and if, the Court's membership is altered again with appointments that may (or may not) lean in the direction of favoring greater protection for states' rights and sovereignty interests.

Notably, too, the way in which new federalism is *interpreted* as a legal doctrine or as a statement of public policy has been transformed since the 1970s. In its original formulation, the Nixon administration envisioned new federalism as a vehicle to construct a domestic economic policy agenda that reconciled "the contradictory demands of dual sovereigns trying to coexist in one polity"[16] through a system of administrative decentralization that is

---

14 See *id.,* at 88.

15 As one Congressional Research Report concludes, "the limited number of cases in which [Gorsuch, as a Tenth Circuit Judge] has ruled on other aspects of federalism and the scope of federal power vis-à-vis the states makes it difficult to conclude with certainty that he would, if confirmed to the Supreme Court, be as receptive to federalism based arguments as was Justice Scalia. What is apparent, however, is his clear interest in upholding the 'essential principles of federal-state comity' in furtherance of a cooperative federalism by deferring to the states when circumstances so warrant." ANDREW NOLAN, ET AL., JUDGE NEIL M. GORSUCH: HIS JURISPRUDENCE AND POTENTIAL IMPACT ON THE SUPREME COURT *Congressional Research Report R44778* (March 8, 2017), https://fas.org/sgp/crs/misc/R44778.pdf at 73. As the report makes clear, however, given his jurisprudential leanings Gorsuch may have an influence on shaping the ideological direction of a variety of public policy issues that are featured in this book, including cases involving environmental protection, criminal procedure, LGBT rights, and civil rights and liberties. See generally *id.*

16 BANKS AND BLAKEMAN, *supra* note 13 at 51.

more in line with a cooperative federalism framework. But, as the introductory chapter and the discussion by Lund (Chapter 2), Banks (Chapter 3), and Dinan (Chapter 5) show, state officials, stakeholders, and advocacy interests have used the language or substance of new federalism principles to craft legal and policy arguments (or enact laws) that safeguard state interests and limit federal powers in a variety of non-economic contexts, including religious liberty and gun rights litigation, as well as in the areas of national security and health care administration. In contrast, as Knauer (Chapter 6) observes, landmark Supreme Court precedents interpreting the scope of LGBT rights can impose constitutional restraints on state governments seeking to advance their own conception of permissible marriage relationships in a highly volatile political environment.

For example, Lund's analysis indicates that the lower courts' response to the landmark gun rights cases of *District of Columbia v. Heller*[17] and *McDonald v. City of Chicago*[18] have so far enabled the states to have a relatively free hand in enacting gun laws without federal interference. For Banks, and in contradiction to the position taken by red states, blue states and their attorney generals, institutions, businesses, and citizens have challenged the Trump travel ban through pleadings and legal briefs that asserted, among other things, that the executive orders gave rise to justiciable claims of injury that violated Tenth Amendment and anti-commandeering principles, along with First Amendment, due process, and equality freedoms. Dinan, on the other hand, argues that the Supreme Court's decision in *National Federation of Independent Business v. Sebellius*[19] created an opportunity for state officials to gain leverage over the federal government over how they would implement Medicaid expansion after the Court ruled held that Obamacare's expansion provision was an illegitimate exercise of Congress's spending authority. In these respects, as Epstein and Kobylka's work has demonstrated,[20] the ability of state-centric interests in federalism cases to fashion their legal and policy arguments around their interpretations of controlling precedents are important variables that potentially empower the states and increase the judiciary's capacity to become an agent of public policy change. Still, as Knauer explains, *Obergefell v. Hodges*[21] reminds us that state laws defining and regulating marriage relationships are only constitutionally valid if they comport with due process and equality standards in accordance with the fundamental rights analysis of the Fourteenth Amendment.

From an *analytical* perspective, these chapters have some resemblance to the political safeguards approach that posits that the states can use the democratic (and legal) process to achieve their goals and policy preferences without the necessity of having the judiciary play the zero-sum or reductionist game of wielding its authority to stop the federal government from eroding state rights, sovereignty or "dignity."[22] While they may not always succeed in their efforts, state officials can use lobbying pressure through their own regional associations and intergovernmental organizations to exert an influence on the federal policymaking

17 554 U.S. 570 (2008).
18 561 U.S. 742 (2010).
19 National Federation of Independent Business v. Sebelius, 132 S.Ct. 2566 (2012).
20 EPSTEIN & KOBYLKA, *supra* note 2 at 310–312.
21 Obergefell v. Hodges, 135 S.Ct. 2071 (2015).
22 See, e.g., Federal Maritime Commission v. South Carolina State Ports Authority, 535 U.S. 743 (2002) (finding that state sovereign immunity, whose "preeminent purpose" is to "accord States the dignity that is consistent with their status as sovereign entities," prohibits the Federal Maritime Commission from hearing a private party's adjudication against a nonconsenting State).

process.[23] Still, as Kamin (Chapter 7), Glicksman (Chapter 8), and Gulasekaram (Chapter 9) show, the dynamics imposed by the political system present a number of challenges to the states in regulating marijuana, protecting the environment, and securing immigration control. Whereas Kamin and Glicksman agree that the interests of the national government and states in regulating marijuana and environmental protection are accommodated better through a cooperative federalism paradigm, Gulasekaram (and Glicksman) suggest that the Trump administration's devolutionary and restrictionist approach to the environment and immigration policies will impede the capacity of state governments to advance their interests without federal overreaching. Glicksman, moreover, adds the important point that the threat to maintaining a cooperative relationship between the federal government and the states does not really come from an antagonistic judiciary; rather, the balance between sovereigns may be upset more dramatically by the Trump administration's bureaucratic retrenchment of the federal government's powers which, in turn, will diminish its efforts to work with the states on environmental issues. Similarly, Banks' chapter (3) on the constitutional implications of the Trump travel ban reveal that the exercise of executive power in the context of national security may have an adverse effect on States that have a sovereign interest in placing less restrictions on foreign nationals and refugees from entering the United States.

Lastly, and from a more *critical* perspective, Atwell (Chapter 4) and Tolson (Chapter 10) argue that the Supreme Court's interpretation of its capital punishment and voting rights precedents will place additional burdens on the states or federal government to control or manage punishment regimes and electoral processes. For Atwell, the internal divisions on the Court over the meaning of "the evolving standards of decency" relative to the Eighth Amendment, and whether foreign law should be a part of interpreting the U.S. Constitution, has undermined the efforts to construct a national consensus in the states about the scope and application of the death penalty. Similarly, Tolson's critique of *Shelby County v. Holder* (2013)[24] argues that the structural principle of equal sovereignty that the Court used to nullify the preclearance formula in the Voting Rights Act of 1965 is an aggressive, process-based "federalism sub-doctrine" that has erroneously taken away the federal government's power to regulate elections in the states in accordance with anti-discrimination laws. Notably, the inclination of the Roberts Court to adopt process federalism as a means to limit congressional will by increasing its legislative fact-finding burden is analogous to the Rehnquist Court's behavior that availed itself of using clear statement rules to achieve policy outcomes that preserved State choices and sovereignty interests.

Together, the essays compiled in this book thus present interpretative, analytical, and critical perspectives about the Supreme Court's relationship to state governments in a political system that is increasingly polarized over matters of controversial public policy. While the Court sometimes takes the lead in fashioning precedents that aggressively impose limitations on the federal government, the constitutional and statutory construction standards it sets merely establishes the legal framework that permits litigants and stakeholders to advance their respective ideological interests in a political system of divided government. In this sense, the scope and application of new federalism principles, which were originally designed to largely advance economic regulatory goals in a system of cooperative federalism under the Nixon administration, is now routinely co-opted for partisan gain that may or

23 See NUGENT, *supra* note 1.
24 Shelby County. v. Holder, 133 S.Ct. 2612 (2013).

may not always advance state interests in non-economic matters of social policy. While the Supreme Court's role is critical in setting the legal and constitutional boundaries of partisan debate over federalism disputes, it more often than not merely a catalyst, and not necessarily the origin of, social policy change. And, as most of the essays suggest, the partisan manipulation of the Supreme Court's federalism decisions yields unpredictable policy outcomes that could fall on either side of the ideological spectrum which, of course, is an unintended consequence that in all likelihood would disappoint those who wish to use the law for the conservative purpose to limit federal control and vindicate state sovereignty interests.

Index

Note: 'n' indicates footnotes.